CONCEPTION OF MATTER ACCORDING TO NYĀYA-VAIŚEṢIKA

CONCEPTION OF MATTER ACCORDING TO NYĀYAV-AIŚEṢIKA

By
DR. Umesha Mishra

With a foreword by
Mm. Ganganatha Jha
And An Introduction By
Mm. Gopinath Kaviraj

Conception of Matter
According to Nyāya-Vaiśeṣika

First Published 1987, reprint 2013 in India by
Gyan Publishing House
23, Main Ansari Road, Daryaganj,
New Delhi - 110002
Phones : 23282060, 23261060
Fax : (011) 23285914
E-mail: books@gyanbooks.com
website: gyanbooks.com

Printed at : Sagar Color Scan, New Delhi.

FOREWORD

Paradoxical as it may seem, the author of the book is its worst enemy. He has named it 'Conception of Matter'. This name implies the idea that the work confines itself to the *material* aspect of things. On looking into it, however, one finds that it deals, not only with the material, but with all conceivable aspects of things. Unless, therefore, 'matter' is understood in its widest connotation—standing for 'things' or 'beings',—it is misleading.

The reader will find that the writer has taken great pains over the work; he does not seem to leave unnoticed any work that is available on the subject. One would wish he had been less generous' in the choice of his authorities. Everything that has been written is not necessarily 'authoritative'. The writer has himself found this to his own cost in several places, where he would have saved himself much bewilderment if he had been more discriminating in the use of the materials at hand. He would have achieved this end if he had concentrated upon the *ākaragranthas* and omitted the manuals,— especially the later ones,— but perhaps the work would have been less 'full and complete' than it is. It is hoped that serious investigators in the same field will have reason to thank him for having made their work lighter.

There are one or two points, which deserve some attention—

1) We are told on page 50, that while Naiyāyikas are worshippers of *Çiva*, Vaiçeṣikas are worshippers of *Maheçvara* and *Paçupati*, and this is mentioned as indicating the difference in the 'religion' of the two sys-

tems. This point needs further elucidation. The ordinary reader cannot find any difference between *Çiva* and *Maheçvara*, or even any difference in the 're- ligion' of persons worshipping God under one or the other name. It should be the business of the philoso- pher to find unity even where there is disunity—not to find disunity where there is none.

2) The treatment of the Law of Karman—which forms the keystone of Indian Philosophy—should have been more illuminating. On p. 272, we read "For each and every action, there is responsibility"; and this is immediately followed by the statement— "almost all of them are pre-determined". One fails to understand how there can be 'responsibility' along with "Determinism". The point needed to be clari- fied.

3) Lastly, there is the fashionable statement that '*Ātman*' is '*jaḍa*';—I confess that I have never understood this assertion, which, to my mind, appears to confuse '*Cetana*' with '*Caitanya*'. However, this has become so fashionable and received acceptance in such high quarters that it must stand. It is with some trepidation that I have expressed my disagreement.

Our lexicons have declared '*doṣajña*'—'one who detects defects'—to be synonymous with '*Paṇḍita*'— the 'wise or learned man'. It is as a '*doṣajña*' therefore that I have noted the above three points. Now as a 'wise' man, I proceed to commend the book to all serious students of Indian Philosophy. We have lately had a number of excellent accounts of 'Indian Philo- sophy'; but to the best of my knowledge, we have not as yet, had any such full and complete account of any one system as the one that we find in the present work. As already pointed the writer has exhausted all the material available—not only in print, but also in manus- cripts. No student of the system, therefore, can do without this excellent work. We wish we had similar handbooks on the other philosophical systems also—as fully documented as Dr. Umesha Mishra's work is.

It is hoped that the work will find readers to profit by it, and to emulate the example set by it.

ALLAHABAD GANGANATHA JHA

November 1, 1936

INTRODUCTION

The study of Indian Philosophy has emerged, with the slow publication of hitherto obscure texts and with the gradual widening of interest in original researches, from its general and rudimentary stage of the previous century into a critical and systematised form today. The following pages represent a brilliant attempt of this kind and the writer is to be heartily congratulated on the manner in which he has made his learning bear on the subject.

The subject chosen for a special study is the Conception of Matter in Indian Philosophy. It is an interesting theme and as it covers a wide field the writer has done well to restrict himself to a single system only, viz., that of Nyāya-Vaiçeṣika, though he has taken the liberty of going afield on occasions for purposes of comparison and illustration. It may be hoped that other writers will, in due course, supplement the work, bringing together in a systematised way all that other thinkers have got to say on the problem of Matter.

The Conception of Matter is elastic as a study of the history of Western Philosophy will show. And even in science the conception has gone through a series of rapid developments into its recognised meaning of the present day physics. Before going further into the question it would be proper to take into account the meaning the writer himself attaches to the term in dealing with the subject. It seems that in his opinion the entire world is divisible into Self or *Ātman* and things other than Self or *Acetana*. What he understands by Matter is really the entire Not-Self, with all that it implies. The implications of the Not-Self of course differ according to the difference in the system of thought.

Every school of thought has had to tackle this question in its own way. The *Prakṛti* of Sāṅkhya, the *Māyā* of Çaṅkara-Vedānta, the *Bindu* of Southern Çaivaism and the *Acit* of Rāmānuja-Vedānta are only the diverse views on this very question. Everywhere except in the extreme views of Monistic Materialism and Monistic Spiritualism there is a sort of dualism between Spirit and Matter. The Cārvākas who admit nothing but matter in its densest form are monists in the sense that to them everything else, including conscious and other psychic phenomena—indeed the whole paraphernalia of the so-called spiritual life,—is a function of matter. Being advocates of the Doctrine of Chance and opponents of Causality they find no room for a transcendent principle in their outlook on Reality. What is believed to be immaterial has either no existence at all or is, in fact, reducible to a function of matter. The Spiritual Monism, on the other hand, entertains a different opinion, viz. that matter is only a passing semblance and that pure consciousness alone is real. The Buddhist Idealists, the Advaitaism of Çaṅkara's school, the monistic thinkers of the Kashmira Çaivāgama—though widely divergent in their general outlook—agree in this that nothing but *Caitanya* is real in the true sense, whether it is conceived as *vijñāna* which is momentary or as *Brahman* or as *Çiva-Çakti* (*Prakāça-Vimarça*) which is eternal. There is therefore no true parallelism of Matter and Non-matter here. But even in these systems the Conception of Matter is not everywhere the same. To the Yogācāra the material is only a bye-product of *Vijñāna*, appearing spontaneously through its internal potency under the stress of *Vāsanā*. To Çaṅkara Matter in its primordial form is nothing but a synonym of the Original Nescience which erroneously but mysteriously attributes itself to the Supreme Intelligence or Pure Spirit. To the Trika Matter is nothing but the Veiling Power of the Spirit through which the Pure Self conceals itself and projects forth the universe as an objective reality. It is the Power in the Subject by means of which it is able to objectify itself.

In the dualistic systems however the material principle has an independent existence as distinct from spirit, so that in whatever manner it is conceived its eternal character is vouchsafed. If, for instance, in Sāṅkhya *Puruṣa* is eternal, *Prakṛti* is no less so. Similarly in Çrī-Vaiṣṇavaism *Acit* is as real as *Cit* and *Içvara*, and in Southern Çaivaism *Bindu* is co-eternal with *Çiva* and *Çakti*. The other schools including Nyāya-Vaiçeṣika are similar. Consequently, even when the Self is freed from the limitations incidental to its mundane existence and becomes restored to its pristine purity the material principle—*Prakṛti*, *Acit* or *Bindu*—persists as before. Only the association between the two which caused all the trouble disappears.

It is clear that in every system of thought Hindu, Buddhist or Jaina, except Cārvāka, the material principle is recognised as evil. Conceived as a power or potency only or even as an entity it is the source of all misery and tribulation. Every school advocates therefore that the Self to be released from the bondage of the world must be freed in every way from its association with matter. *Mokṣa* is impossible so long as Matter sways the Spirit through its functions. Every code of ethico-spiritual discipline is so designed as to ensure gradual purification of the Self from the dominating effects of accumulated matter in the form of error, doubt, *vāsanā*, *karmans* etc. and guarding the purified Self against further inroads of the latter.

It is very difficult to define Matter in its widest sense and to differentiate it from the Self. In the

Sāṅkhya system spirit is all consciousness and matter is the universal background, eternally existing in a state of stable equilibrium as a potentiality of multiple phenomena and sometimes also as a light medium for the expression as it were of the Conscious Principle endowed with the properties of motion and resistance. If it veils, it also unveils, and both the functions are effected through motion. The Rāmānujas—in fact all the Pāñcarātrites—conceive of matter as pure and impure; and they hold impure matter (that is, *Prakṛti*) to be responsible for the conscious souls' limitations, but pure matter or *Çuddha Sattva* is compatible with the pure spirit (*Cit* and *Īçvara*), so that it is believed to persist on the spiritual plane—which plane itself is made of pure matter. This form of matter does not obstruct knowledge and bliss and attaches to the Self for ever. The necessity of assuming such matter is that of extension—as without this there could be no space or objective existence. All the Vaiṣṇava philosophies have had to admit this. The Tāntrists also—Çaivas, Çāktas etc.—admit this. The Southern Çaivaism believes in *Bindu* which as pure is *Mahāmāyā* and as impure is *Māyā*. *Mahāmāyā* is pure matter—the constitutive substance of the pure planes. The Advaitins—Aupaniṣada, Çākta, Çaiva, or Buddhist—conceive of Matter as an obscuring or limiting power of Reality which has therefore to be transcended.

It is hard to say that lack of consciousness is characteristic of matter, for in that case the Pure Self would have to be described as material. The Vaiçeṣikas are usually subjected to a bitter criticism on account of their view that the Self in its pure condition or *Mukti* is without consciousness and hence it is tauntingly likened to a log of wood or a block of stone and nothing more. To the Nyāya-Vaiçeṣika consciousness etc. are indeed qualities of the Self, but they are not essential; they are produced in the Self on account of its special contact with the mental principle in motion and the presence of certain preliminary conditions. If these conditions happen to be absent, as these do in *Mukti*, no consciousness as a quality can possibly arise. As with consciousness so with the other attributes of the Self. That consciousness etc. have been described as bearing an intimate relation to the Self in which, whenever they are generated, they are said to inhere (*samavāya*) does not mean that they are essential to the Self, for in that case they would never disappear in *Mukti* when the Self is in its purest condition. They differentiate the Self from the Not-Self or material principles during *Saṅsāra* only. It has still to be admitted that the Self is unique by virtue of the *svarūpayog yatā* regarding its *viçeṣaguṇas*. In other words, consciousness etc. characterise the Self, sometimes by their presence (as in *Saṅsāra*) and sometimes by their potentiality (*svarūpayogyatā*) as in *Mukti*, and these attributes are never associated with Not-Self or Matter. This being the case, the criticism of the Vaiçeṣika position as mentioned above loses its sting. On the contrary, the Sāṅkhya and Vedānta views too, if analysed from this standpoint, would be reduced to a like position. For in these consciousness etc. as attributes never pertain to the Self—neither in *saṅsāra* nor in *Mokṣa*; they belong to the mind (*Manas*) and are ascribed wrongly to the Self through the error consisting in the identification of the Self with the mind. Consequently, when the false identification disappears the ascription also ceases; and as a matter of fact at this stage these phenomena are unable to emerge into being and the mind itself ceases to function and to exist. To say that the Self, in Sāṅkhya and Vedānta, is conceived as Self-luminous and that even though consciousness etc. do not pertain to it it retains its unique character in *Mukti* which differentiates it from the Not-Self or Matter is simply to take an evasive turn. The statement is true, but to the empirical consciousness the Self-luminousness of the Self spoken of above has no meaning. It is as good for it as absence of consciousness etc. familiar to it.* Hence, in the last analysis the Vaiçeṣika position and the Sāṅkhya-Vedānta positions do not substantially differ except in the mode of presentation. And it may be observed that we actually find a similar fling cast at these systems also, much like the aspersions of these on the Vaiçeṣikas, by the Tāntrists, who make no secret of their attitude. The term *Çāntabrahmavāda* is not a laudatory one. Bhartṛhari plainly says that *Brahma* without *Çakti* is as good as Matter. That is, the self-luminous character assumed in *Brahman* (or *Puruṣa*) means that *Çakti* is associated with it, without which it would be devoid of all consciousness and power.† But even in the Āgamas there is a hint at the existence of a transcendent condition when the *Vimarça* is withdrawn into *Prakāça* (*antarlīnavimarça*) or more properly the two are merged in Unity which is entirely ineffable and unpredicable in terms of discursive thought. To this Pure Self—so it is called—consciousness etc. as attributes cannot be ascribed. Thus the criticism of the Vaiçeṣika by its opponents proves to be suicidal in the long run.

It has been said that matter defiles. But pure matter too is recognised in certain systems. The

* Udayana himself makes this position clear in the following extract from the Ātmatattvaviveka: *Ātmā tu kiṃ svaprakāçasukhasvabhāvo'nyathā veti pṛcchāmaḥ. Çrāddho'si cet upaniṣadaṃ pṛccha, madhyastho'si cet anubhavaṃ pṛccha, naiyāyiko'si cet na naiyāyikasukhajñānātiriktasvabhāva iti niçcinuyāḥ. Tadatirikte tu sukhajñānavyavahārabījābhāvāt tadvyavahārābhāvaḥ. Anugrahābhiṣvaṅgendriyaprasādādilakṣaṇakāryaṃ hi tadvyavahārabījaṃ*—P. 96. Madanamohana Tarkālaṅkāra's edition.

† *Vāgrūpatā cedutkrāmedavabodhasya çāçvatī* ı
Na prakāçaḥ prakāçeta sā hi pratyavamarçinī ıı
—Vākyapadīya, I. 125.

names of Vaiṣṇava Āgama or Pañcarātra (including all the later Vaiṣṇava schools), of Çaiva Āgama (dualistic, monistic etc.) and Çākta Āgama have been referred to already in a general manner. The Buddhists too recognise pure matter. The lowest of the three planes of being, viz. *Kāmadhātu*, represents matter in the impure state, but the two higher planes of *Rūpa* and *Arūpa* with all their graded subdivisions stand for pure matter though of a more and more attenuated character. It is the state of *Nirvāṇa* only which affords emancipation from the entanglements of matter altogether.

The conception of *akliṣṭa-ajñāna*, as distinguished from *kliṣṭa-ajñāna*, in Buddhist Philosophy also shows that so long as there is *ajñāna*, even though it may not be conducive to *kleça*, matter continues, and it has to be transcended in order that Supreme Buddhahood may be realised. And the process of *āçrayaparāvṛtti* described and insisted on by Asaṅga and other Mahāyāna teachers is really the process of transcendence of matter through gradual purification. It is indeed a process of transmutation pure and simple. The *bhūta-çuddhi* and *citta-çuddhi* of the Tāntric *upāsanā* imply a similar process of purification. The recognition in Patañjali's system of *akliṣṭa-vṛtti* which in its tendency is subversive of the dominating influence of the *guṇas* and conducive to *Nirodha* points to the fact that this system also believes in the existence and working of pure matter (symbolised by *Sattva* disengaged from the other *guṇas*) as against the accumulated tendencies brought on by the action of impure matter (e.g. *Tamas**).

* *Rajas* represents the principle of action and allies itself to both pure and impure matter. It is in a sense the link between the two. In manifestations of Nature, however, all the three principles are inter-related, and any one of them divorced from the other two is an absurdity. But beyond manifested Nature the system recognises the existence of *Sattva* which is never associated

The nature of pure matter is marvellous. In Christian theology it is described as spiritual matter.* Heavens and the bodies of angels, arch-angels etc. consist of this. In the view of Vaiṣṇava Ācāryas too the bodies of liberated beings (those who are not in a disembodied condition), of beings who are eternally free and all the higher celestial planes of existence are pure.

The four states of *guṇas*, viz. *viçeṣa*, *aviçeṣa*, *liṅga* and *aliṅga* and the five states of each of the elements (viz. *sthūla*, *svarūpa*, *sūkṣma*, *anvaya* and *arthavattva*) or senses (viz. *grahaṇa*, *svarūpa*, *asmitā*, *anvaya*, and *arthavattva*) represent from different points of view the different degrees of what might be called materiality in matter.

The problem of Matter is intimately connected with that of motion conceived either as *kriyā* or as *spanda*, and with that of Energy or *çakti*, and may be approached from varied angles of vision. A thorough study of the question cannot therefore be expected in a single treatise, however carefully devised, intended to represent only a particular line of thinking.

Sanskrit students owe a deep debt of obligation to the writer of the present monograph for his highly creditable and useful contribution to a study of this vexed problem from the point of view of a particular school of Indian Philosophy, a school which on account of its advocacy of realism and commonsense in its outlook is calculated to have a universal appeal to the modern mind. It is possible that there is scope for

with *Rajas* and *Tamas* and which in a sense is supernatural. It is described as the *upādhi* of *Içvara* and known as *Prakṛṣṭa-Sattva*. This is pure matter in the truest sense, and has no place in Kapila's school as interpreted by Içvarakṛṣṇa, but is recognised by Patañjali and his system. The *Aprākṛta-Sattva* (=*Çuddha-Sattva*) of the Vaiṣṇavas is an allied conception.

* There are some Çrī-Vaiṣṇava scholars who hold that *Çuddha-Sattva* is not *acit* or matter at all, but is an aspect of *Caitanya* The two views of the Çrī-Vaiṣṇavas are well-known.

difference of opinion or interpretation from him on disputed issues here and there, but the extensive knowledge of original Sanskrit texts (in print or in manuscript) which the author has brought to bear upon his work is admirable and the full references furnished in the copious foot-notes will be greatly serviceable to all serious students of the subject. The writer in his thesis has specially stressed the physical and metaphysical viewpoint of the subject and there is no doubt that he has brought together a vast mass of informative and illuminating material relevant to the topic. He has gone beyond the ground traversed by most of his predecessors in the field, e.g., Bodas, Suali, Faddegon, Keith and others and though there is not much room for original thinking in a subject like this it seems that in certain interpretations he has displayed sufficient critical insight and power of synthetic imagination.

Some scholars may be inclined to think that the writer should have confined himself to the ancient authorities only, but it seems to me that the procedure adopted by him in taking note of every view associated with the school, however divergent from the original tradition or comparatively recent and insignificant, has much to recommend itself. A thorough study cannot afford to ignore after-thought or supplementary growth in the same way as it cannot lose sight of the vague adumberations of the earlier unsystematic stages, provided the views concerned are not inconsistent with the basic unity of the school. Broad and hasty generalisations, based on insufficient data of a localised character are apt to be misleading, and it is refreshing to find that the writer has been very particular in attending to and noting the minutiae and details of the data utilised, enabling the reader himself to look up the references conveniently and draw his own conclusions, whenever necessary.

The work, even as it is, represents a highly useful

addition to the literature on Indian Philosophy and wi
I hope be greatly appreciated by all students of the sub
ject.

Gopinath Kavir

Government Sanskrit College
Benares

November 1, 1936

PREFACE

It was in the year 1922 that I began my higher studies in Indian Philosophy, especially in Nyāyā and Vaiçeṣika as these are some of those systems which do not generally attract the attention of modern scholars on account of their stiffness and intricacies. I continued, however, my studies under the careful guidance of my father the late Mahāmahopādhyāya Paṇḍita Jayadeva Mishra and some of the best scholars of Nyāya-Vaiçeṣika of Benares, such as, the late Mahāmahopādhyāyas Paṇḍitas Vāmācaraṇa Bhaṭṭācārya and Ambādāsa Shāstrī and Mahāmahopādhyāya Paṇḍita Phaṇibhūṣaṇa Tarkavāgīsha. With the help of these big veterans I proceeded with my studies on sound orthodox lines. I was at the same time fortunate enough to get the assistance of Mahāmahopādhyāya Paṇḍita Gopīnātha Kavirāja, Principal, Government Sanskrit College, Benares, with whom I have had the good fortune of reading several philosophical works on modern critical lines. In fact, I owe every bit of my critical knowledge to Kavirājajī; and I have no hesitation in saying that without his guidance perhaps it would have been extremely difficult, if not impossible, for me to place before the scholarly world this humble present.

Under the sound and continued supervision of Kavirājajī, I continued my studies even when I joined the University of Allahabad as a lecturer in Sanskrit Department to teach Indian Philosophy. With his advice I then selected the subject for my special study—'Conception of Matter in Nyāya-Vaiçeṣika Philosophy', which I, later on, supplicated for the degree of 'Doctor of Letters' of the University of Allahabad.

After a continuous work for over twelve years the result of my specialised study is presented to the scholarly world for the first time in print. Originally, the thesis contained only ten chapters including the chapter on 'Conclusion', but later on, it was realized that the exhaustive treatment of 'Matter' would remain incomplete until and unless it is supplemented with the treatment of 'Not-Matter', that is, 'Spirit' or '*Ātman*'. Hence a very brief treatment of it also has been added to the book in a separate chapter. This addition has not only added to the better understanding of the idea of 'Matter', but also has made the book complete in a way; so that the book now would give a complete survey of the substances (*dravyāṇi*) recognised in this joint system.

My aim in writing this book is to give a clear and exhaustive account of the idea of 'Matter' according to Nyāya-Vaiçeṣika Philosophy. Hence, not only almost all the works, both in print and in manuscript, dealing with the subject have been utilised for the purpose, but, as is clear from the bibliography given at the end of the book, standard works of other systems also have been often made use of. References of Nyāya-Vaiçeṣika doctrines found in works of other systems have helped me sometimes to elucidate them more clearly and also to meet the criticisms advanced against them by rival schools.

In interpreting the various doctrines of the systems I have ever been careful to keep in mind the angle of vision which these two systems represent in the realm of Indian Philosophy. And it is needless to say that efforts have been made to represent the problems in a clear and dispassionate manner so as to enable every student of Indian Philosophy to understand them more easily, but as the treatment of philosophical systems, especially that of Nyāya-Vaiçeṣika, is so intricate and sometimes obscure that I am afraid I may not have achieved my end in every case. Besides, I am fully aware of my other shortcomings which may have found their place in the book also for which I only crave pardon of my impartial and generous readers.

I have expressed in these pages the viewpoint of Nyāya and Vaiçeṣika without having any preconceived idea in my mind. I have tried to represent the problems on rational basis and on more or less original lines. Every care has been taken to find out authoritative statements from the original texts to support each interpretation. As it is purely a representation of the Nyāya-Vaiçeṣika point of view I have not tried to give any comparative idea either from the rival schools of Indian Philosophy or from the Western thoughts.

I must express my most sincere gratitude to my revered teachers Mahāmahopādhyāya Dr. Gangānātha Jhā, ex-Vice-Chancellor of the Allahabad University and Paṇḍita Gopīnātha Kavirāja, Principal, Government Sanskrit College, Benares who with their usual kindness have always helped me in removing my difficulties while writing this book and have done me great honour by kindly writing the Foreword and the Introduction of this book respectively.

I am much indebted to Dr. A. Berriedale Keith of Edinburgh and Mahāmahopādhyāya Paṇḍita S. Kuppusvāmī Shastrī, I.E.S. (Retd.), Madras, who were good enough to go through the Ms. and favour me with their valuable suggestions. My thanks are also due to Paṇḍita Amaranātha Jhā, M.A., Professor of English, the University of Allahabad, for reading portions of the Ms. and giving me his friendly advice for its improvement. I am also obliged to all those friends of mine who have constantly encouraged me in preparing this book. I must thank the Manager, Allahabad Law Journal Press, who has taken every care to see the book through the Press.

CONTENTS

CHAPTER II

CHAPTER III

PAGE

CHAPTER IV

CHAPTER X

CHAPTER XI

LIST OF ABBREVIATIONS

AG——Abhinava Gupta.
AUS——Allahabad University Studies.
ĀV, or ĀTV.——Ātmatattvaviveka.
BG——Bhagavadgītā.
Bhā or BhāP——Bhāṣāpariccheda.
BhāC——Bhāṣyacandra.
BṛU——Bṛhadāraṇyakopaniṣad.
BS——Brahmasūtra.
ChāU—Chāndogyopaniṣad.
CK——Caturakallinātha's Commentary.
DK or NSMD——Dinakarī.
DP——Dravyaprakāçikā.
DS——Dravyasangraha.
DSV——Dravyasangraha-Vṛtti.
DSR——Dravyasārasangraha.
DÇ——Daçaçlokī.
GBha——Gāgābhaṭṭi.
Guṇa——Guṇaratna's Commentary.
HIL or ILV- —History of Indian Logic.
IP——Īçvarapratyabhijñā.
IPV——Īçvarapratyabhijñāvimarçinī.
IPM——Introduction to Pūrva—Mīmāṃsā.
IPR——Indian Philosophy by S. Radhakrishnan.
IPOK——Introduction to Philosophy by Oswald Külpe.

JBBRAS——Journal Bombay Branch Royal Asiatic Society.
Kaṇṭha——Kaṇṭhābharaṇa.
KKH——Kusumāñjali-Kārikā along with Haridāsī.
KM——Karma-Mīmāṃsā.
KP——Kusumāñjaliprakaraṇa.
KPP——Kusumāñjaliprakaraṇaprakāça.
KR——Kaṇādarahasya.
KU or KV——Kiraṇāvalī by Udayana.
KUBhā——Kaṭhopaniṣad-Bhāṣya.
KVBhā——Kiraṇāvalībhāskara.
KVPA——Kiraṇāvalīprakāçikā.
LU or LV——Lakṣaṇāvalī by Udayana.
LVM——Nyāyamuktāvalī on Lakṣaṇāvalī.
MNSā——Nyāyasāra by Mādhavadeva.
MS——Mīmāṃsā Sūtra.
MSS——Madhvasiddhāntasāra.
MU——Muṇḍakopaniṣad.
NAV——Nyāyāvatāra.
NAVV——Nyāyāvatāravivṛti.
NB——Nyāyabodhinī.
NBhā——Nyāyabhāṣya.
NC——Naiṣadhacarita.
NK——Nyāyakoça.
NL. or NLV——Nyāyalīlāvatī by Vallabha.
NLK——Nyāyalīlāvatīkaṇṭhābharaṇa.
NLPV——Nyāyalīlāvatīprakāçavivṛti.
NM——Nyāyamañjarī.
NMJ——Nyāyasiddhāntamañjarī by Jānakīnātha.

NMV or NMuktā——Nyāyamuktāvalī by Viçvanātha.

NMÇ——Nyāyamuktāvalī by Çeṣa-Çārngadhara.

NP——Nyāyapariçuddhi.

NPP——Nyāyapariçuddhiprakāça.

NS——Nyāyasūtra.

NSM——Nyāyasiddhāntamālā.

NSMM——Nyāyasiddhāntamuktāvalī-mañjūṣā.

NSMR or RR——Rāmarudrī.

NSVṛ or NVṛ——Nyāyasūtravṛtti.

NV——Nyāyavārtika.

PC——Padārthacandrikā.

PD——Padārthadīpikā.

PH. or PHṛ——Pratyabhijñāhṛdaya.

PKSS——Pañcāstikāyasamayasāra.

PP——Prakaraṇapañcikā.

PPP——Pramāṇādipadārthaprakāçikā.

PPBhā——Praçastapādabhāṣya.

PR——Prasthānaratnākara.

PRM——Padārtharatnamālā.

PRY——Pratāparudrayaçobhūṣaṇa.

PS——Pāṇini Sūtra and Padārthasangraha.

PSAH or PSH——Positive Sciences of the Ancient Hindus.

PSPM——Prabhākara School of Pūrva-Mīmāṃsā.

PTN——Padārthatattvanirūpaṇa.

PTNR——Raghudeva's Commentary on PTN.

PTVP——Padārthatattvavivecanaprakāçikā.

PV——Padārthaviveka.

PWSS——Princess of Wales Sarasvatībhavana Series.
RP——Ratnaprabhā.
RS——Rasasāra.
SB——Siddhāntabindu.
SC——Siddhāntacandrodaya.
SD——Siddhāntadarçana.
SDS——Sarvadarçanasangraha.
ṢDS——Ṣaḍdarçanasamuccaya.
SK or SS——Sāṅkhyakārikā.
SLS——Siddhāntaleçasangraha.
SP——Saptapadārthī.
SPM——Mitabhāṣiṇī on SP.
SPBhā——Sāṅkhyapravacanabhāṣya.
SR——Siddhāntaratna (and Sangītratnākara on p. 201).
SSS——Sarvasiddhāntasangraha.
ST——Siddhitraya (and Siddhāntatattva on p. 139).
STV——Siddhāntatattvaviveka.
ÇB——Çabarabhāṣya.
ÇBhā——Çaṅkarabhāṣya.
ÇD——Çāstradīpikā.
ÇK——Çabdakalpadruma.
ÇM——Çuddhādvaitamārtaṇḍa.
ÇS——Çāstrārthasangraha.
ÇV——Çlokavārtika.
TBhā——Tarkabhāṣā.
TBhāNP——Tarkabhāṣā-Nyāyaprakāça.
TC or CM——Tattvacintamaṇi.
TD——Tarkadīpikā.

TK——Tarkakaumudī.
TP——Tarkaprakāça.
TPP——Tarkapradīpa.
TR——Tārkikarakṣā.
TS——Tarkasangraha.
TT——Tattvatraya.
TTBhā——Tattvatraya-bhāṣya.
TV——Tattvavaiçāradī.
VB or Vedā——Vedāntatattvabodha.
VBhā——Vaiçeṣikasūtra-bhāṣya.
VEP——Vedāntaparibhāṣā.
VKT——Vedāntakalpataru.
VKTP——Vedāntakalpataruparimala.
VP——Vākyapadīya.
VPS——Vedāntapārijātasaurabha.
VRM——Vedāntaratnamañjūṣā.
VS——Vaiçeṣikasūtra.
VSS——Vedāntasāra by Sadānanda.
VSM——Vedāntasiddhāntamuktāvalī.
VU——Vaiçeṣika-Upaskāra.
VV——Vaiçeṣika-Sūtra-Vivṛtti and Vivekavilāsa.
VVV——Vaiçeṣikasūtra-Vaidika-Vṛtti.
Vyom——Vyomavatī.
YBhā——Yogabhāṣya.
YMD——Yatipatimatadīpikā.
YS——Yogasūtra.
YV——Yajurveda.

CHAPTER I

INTRODUCTORY

I

GENERAL OBSERVATIONS REGARDING DARÇANA

1. *Darçana—its concept and aim*

PHILOSOPHY is generally considered to be merely speculative. But this is not true of Indian philosophy. In India, it is not merely speculative but it has both theoretical and practical aspects. Truly speaking, no scientific study can neglect either. Moreover, speculation, unless it is based on and has a counterpart in practical experience, is worse than useless.

This idea is borne out by the use of the word *Darçana* for a system of philosophy in India. The word *Darçana* is derived from the root *dṛçir* (to see) with the affix *lyuṭ* and means—the act of perception. This may be either physical or intuitive. Here in the present context, it should be understood in the latter sense. In other words, only that system of thought deserves to be called *Darçana* which gives us a true picture, fragmentary but faithful, of the whole truth, of course through the act of intuitive perception. Hence, the different schools of *Darçana* in Indian thought represent the varied phases of the *truth* viewed from different angles of vision. Thus it is clear from the above that the use of the words—philosophy, system, school, etc. for *Darçana* is quite misleading unless we bear in mind the fundamental difference between the concept of *Darçana* and those of philosophy, system, school and others.

Now, it may be asked here: What is the *truth* which a *Darçana* helps us to realise? The only *truth* —the final aim of Indian thought—is the perception—the direct realisation—of the *Ātman*. All the *Darçanas* aim at the true knowledge of the *Ātman* according to their own angles of vision. And almost all the *Darçanas*, accordingly, follow the common line of treatment for achieving their end. So says, the *Çruti: Ātmā vā are draṣṭavyaḥ çrotavyo mantavyo nididhyāsitavyo Maitreyi, Ātmā vā are darçanena çravaṇena matyā vijñānena idaṃ sarvaṃ viditam.* That is, the *Ātman* is to be perceived; it is the *Ātman* of which we should hear from the *çrutis*, it is the *Ātman* about which we should reason and upon which we should meditate; O Maitreyi! it is through the direct realisation of the *Ātman*, achieved through *çravaṇa*, *manana* and *nididhyāsana* that everything is known.[1] In other words, it is through the process of *çravaṇa*, *manana* and *nididhyāsana* that the *darçana* of the *Ātman* takes place.

By *çravaṇa* we mean learning the truth about the *Ātman*—the *truth* itself—from the *çrutis*. Now, had the enquirer after the truth had full faith (*çraddhā*) in the words of the *çrutis*, he would have at once got the illumination needed.[2] But as a human being, he is beset with doubts and wrong notions, which stand in the way of his immediate conviction. He then sets about collecting arguments in support of what he has heard from the *çrutis*. This stage of reasoning, as based upon the premisses supplied by the *çrutis*, is known as *manana*. This iswhat speculative philosophy in India attempts to represent.[3] But, as pointed out above, mere speculation cannot lead us to the *truth*. It seems

[1] BṛU, II-iv-5.

[2] (1) *Çraddhāvān labhate jñānam*—BG, 4-39; (2) *Çraddhā ca brahmavijñāne paramaṃ sādhanam*—ÇBhā on BṛU, II-i-1.

[3] *Çrutasya parīkṣā nyāyenaivāvasthāpanaṃ yāmāhurmananamiti. Sā cānvīkṣikyāmāyatate*—Tāt., under NS., I. i. 2; p. 70.

quite possible that the conclusions arrived at through speculation might be overthrown at any moment by counter-reasoning of a stronger nature.[4] Examples of such supersession abound in both science and philosophy. The enquirer cannot rely upon this. It is necessary, therefore, to verify the rational conclusion through practical experiments; just as in geometry, demonstration is supplemented by experimentation. This practical verification is reached through *nididhyāsana*. The conclusions of the previous stage are hereby realised as true and unassailable. These are the steps which are recognised in Indian philosophy and which lead to the direct realisation of the *truth*, that is, the *Ātman*.[5]

This makes it quite clear that by philosophy (*Darçana*) in India one understands something more than mere speculation. It is, therefore, wrong to use even the term 'Philosophy' for *Darçana*. But for want of a more appropriate word we are constrained to retain the term, but we must not lose sight of the distinction noted above.

It is also a well-known fact that the origin of *Darçana* in India is almost forgotten. We do not possess any chronological account as to when the great *Ṛṣis* and *Yogins* began to dream of philosophy. In the absence of such a record we can only depend upon

[4] (1) KUBhā, I-ii-8; (2) *Itaçca nāgamagamyerthe kevalena tarkeṇa pratyavasthātavyam. . . .yasmānnirāgamāḥ puruṣotprekṣāmātranibandhanāstarkā apratiṣṭhitā bhavantyutpreksāyā niraṅkuçatvāt. Tathā hi kaiçcidabhiyuktairyatnenotprekṣitāstarkā abhiyuktatarairanyairābhāsyanta iti na pratiṣṭhitatvaṃ tarkāṇāṃ çakyaṃ samāçrayitum puruṣamativairūpyāt* etc.—ÇBhā. on BS, II. i. 11.

(3) *Yatnenānumito'pyarthaḥ kuçalairanumātṛbhiḥ* ।
Abhiyuktatarairanyairanyathaivopapādyate ॥ VP, I-34.

(4) *No khalu diṅmūḍhaḥ sahasreṇāpyanumānairviparyayasaṃskāramapanayati*—Tāt., p. 49.

[5] *Çruteḥ çrutvātmānaṃ tadanu samanukrāntavapuṣo*
viniçcityanyāyādatha vihitaheyavyatikaram ।
Upāsīta çrutvā çamadamavirāmaikavibhavo
bhavocchityai cittapraṇidhivihitairyogavidhibhiḥ ॥ ĀV, p. 131.

hypotheses helped by *anumāna* of the type of *çeṣavat*, meaning, inferring the cause from the effect. Thus we know that the earliest form of systematised thoughts is represented by the Sūtras of the different philosophical systems. This itself presupposes a stage when there was no systematisation of these thoughts, which is quite evident from the study of the pre-Upaniṣadic literature and the Upaniṣads. In these we do not see any systematic arrangement of the ideas and the views represented later on by different schools of thought. It appears that the thoughts contained in these were the common property of the intellectual community of the country. Perhaps, there was no need of systematisation at that time. But later on, due to intellectual degeneration or some other inevitable cause the current ideas were assimilated in certain cases by different schools and formed the backgrounds of distinct lines of thinking in subsequent ages. As time went on such lines of thinking multiplied in number and began to develop each its own individual character. Many of the ideas which are inseparably associated with certain systems at present had then been in a floating condition. But these ideas and the views are no doubt demonstrated truths; and as such, they give evidence of a stage when there had been going on intellectual deliberations amongst the then existing scholars in order to come to certain truths. In this way, we can trace the origin of Indian philosophy to a certain extent.

2. *Varieties of Darçana*

While dealing with the *Darçanas* it will not be out of place, it seems, to consider the number of *Darçanas* recognised from time to time in India. We have been hearing much of the six *Darçanas*. But which are these six *Darçanas*? As to this there is no agreement amongst the writers of philosophical compendia. Thus Haribhadra Sūrin, a Jaina writer, of about 1168 A.D. means by six systems Bauddha, Naiyāyika, Kapila, Jaina, Vaiçeṣīka and Jaiminīya.

Another Jaina writer named Jinadatta Sūrin, of about 1220 A.D.,[7] includes Jaina, Mīmāṃsā, Bauddha, Sāṅkhya, Çaiva and Nāstika under the six *Darçanas.*[8]

The next Jaina philosopher, Maladhāri Çrī Rājaçekhara Sūrin, of about 1348 A.D.,[9] enumerates another kind of division, namely, Jaina, Sāṅkhya, Jaiminīya, Yoga,[10] Vaiçeṣika and Saugata.

Turning towards the references of the Brahmanic writers, we find that according to the son of the well-known commentator, Mallinātha, who must have flourished in the 14th century A.D.,[11] *Ṣaḍdarçana* includes Pāṇini, Jaimini, Vyāsa, Kapila, Akṣapāda and Kaṇāda.[12]

Jayanta Bhaṭṭa, who must have lived before the 11th century,[13] appears to include under *Ṣaṭtarkī*[14] Mīmāṃsā, Nyāya which includes Vaiçeṣika, Sāṅkhya, Ārhat, Bauddha and Cārvāka.

In the Hayaçīrṣa-Pañcarātra, a Brahmanic work,

[6] *Bauddhaṃ naiyāyikaṃ sāṅkhyaṃ jainaṃ vaiçeṣikaṃ tathā* ।
Jaiminīyañca nāmāni darçanānāmamūnyaho ॥ ṢDS, Verse 3

[7] HIL, p. 152.

[8] *Jainaṃ maimāṃsakaṃ bauddhaṃ sāṅkhyaṃ çaivañca nāstikam* ।
Svasvatarkavibhedena jānīyāddarçanāni ṣaṭ ॥ VV.

[9] HIL, p. 153.

[10] The expressions *Yogamata* and *Çaivamata* appear to be used for the same school, namely, Nyāya. The use of the word *Yoga* in this sense is also found in the Nyāya-Bhāṣya 1-i-29. It appears to have been wrongly interpreted in the sense of Vaiçeṣika—Khadyota by Dr. Jhā on ibid.

[11] HIL, p. 380.

[12] *Pāṇinerjaiminneçcaiva vyāsasya kapilasya ca* ।
Akṣapādasya kaṇādasya......in his Comm. on the PRY of Vidyādhara.

[13] HIL, p. 147. The earliest reference of Jayanta is found in Gaṅgeça's TC, Upamāna, p. 61, wherein the former has been called *Jarannaiyāyika.* This Gaṅgeça is put in the 13th century—PWSS, Vol. III, p. 133.

[14] NM, Vol. I., p. 4.

supposed to have been introduced in Bengal by Rājā Ballāla Sen (about 1158-1170 A.D. or earlier) as well as in the Gurugītā of the Viçvasāra Tantra, the six systems are: Gautama, Kaṇāda, Kapila, Patañjali, Vyāsa and Jaimini.[15]

The compiler of the Sarvamatasaṅgraha divides the schools of Indian thought under two main heads: *Vaidika* and *Avaidika*. The former is subdivided into Mīmāṃsā, Sāṅkhya and Tarka and the latter into Bauddha, Ārhata and Lokāyata.[16]

The author of the Arthaçāstra appears to include under the philosophical systems Sāṅkhya, Yoga and Lokāyata.[17]

The Sarvasiddhāntasaṅgraha, attributed to Çaṅkarācārya, enumerates a different classification: Lokāyatika, Ārhata, the four Buddhist schools, Vaiçeṣika, Nyāya, the two schools of Pūrva-Mīmāṃsā, Sāṅkhya, Patañjali, Veda-Vyāsa and Vedānta.

Mādhavācārya in his Sarvadarçanasaṅgraha enumerates many more, namely, Cārvāka, Bauddha, Ārhata, Rāmānuja, Pūrṇaprajña, Nakulīça-Pāçupata, Çaiva, Pratyabhijñā, Raseçvara, Aulūkya, Akṣapāda, Jaimini, Pāṇini, Sāṅkhya, Pātañjala and Çāṅkara.

Madhusūdana Sarasvatī in his Prasthānabheda divides *Darçana* into *Āstika* and *Nāstika*. Under the former he includes Nyāya, Vaiçeṣika, Karma-Mīmāṃsā, Çārīraka-Mīmāṃsā, Pātañjala, Pañcarātra and Pāçupata; while under the latter, he includes the four schools of Buddhism, Digambara school of Jaina, and the

[15] *Gautamasya kaṇādasya kapilasya patañjaleḥ* ।
Vyāsasya jaimineçcāpi darçanāni ṣaḍeva hi ॥ HIL, p. 153, Ft.n. 3.

[16] *Iha hi dvividhāni vicāraçāstrāṇi vaidikāvaidikabhedāt. Tāni ca pratyekaṃ trividhāni—mīmāṃsāsāṅkhyatarkabhedāt bauddhārhatalokāyatabhedācca*—pp. 14-15.

[17] I-i-1., p. 6.

school of Cārvāka.[18] But in his Siddhāntabindu,[19] a commentary on Çaṅkarācārya's Daçaçlokī, he speaks of the schools of Cārvāka, namely, Dehātmavāda, Pratyeka-Indriyātmavāda, Militendriyātmavāda, Ātma-Manovāda and Prāṇātmavāda, of Saugata (Vijñānavāda), Mādhyamika, Digambara, Vaiçeṣika, Tārkika, Prābhākara, Bhāṭṭa, Sāṅkhya, Patañjali and Aupaniṣad (Çaṅkara-Vedānta). Gauḍa-Brahmānanda, while commenting upon it, includes Vaibhāṣika and Sautrāntika under Buddhism and says that the six *Nāstika-darçanas* are: Cārvāka, the four schools of Buddhism and the Digambara school of Jaina while Vaiçeṣika and others represent the six *Āstika-darçanas*.[20] But this is possible only when the two Mīmāṃsā schools are not taken separately.

Puṣpadanta, however, like an old writer, as he undoubtedly is, thinks that there are only four schools of philosophy, namely, Sāṅkhya, Yoga, Paçupatimata and Vaiṣṇava.[21] It may be pointed out that the author refers to the *Āstika-darçanas* alone in the above enumeration.

The author of Nyāyakoṣa is of opinion that there are only six *Darçanas*, namely, two Yogas, meaning, Sāṅkhya and Pātañjala, two Mīmāṃsās, meaning, Pūrva and Uttara Mīmāṃsās, and two Tarkas, that is, Nyāya and Vaiçeṣika.[22] This also is, undoubtedly, said of the *Āstika-darçanas*.

The author of Sarvamatasaṅgraha is of opinion that the Indian thought (*Vicāraçāstra*) is divided into two—*Vaidika* and *Avaidika*, each consisting of three subdivisions, namely, Mīmāṃsā, Sāṅkhya and Tarka

[18] A comm. on the Mahimnaḥstotra of Puṣpadanta, Verse 7.

[19] Verse. I.

[20] p. 110.

[21] Mahimnaḥstotra, Verse 7.

[22] *Dvau yogau dve ca mīmāṃse dvau tarkāviti ṣaḍbudhāḥ.*—Ft. n. 2, pp. 317-18.

under the former head while Bauddha, Ārhat and Lokāyata under the latter.[23]

These are the various divisions and subdivisions of Indian *Darçana*. The Jaina writers and some Brahmanic writers also have taken into account both the orthodox and the non-orthodox schools. But it is difficult to say on what basis these divisions are made.

II

METAPHYSICAL POSITION OF VARIOUS SCHOOLS OF INDIAN THOUGHT

The points of difference between the various schools of *Darçana* may be of several kinds. Here an attempt is made to determine the relative place of various systems of thought on the basis of the triple relation between 1. the subject and the object (*Jñātā*-knower and *Jñeya*-knowable), 2. the subject and the knowledge (*Jñātā* and *Jñāna*), and 3. object and the knowledge (*Jñeya* and *Jñāna*).

The mutual relation of the terms may be studied in the following manner:

(1) *Jñātā* versus *Jñāna*,

(2) *Jñāna* versus *Jñeya*, and

(3) *Jñātā* versus *Jñeya*.

Of these, the first may be split up, thus—

(*a*) *Jñātā* same as *Jñāna*, and *Jñātā* distinct from *Jñāna*, while

The second as—

(*b*) *Jñāna* same as *Jñeya*, and *Jñāna* distinct from *Jñeya*.

[23] pp. 14-15.

The third—It will be seen that the possibilities of this form would follow naturally from the above mentioned two forms.

Now, to find out the place of a particular school of Indian thought we should take each of the two forms under (*a*) and (*b*) separately and study it in detail.

I.—Thus to begin with the first variety, we find that *Jñātā is either identical with Jñāna or is different from it.*

1.—In the former case, prominence (*prādhānya*) may be given sometimes to one and sometimes to the other.

(1) Thus when *Jñātā is prominent*, real and eternal, while *Jñāna* is but a subsidiary, the former (*Jñātā*) may be looked upon either as essentially both *dṛkçaktyātmaka* and *kriyāçaktyātmaka* by which the *Jñātā* is both the absolute consciousness (*draṣṭā*) and the doer (*kartṛ*)[24] or essentially *dṛkçaktyātmaka* (absolute consciousness itself) alone, according to which the *Jñātā* is only the absolute consciousness and not the doer.[25] The former represents the Kashmir Çaivaism while the latter is represented by Sāṅkhya-Yoga. In the former case, the *Jñātā*, is prominent, real and eternal and is also entirely free (*svatantra*) and as such, is the doer (*kartā*)[26] as well. Therefore, when it so desires, it manifests itself into two aspects—one representing the *Jñātā* which is then essentially the doer (*kartā*) and the other the *Jñāna* which represents both the consciousness and the doership (*kartṛtva*). In spite of the fact that *Jñāna* is subsidiary to *Jñātā* it is in no way less real and less eternal. It is almost the same. The *Jñātā* is either the *Çiva* in Whom consciousness is unlimited and so is His doership (*kartṛtva*) or is the *Puruṣa* in which case both the consciousness and the doership are limited as it is within

[24] *Citkriyā citikartṛtā*—IP., I. v. 12., p. 200; *citiçaktir-dṛçiriti, sā cetanakriyā citikartṛtaiva*—AG on Ibid; IP., I. i. 2-3; I. vi 11; I. viii. 1.

[25] YS., II. 2; SK., 19, 65.

[26] PH., Sūtras 1-2; PS, I. iv. 54.

the influence of *Māyā*.[27] The *Jñāna* aspect is nothing but the *Çakti* which is essentially of the form of *dṛk* and *kriyā*.

In the latter case the *Jñātā*, which is no other than the *Puruṣa*, is only an uninterested spectator (*draṣṭā*). It has no *kartṛtva*,[28] as is also clear when it is said—*draṣṭā dṛçimātraḥ*.[29] The prominence belongs to this very Seer. It is also real and eternal.[30] The consciousness (*dṛçi*) which is the very nature of the *Jñātā* is here made to represent the *Jñāna* aspect as subsidiary to the *Jñātā*. But its real nature should not be overlooked. It is equally real, eternal[31] and free from *kartṛtva*.

(2) All this is when *Jñātā* is identical with *Jñāna* and the prominence is given to the former. Now, when *Jñāna predominates* and *Jñātā* follows it, *Jñāna* is real, but it may be either *kṣaṇika*, momentary, or eternal. In both cases it is polarised into *Jñāna* and *Jñātā*. In the former case, it represents the Buddhist Vijñānavāda school and in the latter, the Çaṅkara school of Vedānta.

In the former case, *Jñāna* is represented by the *Pravṛttivijñāna*, while *Jñātā* by *Ālayavijñāna*. In the latter case, on the other hand, *Jñāna* means *Brahman*, that is, *Caitanya*, while *Jñātā* is represented by *Içvara* or *Jīva*.

2.—*When Jñātā, on the other hand, is distinct from Jñāna*, even then both may be real and inseparably associated together.

(1) Here also, when *Jñātā* is made prominent, it may be either eternal or non-eternal. The former may be, again, conceived as *jaḍa* or *ajaḍa*. The *jaḍa* form

[27] PH., Sūtras 9-10.
[28] SK., 19, 65.
[29] YS., II. 20.
[30] SK., 11.
[31] YBhā on YS., II. 2.

of *Jñātā* is either self-illumined (*svaprakāça*) or enlightened by others (non-*svaprakāça*). The *svaprakāça-Jñātā* is represented by the two schools of Pūrva-Mīmāṃsā, namely, Bhāṭṭa[32] and Prābhākara.[33] The non-*svaprakāça* aspect is represented by Nyāya and Vaiçeṣika schools. The non-eternal form, on the other hand, is represented by the Materialistic school of Cārvāka.

Now, when the *Jñāṭā* is *ajaḍa*, it may be subdivided into atomic (*paramāṇu-parimāṇa*), intermediary (*madhyama-parimāṇa*) and all-pervasive (*vibhu-parimāṇa*). Of these, the all-pervasive form does not include any system of Indian thought. The intermediary aspect represents the Jaina school. According to it the *Jñātā* is the support of *Jñāna* and as such, is different from the latter though they are inseparably connected with each other.[34] Both are eternal.[35] The dimension of the *Ātman* which is the *Jñātā* is of the size of the organism wherein it takes its abode for the purpose of experiencing pleasure and pain.[36]

The atomic form of *Jñātā* may, on the basis of the relation between the individual self (*Jīva*) and the *Içvara*, be further split up as possessing difference

[32] ÇV, pp. 690; 693. SB, p. 110; Pañch, chitradīpa. The DSV is of opinion that the *Ātman* according to Bhaṭṭa being of limited-dimension (*mūrta*) differentiates itself from that of Prabhākara. But we know that this is quite inconsistent with the Mīmāṃsā conception of the *Ātman*. The conception of *vibhutva* is quite incompatible with that of *mūrtatva* (ÇV, p. 693).

[33] ÇV, Ātman-section, Verses 142-45; SB., p. 110; IPM., pp. 91-94, 100; SD., p. 122; M. M. Anantakṛṣṇa Çāstrī's intro. to Prabhākaravijaya, p. 27.

The *Ātman* is always a subject and never an object of *ahampratīti*; as a matter of fact, there is no such thing as pure *ahampratīti* other than the *pratīti* of objects in which the *Ātman* reveals itself just like the object. Hence, the *Ātman* may be assumed to be *svaprakāça* according to Prabhākara.

[34] NAV., 30; NAVV., p. 48.

[35] PKSS., p. 40, quoted in DS., p. 9.

[36] DS., Gāthā 2.

(*Jīveçvarabheda*), or identity (*Jīveçvarābheda*), or both difference and identity (*Jīveçvarabhedābheda*). The first may be subdivided into two—one when the *Jīva* forms an *aspect* of *Içvara* and the other when it is not so. The former represents the Rāmānuja school according to which the *Cit*, which is the *Jñātā*,[37] is distinct from *Jñāna*[38] which is clear from the fact that the *Jñātā* illuminates itself even without the help of the *Jñāna*.[39] The *Jñātā* is eternal,[40] self-illuminating (*ajaḍa*)[41] and atomic[42] in nature. The *Jīva* is different from *Içvara* who is the *niyantā* of the former.[43] It has been recognised as a separate entity although dependent upon, rather an aspect of, *Içvara*.[44] The very name *Viçiṣṭādvaita* given to this system lends a support to the above fact. The latter, that is, when the *Jīva* is not an aspect of *Içvara*, may be subdivided into two—one when the *Jīva* is a *Çakti* of the *Içvara*[45] in which case it represents the Caitanya school of Vaiṣṇavaism and the other when the *Jīva* is not so. In this aspect it represents the Mādhva school. In the former case, the *Jīva* is the *Jñātā*.[46] Although *Jñāna* is the very nature of the *Jīva* yet the former should be taken to be an inseparable attribute of the latter, which shows that they are different from each other.[47] The *Jīva* is both eternal and self-illuminating.[48] It is also atomic[49] and is different

[37] TT., p. 18.
[38] TT., pp. 5, 22, 35.
[39] TTBhā., p. 22.
[40] TT., pp. 5, 10.
[41] TT., pp. 5, 10.
[42] TT., pp. 5, 12-13; YMD., p. 73.
[43] TT., pp. 5, 23.
[44] TT., pp. 5, 10.
[45] SR., p. 334.
[46] SR., p. 329.
[47] SR., pp. 16, 302, 329.
[48] SR., pp. 320, 329-30.
[49] SR., p. 329.

from *Içvara*[50] of Whom it is only a *taṭastha-çakti.*[51] The latter refers to the Mādhva school. According to this school also the *Jīva* is distinct from *Jñāna.* It is eternal[52] and self-illuminating.[53] It is atomic in nature.[54] Although *Jīva* is an aspect (not in the form of a *çakti*) of *Içvara* yet it is different from Him.[55]

The second aspect of the atomic form of the *Jñātā* represents the Vallabha school. It also holds, like other Vaiṣṇava schools, that the *Ātman* is distinct from *Jñāna* though they are inseparably connected with each other.[56] The *Jñātā* is eternal,[57] self-illuminating[58] and atomic.[59] But the system differs from all other Vaiṣṇava schools in holding the identity between *Jīva* and the *Içvara.*[60] Hence, it is called *Çuddhādvaita.*

The last subdivision, namely, that which believes both in the difference and the identity existing between *Jīva* and *Içvara,* may be further subdivided into two aspects—one when *Içvara,* that is, *Brahman,* is regarded to be manifesting Himself (*pariṇāmī*) and the other when it is not so. The former refers to the Bhāskara school of Vedānta while the latter represents the Nimbārka school. Both these schools are supporters of the *bhedābhedavāda.*[61] Both believe in the eternity, self-illuminating[62] and atomic[63] nature of the *Jñātā,* and

[50] SR., p. 298; Siddhāntadarçana, p. 41.
[51] SR., p. 334.
[52] SDS., p. 139, B. O. R. I. Edition.
[53] Ibid.
[54] PS., p. 74b along with MSSS.
[55] PS., and MSSS; pp. 24b, 32a, 142b; SDS., p. 128
[56] Nirṇayārṇava of Bālakṛṣṇa Bhaṭṭa, pp. 20-21, 63-65.
[57] Ibid.
[58] Subodhinī, I. ii. 23, p. 27; Prasthāna., p. 59.
[59] Nirṇayārṇava, p. 160.
[60] Çuddhādvaitamārtaṇḍa of Giridharajī p. 8.
[61] Bhāskara, I. i. 4; pp. 16-18; SR., p. 345; Vedā., p. 32; VRM on DÇ., pp. 91-92; ÇM., Verse 36.
[62] VRM., on DÇ., p. 3.
[63] Bhāskara, IV. iv. 15, p. 247; VRM on DÇ., p. 3.

in so far they agree with the above mentioned schools of Vaiṣṇavaism. The only point of difference between the Bhāskara and the Nimbārka schools is that the former believes in the manifesting nature (*pariṇāmitva*) of *Içvara*[64] while the latter does not.

(2) With regard to the other possible alternative, namely, that the *Jñātā* is distinct from *Jñāna* which is prominent, it may be said that there is no system under Indian thought where *Jñāna* is recognised as different from the *Jñātā* as well as prominent having the *Jñātā* as a subsidiary. Hence, the treatment of this aspect cannot be attempted here.

In the same manner, the relation and nature of *Jñāna* and *Jñeya* can be found out with a view to differentiate one school from another.

3. Thus *Jñāna may be looked upon as the same as Jñeya or distinct from it.* In the former case, again, prominence may be given either to *Jñāna* or to *Jñeya*.

(1) Now, when prominence is given to *Jñāna* it is either momentary (*kṣaṇika*) or non-momentary. The former is represented by the Buddhist school of Vijñānavāda according to which there is no difference between *Jñāna* and *Jñeya* which, in its turn, is nothing but forms of cognition.[65] This itself shows that the *Jñāna* is prominent while the *Jñeya* is its subsidiary. This *Jñāna* is also momentary.[66] The non-*kṣaṇika* aspect may be, again, subdivided according to the nature of *Jñāna* which is either essentially active or essentially non-active. In the former case *Jñāna* is really the creative agent of the empirical world, as both *icchāçakti* and *kriyāçakti* belong to it.[67] This aspect is represented by Kashmir Çaivaism. In the latter case, on the other hand, it is not at all active. In fact, it is

[64] Bhāskara, pp. 85, 96, 103-104, 164.
[65] SSS., Verse 6, p. 12.
[66] SSS., Verse 9, p. 12.
[67] PH., Sūtra 5, p. 13.

only the *adhiṣṭhāna* or the substrate of the empirical world. It is, therefore, that the *Brahman* is known as *adhiṣṭhāna-caitanya*. This represents the Çaṅkara school of Vedānta.

(2) With regard to the other aspect it may be pointed out that under this head there is no school in Indian thought according to which *Jñeya* may be regarded prominent and identical with *Jñāna*. *Jñāna* can in no way be regarded as a subsidiary. Hence, no attempt can be made to deal with this aspect here.

4. (1) Coming to the other variety, namely, *when Jñāna is regarded as distinct from Jñeya*, prominent and eternal,[68] it may be either *svaprakāça* or non-*svaprakāça*. The former is represented by the school of Jaina while the latter refers to the schools of Rāmānuja and Mādhva. As for the Jaina school it is true that it differentiates *Jñāna* from *Jñeya*.[69] *Jñāna* is both eternal[70] and self-illuminating.[71] According to the Rāmānuja school the *Jñeya* aspect is unconscious (*acit*)[72] and is, consequently, different from *Jñāna* which belongs to the *Ātman* alone.[73] This *Jñāna* is non-self-illuminating.[74] The Mādhva school agrees with the schools of Rāmānuja and Jaina in holding that *Jñāna* and *Jñeya* are two distinct entities[75] and that the former is, in this connection, prominent and eternal. But it differs from the Jaina in holding the *Jñāna* to be not self-illuminating.[76]

(2) When *Jñeya*, on the other hand, *predominates*, it may be looked upon as eternal or non-eternal. The

[68] TT., p. 35.

[69] NAVV., p. 48; Guṇa. on ṢDS, pp. 138, 161.

[70] NAV., verse 32.

[71] *Pramāṇaṃ svaparābhāsi jñānam*—NAV., p. 1; NAVV., p. 31.

[72] TT., p. 41.

[73] TT., p. 22.

[74] *Svavyatiriktaprakāçakam*—TT., p. 35; *Svayamprakāçarahitattvam*—TTBhā., p. 35.

[75] PS., and MSSS., p. 81b.

[76] SDS., p. 71, Calcutta edition.

former may be divided into *jaḍa* (unconscious) and *ajaḍa* (self-illumining). The latter aspect represents the schools of Bhāskara and Vallabha. According to Bhāskara the *Jñeya*, which represents the extra-mental world, is the manifestation of the *Brahman* itself,[77] and as such, it possesses real existence.[78] The difference between the two is due to *upādhis*.[79] As the empirical world (*prapañca*) is an effect of *Brahman* it is said to be *ajaḍa*.[80] Similarly, according to the school of Vallabha the *Jñeya*, which is eternal,[81] is of the very nature of *Brahman* even in the empirical state.[82] It is also, on this very account, *ajaḍa*.

The *Jaḍa* aspect of the eternal form of *Jñeya* may be split up into two aspects—one evolving and the other non-evolving. The former refers to the Nimbārka school according to which the *Jñeya* is eternal[83] and different from *Jñāna* which is the *dharma* of *Jñātā*.[84] Further, the school believes in the evolving nature of the empirical world.[85] The latter, that is, the non-evolving aspect may be cognisable through the direct means of right cognition and inference, or through the direct perception, inference, analogy (*upamāna*) and valid testimony (*çabda*), or through direct perception, inference, analogy, valid testimony and implication (*arthāpatti*), or through the above mentioned five means of right knowledge and the non-perception (*anupalabdhi*) which is also another means of right cognition. The first refers to the Vaiçeṣika school[86], the second

[77] Bhāskara, p. 17.
[78] Bhāskara, pp. 10, 17, 19, 20.
[79] Bhāskara, IV. iv. 4, p. 243.
[80] Bhāskara, pp. 19, 89, 164-65.
[81] PR., p. 54.
[82] PR., p. 54.
[83] VB., p. 25. IPR., Vol. II, p. 752.
[84] *Jñānāçrayaḥ*—VRM. on DÇ., Verse 1. p. 4; Ibid., pp. 40, 44.
[85] VB., p. 25; VRM. on DÇ., Verse 3.
[86] TR., p. 56.

to the Nyāya,[87] the third to the Prābhākara Mīmāṃsā[88] while the fourth to the Bhāṭṭa school of Pūrva-Mīmāṃsā.[89]

Under non-eternal type of *Jñeya* we may have two subdivisions, namely, momentary (*kṣaṇika*) and non-momentary. The latter represents the school of Cārvāka. The former may be either looked upon as cognisable through direct means of right knowledge (*pratyakṣagocara*) mainly or as cognisable through inference. The former includes the Vaibhāṣika[90] school while the latter the Sautrāntika[91] school of Buddhism.

[87] NBhā., I. i. 1.
[88] PP., p. 44.
[89] ÇD., pp. 37, 59, 72, 74, 76, 83
[90] SSS., p. 14.
[91] SSS., p. 13.

The following are the charts to illustrate the differences between the various schools of Indian thought as explained above:—

I.

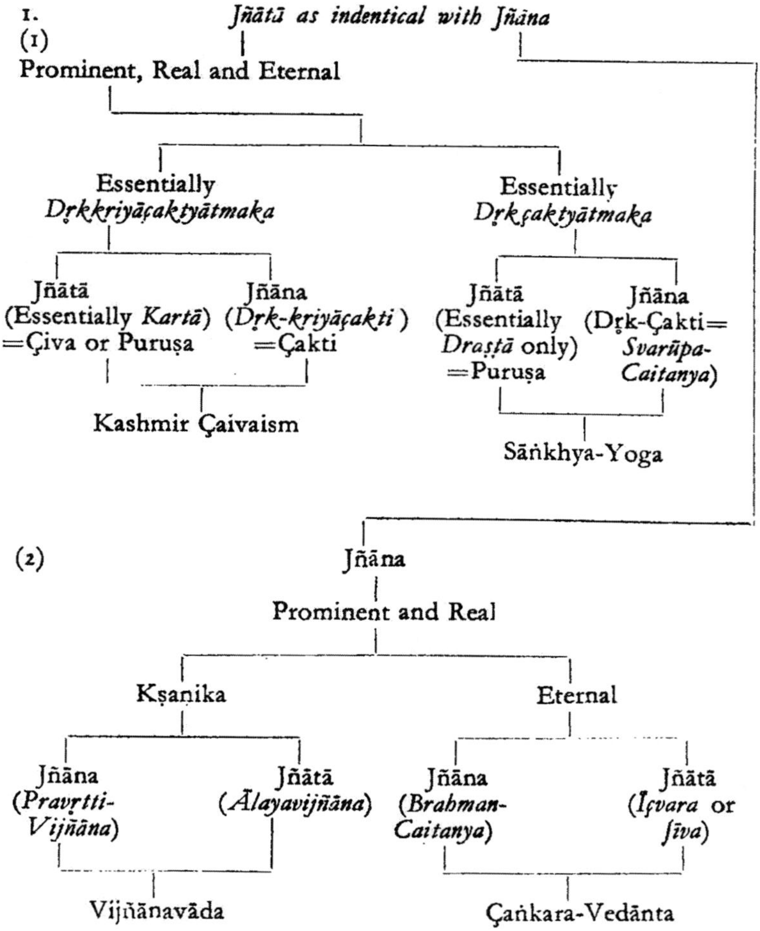

2.

(1) *Jñātā as distinct from Jñāna*

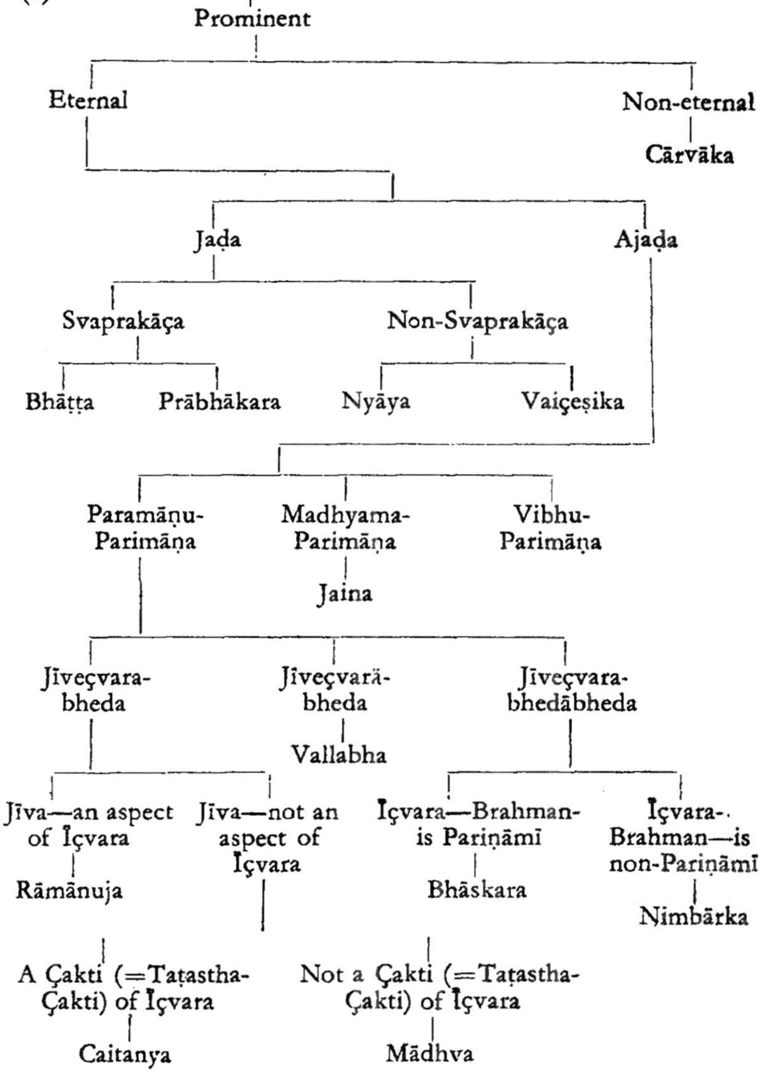

(2) With regard to the other possible alternative it may be said that under no system of Indian thought it

is possible to recognise *Jñāna* as prominent and *Jñātā* as its subsidiary when both are different from each other. Hence, no chart is possible here.

3.
(1)

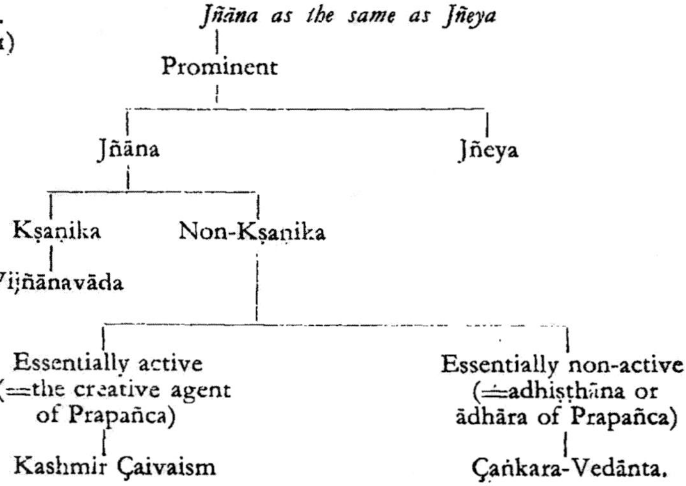

(2) Under this head there is no system in Indian thought where *Jñeya* can be regarded as prominent and *Jñātā* as its subordinate. Hence, this aspect cannot be treated here.

4.
(1)

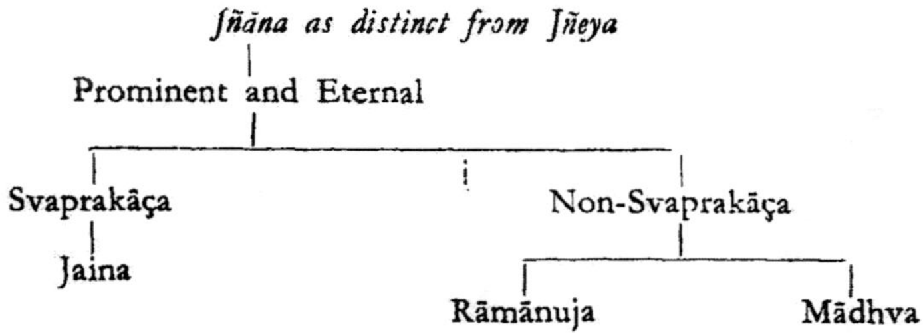

(2) *Jñāna as distinct from Jñeya*

- Prominent and Real
  - Eternal
    - Jaḍa
      - Evolving
        - Nimbārka
      - Non-evolving
        - Pratyakṣānumāna-gocara
          - Vaiçeṣika
        - Pratyakṣānumānopa-mānaçabdagocara
          - Nyāya
        - Pratyakṣā-numāno-pamāna-çabdārthā-pattigocara
          - Prābhākara Mīmāṃsā
        - Pratyakṣā-numāno-pamāna-çabdārthā-pattya-nupalabdhi-gocara
          - Bhāṭṭa Mīmāṃsā
    - Ajaḍa
      - Bhāskara
      - Vallabha
  - Non-eternal
    - Kṣaṇika
      - Pratyakṣa-gocara
        - Vaibhāṣika
      - Pratyakṣāgocara (=anumānagamya)
        - Sautrāntika
    - Non-Kṣaṇika
      - Cārvāka

III

IDEALISM, REALISM AND MATERIALISM DEFINED, DESCRIBED AND DISTINGUISHED

Now, all these schools of thought can be classified under three broad heads on the same basis, that is, the relation between *Jñātā*, *Jñāna* and *Jñeya*. Thus the line of thought, which deals with *Jñeya* as identical with *Jñāna* and does not attribute any independent reality to it, is represented as Idealism; that according to which *Jñeya* is real and distinct from *Jñāna* is represented as Realism; and the line of thought which stresses *Jñeya* into prominence and does not allow an independent existence to *Jñāna* may be taken as representative of Materialism.

1. *Idealism*

The line of thought, which speaks of *Jñeya* as identical with *Jñāna* and does not attribute any reality to it, is known as Idealism. According to this school of thought, *Jñāna* is all in all. The existence of the entire objective world is unreal and is merely a form of *Jñāna*. As for instance, according to the Māyāvādins the objective side is merely illusory; in fact, there is only one Reality which is all-*Jñāna* and which is in the background of this illusory appearance. In like manner, according to the Yogācāra school of Buddhism, there is nothing except *Jñāna*. What appears as an external object is its own form.

2. *Realism*

Realism may be defined as a school of thought which holds that there are things which have their real existence in the objective world as objects of our cognition (*Jñeya*) and are quite independent of the corresponding *Jñāna*. In other words, to the Realists the external world has an objective extra-mental value.[92] Such objects of our cognition exist apart from and independent of their corresponding *Jñāna* and are cognised either through the instrumentality of the external sense-organs or through the internal sense-organs, namely, the *antaḥkaraṇas*. Both the external and internal objects of our cognition, being different from their corresponding cognitions, are equally included under the sensible world which represents the *Jñeya* aspect.

It has been said above that the objective world is cognised either through the help of the external sense-organs or through the help of the *antaḥkaraṇas*. In the former case, the objects of cognition are naturally grosser, while, in the latter case they are subtler. In other words, in the former case, the external objects of cognition are mainly the respective specific attributes of the five *Mahābhūtas* namely, *rūpa*, *sparça*, *gandha*, *rasa* and *çabda* which have enough affinity with their respective sense-organs through which they are cognised. In the latter case, where the objects of the sensible world are cognised through the instrumentality of the *antaḥkaraṇas* the objects of cognition are all those subtler elements which are beyond the reach of our physical eyes, namely, *paramāṇus*, *tanmātrās*, desire, pain and pleasure etc.

This makes it clear that Realism presupposes an objective world, having an independent and real existence as opposed to mere appearance (*Ābhāsa*) as the Idealists are inclined to believe, and as such, being distinct from *Jñāna*. Realism as defined above would include the following schools: Nyāya, Vaiçeṣika, the two schools of Pūrva-Mīmāṃsā, namely, Bhāṭṭa and Prābhākara, Sāṅkhya, Rāmānuja, Mādhva, Çaivaism of Kashmir, and even Çaṅkara-Vedānta in its empirical (*vyāvahārika*) aspect from the orthodox side, while

[92] The World as Power: Reality, pp. 25-27.

Cārvāka, Jainas, and the two schools of Buddhism, namely, Vaibhāṣika and Sautrāntika from the non-orthodox side.

3. *Materialism*

Lastly, the line of thought, which holds that the only reality is *Jñeya* and everything else is its product or its own function, is called Materialism. According to this the external and the internal worlds are forms of gross matter; so that, even *Jñāna* is but a product or by-product of the *bhūtas*. The reality consists, therefore, of the forms of matter (non-*cetana*)[93] alone. The propounders of this thought in India are generally known as Lokāyatikas or Bāhyas.

About the use of the term materialism I quote here the relevant statement of a Western scholar. Thus he says, "The name materialism is often employed in a loose sense as synonymous with atheism, or indeed as a term of abuse for any philosophy which does not square with the prevailing orthodoxy. But to us it has its stricter meaning—a belief that dead matter, in the hard unyielding lumps pictured by common sense, or the solid impenetrable Newtonian particles, is the sole ultimate reality of the universe; that thought and consciousness are but by-products of matter; and that there is nothing real underlying it or existing beyond it."[94]

4. *Realism and Materialism distinguished*

Both Realism and Materialism lay emphasis on the separate and independent existence of *Jñeya*. Matter forms an important aspect of both kinds of thought. It is, therefore, essential to distinguish between these

[93] In this book the term 'Matter' is used in the sense of 'non-*cetana*,' which includes all the *dravyas* except the *Ātman*.

[94] A History of Science and its relation with philosophy and religion, by William Cecil Dampier, Dampier-Whetham, p. 275.

two schools by referring to the salient points of difference.

We have seen above that under Realism *Jñeya* has been asserted to be quite distinct from *Jñāna*. The objective world is neither identified with *Jñātā* nor with *Jñāna*. It is neither a form of *Jñāna* and nor does it depend upon *Jñātā* or *Jñāna* for its existence. This aloofness of the *Jñeya* proves the existence of a Realistic thought. No doubt, according to this school of thought, stress is laid on the material (*acit*) aspect of the universe but the importance of the non-material (*cit*) aspect, as quite distinct in nature and having an independent existence, has not been denied. For, in Realism its existence is as important and essential as the very existence of matter. Without it the very existence of the cosmic world upon which Realism depends is impossible. There is a sort of harmonious co-operation between *Jñātā* and *Jñeya* in spite of the fact that the former is conscious and the latter is unconscious. In other words, Realism attaches equal importance to the conscious (*cit*) as well as to the unconscious (*acit*). In a way, it assumes a dualistic form.

As for the Materialism, on the other hand, we are aware that it is altogether a different type of school. It does not believe in the separate and independent existence of the conscious aspect, that is, the *Ātman*. According to this school of thought, matter is all in all. Both the mental and the extra-mental phenomena, if we can use the terms freely in the present context, are explained in terms of matter. Consciousness, which helps us to establish the existence of the *Ātman*, is also a by-product of matter alone. A peculiar collocation of certain *paramāṇus*[95] or *bhūtas* produces

[95] There appears to have been a class of people of this school who thought that the various *paramāṇus* separately possessed consciousness. But as there was no thorough proof the view was discarded. VBhā, Notes, p. 396. PWSS., Vol. III, p. 70, Ft. n.

consciousness. The *Ātman* is nothing but an organism endowed with the property of consciousness.[96]

5. *Realism subdivided*

Having given in brief the idea of the divisions of the schools of thought under Indian metaphysics, I now pass on to the details of the school of thought with which the present work is directly connected, that is, Realism.

According to the definition of Realism given above all those schools of thought, which hold that *Jñāna* is distinct from *Jñeya* and the latter is as much real as anything else, are all included under Realism. This includes the two schools of Pūrva-Mīmāṃsā, namely, Bhāṭṭa and Prābhākara; Sāṅkhya; Rāmānuja; Mādhva; Çaivaism of Kashmir; and Nyāya-Vaiçeṣika. I would like to go even so far as to include the school of Çaṅkara-Vedānta in its empirical (*vyāvahārika*) aspect under Realism. This is from the orthodox side. From the non-orthodox side, on the other hand, we have the school of Cārvāka; the school of Jainas; and the two schools of Buddhism, namely, Vaibhāṣika and Sautrāntika.

As to the realistic nature of these schools there is hardly any doubt; for, all of them believe in the reality of *Jñeya* and its difference from *Jñāna* and *Jñātā* as shown above.

[96] This view is the most crude form of Materialism. But history shows that there is a gradual improvement in thought; so that, the propounders came to recognise in turn *Indriya*, *Prāṇa* and lastly, *Manas* as the *Ātman* one after another. These views are based on the different substrata of the consciousness and bodily activities. They also thought along with it the question of *independence* to which the superiority was attributed, and that which was proved to be independent was called *Ātman*-VSS., pp. 73-76. ST., Ātmasiddhi, pp. 7-14.

IV

A BRIEF ACCOUNT OF THE REALISTIC SCHOOLS OF THOUGHT

1. *Orthodox Schools*

(1-2) *Pūrva-Mīmāṃsā Schools—Bhāṭṭa and Prābhākara.*

In the Mīmāṃsā schools we do not easily find any reference in the sūtras to the problem of Realism. But a close study of the Sūtra-*Satsamprayoge*[97] etc., in which it is said that the *Jñāna* is produced when the sense-organ comes in contact with *artha*, shows quite clearly that the Sūtrakāra believes in the separate and independent existence of *Jñāna* from *Jñeya*, which is referred to here by the term *artha*. In the Bhāṣya of Çabara[98] also we find that while criticising the view of the Çūnyavādins, Çabara says that the objective reality is quite independent of *Jñāna* or *Buddhi*, which in its turn, really depends upon the external reality for its occurrence. Later on, both the schools of Bhaṭṭa and Prabhākara have dealt with this problem at great length in their respective works. It is, therefore, that both the schools of Pūrva-Mīmāṃsā are classed under Realism.

As regards the nature and relation of *Jñeya* with *Jñātā* or *Jñāna*, we have seen above that there is hardly any difference between the two schools; but somehow or other a difference can be made out between these on the basis of the nature of *Jñātā* and *Jñāna*, as has been pointed out above also. It is on this very basis that these two schools can be differentiated from all other schools under Realism.

(3) *Sāṅkhya School*

After this we come to the Sāṅkhya system. It also represents an aspect of Realism. It posits that there

[97] MS, I. i. 4.

[98] Bhāṣya on Ibid., I. i. 5, pp. 7-8.

are two ultimate entities, namely, *Puruṣa* and *Prakṛti* both of which are eternal and different from each other. *Puruṣa* is consciousness itself while *Prakṛti* is *jaḍā*. *Puruṣa* is *draṣṭṛ* (*sākṣin*) and *bhoktṛ* while *Prakṛti* is *dṛçyā* or *bhogyā*.[99] As such, *Puruṣa* is the *Jñātā* and *Prakṛti* is the *Jñeya*. But as Realism mainly deals with the empirical aspect it would be better if the transcendent *Puruṣa* is left alone as it does not serve any practical purpose under Realism. Therefore, we should come to the *Prakṛtigarbha*. Here we find that the *Buddhi-tattva* represents *Jñātā* and its *Vṛtti Jñāna*. These two can be separated if we want it. The other evolutes represent the *Jñeya* aspect.

These evolutes differ from one another only because of the difference of the collocation of the three *guṇas-sattva*, *rajas* and *tamas*. These three *guṇas* are the constituents of *Prakṛti* and all the *vikṛtis*; hence, it is said that the three *guṇas* alone represent the objective world.[100] Although these evolutes are the modifications of *Prakṛti* alone and finally become dissolved into *Prakṛti* itself, yet their separate real existence cannot be gainsaid. They are real and different *tattvas* and, as such, are differentiated from mere appearance (*ābhāsa*). It is needless to say that the evolutes representing *Jñeya* are in a sense different from *Jñāna*. This is enough to prove the Realistic nature of this school. The only point to note here, as referred to already, is that the *Jñeya*, according to Sāṅkhya, is subtler than that of the Nyāya-Vaiçeṣika and some other schools of thought.

We know that there is no other system under Realism according to which *Jñeya* being *jaḍa* and *triguṇātmaka* acts as if it were conscious. This is the characteristic which differentiates it from all other schools under Realism. It may be suggested on this very ground to designate this school as *Guṇa-Realism*.

99 SS., verse 19.

100 SS., verse 19; Gunaratna's comm. on ṢDS., p. 98.

(4) *Rāmānuja School*

I next pass on to the school of Rāmānuja. The school of Rāmānuja is one of the systems of thought based on Pāñcarātra and represents the Çrīsampradāya, as *Çrī* or *Lakṣmī* is considered to be the original propounder of this school. According to this school *Jñātā* is the *Cit-tattva* which is the substratum of *Jñāna*.[101] Both *Jñāna* and *Jñātā* are eternal[102] and are inseparably connected together.[103] It is, therefore, that the *Cit-tattva* is called *Jñānsvarūpa*.[104] *Jñāna* is all-pervading.[105] It is *ajaḍa* and *ānandarūpa*, that is, of blissful nature.[106] It is capable of *saṅkoca* and *vikāça* (contraction and expansion).[107] It illumines things other than itself.[108]

Jñeya is divided into three kinds:—(a) that which possesses *sattva* only; (b) that which has all the three *guṇas*; (c) and that which does not possess any of the three *guṇas*. It is eternal,[109] distinct from *Jñāna* and is free from consciousness.[110] It is subject to change.[111]

This is enough to show the realistic nature of the system. It is the only school under Realism according to which the *tattvas*, included under *Jñeya* which being *jaḍa* and of the nature of change, are of three different natures as pointed out above. Hence, it represents an entirely different aspect of Realism and may be designated as *Guṇāguṇa Realism*.

[101] TT., p. 17.
[102] Ibid., pp. 5, 35.
[103] Ibid., p. 17. cf. Bhāṣya on it.
[104] Ibid.
[105] Ibid., p. 35.
[106] Ibid.
[107] Ibid.
[108] Ibid. cf. Bhāṣya on it.
[109] Ibid., pp. 41, 45, 74.
[110] Ibid., p. 41.
[111] *Vikārāspadam*—TT., p. 41.

(5) *Mādhva School*

Next, I proceed to the Mādhva school of Vedānta. It is a perfectly dualistic school of thought. It believes in the eternity and reality of *Jñeya*, which is *jaḍa* and, as such, is different from *Jñāna*. Of course, *Jñātā* is different from both *Jñāna* and *Jñeya*. This much is enough to prove the realistic nature of this system. It is differentiated from all other schools under Realism.

(6) *Kashmir Çaivaism*

According to this school of thought the only persisting entity is *Parama Çiva*. All the evolutes are the manifestations of Him. It is believed that all the evolutes are also *jñānasvarūpa*. In spite of this the evolutes are as real as *Parama Çiva* Himself. The distinction between *pramātā* and *prameya* is only possible when the *pramātṛ* aspect is obscured;[112] and it is only then that *prameya* can be said to be distinct from *pramātā*.

Now, considering the fact that there is ultimately only one Real Entity and the rest are its manifestations, this system is sometime wrongly identified with the Çaṅkara-Vedānta, according to which also there is only one Reality, namely, *Brahman* and the rest are all manifestations. But if we closely study the two systems it would become clear that there is a vast difference between the two schools. Thus we find that the manifestations in Çaivaism are not mere names and forms, illusory and unreal appearances (*anirvacanīya*) as it is in Çaṅkara-Vedānta, but they are real manifestations (*satya*). All these real manifestations are present potentially in *Parama Çiva* Who, when, He so desires manifests Himself into the universe.[113]

[112] *Vastutaḥ hi atra yo'yam pramātāpi sa prameya eva, sa tu pramātrīkriyamāṇa ācchāditaprameyātmaka evocyate.* IPV., p. 211.

[113] *Antaḥ sthitavatāmeva ghaṭate bahirātmanā*—IP., p. 13.

This is all to show the realistic nature of this school of thought. The peculiar nature of the *prameyas*, that is, the nature of their being *jñānasvarūpa* and the realistic nature of the school differeniate it from all other schools under Realism. It is due to this very nature of *prameya* that it is suggested to name this system as *Ideo-Realistic School.*

(7) *Empirical School of Çaṅkara-Vedānta*

The conception of Realism given above makes it clear that almost all the orthodox schools of Indian thought, including the Advaita-Vedānta of Çaṅkara, are in some form or other, realistic in nature. Thus when we come to the Advaita-Vedānta of Çaṅkara, we find that there are two distinct views, namely, *dṛṣṭisṛṣṭi* and *sṛṣṭidṛṣṭi*.[114] The former holds that the objective world has no existence apart from its cognition in which it reveals itself like the dream-appearances. The jar, for instance, perceived by one just now has no existence in itself; but it exists in so far as it is perceived and ceases to exist as soon as it ceases to be perceived. In other words, the perception of a thing is, as a matter of fact, its own creation and that there is no phenomenon apart from its perception.[115] This view represents the extreme orthodox Idealistic view. Realism has nothing to do with this theory.

The latter is the pragmatic Vedānta view, according to which the objective world representing merely name and form (*nāmarūpa*) has got an existence even apart from our perception of it. In fact, the view that the *esse* of a thing is its *percipi* is opposed to common sense and is also inconsistent with the Vedāntic position recognising three kinds of existence (*sattā*), namely, *Pāramārthikī*, *Vyāvahārikī* and *Prātibhāsikī*.[116] The first

[114] SLS, pp. 350-356.
[115] VSM, pp. 30-35; SLS, pp. 350-356.
[116] VSM, p. 25.

implies Unity in Pure *Sattā* which is *Brahman*, the Supreme Eternal Reality, and the unreality of everything else. The second refers to the reality of the objective world. No doubt, *Brahman* is the permanent reality but the objective world also has got empirical existence even apart from our perception of it. The objects of the world are proved to possess an empirical existence through the various means of right cognition. It is a fact that the sensible world is but a manifestation of the *Māyā* and is not real in the sense in which *Brahman* is real, and it is after all illusory. But its unreal nature is not felt during the worldly state (*saṃsāradaçā*). That it is illusory is revealed only when the realisation of the self takes place. So, before the *truth* is achieved the reality of this empirical world is accepted.[117] The third type of existence possesses reality only so long as it is perceived (*yāvatpratibhāsamavatiṣṭhate*).[118] Its erroneous nature is proved just after the sublating knowledge makes its appearance. The perception of snake, which erroneously appears in place of rope seen in the dim-light, and whose *esse* is admittedly *percipi*, is an instance of this type of existence.

The first and the third varieties of the existence do not serve any useful purpose under Realism, for in the former case no reality is attributed to the objective world and in the latter the true knowledge of the real world is prevented from appearance. But when we consider the *vyāvahārika* aspect we find that the objective world is real in the empirical sense. Here we find that the distinction between *Jñātā*, *Jñāna* and *Jñeya* is possible. The *Jīva* or *Īçvara* is the *Jñātā* while the empirical world represents the *Jñeya*. This is enough to prove the realistic nature of the system.

As this triple distinction is possible only under the

[117] VEP, pp. 14-16.
[118] Ibid., p. 95.

influence of *Māyā* which is *Anirvacanīyā*, this realistic school may be designated as the *Anirvacanīya Realism*.

2. *Non-orthodox Schools*

The Vaibhāṣika and Sautrāntika schools of Buddhism belong to that type of Realism according to which *Jñāna* is quite distinct from *Jñeya*, and both *Jñāna* and *Jñeya* are *kṣaṇika* (momentary). As there are differences between these two schools themselves, I would like to deal with each school separately.

(8) *Vaibhāṣika School of Buddhism*

The Vaibhāṣika school belongs to the sect of *Sarvāstivādins*. The very name of this sect shows that it believes in the separate and independent existence of the objective world.[119] Both the external and the internal existences in the forms of *artha* and *Jñāna* are believed to be real.[120] The objective or *Jñeya* side consists of *paramāṇus* which are sometimes cognised through perception and sometimes inferred.[121] *Jñāna* is different from *Jñeya*. This is enough to establish the realistic nature of the school.

As regards the nature of and the relation between *Jñātā*, *Jñeya* and *Jñāna* we know that they are identical.[122] The *vijñānaskandha* which is nothing but a series of *Jñāna* is the knower (*Jñātā*).[123] *Jñeya* is cognised through direct means of cognition and is *kṣaṇika*; hence, the system may be called *Direct Momentary Realism*.

(9) *Sautrāntika School of Buddhism*

Not very much different from the above mentioned realistic school is the other Realistic school of Buddhism,

[119] NSM, MS. Bauddhamata; ṢDS, p. 34.
[120] ILV, pp. 247-248.
[121] SSS, pp. 14-15.
[122] Guṇaratna on ṢDS, p. 139.
[123] Ibid.

namely, Sautrāntika.[124] According to this school there is an external world which is as much real as *Jñāna* itself. Although the objective world is independent of *Jñāna*, yet it is not cognised through direct perception as it is the case with the Vaibhāṣika school. The Sautrāntikas hold that the existence of outside world (*bāhyārtha*) which represents the *Jñeya* side is inferred from the various forms of *Jñāna* which forms would not have otherwise existed.[125] In other words, the Sautrāntikas believe that *Jñāna* assumes various forms which lead us to infer the existence of an external world corresponding to them.[126]

As regards the nature of and the relation between *Jñātā* and *Jñāna* it is the same as in the Vaibhāṣika school. It has already been pointed out that both *Jñāna* and *Jñeya* are momentary even according to the Sautrāntikas. These show the realistic nature of the Sautrāntika school as well.

Although both the above mentioned Buddhist schools hold almost similar views regarding certain vital points, yet there are certain points of difference which easily differentiate one school from the other. Thus according to Vaibhāṣika, *Jñāna* is formless, while it has forms according to the other school; the former believes in the direct perceptibility of the outside world while the latter holds it entirely inferential. In other words, it is clear from the above that the real difference between the two schools, both of which are equally realistic, consists in the attitude in which each looks at the order of the external reality. The burden of emphasis appears to be shifting from the outer to the inner. This is the explanation underlying the difference between the two schools of Buddhism.

Emphasising the point of difference between the

[124] SSS, p. 14.
[125] Ibid., p. 13; Guṇaratna on ṢDS, p. 47.
[126] NSM, MS. Bauddhamata; Guṇaratna on ṢDS, p. 47.

two schools we find, according to the Sautrāntika school, that the cognition of the external world is not through the direct means of right cognition but through inference; hence, we would like to name it as *Indirect Momentary Realism.*

(10) *Jaina School*

Coming to the Jaina school we find that *Jñātā* is different from *Jñāna* but both are co-eternal and are inseparably associated together;[127] *Jñāna*, on the other hand, is also distinct from *Jñeya* and both are eternal.[128] These prove the realistic nature of the system.

According to this system there are two *tattvas*, namely, *Jīva* and *Ajīva*.[129] The former is *upayogamaya* consisting of *Jñāna* and *Darçana*.[130] This *upayoga* which is made up of *Jñāna* and *Darçana* is always inseparable from *Jīva*.[131] *Jīva* is conscious[132] and formless (*amūrta*), is the agent and experiencer. It possesses the same dimension as its abode, namely, physical organism.[133] That is, if the body be large the *Jīva* will, accordingly, be large in size, and if it be small then the dimension of the *Jīva* will be, accordingly, small. This is due to the characteristics of contraction and expansion (*saṅkoca and vikāça*) belonging to the *Jīva*.[134] It is eternal.[135] Being an *āçraya* of *Jñāna*, *Jīva* which is the *Jñātā*[136] is different from *Jñāna*, but as *Jñāna* is inseparably connected with the *Jīva*, it is said to be also identical with the *Jīva* itself.[137]

[127] PKSS, p. 40, quoted in DS, p. 9.
[128] Ibid., pp. 53, 55, 57, 59 and DSV, p. 26.
[129] DS, Gāthā, I.
[130] Ibid, 2.
[131] Ibid, 4 and p. 9.
[132] Ibid, 3.
[133] Ibid, 2, 9.
[134] Ibid, 10.
[135] SDS, p. 69, Poona Ed.
[136] NAV, Verse 31, p. 30.
[137] NAVV, p. 48.

The second *tattva* is the *Ajīva-tattva*. It represents the objective side. It is real.[138] It is of five kinds, namely, *Pudgala*, *Dharma*, *Adharma*, *Ākāça* and *Kāla*. Except *Pudgala* the rest are formless.[139] All these are eternal.[140] This *tattva* is unconscious.

The above description shows that the school is a realistic one. The peculiar nature and the relation of *Jñātā*, *Jñāna* and *Jñeya* make the school quite a different type of Realism.

(11) *Cārvāka School*

The Cārvāka school of thought belongs to that type of Realism according to which both *Jñāna* and *Jñeya* are non-eternal. It holds that the reality consists of the objective world only which constitutes the four *Mahābhūtas*, namely, *kṣiti*, *ap*, *tejas* and *vāyu*.

This objective world which represents the *Jñeya* is different from *Jñāna*, which itself in its turn, is merely a by-product of the peculiar amalgamation of the above mentioned four *Mahābhūtas*, although none of them possesses it separately. The seat of *Jñāna* is sometimes the gross-body and sometimes sense-organs etc. The system lays entire emphasis on *Jñeya* which is real. This proves the realistic nature of the school.

Jñātā according to it is the body, or the vital-air, or the sense-organ, or the *Manas* in accordance with the attribution of activity and predominance to each. That which does not possess any consciousness may be classed under *Jñeya*; so that, *Jñātā*, *Jñāna* and *Jñeya* can be easily differentiated according to this school as well. But we should not forget that they do not believe in anything which is neither a *bhūta* nor a *bhautika*. Hence, even being a realistic school the system is purely materialistic. Hence, we may designate this school as *Bhautika Materialistic Realism*.

[138] Ibid., p. 31.
[139] DS, Gāthā 15.
[140] Ibid., pp. 53, 55, 57 and 59; DSV, p. 26.

V

THE POSITION OF NYĀYA-VAIÇEṢIKA AS A REALISTIC SYSTEM

Having thus briefly described the nature of the Realistic schools in general I now pass on to find out the peculiar position of Nyāya-Vaiçeṣika. It is needless to say that this joint-system holds that *Jñātā*, *Jñāna* and *Jñeya* are distinct from one another. *Jñeya*, which is an important factor in Realism, has been shown above as eternal, non-*kṣaṇika* and cognisable through one or more means of right cognition. While speaking of it as eternal we should remember that it refers to the atomic and ubiquitous forms of matter only and not to the objective world. The above mentioned three characteristics of this school belong to Pūrva-Mīmāṃsā also, so that, as far as *Jñeya* is concerned, there seems to be hardly much difference between these schools. The Nyāya and Vaiçeṣika schools may, however, be distinguished from the standpoint of the nature of *Jñātā* and *Jñāna*. Thus whereas the *Jñātā* of the Bhāṭṭa and the Prābhākara-Mīmāṃsā is *svaprakāça*, that of the Nyāya-Vaiçeṣika is not so. The Prābhākara-Mīmāṃsā holds *Jñāna* also to be *svaprakāça* which is not the case with either the Bhāṭṭa or the Nyāya-Vaiçeṣika school.

VI

INTER-RELATION OF NYĀYA AND VAIÇEṢIKA

It is a well-known fact that the two currents of philosophical thought with which we are dealing here were systematised in course of time as two distinct schools by Gautama and Kaṇāda, the authors of Nyāya and Vaiçeṣika Sūtras respectively. It is difficult to say whether the systems started separately and being allied in general attitude and view-point became mixed up in later ages or an original fund of floating ideas, without the distinct character of a regular school, became with the process of time crystallized into two rival, though allied, systems. But there appears to be no doubt that even in the earliest literature of the schools known to us we recognise distinct and unmistakeable points of affinity between them, not only in the general metaphysical position but even in several minor details. The differences too are equally marked. Some of these latter may be summed up here for facility of a proper appreciation of the distinct nature of each.

1. *Standpoint*

Like almost all other schools of Indian thought, Nyāya and Vaiçeṣika aim at the realisation of *Mokṣa* as their *Summum Bonum*. But they differ in their method of treatment. Nyāya, as represented by Gautama, begins mainly as a logical system emphasizing the means of right knowledge. According to this system true knowledge depends upon the critical examination of objects by means of right knowledge. Hence, the entire importance is laid on the various means of right knowledge themselves, so, says Vātsyāyana, that the true knowledge of the objects is not possible without the means of right knowledge.[141] Further he adds that the very science of reasoning (*nyāya*) consists in the true knowledge of the *artha* by means of right knowledge.[142] Hence, Gautama begins his work with an enunciation of the means of right knowledge as the most important category. The object of knowledge according to him occupies the secondary place. The other fourteen categories[143] of his are the auxiliaries to help the science of reasoning. This fact has been very well illustrated by the

[141] Vide *Pramāṇamantareṇa nārthapratipattiḥ*—NBhā, I. i.1, p. 1.
[142] Vide *Prāmaṇairarthaparīkṣaṇam nyāyaḥ*—Ibid., p. 3.
[143] Vide NS, I. i. 1.

foundation of the neo-Nyāya School which has led to the development of the entire later Nyāya literature on the basis of the means of right cognition alone. This justifies the name given to this school of thought as *Pramāṇa-Çāstra.*

The standpoint of Vaiçeṣika, on the other hand, is entirely different. It lays stress on the ontological aspect of the cosmic order. According to it the critical examination of the six categories[144] into which the entire field of existence is divided leads to the realisation of the *Summum Bonum.* The treatment of the means of right knowledge is only subsidiary.

2. *Pramāṇa*

Nyāya believes in four *Pramāṇas,*[145] while Vaiçeṣika recognises only two.[146]

3. *Pratyakṣa*

It appears that according to Naiyāyikas there are as many kinds of direct perception (*pratyakṣa*) as there are sense-organs; so that, by direct perception we should understand visual, gustatory (*rāsanā*), olfactory (*ghrāṇaja*), tactual (*tvāca-spārçana*) and auditory (*çrāvaṇa*).

[144] It appears that the earlier writers on Vaiçeṣika recognised only six categories, *abhāva*, the seventh category, being implied though unexpressed (cf. Vyom, p. 20 (J); KV, p. 6). The explicit recognition is found for the first time in the work of Çivāditya which is named as Saptapadārthī.

[145] Namely, *Pratyakṣa, Anumāna, Upamāna* and *Çabda*—NS., I. i. 3. But there are certain Ācāryas (e.g. Bhāsarvajña) who seem to deny the independent character of *Upamāna* as a valid source of knowledge—Nyāyasāra, p. 2.

[146] Namely, *Pratyakṣa* and *Anumāna*. The usual Vaiçeṣika view, as represented in the Sūtra of Kaṇāda and the standard works of the school, is that *Çabda*, though a source of valid knowledge, is really a form of inference. PPBhā, p. 213; VU., IX. ii. 3. But teachers like Vyomaçiva and others are in favour of triple *pramāṇa*, holding *Çabda* to be an independent means of knowledge. Vyom., pp. 555, 577.

Vaiçeṣikas, on the other hand, seem to consider that there is only one kind of direct perception, namely, visual. That is, the use of the term *pratyakṣa* should be restricted to that of the eyes alone.[147]

4. *Samavāya*

According to Nyāya *samavāya* (inherence) is cognised through *pratyakṣa*,[148] while according to Vaiçeṣika it is inferential.[149] For those who cannot reconcile themselves to the perceptibility of *samavāya*, the Naiyāyika adduces certain reasons.

The Vaiçeṣika standpoint is summed up by Praçastapāda[150] and by Çrīdhara,[151] who have attempted to show that as *samavāya* cannot be held as related to an object through an independent relation (e.g. *saṃyoga* and another *samavāya*) it must be accepted as constituting its own relation and consequently, supersensuous in character. The senses are capable of cognising positive categories only through one of the relations recognised in the system. They add further that unlike *saṃyoga*, *samavāya* never appears in our perceptual knowledge, inasmuch as its two terms are always perceived as inseparably associated *en masse*, which would not have been the case if it were immediately perceived. The later Vaiçeṣikas[152] further point out that the supersensuous nature of *samavāya* is deduced from the fact that like *Manas*, *Kāla*, etc. it is a positive category distinct from the *Ātman* and does not inhere in anything else.

The Naiyāyikas, on the other hand, criticise the above inferences as intrinsically defective and incapable

147. Mallinātha commenting on the text—*apratyakṣasyāpi vāyoḥ sparçaçabdadhṛtikampaliṅgaiḥ siddhiḥ* (TR., pp. 136-137)—says—*svamate vāyoḥ spārçanatve'pi vaiçeṣiko bhūtvāha*—p. 136.

148. TC, Pratyakṣa. p. 645; Nyāyasāra of Mādhavadeva, pp. 166-170.

149. PPBhā, p. 329.

150. PPBhā, pp. 328-329.

151. Kandalī, pp. 329-330.

152. VU., VII. ii. 28; VV., VII. ii. 28.

of leading to a conclusion. They adduce a counter-argument in support of their own doctrine. The more important point bearing on the question, from their angle of vision, relates to the recognition and function of what is technically known as a *svarūpa-sambandha*[158] in neo-logical literature (*Navya-Nyāya*). They hold that a relation or *abhāva*, of which the *pratiyogī* and the *anuyogī* are capable of direct perception, is itself capable of such perception. An illustration of this is found in the case of absolute non-existence, say, of a jar on a particular spot perceptible to the senses. In the case under consideration the *svarūpa-sambandha* referred to above is known as *viçeṣaṇatā* (or *viçeṣya-viçeṣaṇa-bhāva*). The non-recognition of the *svarūpa* of a category as capable of being conceived as a relation in the ancient literature was responsible, the Naiyāyikas allege, for the peculiar view of the Vaiçeṣikas.

5. *Pāka* (*chemical action*)

Nyāya holds that an object is naturally porous,

[158] It has been defined as "*Sambandhāntareṇa viçiṣṭapratītijananāyog yatvam*," meaning, that it is a relation which must be held to exist in a case where a determinate knowledge (*viçiṣṭapratīti*) could not have been effected by any other relation (namely, *samavāya* and *saṃyoga*). In other words, this relation must be either the subject itself (*anuyogin*) or predicate itself (*pratiyogin*) of the said judgment (*anuyogipratiyog yanyatarasvarūpaḥ sambandhaviçeṣaḥ*). For example, take the judgment '*ghaṭaṃ jānāmi*' wherein there are three factors: (a) *ghaṭa*—the object of knowledge, (b) the knowledge which has *ghaṭa* as its object, and (c) knower, the substrate of the knowledge, represented by the verbal termination '*mip*'. Between b and c there is *samavāya* relation; for knowledge is the attribute of the individual self. But there must be some sort of relation between a and b also, in order that this very judgment rather than any other, e.g. *paṭaṃ jānāmi*, might arise. But the relation cannot be *samavāya*, because the attribute *jñānu* belongs to the self and not to the *ghaṭu*. Nor can it be *saṃyoga*, for this relation holds only between *dravyas*. Hence, the only possible determining cause, *niyāmaka*, of this judgment is the *ghaṭasvarūpa* itself, conceived as a relation. This is what is known as *svarūpasambandha*. Also *vide* TC., Pratyakṣa, p. 646.

and *taijasa* particles can very well enter into an object and produce chemical changes both in and out; so that, the chemical action takes place in an object as a whole without destroying the object into its constituent *paramāṇus*. This view of the Naiyāyikas is known as *Piṭharapāka*.

Vaiçeṣika, on the other hand, is of opinion that it is impossible for the *taijasa* particles to come in contact with each and every part of an object unless that object is reduced to its constituent *paramāṇus*. Hence, the chemical action takes place in the *paramāṇus* alone and not in the *Piṭhara* as the Naiyāyikas think. Hence, it is called *Pīlupākavāda*.[154]

6. *Duration of Karman*

According to Nyāya, *karman* (motion) is sometimes destroyed by the destruction of the substratum and sometimes by the subsequent conjunction; and hence, considering the various causes that lead to *karman*, it is clear that a *karman* exists for three or four moments only.

Vaiçeṣika, on the other hand, considers that sometimes the duration of *karman* is even seven moments. Thus when a pot is thrown into fire, there is produced a *karman* in the *paramāṇus* which had produced the *dvyaṇukas* of that pot; then the disjunction between the *paramāṇus* producing *dvyaṇukas* takes place; then there is the destruction of the conjunction; then the destruction of the *dvyaṇuka* followed by the disjunction between the *paramāṇus* and the *Ākāça*; then there is the destruction of the conjunction existing between *Ākāça* and *paramāṇus*; then there is the subsequent conjunction of the *paramāṇus;* and then there is the destruction of the *karman*.

But when the *Vibhāgaja-Vibhāga* (disjunction caused by another disjunction) is produced simultaneously

[154] By *Pīlu* we mean a *paramāṇu*.

with the destruction of the substance then the duration of the *karman* is only six moments.[155]

7. *Hetvābhāsa*

Nyāya believes in five kinds of *hetvābhāsa*, namely, *asiddha*, *viruddha*, *anaikāntika*, *prakaraṇasama* and *kālātyayāpadiṣṭa*; and accordingly, believes in the five conditions necessary for a good *hetu*; namely, *pakṣasattva*, *sapakṣasattva*, *vipakṣāsattva*, *asatpratipakṣatva* and *abādhitatva*. Vaiçeṣika holds that there are only three *hetvābhāsas*, namely, *viruddha asiddha* and *sandigdha*, as is said "*Viruddhāsiddhasandigdhamaliṅgaṃ kāçyapo-'bravīt*"; and accordingly, there are only three conditions of a good *hetu*, namely, *pakṣasattva*, *sapakṣasattva* and *vipakṣāsattva*. Sometimes, they make out the fourth *hetvābhāsa*, namely, *anadhyavasita* from the above statement.[156]

8. *Vegākhya-saṃskāra* (*Velocity*)

Nyāya considers that since the beginning of the discharging of an arrow from the bow up to the hitting of the mark there are several *vegas* and several *karmans*. That is, the first *vega* produced in the arrow is due to motion; that *vega* produces another motion which, in its turn, produces another *vega* and so on till the arrow reaches the mark. Vaiçeṣika, on the other hand, holds that there is only one *vega* throughout. In other words, the first motion is produced in the arrow by the impulsion (*nodana*) which produces velocity, and this velocity produces a series of motion in succession till the arrow reaches the mark. There is no need in believing in more than one *vega* like the series of *karman* in succession; for, it will be a case of *gaurava*[157] only.

[155] PRM, p. 42.
[156] PD, p. 25.
[157] VU, V. i. 17; KR, p. 132.

9. *Sakhaṇḍopādhi*

The New School of Nyāya believes in a particular kind of *dharma* called *sakhaṇḍopādhi* as quite distinct from the recognised seven categories of the Vaiçeṣika. The *sakhaṇḍopādhi* form of *dharma* is to be had in two ways:—(1) That *dharma* which is always and necessarily apprehended through something else is called *sakhaṇḍopādhi*. As for instance, the *dharmas-pratiyogitā*, *anuyogitā*, *ādhāratā*, *ādheyatā* etc. are apprehended only through *pratiyogitātva*, *anuyogitātva*, *ādhāratātva*, *ādheyatātva* etc. respectively and not alone. Hence, the *dharmas-pratiyogitā* etc. are known as *sakhaṇḍopādhis*. (2) Again, that *dharma* also, which is the outcome of several things (*padārthas*), is called *sakhaṇḍopādhi*. In the instance, 'the mountain is smoky; because, it is fiery,' the probans (possessing fire) also belongs to a hot piece of iron where there is no smoke. Hence, the argument is fallacious and is classed under the *sādhāraṇa* type of fallacy. This *sādhāraṇa* is an outcome of several *padārthas*; hence, it is a case of *sakhaṇḍopādhi*, and, as such, is apprehended through something else. Again, in the instance, 'Sound is non-eternal; as, it possesses soundness,' there is the fallacy of *asādhāraṇa*. This *asādhāraṇatva* also, similarly, is a case of *sakhaṇḍopādhi*. Hence, according to Nyāya this is given a separate place.

Vaiçeṣika, on the other hand, thinks that it can be easily included under some of the already recognised seven categories. Thus, *pratiyogitā*, for instance, is nothing but the *pratiyogī* itself. It can be also of the nature of *abhāva* itself. Thus the *pratiyogitā* belonging to the *ghaṭa* (jar) is sometimes of the nature of *ghaṭa* itself, or sometimes of the nature of *ghaṭatvajāti*, or sometimes of the form of *ghaṭābhāva*. Similarly, in the case of the *sādhāraṇa* kind of fallacy given above the *dharma-sādhāraṇatva* is of the nature of *contact*. In the case of the *asādhāraṇa* fallacy, the *dharma* is of the nature of *çabdatva-jāti.*' In this way, it is seen that the *sakhaṇḍopādhi* is not a separate entity at all.[158]

10. *Vibhāgaja-Vibhāga*

According to the Vaiçeṣikas disjunction is of three kinds, and disjunction caused by disjunction (*vibhāgaja-vibhāga*) is one of these. This variety of disjunction, in its turn, is of two kinds: one—the disjunction of cause and non-cause due to the disjunction of cause alone (*kāraṇamātra-vibhāgāt kāraṇākāraṇavibhāgaḥ*) and the other—the disjunction of effect and non-effect produced by the disjunction of cause and non-cause (*kāraṇākāraṇa-vibhāgāt kāryākāryavibhāgaḥ*). The former may be illustrated as the disjunction existing between *kapāla* (half of a pot) and *Ākāça* (not related as cause and effect) due to the disjunction between the two-halves of a pot—*kapālas*—which are its (pot's) cause. The latter may be illustrated as the disjunction of the hand and the tree followed by that of the body and the tree caused by the disjunction of the finger and the tree.[159]

The disjunction in both the cases is, no doubt, brought about by motion produced in the *kapāla* and the finger. In the latter case, however, as the motion thus produced rests in the finger while the disjunction is in the hand or in the body, it is called a case of *vyadhikaraṇa;* so that, this motion cannot be the cause of the disjunction existing between the body and the tree. No motion can be attributed to a composite unless it inheres in all the constituents of that composite. Hence, it is held that the disjunction of the effect (e.g. hand and body) and the non-effect in the latter instance, is produced by the disjunction of the cause (e.g. finger) and the non-cause (e.g. tree) and not by any motion.[160] In this way, the necessity of disjunction

[158] Setu., pp. 102-103.
[159] VU., VII. ii. 10.
[160] VU., VII. ii. 10; NM., pp. 558-59; PPBhā. and Kandalī., pp. 151-164.

caused by another disjunction (*vibhāgaja-vibhāga*) is established by the Vaiçeṣikas.

The Naiyāyikas, on the other hand, do not see any necessity in accepting the above view. They hold that the very motion which separates the finger from the tree and inheres in the former (e.g. finger) is itself capable of destroying the indirect conjunctions existing between the hand and the tree and also that which exists between the body and the tree.[161]

It should not be held here that if the same motion be believed to cause the disjunction of the body from the tree, then there is the danger of its lasting for a longer period or becoming eternal if it is found in any eternal substance; for, a motion is always destroyed by the subsequent conjunction which is possible here by the conjunction caused by this very motion between the body and the *Ākāça*. There is nothing to prevent the motion to produce the conjunction after destroying it in connection with something else; just as the same heat-contact which destroys the attributes of an earthly object by the chemical action is also capable of producing the same. On these grounds the necessity of the disjunction caused by another disjunction is rejected by the Naiyāyikas.[162]

11. *Dvitva*

Vaiçeṣika is of opinion that the qualities *dvitva*, *tritva* etc. are produced by the *apekṣābuddhi* which is a kind of mental necessity giving rise to the notion of number and which is expressed by the proposition

[161] The author of Upaskāra on VS., VII. i.6 attributes this view to Bhāsarvajña, one of the most famous orthodox writers of the middle ages. But this view is not found in this Nyāyasāra which is the only work of his known to us so far. This suggests that there might be some other work of his which is still undiscovered.

[162] NM., pp. 559-60.

'this is one, this is one' etc. The process of the origin of one of these qualities is described as follows:—

First, there is the contact of the sense-organ with the object, that is, each of the two pots, for instance; then there is the cognition of the generality of *ekatva* (*ekatvasāmānyadhīḥ*); then there is the *apekṣābuddhi* which conveys the thought of *ekatva* in each of the two objects in the form of 'this is one', 'this is one'; then the *dvitva* is produced by the combination of the two separate *ekatvas*.[163]

But Nyāya is of opinion that the *apekṣābuddhi* does not produce the *dvitva* etc. but only manifests (*jñāpyate* or *vyañjyate*) it.[164]

12. *Ajasaṃyoga between Vibhus*

Relation (*sambandha*) is of two kinds: inherence (*samavāya*) and an ordinary relation in the form of the combination of two or more separated substances (*saṃyoga*). The former exists between such inseparable pairs which are related as (1) supporter (*ādhāra*) and supported (*ādheya*), (2) as effect and cause, and (3) as non-effect and non-cause.[165] The latter, on the other hand, is possible between such separated pairs of which (1) either one or both possess separate motion (*pṛthaggamana*), as in the case of eternal substances and also of which (2) either one or both are separately related as supporter and supported being mutually exclusive, as in the case of non-eternal substances.[166] Amongst the eternal substances, the condition laid down above is possible either between atomic substances themselves or between one or more atomic and the ubiquitous substances. No third alternative is possible.

[163] LV, p. 58; KV, p. 200; KR, pp. 68-69.
[164] KV, p. 200; KR, pp. 68-69.
[165] PPBhā., p. 324.
[166] PPBhā., p. 141; Vyom., p. 495; Kandalī, p. 150.

As it is essential to have the combination between two or more *separated* things, eternal conjunction (*ajasaṃyoga*) between two or more ubiquitous forms is not possible. Moreover, as the relation necessitates the presence of the capacity of combining and separating themselves, which, again, indicates that there must be motion either in one or both of the combining substances, the Vaiçeṣikas consider it impossible to hold any relation between the ubiquitous substances.[167]

The Naiyāyikas, on the other hand, are of opinion that there is some sort of conjunction between the ubiquitous substances also. They adduce the argument that all-pervading substances have undoubtedly got conjunction with limited substances (*mūrtas*) through which they themselves come to possess mutual combination. And this mutual combination is known as *ajasaṃyoga*.[168]

13. *Nature of the Ātman in the state of liberation*

It is a well-known fact that there is a difference of opinion as to the presence of bliss in the liberated *Ātman* between the schools of Nyāya and Vaiçeṣika. As this topic has been dealt with at great length in Chapter XI of this book, it is not treated here.

14. *Artha*

Nyāya uses the term *artha* in the sense of *gandha*, *rasa*, *rūpa*, *sparça* and *çabda*,[169] which are varieties of qualities (*guṇas*), while Vaiçeṣika understands by it all the *guṇas* as well as *dravyas* and *karmans*.[170]

[167] Vyom., p. 505; Tāt., II. i. 36, p. 401.

[168] Vyom., p. 494; Kandalī, p. 150.

[169] NS, I. i. 14.

[170] The categories of *sāmānya*, *viçeṣa*, *samavāya* (and *abhāva*) are excluded from the scope of this technical designation, VS, VIII. ii. 3.

15. *Number of relations in drawing inference*

Vaiçeṣika holds that inference is drawn through one of the five relations, namely, *kārya*, *kāraṇa*, *saṃyogī*, *virodhī* and *samavāyī*. That is, an inference is drawn sometimes through the *liṅga* in the form of *kārya*; as for example, from the perception of smoke or light we infer the existence of fire; sometimes through the *liṅga* in the form of *kāraṇa*; as for instance, the inference of sound from the particular kind of contact of a stick with a drum by a deaf-man; sometimes, again, through the *liṅga* in the form of *saṃyogī*; as for example, the inference of the organ of touch (*tvak*) from the perception of the body connected with it; sometimes, again, inference proceeds from a contradictory or an antagonistic object; as for instance, the inference of the presence of a mungoose hidden behind the bush etc. at the sight of a furious snake; and lastly, inference results from having *samavāyin* as the mark; as for instance, the inference of the existence of *tejas* in water from the heat present in water.[171]

Nyāya, on the other hand, thinks that the classification[172] of *sambandhas* as given in the Vaiçeṣika works is entirely useless; for, by the use of the single term *sambandhin* all others can be understood.[173]

16. *The generalities of Sukumāratva and Karkaçatva*

Nyāya holds that the generality of tenderness (*sukumāratva*) is quite separate from that of the hardness (*karkaçatva*). They inhere in conjunction (*saṃyoga*) which itself inheres in earth alone, while Vaiçeṣika

[171] VU, VV, on VS, IX. ii. 1.

[172] This sūtra is read by Vācaspati Miçra as follows: *Asyedaṃ kāryaṃ kāraṇaṃ sambandhyekārthasamavāyi virodhi ceti laiṅgikam*. And he divides it into four—*yacca Vaiçeṣikaiḥ catuṣprakāraḥ* etc., Tāt., p. 164.

[173] Ibid.

thinks that they inhere in touch (*sparça*) and not in the conjunction.[174]

17. *Religion*

The Naiyāyikas are the devotees of *Çiva*, while the Vaiçeṣikas are the worshippers of *Maheçvara*[175] or *Paçupati*.[176]

18. *Organism*

Raghunātha Paṇḍita says that there are two kinds of physical organism: viviparous (*yonija*) and non-viviparous (*ayonija*). The former is further subdivided into *jarāyuja* and oviparous (*aṇḍaja*). He further adds that the *udbhijja* class of organism which the Vaiçeṣikas include under the non-viviparous is not recognised as an organism at all by the Naiyāyikas.[177]

But this seems to be only a partial view; for Praçastapāda does not include the *udbhijja* class under the non-viviparous. Its being a physical organism is itself denied by Praçastapāda who includes it under the immoveable (*sthāvara*) type of *viṣaya*.[178]

19. *Dream-Cognition*

According to Nyāya dream-cognition is both true and false. If it is produced from merits then it is true and if from demerits then it is included under erroneous cognition. But according to Vaiçeṣikas it is always a variety of false knowledge (*avidyā*).[179]

[174] PRM., p. 32.
[175] *Vide* the last verse of the Praçastapādabhāṣya.
[176] Guṇaratna on ṢDS., p. 51.
[177] PRM., p. 21.
[178] PPBhā., p. 28.
[179] PRM., p. 34; PPBhā., p. 172; AUS, Vol. V., pp. 278-280.

VII

PROBLEM OF MATTER IN NYĀYA-VAIÇEṢIKA

The universe appears to us a complexity of contradictions—unity and diversity, passivity and activity, perfection and limitation, and so on. Each and every philosopher has to face these contradictory principles and has to give his own solution for each and every problem of the universe. After an enquiry into the nature of these, it is found that the universe may be divided under two distinct heads—mental and extramental, or in the terms of Indian thought, *Cetana* and *Jaḍa*. Philosophical studies, which aim at explaining things, as they exist, cannot neglect either side. Even the *Bhautika* Materialistic Realism has to accept the *cetana* aspect in some form or other.

The extramental side represents the material world mostly, which is produced out of matter and its products. Matter and its forms occupy our attention at the very first stage of production (*sṛṣṭi*). We know that attempts have been made by thinkers to explain the essence and function of *matter* from time to time, but the explanations till now supplied are of a divergent character and not adequate in all cases.

The *jaḍa* aspect of the universe represents the objective world; and it is with this that the Realistic thought has mainly to do. Hence, the problem of matter forms one of the most vital problems of the Realistic thought.

It is an admitted fact that the definition of *Matter* has varied with every philosopher in the West and there does not appear any common solution of the problem, as is clear from the following: "The idea of matter, which plays so large a part in materialistic thinking, has neither met with such general acceptance nor admits of such certain proof as to take rank, without further discussion, as a firm and adequate foundation for our direct conscious experience. The conflict between the mechanical and dynamical views of nature is not yet over and the latter eliminates the idea of matter altogether. That is, the mechanist defines the atoms as Material extended particles; his opponent makes them centres of force, unextended points of reference, for the effects of force."[180]

But the case of Indian philosophy is altogether different. The problem of matter, like all other problems of thought, has been discussed and final solutions have been arrived at in different ways according to the different outlooks and aims of the different systems of thought. All the details are found worked out there. Beginning with the grossest form of matter we gradually enter into its subtle forms by slow degrees. The joint-system, with which we are concerned, deals with all the forms of gross matter in the most natural way so as to satisfy the common-sense of man and be in agreement with the actual reality and the conventions of the external world (*vyavahāra and pratīti*). But at the same time it talks of *paramāṇus* and *dvyaṇukas* also which shows that the system deals with even those forms of matter which are beyond the scope of common-sense view.

Like almost all other Realistic schools, Nyāya-Vaiçeṣika attaches much more importance to matter. The only non-material entity here is the *Ātman* which alone is conscious. All the rest are *jaḍa* and represent the various phases of matter. Matter alone manifests the consciousness which is a *dharma* of the *Ātman*. Hence, we may say that as far as the objective world is concerned the place of matter, in Nyāya-Vaiçeṣika, is as important as that of the *Ātman*. But at the same time we should remember that the *cetana* aspect is in no way less important.

[180] IPOK., pp. 122-123.

VIII

MATTER AND SPIRIT

We have seen above the importance of the sensible world under Realism. It is also a fact that even laying full stress on the non-conscious aspect of the physical world, the Realistic thought cannot neglect the subjective aspect of it, namely, the *Ātman*. By non-conscious aspect of the world we understand all that is included under *jaḍa*, which is entirely free from consciousness. Thus '*Matter*', as used in the present work, may be defined as that which is other than the substratum of *Jñāna* and possesses or has the capacity to possess an attribute (*Jñānadhikaraṇātiriktatve sati guṇavat*). This excludes the spirit (*Ātman*) and includes all other *dravyas* recognised by Nyāya and Vaiçeṣika.

Both these aspects are essential for explaining phenomena. According to Nyāya and Vaiçeṣika both matter and spirit as defined above are equally eternal. None of these two depends upon the other for its existence. But there is a peculiar relation between the two in so far as the existence of one is manifested through the help of the other. Thus we find that there is a sort of intimate relation, something like causal sequence, between our thoughts and the external realities. That there are thoughts of the external world in our mind is proved by our worldly usages (*vyavahāra*). Now, it may be asked as to what is the substratum of these thoughts: thoughts being attributes must have a substratum to inhere in. The material substances cannot be the desired substratum; so that, it must be something other than material. Thus the inferred substratum which possesses these thoughts is known as the spirit or *Ātman*. Again, the Divine existence is also proved by the necessity of imparting motion to the ultimate particles for grouping together during the *Pralaya* so as to form the cosmic world. In these ways matter manifests spirit. Again, there can be no thought without the existence of the external reality, nor can there be any Divine Will to help the production of the cosmic order if there be no matter in some form or other. Hence, directly or indirectly it is through the spirit that the existence of the external world is manifested.

It will not be out of place here to refer to the views which deny consciousness in the *Ātman* but affirm it in the physical organism, the vital airs, the sense-organs, the *Manas*, or the *paramāṇus* taken collectively or separately. But it will be seen that all these views are untenable.

Thus, it is well-known that the physical organism, though constantly in a state of flux, continues to persist for a time even after death, but without any consciousness. If consciousness were the normal function of the organism as such, there is no reason why it should disappear even when the organism of which it is believed to be a quality persists. For it is observed that qualities and substances continue together as mutually related. Then again, the fact of recognition (*pratyabhijñā*), which implies the co-ordination of two moments in temporal sequence on the basis of a persistent unity, coupled with the fact that the nature of the organism is always changing, indicates that there must be an eternal substance distinct from the body as known to us in which consciousness may inhere as its inalienable property. The assumption of consciousness in *matter* would lead to an absurd logical position. It may be held to belong to the ultimate constituents of matter (either severally or collectively) or to the material product. In the first alternative of the former case there would be as many consciousnesses as there are particles in an organism, and this would make life impossible, for the simple reason that the several unrelated or discordant consciousnesses could not lead to a harmony of effect. In the second alternative there would be no ground for differentiating one group-particles (e.g. living organism) from another (e.g. a piece of stone). The latter case, which presupposes organisation, would involve the pre-existence of consciousness and life in the particles concerned, because what is absent in the cause cannot appear in the effect. And the difficulties in consequence of this position would be the same as those to which reference has already been made.

In like manner, consciousness cannot be the attribute of the sense-organs. In the same manner, *Manas* also cannot be the seat of consciousness, unless we hold it to be all-pervading and presuppose the existence of an eternal *karaṇa* distinct from it, in which case, the difference between the *Ātman* and the *Manas* will be only a verbal one.

Such an *Ātman* is different from '*matter*.' But without the help of the latter its own existence cannot be easily proved. The nature and operation of the *Ātman* are also known through '*Matter*' alone. Although these two are opposite entities yet they co-operate in such a harmonious manner that our life and the dealings of the world become quite smooth.

The relation between '*Matter*' and the *Ātman* is *vyaṅgya-vyañjakabhāva*; so that, the harmony of the *saṃsārayātrā* under the influence of *adṛṣṭa* becomes possible. But it may be asked: When did this relation begin? To this it may be said that the *saṃsāra* is believed to be beginningless and the primary elements, out of which the products of the objective world are formed, are eternal. The *Ātman* also is eternal. Similar is the case with *Manas* which brings about the relation between the two. Under the circumstances, it is impossible to fix the time of the beginning of the relation (for the purpose of experiencing pleasure and pain) between the *Ātman* and the *Matter*.

IX

DIVISIONS AND SUB-DIVISIONS OF MATTER

The present work deals with the problem of '*Matter*' conceived as non-*cetana*, that is, as a substance in which consciousness and other allied psychic qualities do not inhere. The following table will show the various divisions and subdivisions of matter as understood above, and followed in the present work.

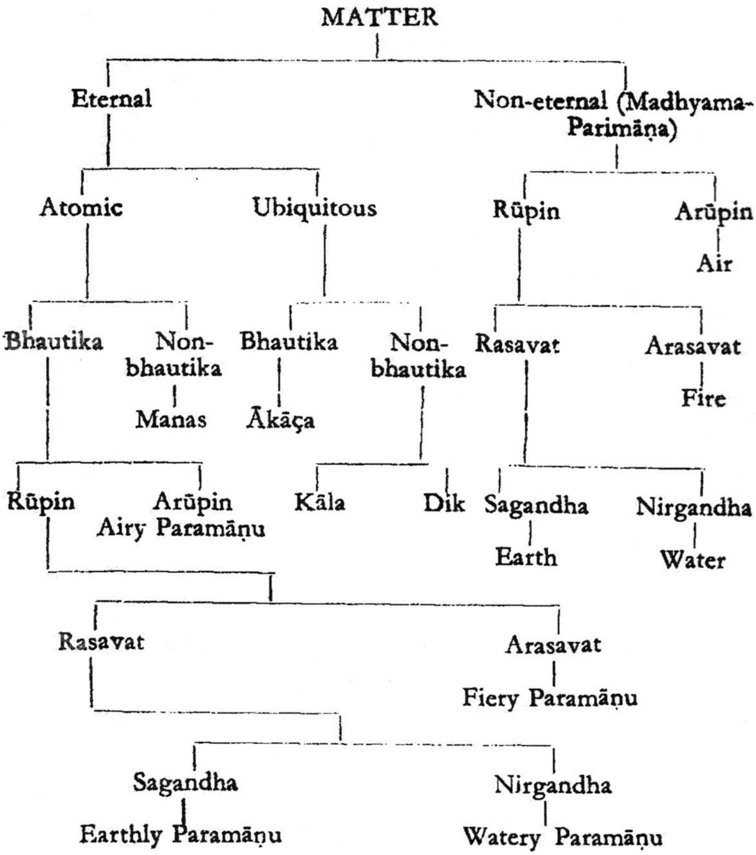

CHAPTER II

GENERAL TREATMENT OF MATTER

I

INTRODUCTION

It has been shown in the previous chapter that belief in the existence of the objective world is indispensable for Realism. Now, when we come to study the nature of this objective world in all its aspects we find that it cannot exist without the help of a conscious element. In every kind of product, whether individual or collective, the necessity of a conscious agent cannot be gainsaid. This conscious active element is either the *Jīvātman* or the *Paramātman*. The remaining factors contributing to the origin of the world are, as a matter of course, unconscious elements, comprising eight forms of matter (five atomic and three ubiquitous in nature) and their qualities. Matter, in its atomic or discrete form, consists of (1) four productive elements (*bhūtas*) which enter into the composition of the world and (2) mind (*manas*) which, conceived as an eternal substance and associated with the individual self (*Jīvātman*), helps in the organisation of the productive matter into structures capable of experiencing pleasure and pain under the stress of moral necessity and retributive justice. The other form of matter which is looked upon as a continuum (being substantive in character) is the eternal background of the creative process (viz. time or *Kāla* and space or *Ākāça*[1]) and of the relative position involved therein (viz. *Dik*).

[1] *Sarveṣāṃ saṃyogināṃ mūrtadravyāṇāmākāçaḥ samāno deça eka ādhāra ityarthaḥ......iha tu sarveṣāmādhāra ityucyate*—Kandalī, p. 22.

The nature and characteristics of the *Ātman* are described at length in Chapter XI of this book. The following pages are, therefore, devoted to a consideration of the various forms of matter as mentioned in the preceding paragraph.

II

COMMON CHARACTERISTICS OF ALL THE FORMS OF PREDICABLE EXISTENCE

Before we proceed to study in detail the general character of matter it would be well to have, if possible, a clear idea from the Vaiçeṣika point of view of the properties which characterise every form of existence, material or immaterial. It is held that everything having an existence must have a nature of its own by virtue of which it is said to exist (*astitva*)[2] and which constitutes so to say its self-identity. But existence, to have any meaning at all, presupposes knowledge in which it is revealed (*jñeyatva*) and language in which it finds an expression (*abhidheyatva*),[3] and *vice versa*. To a realist what can be known or spoken of cannot but have an existence of its own. Really speaking, the existence of a thing and its knowable and predicable character are co-existent in nature.

III

SIMILAR CHARACTERISTICS OF MATTER

It has already been pointed out that according to Nyāya-Vaiçeṣika the self forms the basis of psychic life; so that, consciousness, will and other qualities, which

The same idea is expressed by Bhartṛhari in his Vākyapadīya—*Ādhāraçaktiḥ prathamā sarvasaṃyoginām matā*—Kāṇḍa 3, Verse 4, p. 279.

[2] Kandalī, p. 16.

[3] FPBhā., p. 16.

mark psychic existence, are held to be its attributes.[4] Viewed in this light matter is what may be described as intrinsically unconscious and essentially substantive (*dravya*).[5] On further analysis, a number of other properties will be found to pertain to the different forms of matter in common. Of these, the most important seem to be inherent causality (that is, capable of generating an effect within itself as its cause—*svātmanyārambhakatva*), an individual character in each of its ultimate forms which are eternal (*antyaviçeṣavattva*) and in its emergent aspect incapability of being destroyed, as an effect, by the cause concerned (*kāryakāraṇāvirodhi*).[6]

The above mentioned characteristics are in common with the self. Hence, for the facility of finding out the similarities and dissimilarities of matter its eight forms may be grouped under two broad heads, viz. *bhautika* and non-*bhautika*. Each of these is subdivided into two groups again, viz. atomic (e.g. earth, water, *tejas* and air[7] in the former and *Manas* in the latter) and ubiquitous (e.g. *Ākāça*[8] in the former and *Kāla* and *Dik* in the latter).

Now, more important characteristics of each of these are given below:

As regards earth (*pṛthvī*) it is found that it has motion (*kriyā*)[9] which generates velocity (*vega*);[10] so that, when any earthly object, an arrow for instance, moves on it continues to move only because it possesses velocity which helps the existence of motion in that object for a certain length of time according to the strength of the impetus imparted to that object. But when that strength is exhausted the arrow does not

[4] PPBhā., p. 70.
[5] PPBhā., p. 20.
[6] PPBhā., p. 20; Kandalī, p. 21.
[7] PPBhā., p. 22.
[8] PPBhā., p. 22.
[9] VS., V. ii. 1; PPBhā., p. 21.
[10] VS., V. i. 17; PPBhā., p. 21.

move forward but falls down. This falling down of the arrow shows that it possesses weight (*gurutva*)[11] which is the necessary condition of the falling of the arrow. Hence, falling down (*patana*)[12] is also one of the characteristics of earth.

Earth is by its very nature solid. But under certain conditions when it comes in contact with heat it is reduced to atoms (*paramāṇus*) wherein a certain attribute called liquidity (*dravatva*) is produced.[13]

Earthly particles produce a sense-organ through which they themselves (through the law of affinity), in the form of an object, become manifest.[14]

Water (*jala*) possesses all the characteristics noted above[15] with only this difference that the liquidity possessed by it is natural.[16]

Tejas also possesses all the characteristics in common with earth and water[17] except weight,[18] due to the absence of which the *taijasa* particles do not naturally fall down. They always move upwards.[19] The liquidity present in it, as revealed in molten gold,[20] is not intrinsic.[21]

Coming to air (*vāyu*) it is found that it possesses oblique or transversal motion (*tīryaggati*)[22] but no

[11] VS., V. i. 18; PPBhā., p. 24; KV., p. 37.
[12] KV., p. 37.
[13] VS., II. i. 6-7; PPBhā., p. 25.
[14] VS., VIII. ii. 5; PPBhā., p. 22.
[15] VS., V. i. 18; V. ii. 12; PPBhā., pp. 21-22, 24.
[16] PPBhā., p. 25.
[17] PPBhā., pp. 21-22, 24-25.
[18] PPBhā., p. 24.
[19] VS., V. ii. 13.
[20] According to Nyāya-Vaiçeṣika gold is considered to be a *taijasa* object, because its liquidity is not destroyed however strong heat may be applied to it, which characteristic is not, however, found in any other substance.
[21] PPBhā., p. 25.
[22] VS., V. ii. 13.

weight.[23] It does not, therefore, naturally come down, and consequently, there is nothing to check its movement which ever continues to get impetus from the velocity the air possesses.[24] Hence, air is said to be always in motion (*satatagati*). Amongst the *bhautikas* it has the swiftest motion.

Each of these four substances has got two forms—one eternal in the form of *paramāṇus* and the other non-eternal as products (*kāryadravyas*). These products are non-existent before their production and also after their destruction. Prior to the production and after destruction all these four substances have a permanent form. Out of this permanent form every time a fresh production is made. This is at the root of the theory of *Ārambhaka*[25] expounded by Nyāya and Vaiçeṣika.

The last *bhautika* substance is the *Ākāça*.[26] The only point it has in common with the other *bhautikas* is that it provides a sense-organ through which alone its own property can be revealed.[27] Like the other ubiquitous forms of matter it is also all-pervasive and constitutes a basic principle of creation.[28]

Amongst the non-*bhautikas* we have *Manas* which is atomic and possesses motion and velocity[29] like all the non-ubiquitous forms of *bhautika* matter, with this difference that its motion is the quickest of all.

Time (*Kāla*) and what may be described as the background of relative position (*Dik*) are recognised to be at the bottom[30] of the entire cosmic order in which aspect they agree with the *Ākāça*.[31]

23 PPBhā., p. 24.
24 PPBhā., p. 21.
25 PPBhā., p. 24.
26 PPBhā., p. 22.
27 PPBhā., p. 22.
28 PPBhā., p. 22.
29 PPBhā., p. 21; VS., V. ii. 13.
30 PPBhā., p. 22.
31 PPBhā., p. 22.

These are the more important points of similarities in the various forms of matter.

IV

EXISTENCE OF ATOMIC AND ALL-PERVASIVE DIMENSIONS PROVED

Whenever anything is not directly perceived doubts are felt about its very existence. Both the atomic and the all-pervasive dimensions mentioned in the previous section are not perceptible through our physical senses. Hence, arguments have to be adduced to prove their existence.

Following very closely the common-sense view Nyāya-Vaiçeṣika finds that there are three possible dimensions, namely, the smallest, the largest and the intermediate. It is a fact that a *product* before its creation and after its destruction has no existence of any kind. But this does not mean that nothing pre-exists and that production takes place out of void. Nor does it mean that the destruction of the product means an absolute negation of the entire substance. According to Nyāya and Vaiçeṣika, therefore, every product is a fresh one which in no form exists before and after. It is believed that there is an ultimate substance or series of substances out of which through the operation of causal and instrumental agencies an object is produced. This ultimate substance consists of indivisible particles, called *paramāṇus*. These particles, being incapable of further analysis, are held to be eternal and represent the smallest fraction of creative substance. It is not possible for the process of destruction to continue *ad infinitum*; for, they hold that inasmuch as every material product would consist of an equally endless number of constituents there would be no difference of dimension amongst the various products. But that there is such a difference cannot be denied. Hence, it is necessary to hold that the process of destruction stops at a certain definite stage which, being incapable of further division, is eternal. Besides, there is also the *āgama* '*aṇoraṇīyān*' etc. to support the above view.

This is about the atomic nature of the *bhautika* type of ultimate and eternal particles. There is another non-*bhautika* substance which also possesses atomic nature. Just as it is essential to have an instrumental cause (*karaṇa*) to produce an external object, so it is necessary to have an internal instrumental cause for the genesis of cognition, desire, etc., which are psychic products. This internal instrumental cause, called *Manas*, cannot be of an intermediate dimension, as it would make it composed of parts and consequently, non-eternal. In the latter alternative, the creation and destruction, times without number, of an infinite number of *Manas*, to account for psychic phenomena, would have to be posited, which would naturally involve logical absurdities of a complex nature. It is through the help of this *Manas* that organism, capable of experiencing pleasure and pain under the demands of moral justice, is formed. This mind-substance cannot but be atomic, as otherwise, no knowledge would possibly arise, or if it arises at all, there would be simultaneity in it, which is inconsistent with the records of human experiences. States of consciousness, however quick they may be, appear only in succession, which is not in any other way possible. Hence, it is necessary that the nature of *Manas* must be atomic.

The very fact that creation exists implies that there must be some necessary conditions to form its background. These conditions cannot but be ubiquitous and eternal in nature. Hence, time, space and that which may be described as the relative position (*Dik*) have been accepted as all-pervasive.

CHAPTER III

ETERNITY AND MATTER—ATOMIC

A

BHAUTIKA MATTER

AFTER the general treatment of matter we proceed to deal with each of the forms of matter in detail. Proceeding in the order in which the forms are classified above the *bhautika* form of atomic matter is taken first for detailed study.

I

PARAMĀNU

1. *Defined and existence proved*

Paramāṇu has been defined as the ultimate particle of each of the four *Mahābhūtas*. Such a particle is necessarily supersensuous, and as such, its existence is sometimes questioned. That a *paramāṇu* is not perceived need not imply its non-existence, for it may as well be due to the action of certain factors[1] which stands in the way of its perception. According to Nyāya-Vaiçeṣika, the presence of magnitude (*mahattva*) in an object is one of the conditions of its perception; and as there is no magnitude in the *paramāṇu*, it is not perceived. Its existence, therefore, is proved through inference as shown below:

The motes, observed floating in the sun-beam entering a room through a little chink, are called *trasareṇus* and represent the ultimate particles of matter in

[1] *Ṣaḍbhiḥ prakāraiḥ satāṃ bhāvānāmanupalabdhirbhavati—*
atisannikarṣādativiprakarṣānmūrtyantaravyavadhānāt ।
tamasāvṛtatvādindriyadaurbalyādatipramādāt ॥
Mahābhāṣya on PS., IV; i. 1; SS; Verse 7.

so far as they are visible. Possessed of magnitude and being amenable to sense perception, these particles must be held to have component parts which, called *dvyaṇukas*, must, in their turn, possess similar constituents of their own for identical reasons. The components of these *dvyaṇukas* are called *paramāṇus*[2] which are indivisible by nature and incapable of further analysis. The assumption of the possibility of further division of these particles on the analogy of grosser matter would lead to a *regressus ad infinitum*. Besides, inasmuch as every material product would, in that case, consist of an equally endless number of constituents, there would be no actual difference in the dimension of the various products; so that, the dimension of the highest mountain of the world would be equal to that of a mustard seed. But that there is such a difference cannot be denied.[3] Hence, a *paramāṇu* cannot be further divided.

2. *Attributes of Paramāṇu*

The more important characteristics of the *bhautika-paramāṇus* are:

(1) They are eternal and indivisible.[4]

(2) By themselves they cannot produce anything;[5] else their eternal character would involve a continuous process of production.

(3) Each of the four kinds of *paramāṇus* possesses its specific attributes, namely, smell, touch, taste and colour. That is, the earthly *paramāṇu* has smell, the airy touch, the watery taste and the fiery colour.[6]

(4) They cannot be perceived through any of the organs of sense perception. Thus, for want of

[2] NV., IV. ii. 17; VS., IV. i. 2.

[3] PPBhā and Kandalī., p. 31; NM on LV., p. 23.

[4] VS., IV. i. 4; Vyom., p. 22?; VS., IV. i. 1; KVBhā., p. 78., VV., II. i. 13.

[5] Kandalī, pp. 31-32.

[6] VS., IV. i. 3.

magnitude and manifested colour[7] in them, there can be no visual perception; for want of magnitude and manifested touch, they cannot be felt through the tactual sense-organ, and so on.[8] But this does not mean that a sense-organ does not come in contact with *paramāṇus*;[9] for, they are perceived by the *yogins*.[10] In other words, in the case of the *yogins* also, the direct perception of the *paramāṇus* is through the sense-organ and object-contact. This does not deny the possibility of the intuitive perception of the *paramāṇus* by the *yogins*.[11]

(5) The attributes inherent in the *paramāṇus* are also eternal except in the case of the earthly *paramāṇus*.[12]

(6) The *paramāṇus* are the ultimate material cause (*upādānakāraṇa*) of the universe.[13]

(7) They are, both collectively and individually, imperceptible.[14]

(8) They possess quiddity (*antyaviçeṣa*) which differentiates one *paramāṇu* from the other.[15]

3. *Dimension and Paramāṇu*

Dimension (*parimāṇa*) has been defined by Praçastapāda as an attribute which is the cause of all measurements. It is of four kinds: small (*aṇu*), large (*mahat*), long (*dīrgha*) and short (*hrasva*).[16] Vallabha, on the other hand, is of opinion that *hrasva* and *dīrgha* are not separate dimensions but the subdivisions of *aṇu* and *mahat*

[7] NS., II. i. 36., VS., IV. i. 6; NSM., p. 35; TP, a comm. on NSM., MS. Fol. 26b; TPP., MS. Fol. 2a; a comm. on PC., MS. Fol. 47b.

[8] TPP., MS. Fol. 2b.

[9] NV., II. i. 33, p. 230.

[10] VU., VIII. i. 2.

[11] VU., VIII. i. 2.

[12] VS., and VU., VIII. i. 3.

[13] NV., IV. i. 21, p. 457.

[14] NLV., p. 8; Prakāça on NLV., p. 122.

[15] PPBhā., pp. 321-22.

[16] PPBhā., p. 131; Kandalī, pp. 133-34.

respectively.[17] Of these, *aṇutva* is both eternal and non-eternal according to the nature of the object to which it belongs. Thus, the *aṇutva* belonging to a *paramāṇu* is eternal, while that which belongs to a *dvyaṇuka* is non-eternal. About *hrasvatva* it is said that it belongs to that object wherein *aṇutva* is produced. In other words, *hrasvatva* is not present in an eternal object.[18] But Udayana holds that like *aṇutva*, *hrasvatva* is also of two kinds—eternal and non-eternal. The former belongs to a *paramāṇu* and the latter to a *dvyaṇuka*. That which is found in a *paramāṇu* is called *paramahrasvatva*.[19] Thus, a *paramāṇu* possesses both the smallest and the shortest possible dimensions.[20] The dimension of a *paramāṇu* is known as *parimaṇḍala* and is eternal.[21]

About the meaning of *parimaṇḍala*, it may be said that the word '*maṇḍala*' is used in the sense of a circular shape. Even circular objects appear to possess length to persons who stand on only one side of the object and whose eyes come in contact with a certain part of that object only. *Paramāṇu*, on the other hand, appears, from all quarters, spherical, and neither long nor crooked from any side; as it does not possess any part. The attribute '*maṇḍala*' would suggest the idea of having parts, but a *paramāṇu*, being partless, is unique in character. Thus *parimaṇḍala* here means the attribute of possessing *prakṛṣṭa-aṇutva*, the smallest possible dimension.[22]

4. *Partless character and eternity of Paramāṇu discussed*

The partless nature of a *paramāṇu* and its eternity have been objected to mainly by the Buddhists in various ways. It will be clear from the arguments of both the

[17] PRM., p. 31.
[18] PPBhā., p. 131; Kandalī, pp. 133-34.
[19] KV., p. 212.
[20] KR., pp. 72-73; PD., p. 12; TPP., MS. Fol. 8b; PRM., p. 31.
[21] VS., VII. i. 19-20.
[22] Mañjūṣā on NMV., pp. 178-79; Kandalī, p. 133.

schools given below that the objections of the Buddhists are more natural and serious in nature, while the answers given by Nyāya and Vaiçeṣika, in order to defend their position, are, apparently, not quite so strong. But if we remember that their stand-points, being quite different, each of them looks at the question entirely from a different angle of vision, we shall be able to know that the arguments of each of the schools are quite reasonable within the limits of its own sphere. As the Nyāya and Vaiçeṣika identify their view-point with the common-sense view and the worldly usage (*laukikapratīti*), they cannot go beyond their limits, and it is perhaps for this that at a certain stage their arguments appear to be not so strong as those of the other schools. If the critics bear these points in their mind when trying to follow the arguments of Nyāya and Vaiçeṣika, they will be in a better position to realise the view-point of Nyāya and Vaiçeṣika, or even that of the Buddhist, or of any other school.

The Nihilist school of the Buddhist, which holds that void is the only real entity, cannot imagine the possibility of the existence of a substance which has no constituent part and is eternal. The argument put forth in support of the above view is that *Ākāça*, being all-pervading, must permeate the *paramāṇus* both 'in' and 'out'. This permeating of the *Ākāça* shows that a *paramāṇu* possesses parts, as without this it is not possible to speak of it as having 'in' and 'out'. If, again, *Ākāça* does not permeate the *paramāṇus*, it loses its characteristic of being all-pervasive. Therefore, holds the Buddhist, the Nyāya-Vaiçeṣika should either believe that the *paramāṇus* have parts and are non-eternal, or that *Ākāça* is not all-pervasive.[23]

This argument of the Buddhist contains two parts: (1) that the *paramāṇu* has got parts and that it is non-

[23] NBhā. IV. ii. 18-19.

eternal; (2) and that *Ākāça* is not all-pervasive. As regards the first objection, the Nyāya-Vaiçeṣika view is that it is untenable; for, the expressions 'in' and 'out' in regard to an object refer to the parts of that object, but as the *paramāṇu* is conceived to have no parts, it is not possible to talk of it as having 'in' and 'out'. Hence, the expression *vyatibheda* (permeating both in and out) is not applicable to a substance like *paramāṇu*.[24]

Regarding the second part, although it is out of place to discuss it here, the only answer, which can be adduced now at this place, is that all-pervasiveness means that a substance having all-pervasive nature should be in contact with each and everything having limited form (*mūrtimat*) and not that it should also be in contact with a thing which has no existence. How can, therefore, we assume that *Ākāça* will not remain all-pervading if it is not held to be in contact with 'in' and 'out' sides of the *paramāṇu* which are non-existing? Therefore, this objection also, like the other one, falls to the ground.[25]

It is to be noted here, however, that Nyāya and Vaiçeṣika have finally decided that a *paramāṇu* is an ultimate and indivisible particle of a *bhūta* and is eternal. Being fully convinced of their position they would not allow any objection against this conviction. Hence, most of the objections raised by the opponents are thrown aside only because these objections refer to a *paramāṇu's* having parts, which of course, it cannot possess as has been shown in the previous chapter.

Thus, the objection that as objects, having limited form and possessing touch sensation, occupy space and possess parts, a *paramāṇu* also which possesses a limited form and touch sensation should occupy space and have parts is rejected on the ground that if it were so,

[24] NS., IV. ii. 20.
[25] NV., IV. ii. 20, p. 512.

then a *paramāṇu* could not be the ultimate indivisible particle.[26]

The next objection is that as *paramāṇus* combine together, they must possess constituent parts, like threads, for instance. In other words, when one *paramāṇu* comes between two other *paramāṇus* and combines with them, it really has two aspects corresponding to the two *paramāṇus* with which it combines. From this mediation it is inferred that the front part of the intervening *paramāṇu* has come in contact with the *paramāṇu* in the front, while the rear part has combined with the *paramāṇu* at the back. Now, these front and rear parts naturally refer to the two constituent parts of the intervening *paramāṇu*. Likewise, the mediating *paramāṇu* will combine simultaneously with other *paramāṇus* put on all other four sides. In this way, the *paramāṇu* in the middle will join others on six sides. As conjunction is an attribute, it must have a substratum, and, again, as it does not pervade over the whole of its substratum, there must be parts in its substratum. This shows that a *paramāṇu* has parts.[27]

To this it is said that the contact of the *paramāṇu* in the centre with the other *paramāṇus* is due to the fact that a *paramāṇu* possesses a limited form (*mūrta*) and not because it has parts. And, again, a substance which has parts inheres in another substance, but as a *paramāṇu* does not inhere in any substance, it has no parts; hence, it is wrong to hold that there are parts in a *paramāṇu* with which other *paramāṇus* combine.[28]

There are other similar objections against the partless nature of a *paramāṇu*, such as, possessing motion, being the productive of *dravyas*, being the substratum of the *saṃskāra* which is the cause of motion, and also being in possession of priority and posteriority. All

[26] NS. and NBhā., IV. ii. 23; NM., p. 551; Vyom., p. 207.
[27] NV., IV. ii. 25, pp. 516-17; Tāt., IV. ii. 24-25, p. 651.
[28] Tāt., IV. ii. 24-25, p. 651.

these objections, when put in the form of syllogisms, are found to be beset with the fallacies of *viruddha*, *asiddha* and *anaikāntika* etc., just as the probans '*mūrtimatva*' is found to possess the fallacies of *pratijñā* and *hetu*.[29]

Kamalākara Bhaṭṭa, the mathematician, also refutes the partless nature of a *paramāṇu* through the help of a Geometrical theorem. According to the 29th theorem of Geometry, it is held that the square on the hypotenuse is equal to the sum of the squares on the two other sides of a right-angled triangle. Now, if the side *a*, in the following figure, be assumed to consist of two *paramāṇus* and the side *b* equal to it, then it is clear that a^2+b^2 is equal to c^2; that is, $2^2+2^2=c^2$; or 4 and 4 together are equal to c^2. In other words, c^2, or the square on the hypotenuse, is equal to 8 *paramāṇus*. Thus, the value of the line *c* being the square root of 8, we find that it contains more than two and less than three *paramāṇus*. This is possible only when a *paramāṇu* can be split up into parts. Thus, it is wrong to hold, says Kamalākara, that *paramāṇus* are partless.[30]

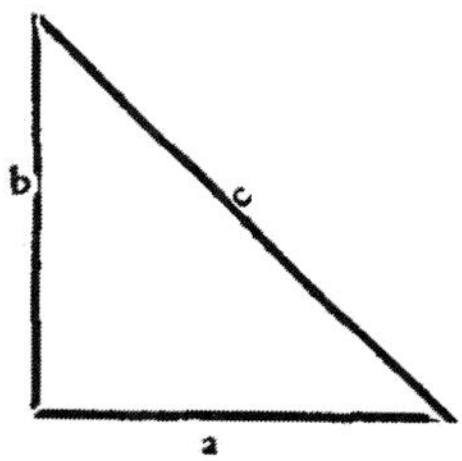

To this objection it may be said that the view-point adopted above seems to be based on the assumption that a straight line consists of a series of points (*paramāṇus*). But, as a matter of fact, it is not so according to Nyāya and Vaiçeṣika, which seem to hold that a straight line is an unit in itself like a point (*paramāṇu*). The difference between a straight line and a point is that of the possession or otherwise of motion; that is, a straight line is in motion, while the point is at rest; so that, from the Nyāya-Vaiçeṣika point of view the question raised by the great mathematician, does not rise at all.[31]

[29] NV, p. 518; Vyom., pp. 224-225.
[30] STV., spaṣṭādhikāra, after Verse 21.
[31] It should be noted down here that in case a straight line is

5. *Paramāṇu and Motion*

Before we take up the question of the formation of a composite whole (*avayavin*) from *paramāṇus*, we should know something about motion which plays an essential part in its formation. A composite is formed out of conjunctions which are brought about by motion (*karman*) which is the cause of conjunction and disjunction. Motion inheres in a substance having limited form and is produced by weight (*gurutva*), liquidity, effort and conjunction. It is always a non-material (*asamavāyi*) cause and never an instrumental one, like attributes.[32]

Such a motion is very essential both for the production and the destruction of the sensible world. As the universe (*saṃsāra*) is beginningless and everchanging, all its products must undergo change. Changes are brought about by motion. According to Nyāya and Vaiçeṣika, motion is not intrinsic but comes from without. Hence, either through human effort (in the case of individual destruction), or through Divine Effort (in the case of universal destruction) a motion is produced in the object, and through a regular process the motion brings about the destruction; so that, all the non-eternal objects are ultimately reduced to various *paramāṇus* through motion. These *paramāṇus* remain, during the period of dissolution (*pralaya*), separated from one another; so that, they cannot bring into existence any product for sometime[33] till the commencement of the cosmic order sets in. Even during this period there exists, according to some, a sort of motion which is non-productive of any conjunction.[34] It is caused to

to represent a series of points (*paramāṇus*), it cannot be continuous; for, the points, thus placed together so as to form one continuous straight line, will certainly leave inter-space between each and every pair.

[32] PPBhā. and Kandalī, pp. 290-91.

[33] KV., p. 92.

[34] Setu., p. 286.

the *paramāṇus* from the first shock (*saṃkṣobha*) or blow in the objects causing their destruction. This shock produces motion in the *paramāṇus*, which is productive of the impression (*saṃskāra*), called *vega* (velocity). This motion persists even during the dissolution period[35] in the form of atomic vibration.[36]

It may be asked: what is the use of such a motion then? The answer is: the only use of this sort of motion in the *paramāṇus* is to mark the time-limit.[37]

Thus, it is clear that the series of *karmans* present in the *paramāṇus* during the dissolution period are unable to make them group together so as to form any effect. But there must be grouping of that sort; hence, we require another motion. This motion is to be had, like all other motions, from some *cetana* agency. As it is not possible for individual soul (*Jīvātman*) to produce such a motion at that time, we are constrained to assume the presence of a superhuman power, conscious and capable of producing such a motion in the *paramāṇus*. It does this under the influence of the *adṛṣṭa* of the persons or creatures who are to make use of the body or object concerned.[38] But why should the conscious agent be at all influenced by *adṛṣṭa*? for, *adṛṣṭa* inheres in the *Jīvātman*, and *Jīvas* are then in a discarnate and insensate condition. The truth is that as soon as the cumulative *adṛṣṭa* of the *Jīvas* matures for fructification, the Will of God, which is eternal, becomes, as it were, creative, and immediately the *paramāṇus* group themselves round the *Manas* and form organisms one for each. The initiation of motion in *Manas* and *paramāṇus* is attributed to *adṛṣṭa* quickened by the Divine Will.

Thus, there are, so to say, two kinds of motion in

[35] Bodhani on KP., p. 91.
[36] Bodhani on KP., p. 91; KV., p. 92.
[37] "*Kālāvacchedaikaprayojanam*" KP., p. 333.
[38] NM., pp. 192-93.

the *paramāṇus* before any effect is produced out of these. Apparently, one appears to be intrinsic, while the other extrinsic. But when closely observed we find that both have come from without, the only difference being that of time; and in both the cases, the motion is due to some *cetana* element. Both of these motions are produced by effort (*prayatna*) and *adṛṣṭa* helped by Divine Will respectively.[39]

With the help of such a motion *paramāṇus* group together to form bigger parts (*avayavas*) till composites are formed and the cosmos comes to exist.

6. *The four kinds of Paramāṇus along with their respective characteristics*

These *paramāṇus* are of four kinds: earthly, watery, *taijasa* and airy. Their common characteristics have been given above, and now, the individual attributes of each of these are given below:

(1) *Earthly paramāṇu*

The earthly *paramāṇus* possess attributes, of colour, taste, smell, and touch which are all non-eternal;[40] for, these are produced and remain changing due to the application of heat through the process of chemical action (*pākaprakriyā*).[41] These attributes are unmanifest.

Padmanābha Miçra holds that although there is variegated colour and touch in earthly products, yet they do not inhere in *paramāṇus*.[42] But Çaṅkara Miçra, on the other hand, thinks that there is variegated colour at least even in these.[43]

(2) *Watery paramāṇu*

The watery *paramāṇus* possess colour, taste and

[39] VS., V. ii. 13; KP., p. 135.

[40] PPBhā., pp. 104-107; and a comm. on PC. a comm. on SP., Ms. Fol. 19b.

[41] Kandalī., p. 99; KV., p. 166.

[42] Setu., pp. 181-82.

[43] VU. on VS., VII. i. 6.

touch which are all eternal;[44] as, these are not due to any chemical action (*pākajas*).[45]

(3) *Taijasa paramāṇu*

Similarly, the fiery *paramāṇus* possess the attributes of colour and touch which are also eternal;[46] as, they do not possess *pākajaviçeṣa*.[47]

(4) *Airy paramāṇu*

The airy *paramāṇus* possess touch which is eternal;[48] as, there is no chemical action in them.

II

CHEMICAL ACTION (PĀKA)

We have referred to above about the chemical action taking place in earthly *paramāṇus*. But what is it? It is a kind of conjunction of the *taijasa* elements by which the previous colour etc. of the earthly *paramāṇus* are destroyed and another colour etc. are produced in their place. This conjunction of the fiery elements is also of various types; thus, the conjunction which produces colour is different from that which produces taste; again, that which produces smell is different from those which produce colour and taste; similarly, that which produces touch is different from all other conjunctions. According to the difference of the earthly objects there is difference in the conjunction of the *tejas*; so that, when a mango fruit is kept under a collection of straw, owing to the *taijasa* conjunction, the previous green colour of it is destroyed, and another colour of yellow type is produced in its place. But it does not affect the taste of the fruit; for, the previous taste of sourness (*āmlatva*) is still found in it. Sometimes, although the

[44] PPBhā., p. 104; Kandalī., p. 105; KV., p. 181; TPP., MS. Fol. 8a.

[45] KP., p. 138; Bodhanī, p. 53.

[46] Kandalī., p. 104; KV; p. 181.

[47] KP., p. 138.

[48] KV., p. 181.

previous green colour is present, yet a change in the taste is found. This shows that due to the difference in the type of conjunction, which does not affect the colour, the sour taste has been destroyed and has been replaced by the sweet taste. Therefore, we conclude that the cause of the change in taste is different from that of the change in colour. Similarly, the *taijasa* conjunction which produces sweet smell in the mango fruit after destroying the previous smell without affecting the colour and the taste of it, is different from all other conjunctions. In the same manner, the conjunction which does not affect the colour, taste and smell of the fruit, and which, after destroying the hard touch of the fruit, produces the soft touch, must be different from all other conjunctions. It is due to these differences of conjunction that although all the earthly *paramāṇus* are of one class, yet they produce all different sorts of objects. For instance, when the grass grazed by the cow is reduced to *paramāṇus*, they come in contact with a different type of *taijasa* conjunction which destroys the previous colour, taste, smell and touch present in those *paramāṇus*. Then again, a fresh set of colour, taste, smell and touch found in the cow-milk is produced in them by another *taijasa* conjunction. In course of time, these *paramāṇus* form, in a regular process, the *dvyaṇuka* etc. which lead, in their turn, to the production of cow-milk.

Now, out of those very *paramāṇus* from which the cow-milk is formed, we also get curd only with this difference that in the case of curd, the fiery conjunction is of a different type from that which is required for the cow-milk. And, again, it is due to another type of *taijasa* conjunction that from those very *paramāṇus*, which produce curd, we also get cream and other milk-made products.[49]

Çaṅkara Miçra, Bhagīratha Ṭhakkura, Koṇḍa Bhaṭṭa and others, however, hold that the difference in the

[49] NB. on TS., pp. 17-18.

colour, taste, smell and touch due to the chemical action is on account of the difference in the *prāgabhāva* (pre-non-existence).[50]

III

THE PROCESS OF CHEMICAL ACTION

When any earthly object[51] is brought into contact with *tejas*, motion is produced in the ultimate constituents of that object through the forcible contact (*abhighāta*)[52] or impulsion (*nodana*)[53] of the *tejas*. This motion, in its turn, produces disjunctions which lead to the destruction of the conjunctions existing between the various constituents of the composite and finally reduces them to their ultimate particles. Thereafter, these particles come in contact with another group of *tejas* particles which destroy their original attributes.[54] Then, again, a fresh similar contact of *tejas* takes place which produces fresh attributes in place of the old ones, which are known as *pākajas*.

It is clear from the above that the *taijasa* contact which destroys the previous attributes of the product does not produce fresh attributes in place of old ones. Both the functions cannot be performed by a single

[50] NLK; pp. 356-357; NLPV., p. 355; PD., p. 11.

[51] This includes even human body, but, generally, no example is taken from this class, for the simple reason that if any one comes to know of the chemical action taking place in it, he may become disgusted with his own body and his interests may cease towards it—Vyom., p. 446.

[52] It is a form of contact which produces separation between the two connecting objects by producing sound. VU; V. ii. 1.

[53] It is that form of conjunction which causes motion without separating the two objects which are joined together without producing any sound while coming in contact with the object. VU., V. ii. 1.

[54] Vyom., p. 446; KV., p. 183; Kandalī., p. 107; RS., p. 21. Although almost every attribute at every stage of the earthly object is produced by the chemical action, yet the example is taken of one particular stage only—Vyom., p. 446.

taijasa contact; for, that which destroys the old attributes cannot wait till the time of the production of the fresh attributes arrives, as is made clear below:

Simultaneously with the production of the motion through the contact of *tejas* possessing velocity in the ultimate constituents of the product, another motion is produced in the parts of the *tejas* itself through the contact of another similar *tejas*; so that, as soon as there is the disjunction between the two *paramāṇus*, there is the disjunction between the two parts of the *tejas* also. Then there is the destruction of the conjunction of the two *paramāṇus* followed by that of the two parts of the *tejas*. This leads to the destruction of the *dvyaṇuka* and the *tejas*. Then follows the destruction of the colour etc. together with that of the conjunction of the *tejas* and the *paramāṇu* (due to destruction of its material—*samavāyi*—cause, namely, the *tejas*). Now, as the conjunction of the *tejas*, which destroys the colour etc., is absent at the moment previous to the production of the fresh colour etc., it cannot be the cause of the latter. Hence, it is necessary to have another *taijasa*-contact to produce the fresh attributes in the ultimate particles.[55] There are several similar instances to support the above view; as for instance, the production and the destruction of the colour of the thread from two distinct sources,[56] and so on.

Then, again, it has been said above that in order to change the colour etc. of a pot, for instance, the object should be reduced to its *paramāṇus* wherein the change takes place. To this view of the Vaiçeṣikas there have been various objections.

Thus, it is objected that when a pot is put in the furnace and comes in contact with *tejas*, almost all its attributes are changed without its being reduced to its constituent *paramāṇus*, so that, the views of the Vaiçeṣikas are open to serious criticism.

[55] KV., p. 184; RS., p. 24.
[56] Kandalī., p. 108.

To this it may be said, in reply, that as the *taijasa*-contact cannot be with the pot as a whole, the chemical action due to this contact cannot affect it in its entirety unless it is reduced to its constituent *paramāṇus*.[57] If it is held that the pot, like all other earthly products, being porous by nature,[58] there is nothing to prevent the particles of *tejas* to come in contact with each and every part of it and help on the chemical action,[59] the simple rejoinder of the Vaiçeṣikas, is that, as a matter of fact, particles of *tejas* cannot enter into the pot and affect the interior portion of it, without destroying it. In other words, it is not possible for the *dvyaṇuka*, for instance, to possess interstices; for, if it were so, then there could have been no conjunction between the two *paramāṇus* entering into its composition, and the very existence of the *dvyaṇuka* would have been impossible. Interstices may be admitted between two such parts as are not absolutely partless. Hence, a *dvyaṇuka* cannot be held to have interspace in its components. This shows that no substance, which is a product, can be porous by nature. Consequently, the chemical action cannot pervade the entire pot.[60] Moreover, as the various parts of the pot cohere strongly and leave no space unoccupied, it is not possible for the particles of *tejas* to occupy any space between those impenetrable parts, because no two things having limited form can occupy the same space simultaneously.[61]

Udayanācārya says that so strong is the velocity and the sensation of contact of *tejas* due to its being exceedingly light that the motion produced by it causes the product to deprive itself of its previous structure

[57] PPBhā., p. 107; Kandalī, p. 109.

[58] KV., p. 187; Kandalī, p. 109.

[59] That a product like pot is porous is proved by the fact that water, if placed within it, flows out in particles, which would not have been possible otherwise—VU., VII. i. 6.

[60] Kandalī., p. 109.

[61] VU., VII. i. 6.

(*vyūha*) and to assume another structure out of the constituent parts of it. If the *taijasa*-contact does not destroy the structure entirely, then, for instance, milk, water etc. being produced of closely compact parts and there being no pores, it will have to be assumed that the *tejas* does not enter within the milk, water etc., and if it does not enter into it, there should not be the rising up of the boiled milk or water. But it is not the fact.

The opponent says that it is possible in the case of milk or water to destroy the previous structure and produce another, as the conjunction of the parts in these is soft (*mṛdu*), but it is not possible in the case of a pot where the conjunctions, which bring about the product, are harder.

To this, again, the reply is: that softness or hardness does not matter at all; for, even in the case of still harder and the hardest substances the result is the same. In the case of rice, for instance, which is a harder substance, or stone, jewel and adamantine which are the hardest substances, it is found that when heat is applied to these, they break and another structure of these is, again, formed.

Thereupon, again, the opponent says that it is possible even in these cases as some sort of *atiçaya* (specific quality) is produced therein, while the chemical action is going on, but that specific quality being absent in the case of a pot, it is impossible to destroy it by the application of heat.

The answer to this is: that in the chemical action there is no *atiçaya* of any kind. Therefore, just as in the case of an organism etc., the effect of chemical action, although not apparent everyday, yet becomes quite obvious after sometime; similarly, in the case of a pot there is the effect of chemical action in it due to which it is destroyed entirely. Thereby, all the various arguments adduced in favour of the non-destruction of the previous structure, such as, the recognition (in the form that it is the same pot which was thrown into the furnace long before the production of the red colour etc.), perception of the pot in all its stages, placing of some other *mūrta* substance on it, its surroundings, its existence along with other pots etc., number and dimension and the various marks on it, are rejected. In other words, none of the above mentioned arguments can prove that the pot is not reduced to its *paramāṇus*.[62]

It may be also said in support of the *Pīlupākavāda* that before the chemical action, the constituent parts of the pot are very loosely connected, but after it, those loose connections become quite hard. Both the loose and hard connections, being mutually opposed, cannot simultaneously remain in the same substratum. Hence, it has to be assumed that the old structure is destroyed and a fresh one is produced in its place.[63]

Another objection is that no one has ever seen that a pot, for instance, when thrown into the furnace is reduced to its ultimate particles, rather it is seen all the time in the furnace and is recognised as the same old pot even when it is taken out of the furnace after the chemical action has taken place in it.

As regards the perception of the existence of the pot under chemical action, it is said that since the pot is not merely a collection of several *paramāṇus*, it is not reduced to its ultimate particles at once. The process of the destruction of the pot is also similar to that of the production; so that, the destruction is gradual and the pot remains visible till it is completely reduced to its *paramāṇus*. But there never comes a time when one would cease to perceive the pot; for, in the course of the gradual destruction of the pot, those parts, which have been destroyed and reduced to their *paramāṇus*, are also gradually undergoing chemical action and fresh

[62] KV., pp. 187-88; RS., pp. 34-37; KR., p. 60.
[63] Kandalī., p. 109.

products are being produced; so that, both the process of destruction and that of production after the chemical action are simultaneous. This is the reason why sometimes, only a part of the pot is found to have undergone chemical changes. This also explains that the ultimate number of the constituents under both the circumstances remains the same and that no change in the dimension is found.[64]

Çaṅkara Miçra, however, says that even according to the propounders of the theory of *Piṭharapāka*, when certain scratches are made by the point of a needle, for instance, on the pot, those scratches certainly cause disjunctions between three or four *trasareṇus*, at least, of that pot; so that, there being the destruction of the pot as a whole in consequence of the destruction of the conjunctions productive of the pot, they should not raise such ordinary objections against the Vaiçeṣika view.[65]

Moreover, the production of another colour etc. is possible only when their proper substratum in the form of a pot, for instance, is formed beforehand in accordance with the conditions of causation. Here, in the present case, the pot, as existing before the chemical action, is the substratum of blue colour etc. and the same pot cannot be the proper substratum of red colour etc.; so that, in order to produce red colour etc. it is

[64] Kandalī., p. 110.

[65] VU., VII. i. 6. KR., p. 60. It should be noted down here that according to the Mīmāṃsakas, who appear to be perhaps the oldest propounders of the *Piṭharapākavāda*, the pot, even when scratches destroying the conjunctions of certain *trasareṇus* are made on it, remains as such; for, they hold that it is possible for a product to continue to exist by inhering in other constituents whose conjunctions have been destroyed even when certain constituents have been destroyed. Were it no so, recognition of the pot and the rest would not have been possible. This view also has been criticised by the author of Upaskāra on VS., VII. i. 6. For further reference *vide* KV., p. 188; NK., p. 155.

essential to have another pot constructed first. This is not possible unless the pot is reduced to its ultimate constituents and a fresh one is produced in its place.[66]

Again, in order to have red colour etc. produced in the pot, it is essential, according to the law of causation, to have the red colour etc. in their cause also, which is not possible unless the pot is reduced to its *paramāṇus*.[67]

Hence, it is held that an earthly product is reduced to its *paramāṇus* by the force of the *taijasa*-contact wherein the chemical action produces fresh colour etc. after destroying the previous ones. This being done, another motion is produced in those *paramāṇus* due to the conjunction of the *Ātman* and the *paramāṇus* helped by the *adṛṣṭa* of the persons and other creatures concerned which, in the usual course, leads to the production of the final composite (*antyāvayavin*).[68]

Now, again, it is asked: if the entire process of destroying and producing of the pot be due to *adṛṣṭa* or Divine Will, what is the use of having a potmaker then? To this it may be said that both *adṛṣṭa* and the Divine Will help directly only when there is no other help possible and without which the very aim of creation would not have been realised, but not afterwards when such help is possible from other sources. Hence, the utility of a potmaker continues unaffected.

This chemical action affects colour, taste, smell and touch only and not number, dimension etc.; as no peculiarity is found in these latter after the chemical action. We cannot, likewise, hold that there being no apparent difference in touch, chemical action does not affect it also, like number etc; for, that there is the

[66] Kandalī., p. 109.
[67] Kandalī., p. 109.
[68] Kandalī., p. 108.

peculiarity in touch after chemical action is proved by inference.[69]

IV

TIME—LIMITS OF CHEMICAL ACTION

The whole process of chemical action is complete in nine moments, or in ten, or in eleven, according to the difference of opinion about the acceptance of *vibhāgajavibhāga*. Thus, he, who does not believe in it (i.e. *vibhāgaja-vibhāga*), holds that the process is complete only in nine moments, but he, who believes in it, holds that if the disjunction produces another disjunction with reference to the time characterised by the destruction of the conjunction producing the substance, then the process of chemical action is complete in ten moments. If, on the other hand, the disjunction produces another disjunction with reference to the time or the part (*avayava*) characterised by the destruction of the substance, then it is complete in eleven moments.[70] Both the types of process are given below:

1. *The process involving nine moments*

First of all, a sort of motion is produced in the *paramāṇu* productive of the *dvyaṇuka* through the impulsion or the forcible contact caused by the *tejas*; by that motion the disjunction between the two *paramāṇus* producing the *dvyaṇuka* takes place followed by the destruction of the conjunction producing the substance called *dvyaṇuka*.[71] This leads to (1) the destruction of the *dvyaṇuka* followed by (2) the destruction of the blue colour etc. inherent in the *paramāṇu*. Then comes (3) the production of the red colour etc. in that very *paramāṇu*, after which (4) the motion favourable

[69] Kandalī., p. 108.

[70] KR, p. 61.

[71] As upto this the action does not directly affect the composite, these moments are not counted here. The counting of the moments, therefore, begins from the destruction of the *dvyaṇuka*.

to the production of the substance is produced in the *paramāṇu* (5) which causes the disjunction of the *paramāṇu* from the *Ākāça* etc. Then follows (6) the destruction of previous conjunction leading to (7) the conjunction between the two *paramāṇus* producing the *dvyaṇuka*. Then comes (8) the production of the *dvyaṇuka* which then causes (9) the production of the colour etc. in the *dvyaṇuka*. Thus beginning from the destruction of the *dvyaṇuka* up to the production of the red colour etc. in it there are nine moments.[72]

2. *The process which takes ten moments*

The process of ten moments is possible when the disjunction produces disjunction with reference to the time which is characterised by the destruction of the conjunction which produces the effect. Thus, first, there is the motion produced in the *paramāṇus* which produce the *dvyaṇuka* followed by the disjunction between the two *paramāṇus*. Then there is the destruction of the productive conjunction leading to (1) the destruction of the *dvyaṇuka* and to the disjunction between the *dvyaṇuka* and the *Ākāça* due to the disjunction. Then there is (2) the destruction of the blue colour etc. and the previous conjunction causing (3) the production of the red colour etc. and the subsequent conjunction. Then comes (4) the destruction of the motion of the *paramāṇus* produced by the impulsion of the *tejas* followed by (5) the production of the productive motion in the very *paramāṇus* by the conjunction of the *Ātman* and the *paramāṇu* aided by the *adṛṣṭa*. Then follows (6) the disjunction between *paramāṇus* and the *Ākāça* leading to (7) the destruction of the previous conjunction. Then there is (8) the productive conjunction followed (9) by the production of the *dvyaṇuka* wherein then (10) the production of the red colour etc. takes place.[73]

[72] KR., p. 61.
[73] KR., p. 62.

3. *The process which includes eleven moments*

First, there is the motion in the *paramāṇus* producing the *dvyaṇuka*, then the disjunction between the two *paramāṇus*, then the destruction of the productive conjunction, then (1) the destruction of the *dvyaṇuka*, then (2) the disjunction produced by the disjunction with reference to the time characterised by the destruction of the *dvyaṇuka*, then (3) the destruction of the previous conjunction, then (4) the subsequent conjunction, then the (5) destruction of the motion belonging to the *paramāṇus*, then (6) the production of the productive motion in the very *paramāṇus* by the conjunction of the *Ātman* helped by the *adṛṣṭa*, then (7) the disjunction between *Ākāça* and the *paramāṇus*, then (8) the destruction of the previous conjunction, then (9) the conjunction producing a substance, then (10) the production of the *dvyaṇuka*, and then (11) the production of the red colour etc.

A question is raised here: if the productive motion in the *paramāṇus* be believed to be synchronous with the destruction of the blue colour etc., then the number of moments will be reduced; that is, the production of the red colour etc. will take place either in the eighth, or even in the seventh moment.

This view is rejected on the grounds that there cannot be another motion in the *paramāṇu* either without the destruction of the motion produced in it through the impulsion or the forcible contact caused by the *tejas*, or without the production of an attribute etc.; for, there can be no two simultaneous motions in an object; and also because, there cannot be a productive motion in an object where there is no attribute.

Then, again, the opponent holds that if the production of the red colour etc. be simultaneous with the destruction of the blue colour etc. even then there will be a few less moments required in the process of the chemical action.

This view is also rejected as untenable; for, the destruction of the previous colour etc. is itself the cause of the production of the fresh colour etc. and the cause must precede the effect. Therefore, there cannot be both the destruction and the production of the colour etc. simultaneously.[74]

Çaṅkara Miçra adds that if the same conjunction of the *tejas* which produces colour etc. also destroys them, then it will have to be assumed that when the colour etc. and the *tejas* are destroyed, then the *paramāṇu* will have to remain colourless for a long time; if, on the other hand, that which is the destroyer be also the producer, then there can be no production of the red colour by the chemical action. If it be considered that the motion may be produced in another *paramāṇu*, then the production of the attribute due to the chemical action will take place in the fifth, or in the sixth, or in the seventh, or in the eighth, or even in the ninth moment.[75] All these possible varieties are given below:

4. *The process involving five moments*

There is the motion in one *paramāṇu*, then the disjunction, then the motion in another *paramāṇu* together with the destruction of the productive conjunction, then the destruction of the *dvyaṇuka*, then there is the disjunction by the motion of another *paramāṇu*. This whole represents one moment.[76] Then there is the destruction of the blue colour etc. in the *paramāṇu* which is left alone and that of the previous conjunction due to the disjunction. This is another moment. Then the production of the red colour etc. followed by the conjunction producing the substance. This is another moment. In the next moment there

[74] KR., pp. 61-62.

[75] KR., p. 64.

[76] The consideration of a moment, here, appears to be based on a belief that simultaneity of actions is possible.

is the production of the *dvyaṇuka*. And then the production of the colour etc. in that *dvyaṇuka*.[77]

5. *The process including six moments*

If it be held that the motion is produced in another *paramāṇu* simultaneously with the destruction of the substance (*dvyaṇuka*), then the production of the colour will take place in the sixth moment. Thus, there is the disjunction from another *paramāṇu* by the motion of the *paramāṇu*, then the destruction of the productive conjunction followed by the destruction of the *dvyaṇuka*. In the very moment, there is motion in another *paramāṇu*, then simultaneously with the destruction of the blue colour etc. there is the disjunction due to the motion of another *paramāṇu*, then from the simultaneous production of the motion in another *paramāṇu* with the production of red colour there is the destruction of the previous conjunction, then the conjunction with another *paramāṇu*, then the production of the *dvyaṇuka*, and then the production of the red colour.[78]

6. *The process including seven moments*

If the motion be produced in another *paramāṇu* simultaneously with the destruction of the blue colour etc., then the process involves seven moments. Thus, following the previous process (of the five moments), after the destruction of the *dvyaṇuka* there is the destruction of the blue colour etc. In this very moment, there is the motion in another *paramāṇu*, then the disjunction followed by the production of the red colour. This represents one (viz. the sixth) moment. Then the destruction of the previous conjunction, then the subsequent conjunction, then the production of the *dvyaṇuka* and that of the attribute in the *dvyaṇuka* in the next moment. These are the seven moments.[79]

[77] KR., p. 65.
[78] KR., p. 65.
[79] KR., pp. 65-66.

7. *The process including eight and nine moments*

If the motion be produced in another *paramāṇu* simultaneously with the production of the red colour, then the process involves eight moments. If, on the other hand, the motion be produced in another *paramāṇu* after the production of the red colour, then the process includes nine moments only.[80]

8. *The process including two, three and four moments*

Again, it is not possible to hold that after the destruction of a *dvyaṇuka* followed by the production of another *dvyaṇuka* there appear attributes in the second, or in the third, or in the fourth moment. These are, however, explained below: Thus when the motion is produced in another *paramāṇu* simultaneously with the motion favourable to the destruction of the *dvyaṇuka* the process represents two moments only.

When there is the motion in a *paramāṇu* favourable to the production of a substance simultaneously with the production of the destructive motion in another *paramāṇu*, then the process includes three moments.

Again, if the motion be produced in a *paramāṇu* simultaneously with the disjunction unfavourable to the production of a substance, then the process involves four moments.[81] These last three processes are not accepted by Nyāya-Vaiçeṣika.[82]

9. *The distribution of moments in Pāka according to the Kandalī*

The process given in the Kandalī is somewhat different from the above. Thus it says—that the destruction of the *dvyaṇuka*, the destruction of the *tryaṇuka*, the destruction of the blue colour etc., the

[80] KR., p. 66.
[81] KR., p. 66.
[82] KR., p. 66.

production of motion in the two *paramāṇus*, the production of the *vibhāgaja-vibhāga*, and the production of the *taijasa*-contact which produces the red colour etc. all these represent one moment. Then the destruction of the *tryaṇuka*, the destruction of the product of the *tryaṇuka*, the destruction of the blue colour etc., the production of the *vibhāgaja-vibhāga*, the destruction of the conjunction, the production of the *taijasa*-contact productive of the red colour etc., the production of the red colour etc., the destruction of the *taijasa*-contact destructive of the blue colour etc.—these represent another moment. Then the destruction of its effect, the destruction of the product of that effect, the production of the subsequent conjunction, the production of the red colour etc., the destruction of the *taijasa*-contact destructive of the blue colour etc., the production of the motion productive of a substance in another *paramāṇu*, this whole represents another moment. Then the destruction of its product, the destruction of the product of this product, the production of the subsequent conjunction, the destruction of the motion, the disjunction and the *vibhāgaja-vibhāga*, the production of the motion in another *paramāṇu*, the production of the disjunction—all these represent another moment. Then the destruction of its effect, the destruction of the effect of this effect, the destruction of the motion, the disjunction and the *vibhāgaja-vibhāga*, the production of the disjunction from *Ākāça* in the second *paramāṇu*, and the destruction of the conjunction between *Ākāça* and the *paramāṇu*—all these represent another moment. Then the destruction of its product, the destruction of the product of this product, the destruction of the conjunction of the *Ākāça* with the *paramāṇu*, the production of the subsequent conjunction—all these represent another moment of time. Then the destruction of its product, the destruction of the product of this product, the production of the subsequent conjunction of one *paramāṇu* with another, the production of the *dvyaṇuka*, and the destruction of the disjunction and the motion—all these, again, form another moment of time. Then the destruction of its product, the destruction of the product of this product, the production of the *dvyaṇuka*, the production of the colour etc. belonging to the *dvyaṇuka*, the destruction of the disjunction and the motion, and then, in the next moment, the production of another set of attributes in the *dvyaṇuka* according to the attributes belonging to its cause, namely, the *paramāṇus*.

This process is applicable to all the *dvyaṇuka*s (forming one object). As regards the production of the *tryaṇuka* etc. we should not think of any motion; for, these are produced from the conjunction produced by conjunctions. Thus, several *paramāṇus* join together simultaneously, and a *paramāṇu*, which is the cause of a *dvyaṇuka*, comes into contact with another *paramāṇu* which is the cause of another *dvyaṇuka*. The *dvyaṇuka*, on the other hand, combines with another *paramāṇu* which is the cause of another *dvyaṇuka* and after this there is the conjunction between the two *dvyaṇukas*.[83]

The sum and substance of all this is that both the Naiyāyikas and the Vaiçeṣikas believe that the chemical action takes place in the earthly objects. But they differ in the details of it. Thus, the Vaiçeṣikas hold that it takes place in the *paramāṇus*, as it is only then that its products can have the attributes in accordance with the attributes belonging to their cause. Hence, they are called *Pīlupākavādins*. The Naiyāyikas, for reasons given above, do not think it reasonable that a pot previous to the possession of red colour etc. must be reduced to its constituent *paramāṇus* and due to the unseen forces, again, be brought back to its natural shape after the function of chemical action. Therefore, they believe that a pot which is naturally porous remains

[83] Kandalī, pp. 110-111.

as it is and the *taijasa*-contact takes place in the very composite. Hence, they are called *Piṭharapākavādins*.[84]

The importance of the *Pīlupāka* is to prove that consciousness, pleasure, pain etc. cannot belong to any of the *bhūtas*. The reason is that the specific attributes of the earthly composites inhere in them as long as they themselves exist. In order to show this character of *yāvaddravyabhāvitva* present in each and every part of the earthly object, it is essential to reduce it to its *paramāṇus* and show that the attributes inhere in all the constituents. This will reject the possibility of consciousness, pleasure and pain etc. which are not *yāvaddravyabhāvins*, to inhere in earth and other *bhūtas*.[85]

V

UDAYANA ON THE NECESSITY OF CHEMICAL ACTION

If there were no *pākajas*, holds Udayana, then there would have been no difference between the various kinds of touch, taste, colour and smell like the other attributes of number, dimension etc. In other words, just as it is not possible to differentiate between the particular number attributed to a pot and the same particular number attributed to a piece of cloth, so the differentiation between the touch of one thing and the touch[86] of another thing, and so on, would not have been possible otherwise. Thus, there would have been no difference in the pain felt at the touch of particular herbs, namely, cowach (*çūkaçimbi*), *vṛçcikapatra* etc. on the place of snakebite, or where scorpion or any other insect had stinged; and also there would not have been

[84] NS., III. ii. 48-49; TPP., Ms. Fol. 7a-7b.

[85] KR., p. 66.

[86] The question does not arise regarding colour, taste and smell; for, these are found obviously changed due to *Pāka*; but as regards touch no difference is apparently observed; hence, the question.

the cessation of pain at the touch of some particular stone or some particular (snakebite-curing) herb, had there been no difference in the various kinds of touch. Again, nor would there have been any difference between the touch of a cow and the touch of a *Cāṇḍāla*, and accordingly, there would not have been any Vedic or religious injunction or prohibition regarding these varieties of touch; nor would any injunction or prohibition have been laid down regarding every object; nor would there have been any justification for the difference of *Prāyaçcitta* in the case of perception and touch of a *Cāṇḍāla* and smell and taste of wine. Hence, in order to explain these differences the existence of chemical action must be accepted.[87]

Koṇḍa Bhaṭṭa also agrees with the above view and says that there is obvious difference in touch also. It is, therefore, that a hard substance, for instance, becomes soft and *vice versa* by chemical action.[88]

The Mīmāṃsakas raise here an objection against the chemical action itself. They are of opinion that it is the particular kind of *çakti* (capacity) or *saṃskāra* (as in the case of *vrīhīn prokṣati*) belonging to the seed or any other cause of the object, viz. *paramāṇu*, which determines the nature of the product from that cause; just as in the case of the citron tree in which a kind of *çakti* is produced by the watering through the red juice of the lac (*lākṣārasa*), due to which red colour is produced in its flower. Thus, there is no necessity to believe in the chemical action to produce the change in colour etc. of the product.[89]

This view has not been accepted as tenable; for, both the *çakti* and *saṃskāra* are unseen forces; and as such, they should not be preferred to the seen

[87] KV., p. 49.
[88] PD., p. 11.
[89] KP., pp. 133-134; Bodhanī on Ibid, p. 31; NLV., pp. 72-73, Bombay Ed.

forces.[90] And as regards the redness belonging to the flower of the citron tree, in spite of the fact that the watering of the tree is done by the red juice of the lac, it is really due to the conjunction of the heat of the sun, which is not different from the chemical action.[91] The chemical action is a *dṛṣṭa* means and must have preference over the *adṛṣṭa* means.

It is only due to the chemical action that when a particular seed is reduced to its *paramāṇus*, the different objects are produced out of those *paramāṇus* qualified by the peculiarity formed by the chemical action (*pākajaviçeṣaviçiṣṭa*),[92] in spite of the fact that there are no subordinate *jātis* which could have helped the determination of the difference in the products. As for instance,[93] the seed of the paddy is different from that of the barley; the seed (cause) of man is different from that of monkey and others; the cow-milk is different from that of the she-baffalo on account of the difference of the respective *jātis* belonging to them; but their respective *paramāṇus*, from which all these originate, are differentiated by the chemical action alone. In other words, at the earliest stage, objects are differentiated mutually by chemical action alone, while at later stages, they are differentiated by their respective generalities (*jātis*)[94] also.

It is quite impossible to think of the *paramāṇus* to possess attributes entirely different from those of

[90] NM., p. 42; Kandalī, p. 145; VU. on VS. V. ii. 13; Bodhanī p. 31.

[91] Prakāça on KP., p. 134.

[92] Bodhanī makes it very clear in the following way—By virtue of which *pākajaviçeṣas*, separated from the *paramāṇus* productive of paddy seed, the *paramāṇus*, productive of barley seed which have before produced barley seed as different from the paddy seed, produce the barley-sprout. p. 31.

[93] Bodhanī says that here is a proof for the differentiating nature of *pākajaviçeṣas* which alone can differentiate at the time of the production of objects, p. 31.

[94] Ibid.

the products formed out of them. Had it been so, then it would not have been possible to infer the nature of the attributes of *paramāṇus* from that of their products. Hence, there is no place for any kind of *śakti* to be present in them.[95]

VI

PARAMĀNU AND AVAYAVIN

It has been said before that the *paramāṇus* are the ultimate material cause of the universe. Under the influence of *adṛṣṭa* and Divine Will, these are moved into action and cluster together in twos and form the first products, called *dvyaṇukas*, of which, in each case, the two *paramāṇus* serve as the material cause,[96] their combination as the non-material, and *adṛṣṭa*, Divine Will, etc., as the instrumental cause. When three *dvyaṇukas*, being moved again, combine together, they produce a *tryaṇuka*, also known as *trasareṇu*, which produces, in its turn and in a similar manner, a *caturaṇuka*, and so on, till the final product (*antyāvayavin*) comes to exist. This process is common to all the four types of *bhautika* products.[97]

As to the question: whether the two *paramāṇus*, forming a *dvyaṇuka*, belong to one and the same class, or to two different classes, it is said that both the *paramāṇus* are of one and the same class. For instance, in the case of an earthly *dvyaṇuka*, the two *paramāṇus*, representing the material cause of it, belong to earth alone. If, of the two constituent *paramāṇus* of a *dvyaṇuka*, one were held to be earthly and the other of a different class, the resulting *dvyaṇuka*—assuming

[95] KPP., p. 135.

[96] The material cause is always of that class to which the product belongs.

[97] Kandalī., pp. 33-34; TBhā., pp. 113-14.

that a *dvyaṇuka* could be produced out of heterogeneous elements—would not possess any of the specific qualities of the constituent *bhūtas*; for, an attribute by itself cannot produce any effect. Hence, neither the smell belonging to the earthly *paramāṇu*, nor the taste belonging to the watery *paramāṇu*, for instance, is capable of producing either smell or taste in such a *dvyaṇuka*. If it were supposed to be capable, it would continue to produce its effect without ceasing; for, an attribute is always present in the causal substance.

The view—that the capability of producing the attribute constantly is equally possible in the case when the production of a *dvyaṇuka* depends upon more than one *paramāṇu* of the same class—is not correct; for, a *dvyaṇuka*, being produced, there must be the production of a specific quality in it. Such a quality becomes an obstacle in the way of the origin of a fresh quality, which cannot be produced until the earlier quality is destroyed. Hence, there is no danger of constant production in this case.[98]

Again, if a *dvyaṇuka* were produced out of two distinct classes of *paramāṇus*, then it should possess the generalities of both the classes. This would lead to the overlapping of generalities which has not been accepted as valid by the Naiyāyikas.[99] Hence, it is said that the constituents of a *dvyaṇuka* are of the same class.[100] Similarly, in the case of a human organism, which is called *pāñcabhautika*, the ultimate material cause is the earthly *paramāṇus*, while the *paramāṇus* of other *bhūtas* represent the instrumental cause and are called *upaṣṭambhaka*, meaning, a contact producing a composite along with which it remains till that composite exists.[101] In other words, in an earthly

[98] KV., p. 58; KVBhā., p. 87.

[99] KV., p. 33.

[100] KV., pp. 59-60; KVBhā., pp. 86-89; NP., *MS*, pp. 1003-1009.

[101] NSVṚ., III. i. 27.

organism the ultimate material cause is, undoubtedly, the earthly *paramāṇus*, but the contact of other classes of *paramāṇus* cannot be denied. This is the case with every kind of product, whether animate or inanimate.[102] Hence, although the material cause of a *dvyaṇuka* is represented by the two earthly *paramāṇus*, yet the other classes of *paramāṇus*, along with the *Ākāça*, are in close contact with the earthly ones. An illustration of it can be found even in the case of the germinating of a sprout from a paddy seed where it is assumed that the constituents of a paddy seed, growing into a plant, renounce their former composition and take up another; wherein it so happens that the particles of earth combining with those of water and joined by the internal *tejas*, produce juice in it, which, in its turn, operating upon and along with the constituents of the seed, modifies itself into a sprout.[103]

VII

OBJECTIONS AGAINST PARAMĀṆUKĀRAṆAVĀDA AND THEIR POSSIBLE REFUTATION

It has been held by the Vaiçeṣikas that the *paramāṇus* are the ultimate material cause of the universe. This view has been variously objected to by the Vedāntins, mainly, of the Çaṅkara school. An attempt is, however, made in this section to meet all these objections and defend the Nyāya-Vaiçeṣika position.

As to the view that as there is no cause as seen (*adṛṣṭa*), in the form of human effort, etc., or as unseen (*adṛṣṭa*), or as the knowledge or effort of the *Jīvātman*, etc., to produce motion in the *paramāṇus*, during the dissolution period, no combination of the *paramāṇus* is possible, and consequently, there would be no product,

[102] VS., IV. ii. 4 along with VU., VV., VBhā.; NBhā., III. i. 27; NV., p. 371; BhāC., p. 484; VVV., p. 98.

[103] NV., p. 351.

individual or universal, formed out of those *paramāṇus*,[104] it may be said by the Nyāya-Vaiçeṣika that although the above mentioned possible causes may not be operative there, yet there is *Içvara*[105] Who is endowed with eternal knowledge and effort, and Whose Will helps the *adṛṣṭa*, on the point of fructification,[106] which forms the instrumental cause to produce motion in the *paramāṇus* causing them to form products. Hence, there would not be any difficulty in maintaining *paramāṇus* to be the ultimate cause of the universe.

Again, the Vedāntins object to the validity of the relation of inherence assumed by the Naiyāyika to subsist between a material cause and its product, arguing that such a relation is unable to account for the facts of the empirical world unless it is believed to be itself related by a fresh relation to the terms of the original relation. For, an unrelated relation conveys no logical significance whatever. The assumption of a fresh relation, however, would lead on to an assumption of a further relation, and so on; so that, the whole process would pre-suppose a vitiated logical position. To this objection, the Naiyāyika replies that as the relation of inherence is eternal by nature, it does not need the help of another relation (*viz.*, inherence) to connect it.[107]

Again, the Vedāntins urge that an object may be of the nature of having motion (*pravṛtti*), or not having motion (*nivṛtti*), or having both, or having neither. But none of these alternatives is possible

[104] BS., II. ii. 11-12 along with ÇBhā., Bhāmatī and RP.
[105] PPBhā., pp. 48-49.
[106] (1) ĀV., pp. 118-19., NV., IV. i. 21. pp. 464-66; (2) If *Içvara* be insisted upon to have an organism to exercise His Will, then *paramāṇus* themselves should be assumed to form His body—Bodhanī, p. 91; (3) As the point of fructification is nothing but time (*kāla*) to guide the motion, there would not be any constant motion-NV., IV. i. 21; p. 459.
[107] BS., II. ii. 13 along with ÇBhā. and RP.

in the case of a *paramāṇu*; for, the first would make it ever active which would make *pralaya* impossible; the second would make creation impossible; the third, being mutually contradictory, cannot be upheld; while the fourth would mean either the presence of eternal activity (*pravṛtti*), as both activity and non-activity depend upon *adṛṣṭa*, *Kāla*, and the rest, which are ever present, or the presence of eternal non-activity, if they do not depend upon any *nimitta*. Both the cases would make creation and dissolution (*pralaya*) impossible. Hence, the *paramāṇus* cannot be the ultimate cause in either case.[108]

To this it may be replied that a *paramāṇu* is active or inactive according to its association with relevant auxiliary factors. The presence and the absence of the auxiliaries are inferred from the presence or otherwise of the effect. In other words, if the auxiliary is present, then there is the activity, and not otherwise. Both creation and *pralaya* being thus explained, the causality of *paramāṇus* remains unaffected.

Next, to the objection that as a *paramāṇu* possesses colour and other attributes, it is grosser and consequently, has parts (compared with which the *paramāṇu* is called grosser), and therefore, it cannot be the ultimate eternal cause of the universe,[109] it may be said that the possession of colour and other attributes is not at all contrary to the non-possession of cause. Hence, the *paramāṇus* have no parts, and are, undoubtedly, the ultimate cause of the universe.

Again, it is objected that as an earthly object possesses the attributes of smell, taste, colour and touch, and is the grossest of all the *bhūtas*; water possessing colour, taste and touch is grosser; *tejas* having only colour and touch is gross, while air possessing the

[108] BS., II. ii. 14 along with ÇBhā.
[109] BS., II. ii. 15 along with ÇBhā. and RP.

single attribute of touch is subtle, so it may be said of the *paramāṇus* which also would be consequently, grossest, grosser, gross and subtle respectively.[110] To this it may be said in reply that the difference in the size of an object is mainly due to its possessing large or small number of constituents and not to that of the number of attributes. Hence, *paramāṇus*, which have no constituents, are not at all affected.

Lastly, it is urged that as the *paramāṇukāraṇavāda* has not been accepted by authoritative persons even partly, it is totally disregarded by the believers in the Vedas.[111] To this also it may be said in reply that as *Ānvīkṣikī* including the *paramāṇukāraṇavāda* has been accepted as one of the *vidyās*, the above objection does not hold good. This has been supported by the inclusion of the *vākovākya*,[112] in the list of the enumeration of the *vidyās* in the Chāndogya Upaniṣad, which has been explained as referring to *tarkaçāstra*[113] (which stands for the joint-system of Nyāya and Vaiçeṣika) by Çaṅkarācārya himself. Hence, it is not at all proper to reject the theory of the ultimate causality of the *paramāṇus* on these grounds.

VIII

OBJECTIONS AGAINST AVAYAVIN AND THEIR REFUTATION

Avayavin (composite) and *avayavas* (constituents) have been much talked of above. Now, it may be enquired as to what is the relation between the two? Every sensible object consisting of parts has been produced out of some cause. The constituents or the cause are known as *avayavas* of that object, which itself,

[110] BS., II. ii. 16 along with ÇBhā.
[111] BS., II. ii. 17 along with ÇBhā.
[112] ChāU., VII. i. 2.
[113] ÇBhā. under Chāndogya., VII. i. 2.

in relation to those constituents, is called an *avayavin*. The relation between the two is that of cause and effect. The composite which is the effect is said to inhere in its cause, *viz.*, the *avayavas*. Although both are related inseparably by a peculiar relation known as inherence (*samavāya*), yet they are two distinct entities having different attributes and functions. This is the secret of the theory of Origination (*Ārambhakavāda*) propounded by Nyāya-Vaiçeṣika.

This view has met serious objections from the Buddhists.[114] But before entering into the examination of the nature of these objections from the Nyāya-Vaiçeṣika point of view, it would not be out of place to remark that both the schools of thought are quite justified in holding different views within their own spheres. But it is hardly justifiable to criticise the view-point of one particular school from that of another, as it is quite natural that they should widely differ with their different outlooks. This cannot be called a sincere criticism. If we observe with a still wider outlook, it will be seen that both the schools of thought are passing along the same royal road with this difference that one has gone further than the other. Hence, it is quite natural that there should be difference in their points of observation. This being accepted as a fact, the only justification for such criticisms is that each of the schools wants to give a thorough training of its tenets to its students which necessitates the discouraging of the temptations which may be caused by other schools of thought. But sometimes, criticisms also proceed from other than honest and sound reasonings, such as, mutual malice, vindicative nature, temptations

[114] Of the two Buddhist Schools which believe in the existence of the external world, it appears that the objections against the existence of a composite apart from the mere collection of *paramāṇus*, are from the Vaibhāṣikas, as is indicated by Vācaspati Miçra also—*vide* Tāt., II. i. 36, p. 398.

for worldly fame, religious rigidity, and so on. Some of these might have been also responsible for certain criticisms in the case of the Buddhists and others. However, following the traditional procedure attempts are made here to prove the untenability of the Buddhist views against the Nyāya-Vaiçeṣika.

The Buddhists consider that there is no essential difference between a composite and its constituents. The various *paramāṇus*, for instance, when collected together form a composite. To this the reply is that in that case, there would have been no perception of any substance. Nor would any of the other categories of Nyāya-Vaiçeṣika have been perceived; for, each of them becomes visible only when it has got a perceivable object for its substratum, which is not possible, if the grouping of *paramāṇus* form an object. But that these categories are perceived cannot be denied. Hence, it is to be admitted that a composite is something different from the mere collection of *paramāṇus*.[115]

Moreover, if the Buddhists deny the perceptibility of a substance, they would be, thereby, rejecting both the means of right cognition, *viz.*, direct perception and inference, which they themselves believe in.[116]

As to the view—that the perception of a group of *paramāṇus* would be possible just as a collection of hairs becomes visible, it may be said that the analogy is based on a wrong assumption. A hair is not supersensuous by nature, while a *paramāṇu* is naturally supersensuous in every state.[117] Hence, a *paramāṇu*, taken severally or collectively, will always remain supersensuous.

Again, as there is the possibility of catching hold of and drawing an object, it is held that an object is

[115] NS. and NBhā., II. i. 34-35.
[116] NV., II. i. 34; NP., *Ms.* p. 880.
[117] NS. and NBhā., IV. ii. 13-14, 16; Tāt., pp. 646-47.

different from a mere collection of *paramāṇus* which being supersensuous cannot be caught and drawn.[118] As to the objection that catching and drawing of *paramāṇus* being possible by the presence of a sort of coherence (*saṅgrahakāritā*)[119] in them, difference between a composite and its constituents cannot be proved, it may be replied that both catching and drawing are possible only in case of composites, as these are not found in substances like *Ākāça*, *Kāla*, *paramāṇus*, etc., which are all partless; hence, it is clear that a composite is not merely a collection of *paramāṇus*.[120]

Further, the separate existence of a composite is proved also by the fact that an object like a pot, for instance, is looked upon as '*one*', which would not have been possible had the pot been merely a collocation of *paramāṇus*. The notion of *oneness* can never be attributed to a group of many supersensuous objects. As to the objection that such a notion is found to exist in case of an army, a forest etc. which are merely names given to separate groups of several constituents, not visible from a distance, it may be said that as each and every constituent of an army or a forest is naturally sensuous there is no difficulty to attribute oneness to such collections, while a *paramāṇu* being naturally supersensuous remains so, even if collected together in a large number, which prevents the attribution of any number to its group.[121]

It may be further pointed out that the notion of oneness is really attributed to that object alone which

[118] NS. and NBhā., II. i. 36.

[119] *Saṅgrahakāritā* is a particular kind of attribute which is co-existent with conjunction, and which is produced by smoothness and fluidity, as it is found in the case of a pot devoid of chemical action by the contact of water, and in the pot where chemical action has taken place through the *taijasa*-conjunction.-NBhā. II. i. 36.

[120] NV., II. i. 36.

[121] NS and NBhā., II. i. 36.

possesses magnitude (*mahattva*) which being absent in the *paramāṇus* either taken severally or collectively, the notion of oneness cannot be attributed to their collection. But as it is attributed to a pot, it is obvious that a pot is not a collection of *paramāṇus*.[122]

As to the answer given by the Buddhists to the above view that the notion of *mahat* present in the *paramāṇus* grouped together is different from that of Nyāya-Vaiçeṣika and means only a peculiarity (*atiçaya*)[123] which being relative is found to exist when one collection of *paramāṇus* is differentiated from another, and may be attributed to a collection of *paramāṇus* along with the notion of oneness, it may be said in reply that if this interpretation be accepted as true, then as the presence of real magnitude itself has been denied in the *paramāṇus* by the Buddhists also, it will have to be admitted either that no kind of *mahat* is present in the *paramāṇus*, or that if there is any, it is a false notion. Now, even to believe in the presence of the false notion of magnitude in the *paramāṇus*, it would be essential to believe in the presence of the real magnitude somewhere; for, the pre-existence of the *dharmin* is presupposed before any wrong notion about it is affirmed anywhere. But as this magnitude is not possible in the *paramāṇus*, some object will have to be admitted to possess this magnitude, and that such an object is a pot which, under the circumstances, cannot be merely a grouping of *paramāṇus*.[124]

Again, in support of the Nyāya-Vaiçeṣika view, another argument is adduced that when any two objects combine together we perceive the conjunction taking

[122] NS. and NBhā., II. i. 37.

[123] The Tātparya says that this *atiçaya* of the *paramāṇus* is nothing except the production of a substance in the form of an *avayavin* in order to establish the *sthairya* in the *bhāvas*, *viz.*, *paramāṇus*—p. 396.

[124] NS. and NBhā., II. i. 37.

place between those *two* objects which form the substrata of that conjunction.[125] Now, if any of these two objects be merely a collection of *paramāṇus*, then the notion that the combination takes place between *two* objects cannot be valid. But that such a valid notion prevails uncontradicted cannot be overlooked. Hence, a composite is different from its constituents. As to the interpretation of the Buddhists that the number two refers to the *two groups* (*samudāya*) of the *paramāṇus* and not to any composite, it may be said in reply that the word '*grouping*' (*samudāya*) may mean either the conjunction of several (separated) *paramāṇus* or several conjunctions forming one cluster of *paramāṇus*. According to the former alternative, grouping would become a synonym of conjunction;[125] so that, the expression—'two objects combine together'—would be expressed now, as 'two conjunctions combine together'. But this sort of expression is quite against the usage. Hence, the first alternative is not possible. As to the second, it may be said that the expression never indicates that the two groups meet together, rather it shows that the number two is attributed to two definite objects which form the substrate of conjunction. It may be further added that if the substrata of this combination would have been the collection of *paramāṇus*, then as the *paramāṇus* and their attributes are supersensuous, this conjunction also would have become imperceptible, which is not the case. Hence, the interpretation of the Buddhists cannot be accepted. Therefore, the composite ever remains distinct from its constituents.[126]

Nyāya-Vaiçeṣika believes in the independent existence of a category, called generality (*sāmānya* or

[125] The separate and independent existence of conjunction cannot be denied, as it is proved through direct perception and inference—NBhā. II. i. 37.

[126] NBhā., II. i. 37.

jāti), on the basis of there being a common notion belonging to all the objects of one class, however different each of the objects may be in size, shape, colour etc. They also believe in the direct perceptibility of this generality, which is possible only when it has a substratum. The *paramāṇus*, or their collection, cannot be the desired substratum, as both are supersensuous, and as such, they cannot make the generality perceivable. Hence, it is essential to believe that a composite is quite different from its constituents and that it possesses magnitude due to which the generality belonging to it also becomes perceptible.[127]

Uddyotakara adds that the terms '*aṇu*' and '*paramāṇu*' themselves, being relative, indicate that there is some other dimension in relation to which they are themselves so called. Such a dimension is no other than *mahat* (magnitude) which is possessed by a composite.[128]

As to the view that the so-called cloth, for instance, is nothing but a collection of threads; for, had there been any substance like cloth, it would have been perceived independently apart from the threads, and as it is not so, it is concluded that the effect is the same as its cause,[129] it may be pointed out that as the cloth, which is a product, inheres in its cause, namely, threads, it is not ordinarily found apart from the threads. Both, the cause and the effect, would have been separately cognised only if the effect did not inhere in the cause, which is not possible.[130] It is further pointed out that both, the cause and the effect, are independently perceived by those who can penetrate into subtle things, but for an ordinary perceiver, this is not possible. He can only perceive a composite and cognise the

[127] NBhā., II. i. 37.
[128] NV., II. i. 36. (37), p. 250.
[129] NS. and NBhā., IV. ii. 26.
[130] NS., NBhā., NV., and NP., IV. ii. 28.

constituents through inference alone.[131]

The very essence of the theory of Origination is that an effect is a fresh production, and that it had no existence before, and that it is produced through causal operation; hence, both, the cause and its effect, are two distinct things. It is, therefore, that a cloth, for instance, is different from its cause, namely, the threads.[132]

Again, the cause is different from its effect on account of their having different capacities. For instance, a cloth can be used for such various purposes of our daily life which cannot be served by the threads. Again, that function which can be performed by threads cannot be done with the help of a cloth.[133]

It may be further pointed out that as the cause and its effect produce two different cognitions, they cannot be regarded as one.[134] Again, the fact that both are denoted by two different names shows that they are two distinct things.

Believing in the independent existence of the variegated colour (*citrarūpa*), Nyāya-Vaiçeṣika holds that as threads possess various colours separately and not any variegated colour, they cannot be identical with their effect, namely, the cloth, which unlike the threads, does not possess various colours but only the variegated colour. This shows that these are two different substrates and not one.[135]

The Buddhists think that as each and every constituent of a composite does not inhere in the entire composite, on account of their having two different dimensions; and if it does, there being no scope for its combining with any other constituent, the whole would

[131] Tāt., IV. ii. 28, 29. pp. 654-55; NS., NBhā. and NV., IV. ii. 29.

[132] NV., II. i. 36 (37); p. 250.

[133] Tāt., II. i. 36 (37), p. 401., NP. *Ms.* p. 888.

[134] NV., II. i. 36 (37), p. 250.

[135] NV., II. i. 36 (37), p. 250; Tāt., II. i. 36 (37), pp. 401-02.

have consisted of a single constituent, whereby there would have been no true product; and if the same be regarded as such, it would have become eternal; and again, as the constituents do not subsist in any single part of the composite, for, the composite has no other constituents apart from the constituents which it possesses, it is held that there exists no substance which may be called a composite apart from the mere collection of its constituents.[136]

To this the Nyāya-Vaiçeṣika replies that the objection of the Buddhists is entirely groundless; for, no one believes that a cause or any constituent (of an effect) ever inheres in any effect.[137]

As to the objection then that as the composite either wholly or partly does not inhere in its constituents, on account of their having different dimensions, and also because, the composite would then consist of one single constituent which would make the production possible from a single substance leading to the possibility of constant production or making the product eternal in the case of a *dvyaṇuka*, in the former case;[138] and due to the possibility of the composite possessing constituents other than those which produced the composite in the latter case (which it has not), there is no difference between a composite and its constituents, it may be said in reply that there being no diversity in one, the use of the terms denoting difference should not be used regarding that one. In other words, the terms 'wholly' and 'partly' denoting difference cannot be attributed to a composite which forms one definite unit. Hence, the objection does not affect the forming of a composite.[139]

As to the argument that as the composite cannot

[136] NS., IV. ii. 7 along with NBhā., NV. and Tāt.
[137] NV., IV. ii. 10., p. 505.
[138] NS., NBhā and NV., IV. ii. 8.
[139] NS. and NBhā., IV. ii. 11.

remain apart from the constituents, as it is never found so, and also because, in that case, it would become eternal,[140] it is held that there is no composite, it may be replied that the very reasoning adduced above may be used in support of the existence of a composite. For, if a composite had existed apart from its constituents, it would have remained without any substratum, and that which remains without any support should be eternal; so that, a composite would, in that case, become eternal, which is against the reality. Hence, the objection falls down as invalid.[141]

Uddyotakara makes a thorough analysis of this important problem by examining the nature of the possible objections of the Buddhists. After the hair-splitting analysis of almost all the objections, he shows that the Buddhist position is quite untenable. The following is the summary of the objections along with their refutations from the Nyāya-Vaiçeṣika point of view which maintains that a composite is different from its constituents.[142]

As to the argument that the relation of composite and its constituents is possible only when they are not two different things, as is clear from the fact that a cow and a horse are not so related; hence, it is held that a composite is the same as its constituents, it may

[140] NS., IV. ii. 9. There being a different version of the NBhā. here as given below—'*pṛthakcāvayavebhyo dharmibhyo dharmasyagrahaṇāditi samānam*', the query may be put in a different way, that is, just as an attribute is not to be had apart from its substratum, so the composite also cannot be found apart from its constituents; hence, the existence of a composite is denied (*vide* Kāmākhyānātha's edition, Calcutta 1911). Viçvanātha in his Vṛtti explains this sūtra in another way—*Vide* pp. 277-78.

[141] NV., IV. ii. 9 along with Tāt., p. 643.

[142] NV., II. i. 33; pp. 217-39. For further references on this problem one should consult NM., pp. 549-51; Tāt, pp. 385-86; Kandalī, p. 147; Setu., pp. 218-19; Sūkti., p. 198; DSR. *Ms.* Fol. 59-60; ST. on PV., Dravya section, *Ms.* Fol. 12a—b.

be said that the argument, as it stands, has no probans to infer any conclusion. The argument—'because it (thread) is a constituent' (hence, thread should not be different from the cloth) cannot be adduced as a probans; for, the terms—composite and constituents being related, one cannot remain without the other; so that, the probans is really self-contradictory and cannot deny the existence of a composite.

As to the argument that as no composite can be produced from a substance radically different from the composite, like the non-production of a cow or a horse from a man, it is inferred that both, a composite and its constituents, are identical, it may be said in reply that, if the above argument is put in the form of a syllogism, namely, '*paṭaḥ tantubhyo nārthāntaram*, *tebhyaḥ utpatteḥ*', it will be seen that the probans is faulty; for it cannot be denied that a shuttle or a loom, for instance, producing the cloth, is quite different from the effect.[143]

Again, it is argued by the Buddhists that the objects which are different from a composite are such as form the constituents of another composite; as for instance, the wheels being the constituents of a chariot are different from cloth but not from the chariot itself. Hence, if the threads be regarded as different from the cloth, they should form the constituents of something else than the cloth. But as it is not the case, it should be held that both the threads and the cloth are identical in every respect.[144]

To this the rejoinder is that the argument when put in the form of a syllogism is found to be beset with a fallacy. The major premise (*pratijñāvākya*) being the same as before, the probans is 'because the threads are not the constituents of anything other than that cloth' (*tadvyatirekeṇānyānavayavatvāt*). Now, it may be pointed out here that as the threads are not the constituents of

[143] NV., II. i. 33, p. 226.
[144] NV., II. i. 33, p. 226.

threads themselves, the probans involves the fallacy of *viruddha*. It may be further pointed out that the very assumption of the Buddhists that the wheels are the parts of the chariot shows that they are two different things.[145]

Again, it is held by the Buddhists that the two objects admitted to be different from each other are seen to be produced on two different places; as, for instance, a cow is produced in a place different from that of a horse. In the case of threads and a cloth, on the other hand, it is seen that the latter is produced in the place where the former exists; so that, they are not distinct from each other.

To this, again, the answer is that the probans—'because, it is produced in the place occupied by the constituents' (*taddeçotpatteḥ*)—is wrong; for, admitting for a while that both are identical, it will have to be admitted that the thread is produced in place previously occupied by itself, which, however, is not the case. Hence, the probans is a wrong one.

If the production of the cloth be denied then, what is the meaning of the term '*utpatti*' used in the above probans? 'Threads' appearing as 'threads' alone cannot be said to have been produced. Hence, the very term '*utpatti*' shows the coming into existence of something which had no existence before. It is, therefore, clear that a composite is not identical with its constituents.[146]

Further, it is argued by the Buddhists that a composite possessing a particular kind of constituent is entirely different from other constituents (which are different from that composite); as a pot, for instance, possesses constituents which are different from the wheels which, again, are distinct from the pot. As this is not the case with the threads and the cloth, they are said to be identical.[147]

[145] NV., II. i. 33, p. 227.
[146] NV., II. i. 33, pp. 227-28.
[147] NV., II. i. 33, p. 228.

Here, also, the argument of the Buddhists is fallacious like before. The very assumption that there is a composite of another set of constituents shows that the separate existence of a composite is admitted, as the terms—composite and constituent are relative.[148]

Next, the Buddhists argue that things, which are different from something else, are produced from conjunctions other than those which produce that something else; as, for instance, the mat is produced from a conjunction other than that of the threads. As the cloth is not produced from a conjunction other than that of the threads, they are said to be identical with each other.[149]

Here, also, the implied probans—'*tantusaṃyogebhyastadutpatteḥ*'—is fallacious as before. The reason is that the very assumption that the cloth is produced from the conjunctions of the threads admits that both the conjunction and the composite are different from the threads.[150]

Again, the Buddhists may argue that as it is not seen that the attributes of one particular substance can be produced from those of another substance entirely different from the former, as, for instance, the attributes of a horse are never found to be produced from those of a cow,—and as the attributes of the threads are observed to produce those of the cloth, the cloth is not different from the threads which are its constituents.[151]

This argument, also, is untenable from the Nyāya-Vaiçeṣika point of view. The inconsistency lies in admitting that the attributes of threads do produce those of cloth and at the same time rejecting the difference between the cloth and the threads. In fact, it is wrong to assume that the attributes of cloth are

[148] NV., II. i. 33, p. 228.
[149] NV., II. i. 33, p. 229.
[150] Ibid.
[151] Ibid.

produced from those of the threads when it is known for certain that the attributes of the threads cannot be produced from those of the threads themselves.[152]

The last but the most important argument of the Buddhists in support of the identity of the cause and its effect may be that they do not differ in their weight. In other words, as the weight of the constituents does not differ from that of the composite, it is held that both are identical. As for instance, argue the Buddhists, no difference in the form of lowering of the balance or otherwise is seen in the effect when two pieces of clay are put in the balance separately and also when those very two pieces are joined together and placed in the balance in the form of a pot. Therefore, like the separate pieces of clay the joint-pieces also do not produce a different substance. Hence, it is held that the effect is not distinct from its cause.[153]

This argument, also, is held to be wrong as it appears that according to Nyāya-Vaiçeṣika the difference in the weight of the two is admitted.[154]

There may still be yet more minor objections on the part of the Buddhists; these also can be very easily refuted.

[152] Ibid.

[153] Ibid.; Tāt., II. i. 33, p. 392.

[154] *Yaççāyam heturgurutvāntaravattvaprasaṅgāditi? Ayamapyabhyupagamānna kiñcit.* NV., II. i. 33, p. 234—This view seems to be a partial one. Also consult here Tāt., p. 393: Vyom., p. 219; KV., p. 64; Kandalī., p. 148; KVP., p. 258.

IX

DISCUSSION ABOUT THE INTERMEDIARY STAGES IN THE FORMATION OF THE FINAL COMPOSITE

1. *Tryaṇuka*

The separate existence of composite being proved it may be further urged: Why should not a composite be formed directly from *paramāṇus*? To this it may be said, in reply, that had there been no intermediary products like *dvyaṇuka*, *tryaṇuka* and the rest, then when, for instance, a pot is broken, it ought to be directly reduced to its invisible ultimate atoms, but it is not so.[155] It may also be pointed out here that the pot being an effect possessing magnitude necessitates that its cause also should be an effect.[156] Hence, the *paramāṇus* cannot directly produce the *tryaṇukas*.

Gopīnātha Maunin, however, thinks that a *tryaṇuka* can be produced directly out of three *paramāṇus*. He holds that the necessity for believing in the existence of a *dvyaṇuka* is only to produce magnitude in the *tryaṇuka*, but if it were produced by the plurality belonging to the group of three *paramāṇus*, then there is no reason why the existence of a *dvyaṇuka* should be at all accepted.[157]

Appayya Dīkṣita also supports the view that a *tryaṇuka* is produced directly from the three *paramāṇus* whose simultaneous conjunctions and productivity of further effect cannot be denied.[158]

The argument adduced by Amalānand Sarasvatī that that which is of the nature of the class of cause

155 Tāt., III. i. 32, p. 520; KV., p. 64; KVBhā., p. 91; KP., Stavaka V, verse 5, p. 116; NM., p. 503; NLV., p. 97; Bhāmatī, II. ii. 11; p. 503.

156 KV., p. 64.

157 ST., a comm. on PV., *MS*. Fol. 11-12.

158 VKTP., II. ii. 11, p. 504.

(*kāraṇajātīya*) is not productive of that of the class of effect; as for instance, the thread which belongs to the *aṇu* (smaller) class does not produce the effect belonging to the class of cloth; so that, *paramāṇus* belonging to the *aṇu* class cannot produce the effect belonging to the class which possesses magnitude,[159] as to that it may be said that it is not always true; for, a cord (consisting of three threads—*trivṛtsūtra*) is produced sometimes, by three *sūtras* (cords) produced by three threads (*tantus*) and sometimes, directly from three threads.[160] He, however, admits that just as a cord (*trivṛtsūtra*) produced by three threads (*tantus*) is different from that which is produced by three *sūtras* (cords), so the *tryaṇuka* produced directly from three *paramāṇus* may be different from that which is produced out of three *dvyaṇukas*. But even then, it is clear that a *tryaṇuka* can be produced directly out of three *paramāṇus*.[161]

As to the argument that as such a *tryaṇuka* is of the class of *aṇu*, there would be no difference between a *paramāṇu* and the so-called *tryaṇuka* as far as their empirical utility is concerned; and hence, there is no need for such a production, it may be said that the so-called *tryaṇuka* being produced out of three *paramāṇus* (*kāraṇabahutva*) would possess magnitude and would not remain atomic in any way; so that, the above-mentioned objection is quite groundless. Hence, there appears to be no harm, holds Appayya Dīksita, in believing that a *tryaṇuka* is produced directly out of three *paramāṇus*.[162]

This view may be further supported by the fact that almost all the definitions and descriptions of the *tryanuka* found in different texts refer to the number of the *paramāṇus* constituting it and not to that of the *dvyaṇukas*.

[159] VKT., II. ii. 11, p. 504.
[160] VKTP., p. 504.
[161] Ibid.
[162] VKTP., II. ii. 11, p. 504.

Thus, some are of opinion that a *paramāṇu* is the sixth part of a first product;[163] others hold that a *paramāṇu* is the eighth part of it;[164] again, some think that it consists of thirty *paramāṇus*,[165] while others believe that it is out of three *paramāṇus* alone that a *tryaṇuka* is produced.[166] These different views themselves create a doubt as to the exact nature of the constituents of a *tryaṇuka*.

A question naturally rises here: What is the reason that Nyāya and Vaiçeṣika, in spite of these oppositions, stick to the view that a *tryaṇuka* is produced out of three *dvyaṇukas* and not *paramāṇus*? A probable answer of this seems to be that the joint-system, representing the common-sense view, finds it difficult and unreasonable too to reject the production out of two *paramāṇus*. In other words, when the *paramāṇus* are moved, they naturally form first groups of twos and as they are fresh productions they must have a different nomenclature and place in the process of creation. Afterwards, when such groups are formed and the question of further productions comes up in order to attribute magnitude to the fresh productions and make them visible it becomes necessary to have the grouping of three. Now, as there are only *dvyaṇaukas*, the other groups are formed out of these three *dvyaṇukas*.

2. *Dvyaṇuka*

Coming to the *dvyaṇuka* it may be asked: Why only two *paramāṇus* produce it? To this the reply is that a single *paramāṇu* cannot produce anything for obvious difficulties. If three *paramānus* be admitted

[163] TK; TP. *MS.* Fol. 1*a*.

[164] NMÇ. a comm. on LU, p. 23.

[165] ÇK. of Sir Rājā Rādhākāntadeva Bahādura, Vol. I. p. 398, Col. 3; PSH., p. 83. NK., p. 344, 3rd Edition.

[166] DK. with RR., p. 293; DP. of Bhagīratha Ṭhakkura, *MS.* Fol. 127*a*; Çrīmadbhāgavata, III. xii. 5 along with Çrīdhara's comm. on it; NK., pp. 343-44.

to produce a *dvyanuka*, then there being the plural number in the cause, the effect should have possessed magnitude and have become perceptible which it is not. And as there is no reason to go beyond the number three, it is concluded that a *dvyaṇuka* is produced out of two *paramāṇus* alone.

X

DIMENSION AND ITS CAUSES

It has been mentioned above that there are four kinds of non-eternal dimensions, namely, long (*dīrgha*) and short (*hrasva*), magnitude (*mahat*) and atomic (*aṇu*).[167] These are produced by number, dimension and aggregation (*pracaya*)[168] either taken collectively or independently.[169] Of these, the magnitude is produced by all the three causes[170] independently. Thus, the magnitude belonging to a *tryaṇuka* is produced from the number and not out of the other two causes mentioned above. According to the law of causation a *tryaṇuka* has *dvyaṇukas* as its material cause and the conjunction of those *dvyaṇukas* as the non-material cause. The attributes of a *tryaṇuka*, on the other hand, possess the *tryaṇuka* itself as their material cause, while the attributes of the *dvyaṇukas* as their non-material cause. Following this general rule, now, if the dimension of a *dvyaṇuka*, that is, *aṇutva*, were to produce the dimension of a *tryaṇuka* then, as the dimension of the effect should

[167] PPBhā., p. 131.

[168] PPBhā., p. 131; ÇBhā under BS., II. ii. 11; Vyom., p. 474. Although almost all the available editions of the Vaiçesikasūtra read the *sūtra* VII. i. 9 as '*kāraṇabahutvācca*,' yet ÇBhā. under BS., II. ii. 11 and the Vyom. p. 474 read it as '*Kāraṇabahutvāt kāraṇamahattvāt pracayaviceṣācca mahaditi.*' Consult VU. also under VS., VII. i. 9. *Pracaya* is a particular kind of loose conjunction of a substance, as for instance, a lump of cotton-Kandalī, p. 136.

[169] Vyom., p. 474.

[170] By 'cause' is meant here 'non-material cause.'

be of the same class as that of the cause and also larger, the dimension of the *dvyaṇuka* being *aṇu* (atomic), it would not only produce the atomic dimension in the *tryaṇuka* but also comparatively larger than itself which would make the dimension of the *tryaṇuka aṇutara* (smaller). This would not only make the *tryaṇuka* imperceptible but the very aim of the production of it would be frustrated. Hence, the dimension of a *dvyaṇuka* cannot produce that of a *tryaṇuka*.[171] This question does not arise as regards the production of the dimension of a *dvyaṇuka*; for, the dimension of a *paramāṇu* is not the cause of anything.[172] None of the other attributes, namely, colour, taste, smell, touch, oneness, one-separateness, weight, fluidity and smoothness is capable of producing magnitude in a *tryaṇuka*; as these produce similar attributes in their respective effects.[173] Nor can the aggregation be the desired cause; for, it is not possible to have the aggregation present in a *dvyaṇuka*,[174] and moreover, it is meant for producing the magnitude of some specific substances, like cotton, for instance.[175] Hence, according to the method of elimination the cause of magnitude in the *tryaṇuka* is number only.[176]

As to the exact number which produces the magnitude in the *tryaṇuka*, it may be said that one cannot produce anything for obvious reasons, and as the number two produces atomic dimension alone, it should also be rejected. Therefore, it is the plural number three alone which has been admitted by the author of the sūtra also,

[171] KV., p. 214; Kandalī., p. 135; NLV., pp. 99-100; KP. and KPP., stavaka V, under verse 5, p. 112; Jalada on KV., *MS*. Fol. 127.

[172] Vyom., 479; KV., 216; Kandalī., p. 137; Bhā; verse 15; KP., stavaka V, under verse 5, p. 112; KPP., on Ibid.

[173] Vyom., p. 476; KV., p. 214; Kandalī., p. 135.

[174] Vyom., p. 476; KV., p. 214; KP. and KPP., stavaka V, verse 5, p. 116.

[175] Kandalī., p. 136.

[176] Vyom., p. 476; KV., 214; Kandalī., p. 135.

to be the non-material cause of the dimension of a *tryaṇuka*. When the least plural number serves the purpose, there is no sense in going beyond this number. Now, as to how this plural number produces the dimension, it is said that as the number beyond one is produced by an *apekṣābuddhi*, its presence is required here also in order to produce the plurality of number in *dvyaṇukas*.[177] As *dvyaṇukas* are supersensuous this *apekṣābuddhi* should belong to one who can perceive them. He may be *Içvara*[178] whose *apekṣābuddhi* produces the plurality of number, namely, three in the *dvyaṇukas*, which, in its turn, causes the existence of magnitude in the *tryaṇuka*.

It may be urged here that as the number three is produced by the *apekṣābuddhi* of *Içvara*, it cannot be destroyed, as the convention that the effect is destroyed by the destruction of the *apekṣābuddhi* is not applicable in this case; for, the *apekṣābuddhi* of *Içvara* is eternal. But neither is it possible to hold that the number three is indestructible and hence, eternal, nor is it possible to reject the causality of the *apekṣābuddhi* of *Içvara* in the absence of which neither the *tryaṇuka* nor, consequently, the universe would itself be ever produced. To get rid of this dilemma the suggestion to dispense with the *apekṣābuddhi* of *Içvara* and accept, in its place, an inferential one which may belong to any human being, is also untenable; for, it would involve the defect of being mutually inter-dependent; as, the production of human being or anything of the universe and the inference of *apekṣābuddhi* all would depend upon the production of the *tryaṇuka* which itself would now depend upon the

[177] KV., p. 213; KP., stavaka V, under verse 5, p. 119. These *dvyanukas* are called *paramāṇu-dvyaṇukas* as these are produced by the combination of two *paramāṇus*—Kandalī., p. 135; Vyom., p. 475. KV. remarks here that the use of the term '*dvyaṇuka*' here shows that a *tryanuka* is produced from *dvyanukas* and not from *paramāṇus* directly, p.213.

[178] PPBhā., p. 131; Bhāmatī, under BS., II. ii. 11, p. 504.

existence of human beings etc. Hence, it is rejected.[179] As to the other solution advanced here that instead of *apekṣābuddhi* let *adṛṣṭa* itself be the required cause, it may be said in reply that if *adṛṣṭa* be accepted to be the cause everywhere then what would be the use of any *dṛṣṭa* cause. Therefore, this also is not a sound argument.[180]

Thus, the various suggestions having been proved untenable and the dilemma being still present, it is held that this number being a product must be destroyed like all other products. But as there can be no destruction without a cause, and as there is no apparent cause to destroy this number, and also as there is the *adṛṣṭa* to justify its existence (for ever), some other means, namely, the destruction of *adṛṣṭa* etc., may be held to destroy the number three.[181]

The author of Vyomavatī, however, holds that the term *Içvara* does not necessarily mean God. The very root meaning of the term *Içvara* shows that it may be used for any one who possesses miraculous powers as a *yogīçvara*. If this interpretation be accepted as valid, then all the above-mentioned difficulties would be easily solved, as such an *apekṣābuddhi* being non-eternal can be destroyed.[182]

It may be, however, pointed out here that the interpretation of the author of Vyomavatī is possible only when the world comes to exist and fresh *tryaṇukas* are to be produced. But this cannot be applicable to the production of the magnitude in the *tryaṇuka* just in the very beginning of the creation after the *pralaya* when no human being or any *yogīçvara* happens to exist.

However, both the processes of production and

[179] KP. and KPP., stavaka V, verse 5, pp. 119-20.

[180] Ibid.

[181] Vyom., p. 476; KPP., stavaka V, verse 5, p. 120 along with the Makaranda; TP., *MS*. Fol. 8*a*-9*a*.

[182] Vyom., p. 476.

destruction of the number three produced through the *apekṣābuddhi*, are also given below:

When the motion produced in the *dvyaṇukas* produces disjunction then there is the destructivity (*vinaçyattā*) of the conjunction, and simultaneous with it the cognition of the generality *ekatva* is produced. Then there is the productivity (*utpadyamānatā*) of the *apekṣābuddhi* followed by the destruction of the conjunction; then the productivity of the subsequent conjunction followed by the production (*utpāda*) of the *apekṣābuddhi*; then there is the productivity of the *tritva* followed by the production of the conjunction out of two *dvyaṇukas* leading to the productivity of the *tryaṇuka* followed by the destructivity of the disjunction and the motion. Then comes the production of the *tritva* followed by the productivity of the conjunction of the generality *tritva*. Then the *tryaṇuka* is produced followed by the destruction of the disjunction and the motion. Then follows the production of the cognition of the generality *tritva* followed by the productivity of the magnitude (*mahattva*) and the *dīrghatva*. Then appears the destructivity of the *apekṣābuddhi* followed by the productivity of the cognition of the attribute *tritva*; then the production of the *mahattva* and the *dīrghatva*; then the destruction of the *apekṣābuddhi*; then the destructivity of the attribute *tritva*; then the production of the cognition of attribute followed by the productivity of the cognition of the substance; then simultaneously with the cognition of the substance there is the destruction of the *tritva*.[183]

In products beyond *tryaṇuka* the dimension is caused by the dimension of their respective causes.[184] As to the view that the plurality of the number of the cause itself may be held to be the cause of magnitude in every product, it may be said that as there are several products which are produced directly from two parts only and

[183] Vyom., p. 476.
[184] Jalada on KV., *MS*. Fol. 127.

as there is the absence of plurality in such cases, no magnitude would have been produced; for instance, a pot which is directly produced out of the two halves (*kapālas*) only; but if the above view is held, then there would have been no magnitude in that pot. Moreover, when the magnitude is present in the cause how can it be possible to deny its causality.[185]

Similarly, aggregation (*pracaya*), which is a particular kind of loose contact existing in the two bundles of cotton which depends upon the loose conjunctions of the constituents productive of the cotton bundles, or which depends upon the loose conjunctions between parts of one bundle and those of the other, produces magnitude in the product produced out of those two cotton bundles, named, *dvitūlaka*. As there are only two bundles and not more the plurality of the number cannot be the cause of the magnitude of the *dvitūlaka*. Although the magnitude is present in the cause and can produce the required effect, yet its being not self-dependent, as it depends upon the loose conjunctions existing in the two bundles of cotton, cannot be the cause of the magnitude of the *dvitūlaka*.[186]

As to the view that although there is no plurality of the number in the two bundles of cotton, yet taking all the constituents up to *dvyaṇukas* and *paramāṇus* of the bundles into consideration, the plurality can be found to belong indirectly to the constituents of the effect, called *dvitūlaka*; so that, it is really the plurality of number which produces the magnitude in the *dvitūlaka* and not the aggregation,[187] it may be said that if number were to produce the magnitude in the present case, then there ought to have been no difference of magnitude (*mahattātiçaya*) in the product, namely, *dvitūlaka* (a double-lump of cotton),

[185] KV., pp. 214-15.
[186] KV., pp. 215-16.
[187] RS., p. 64; Kandalī., p. 136.

produced by the two separate bundles of cotton having loose contacts and the same, when it is produced out of two cotton bundles having compact contacts (*pracita*), although both contain an equal number of components.

This very reason may be put forth regarding the view that magnitude itself may be the cause of the magnitude of the *dvitūlaka*. But, as a matter of fact, according to Nyāya-Vaiçeṣika, there is the difference in the magnitude of the effect under two circumstances. Hence, it is concluded that neither the number, nor the magnitude is the cause of the magnitude of the effect, called a double-lump of cotton.[188]

As to the view that the two conjunctions belonging to the three *dvyaṇukas* may be the cause of the magnitude of a *tryaṇuka*, it may be said that it would have been possible to hold such a view, if it were held that the conjunctions of the several constituents were the cause; but as it is not possible, the view is rejected as untenable.[189]

Again, as to the argument that a particular kind of *jāti* belonging to the *dvyanuka-parimāṇa* may help the *aṇutva* of a *dvyaṇuka* to become the cause of the magnitude of a *tryaṇuka*, it may be said that had this been the fact, then the magnitude would not have been the cause of another magnitude ever. Moreover, the two dimensions, namely, *aṇutva* and *mahattva*, being mutually opposed, would counter-act each other and would not be able to produce any one class of effect. If, it be, however, urged that the difference in the cause would determine the difference in the effect; so that, the above-mentioned difficulty would not arise, then the rejoinder should be that if it were so, then the magnitude would have been produced in the effect even from several *paramāṇus* directly and also from two *dvyaṇukas*, which would have led to the production of magnitude

[188] Kandalī., p. 136; RS., p. 64.
[189] Kandalī., p. 135.

in the effect of the *paramāṇus* also, like that of a *dvyaṇuka*. Moreover, if it be admitted, then the production of the magnitude being possible from two only, there would be no justification in holding the production from any bigger number, namely, three.[190]

In the like manner, the dimension, called *dīrghatva*, also is produced by the plurality of number, *dīrghatva* and the aggregation of the cause.[191] In other words, the *dīrghatva* in a *tryaṇuka*, for instance, is produced by the plurality of number belonging to the cause; in the effect, called *dvitantuka* (a product formed out of the combination of two threads), it is produced by the *dīrghatva* belonging to the cause, and in the effect, namely, *tritantuka* (a product formed out of the combination of three threads), it is produced by the plurality of number as well as the *dīrghatva* belonging to the cause, while in the case of a treble-lump of cotton (*tritūlaka*), it is produced by all the three causes mentioned above.[192]

The same can be said as regards the production of *mahattva* and *dīrghatva* in a *caturaṇuka*; for, these cannot be produced in a *caturaṇuka* out of the *mahattva* and the *dīrghatva* belonging to a *tryaṇuka*; as, there is a logical convention that the *mahattva* which is not produced either out of the number, or the aggregation, as it is in the case of the *mahattva* of a *caturaṇuka*, can be produced only by the *mahattva* belonging to the constituents of the cause.[193]

As regards the production of the other two dimensions, namely, atomic (*aṇutva*) and shortness (*hrasvatva*), it is said that both are produced in a *dvyaṇuka* out of the number two possessed by the two *paramāṇus* producing a *dvyaṇuka*.[194]

[190] KP. and KPP., stavaka V, verse 5, pp. 114-16.
[191] PPBhā., p. 131; Vyom., p. 479.
[192] Ibid.
[193] PPBhā., p. 131; Vyom., p. 479.
[194] KPP., stavaka V, verse 5, p. 117.

Regarding the question—what is the difference between the two dimensions belonging to a *dvyaṇuka* and a *tryaṇuka*, it may be pointed out that the difference between the *mahattva* and the *dīrghatva* is quite clear from the common everyday usage as expressed in the judgment—'bring a *dīrgha* (large) thing' even when the speaker has got the thing possessing *mahat* and *vice versa*.[195] The author of Vyomavatī adds that this difference is quite obvious from the very appearance of the object.[196] It may be further pointed out here that although a *tryaṇuka* simultaneously possesses both the dimensions, yet that *tryaṇuka*, in the formation of which its constituents are placed in a circuitous manner (*paritaḥ*), appears to be *mahat*, while that, of which the components are placed obliquely (*tīrvak*), seems to be *dīrgha*.[197]

Similarly, the difference, between *aṇutva* and *hrasvatva* belonging to a *dvyaṇuka*, is visible to those who are capable of perceiving it.[198] It may be also added here that the dimension of a *dvyaṇuka* should not be taken to be identicle with that of a *paramāṇu*; for, the former, being an effect, must have some difference,[199] and hence, it is said to have some expansion (*prathimā*),[200] which is not possible in the case of a *paramāṇu*. It is, therefore, that the term *pārimāṇḍalya* has been specially used to denote the dimension of a *paramāṇu*.[201]

Of the four varieties of dimension, the *mahattva* and the *dīrghatva* are always found together, and so is the case with the other two dimensions, namely, *aṇutva* and *hrasvatva*. Some are of opinion that just as *Ākāça*, being in possession of *vyāpakatva*, does not possess *dīrghatva*, so, a *paramāṇu* also, having the *parimaṇḍalatva*,

195 PPBhā., pp. 131-32.
196 Vyom., p. 479.
197 VKTP., II. ii. 11, p. 506.
198 PPBhā., p. 132.
199 KV., p. 212; Kandalī., p. 133; VBhā., VII. i. 10.
200 VBhā., VII. i. 10.
201 VS., VII. i. 20; Vyom., p. 492.

has no *hrasvatva*.[202] And, again, *mahattvatva* and *dīrghatvatva*, or *aṇutvatva* and *hrasvatvatva*, being separate *jātis*, the presence of one is an obstacle in the way of the existence of another in the same substratum and at the same time. Hence, the two dimensions cannot coinhere in a single substratum at one particular time.[203] The Naiyāyikas, however, do not agree with the above mentioned views. They hold, on the other hand, that both, the *parama-dīrghatva* and *parama-mahattva*, are simultaneously present in the *Ākāça*, just as both, the (*parama*) *aṇutva* and (*parama*) *hrasvatva*, subsist in a *paramāṇu*[204] at one and the same time. In other all-pervasive substances also both the dimensions, namely, *parama-mahattva* and *parama-dīrghatva*, co-inhere. In the like manner, in substances of intermediate dimensions (*madhyama-parimāṇa*) there are both, the intermediate *mahattva* and intermediate *dīrghatva*, except in the case of a *dvyaṇuka* where the intermediate *aṇutva* and intermediate *hrasvatva* exist.[205]

Vallabha, the author of Nyāyalīlāvatī, holds that *hrasvatva* and *dīrghatva* are not distinct dimensions, but are the sub-divisions of *aṇutva* and *mahattva* respectively. He, further, adds that if these be held to be independent dimensions, then why should not the other possible varieties of dimension, such as, *vakratva*, *ṛjutva*, etc. be recognised as such.[206] This, again, seems to be only a partial view. Even Çaṅkarācārya, while referring to the general view of Nyāya-Vaiçeṣika, says that *anutva* and *hrasvatva* are the two dimensions which are said to belong to a *dvyaṇuka*.[207]

[202] Kandalī., p. 134.
[203] NLPV., pp. 367-68.
[204] Kandalī., p. 134.
[205] Kandalī., p. 134.
[206] NL., p. 34, Nirnavasāgara edition; PRM., p. 31.
[207] ÇBhā., on BS., II. ii. 11.

XI

VARIOUS OTHER VIEWS REGARDING PARAMĀṆU

The term *paramāṇu* has been variously used in different schools of thought, and it will not be out of place to refer to them here.

1. Thus, *paramāṇus* are regarded as forming a body of *Içvara* being the substrata of His direct effort. It is, therefore, that the motion inherent in them is said to be His breath, as is said in the çruti also—*asya mahato bhūtasya niḥçvasitametat.*[208]

This view has been rejected by Udayanācārya on the ground that such a body cannot be the substratum of sense-organs, as it does not possess the *Manas.*[209]

2. *Paramāṇu* is also a name given to that particular point of time which the sun requires to pass over an atomic object. The mathematical calculation of it, given by Bhāskarācārya, in his Siddhāntaçiromani,[210] will be clear from the following table:

2	Paramāṇus	—	1 Dvyaṇuka
3	Dvyaṇukas	—	1 Truṭi[211]
100	Truṭis	—	1 Tātparya
30	Tātparyas	—	1 Nimeṣa[212]
18	Nimeṣas	—	1 Kāṣṭhā
30	Kāṣṭhās	—	1 Kalā
30	Kalās	—	1 Ghaṭikā
2	Ghaṭikās	—	1 Kṣaṇa[213]
30	Kṣaṇas	—	1 Ahorātra (Day).

[208] Bhodhanī, p. 91.

[209] AV., p. 119.

[210] Ganitādhyāya, Madhyamādhikāra, Kālamānādhyāya, verses 16-17.

[211] *Truṭi* is a synonym for a *tryaṇuka*.

[212] *Nimeṣa* is that length of time which is denoted by the single falling of the eyelashes—KV., p. 118; Kandalī., p. 65.

[213] *Kṣaṇa* is that point of time during which a produced substance remains without an attribute, or a motion; or, that which marks

After calculation, it is found that a day consists of 17,496,000,000 *paramāṇus*. In other words, a single second being equal to 202500 *paramāṇus*, makes one *paramāṇu* equal to $\frac{1}{202500}$ of a second. Hence, Dr. Brajendranātha Seal says that a *truṭi* of time is equal to $\frac{1}{337500}$ of a second, which is nearly the measure of the *paramāṇu* of time as given in the Viṣṇu-Purāṇa.[214]

3. According to some, again, a *paramāṇu* is the smallest aggregation of *sattva*, *rajas* and *tamas*. This view has been refuted by Nyāya-Vaiçeṣika on the ground that the terms, 'smallest' and 'aggregation,' being mutually contradictories, cannot be attributed to a *paramāṇu*.[215]

4. The Saugatas are of opinion that the four kinds of *paramāṇu*, namely, earthly, watery, fiery and airy, are of the nature of being hard and solid (*khara*), viscid (*sneha*), hot (*auṣṇya*) and moving (*īraṇa*) respectively. Of these, the first possesses the attributes of colour, taste, smell and touch; the second has colour, taste and touch; colour and touch are attributed to the third; while, the fourth possesses the only attribute of touch. When these collect together, they are called earth, water, fire and air respectively.[216]

5. The next view is that a *paramāṇu* is nothing but an aggregate of colour, taste and the rest. This view also has been refuted by Nyāya-Vaiçeṣika on the ground that the meaning of the term 'aggregate' (*saṅghāta*) is ambiguous; for, generally the term means a collocation of several such objects as are not related to one another as cause and effect; so that, if a *paramāṇu* be held to be

the interval between the conjunction of the last thread and the production of the cloth, or between the produced motion and disjunction caused by it, or between the presence of the entire material for the production of an effect and the actual production of that effect—KV., p. 118.

[214] PSH., pp. 76-77.

[215] NV., p. 250.

[216] NSMM., p. 283.

an aggregate, there should be particles smaller than *paramāṇus* and possessing colour, taste, etc. to form the aggregate, called *paramāṇu*. But, as *paramāṇus* themselves have been regarded as the ultimate particles, there cannot be yet still smaller particles. Hence, the view is rejected as untenable.[217]

6. Some, again, consider that a *truṭi* itself is a *paramāṇu*. But this view is also untenable; as a *truṭi* is further divisible, while the same is not possible for a *paramāṇu*.[218]

7. The very existence of a *paramāṇu* is denied by Raghunātha Çiromaṇi for want of sufficient proofs to support it. He, further, adds that the use of the term *aṇu*, with reference to an object, is only to show that the particular object is very small, and it is, therefore, that the term is used also for things possessing magnitude.[219]

8. Some not only identify a *paramāṇu* with a *dvyaṇuka*,[220] or a *tryaṇuka*[221], or even a *caturaṇuka*[222], but also make these eternal[223] like a *paramāṇu*. It may be pointed out here that if a *tryaṇuka* and a *caturaṇuka* be held to be perceptible, as they certainly are, then it is not possible to make them eternal. Again, in case, a *tryaṇuka* is visible and non-eternal, its constituents cannot be eternal, as has been made clear in previous sections. Hence, all these views have been rejected by Nyāya and Vaiçeṣika as invalid and untenable.[224]

[217] NV., I. ii. 33, p. 232; Tāt., p. 392.
[218] Ibid.
[219] PTN., pp. 11-15.
[220] KVBhā., p. 90.
[221] KVBhā., p. 90; Setu., p. 206; NSMR., p. 293.
[222] KVBhā., p. 90.
[223] KVBhā., p. 90; Setu., p. 206.
[224] NL., pp. 23-24; Vādīndra, quoted in Nyāyamuktāvalī, a comm. on Udayana's LU., p. 23.

XII

PARAMĀṆU AND QUIDDITY (ANTYAVIÇEṢA)

It has been said that the true realisation of the *Ātman*, the only aim of the *Çāstra*, is possible by the right knowledge of each and every category accepted by the system. This is possible only when every object is distinguished from its homogeneous and heterogeneous classes. Generally, this is done through the help of attributes. But, in the case of *paramāṇus*, particularly of one class, the distinction between one another is not possible through the help of ordinary attributes. But the distinction has to be made even there, not only for the sake of having true knowledge of each of the ultimate particles, but also for the guidance of the future individual and the universal productions. Hence, Nyāya-Vaiçeṣika believes in the existence of a category, called *viçeṣa*, generally known as *antyaviçeṣa*, to differentiate one eternal *paramāṇu* from the other. Similarly, it is essential to make distinction between other eternal substances, namely, *Ākāça*, *Kāla*, *Dik*, *Ātman* and *Manas*.[225] This is also possible only with the help of a quiddity.

As to the view that a sort of differentiating capacity may be assumed to belong to the *paramāṇus* themselves instead of having a different category, called *antyaviçeṣa*, it may be pointed out that the view is groundless, as no such capacity is ever found to be associated with the *paramāṇus*.

Again, as to the view that a series of quiddity will have to be assumed to distinguish one *viçeṣa* from the other in successive cases leading to logical absurdities, it may be pointed out that on account of its having an absolute nature of differentiating, the *viçeṣa* alone through its own nature causes differentiation and does

[225] PPBhā., pp. 321-22.

not require the help of another *viçeṣa* over it.[226] Moreover, if it requires another *viçeṣa*, then the very aim of its existence becomes frustrated. Hence, the view is rejected as groundless.

Again, it may be asked here: Would not the *sāmānya* (generality) serve the purpose of the quiddity? The reply is in the negative, for the following reasons:

1. The *sāmānya* inheres both in eternal and non-eternal objects, while the *viçeṣa* does not subsist in non-eternal things.

2. Again, the *sāmānya* does not exist in substances alone but also in qualities and motions, while the *viçeṣa* inheres only in eternal substances.

3. A single *sāmānya* subsists in innumerable objects belonging to one particular class and differentiates one class of objects from another, while the *viçeṣa* inheres independently in each and every eternal substance and differentiates one single individual from another.

4. The existence of *sāmānya* depends upon a common notion depending upon many objects, while no such notion is required for the existence of a *viçeṣa*.

5. The *sāmānya* is an object of direct perception, while the other is only inferential.

6. The *viçeṣa* is meant for those eternal substances also wherein the *sāmānya* does not exist, such as, *Ākāça*, *Kāla* and *Dik*.

These points of difference show that these are two distinct categories and one cannot be substituted for the other.

Similarly, the *pākaja-viçeṣa* cannot be a substitute for the *antya-viçeṣa* on the ground that the former belongs to the earthly *paramāṇus* alone and that there is no such differentiating nature in it, while the latter is particularly meant for differentiating one eternal substance from another.

226 PPBhā., pp. 321-22.

This *antyaviçesa* does not belong to the qualities and motions possessed by eternal substances; for, the differentiation in those cases is possible through the help of their own intermediate *jātis*, namely, *çuklatva*, *raktatva*,[227] *gamanatva* etc. and also through the *viçeṣas* of the form of their substrata.[228]

Some are of opinion that *Içvara* and *Ākāça* do not possess any quiddity; for, these are distinguished from everything else by their own eternal qualities, namely, consciousness and sound, respectively.[229]

The Neo-Nyāya School does not believe in the *viçeṣa* as an independent category; for, they hold that the differentiation is possible by the very nature of the eternal substances themselves. This view is further supported by the fact that *yogins* also do not perceive such a *viçeṣa*, which is possible only when it does not exist independently.[230]

B

NON-BHAUTIKA MATTER

I

MANAS

1. *Defined and existence proved*

Under the non-*bhautika* form of atomic matter there is only one category, namely, *Manas*. It has been defined as an internal sense-organ which brings about pleasure, pain etc.,[231] and also cognitions of all sorts.[232] In other words, it is that internal sense-organ, the

[227] SPM., p. 12.
[228] NSMD., p. 122.
[229] Ibid.
[230] PTN. along with the comm. of Raghudeva, pp. 30-32; NSMD. on verse 10.
[231] NL., p. 328 (chowkhamba edition).
[232] NBhā., I. i. 9.

absence of which prevents the production of any cognition, even when the sense-organs are in direct touch with their respective objects. It has also been defined in several other ways on the basis of its peculiarities. Thus, some hold that *Manas* is that which does not possess any touch or any specific quality (*viçeṣa-guṇa*), but has a limited form[233] and motion.[234] Çaṅkara Miçra defines it as that whose presence or absence necessitates the production or otherwise of cognitions at the time when the *Ātman* and the sense-organ-contact is present.[235] It has been also defined as that which possesses the atomic nature not coherent with the productive conjunction; or, as that which possesses a limited form which is the substrate of the conjunction, the non-material cause of consciousness; or, again, as that which possesses an impression (*saṃskāra*) and is a sense-organ but is not coherent with any specific quality, and so on.[236]

Such a *Manas*, being supersensuous, is proved to have an existence through inference alone. As regards the probans to infer its existence, Gautama holds the non-production of the simultaneity of cognition alone as the most important one.[237] Vātsyāyana adds memory, inference, verbal testimony, doubt, intuition (*pratibhā*), dream-cognition, imagination (*ūha*), the experience of pleasure and pain, desire and the rest as indicative of the existence of *Manas*.[238] Regarding the form of inference to prove its existence, it is said that every kind of production requires an instrument (*karaṇa*) to cause its existence. Now, that memory, desire, doubt, etc. are psychic phenomena of

[233] LU., p. 49.
[234] Padārthabodha's comm., *MS*. Fol. 5*a*; TD., p. 13.
[235] VU., III. ii. 1.
[236] KR., p. 42.
[237] NS., I. i. 16.
[238] NBhā., I. i. 15; also Vide VS., III. ii. 4.

everyday experience cannot be denied. These are also products, and as such, they also must be preceded by an instrument. And, again, external sense-organs, even when they appear to be in contact with their respective objects, do not produce any cognition about these psychic phenomena. These show that there must be some different type of sense-organ or instrument to produce cognition, desire, memory and the rest. This instrument is named as *Manas*.[239] Again, the fact that even when all the external sense-organs simultaneously appear to be in contact with their respective objects, no simultaneity of cognitions takes place, shows that there is something whose absence prevents the appearance of any cognition, and whose presence would have certainly led to the production of cognitions.[240] This something is no other than the *Manas*. That such a *Manas* is an internal sense-organ is proved by the fact that the psychic products, like desire, pain, pleasure, etc. are all produced by this *Manas* alone.[241] Of course, the agency of the individual self is not denied in any case.

2. *Attributes of Manas*

The following are the more important of the attributes of *Manas*:

(1) It is an admitted fact that our cognitions appear in succession[242] which is possible only, if the most efficient cause of these cognitions which is the *Manas* here, comes in contact in succession with the external sense-organs, in the case of external cognitions, and with the individual self, in the case of psychic products, like pleasure, pain, etc. and does not combine with every limited form simultaneously.[243]

[240] NBhā. and NV., I. i. 16; VS., III. ii. 1.
[240] NBhā. and NV., I. i. 16; III. ii. 56.
[241] PPBhā., p. 89; NBhā., I. i. 16.
[242] TR., p. 125.
[243] VS. and VU., VII. i. 23.

This leads us to assume that *Manas* is atomic in nature.[244] If, on the other hand, it were non-atomic and of intermediary dimension, then beside its becoming a non-eternal substance due to its having constituent parts, it would have combined with more than one sense-organ at one and the same time which would have prevented the production of any knowledge; or, if knowledge were at all produced, then there would have been simultaneity in it, which is quite against the reality. Then, again, the non-eternity of it would have also led to several logical absurdities of a complex nature. Demand for moral justice, which is entirely regulated by the eternity of *Manas*, would have been nowhere; and perhaps, there would have been no regular life; as, the universal creation, which mainly depends upon it, would not have come to exist, and if, at all, it had ever come to exist, it would have been by sheer chance. In both the cases, the cosmic order would have been upset. Hence, to remove the possibilities of such difficulties, it is essential to accept the atomic nature[245] of *Manas* which itself proves its eternity.[246]

(2) As it is atomic, it is not perceived through any external sense-organ of ours.[247]

(3) It, being a sense-organ itself, exists for another. In other words, its existence is mainly meant for helping the *Ātman* to experience pleasure and pain, the very aim of the empirical world.[248] This, again, is possible when the *Manas* comes to possess a physical organism.[249]

(4) As it is not of the nature of any of the *mahābhūtas*, it is called non-*bhautika*,[250] and hence, it does not

[244] NS., III. ii. 59; VS., VII. i. 23.
[245] NS., III. ii. 59; VS., VII. i. 23.
[246] VS., III. ii. 2; PPBhā., p. 16.
[247] VS., IV. i. 6; VIII., i. 2; KV., p. 40.
[248] PPBhā., p. 89; Vyom., p. 428; Kandalī., p. 93.
[249] KV., p. 40.
[250] NBhā., I. i. 4. NM., p. 497. The term '*non-bhautika*' may be explained in two ways: one—'not of the nature of any of the

possess any touch;[251] so that, even when *Manas* comes in contact with any other substance, it does not produce a fresh one, like all other substances having limited form.[252]

(5) Being non-*bhautika* and having motion[253] and velocity (*vega*),[254] it cognises its objects with the quickest possible motion.[255] Its activity is effective on all objects alike. In other words, it comes in contact with any external sense-organ, at any time, and without any restriction, and through it with the objects of the external world. Uddyotakara gives the following reasons to account for its being so effective: (a) because, it is the substrate of the conjunction which is the cause of remembrance, like the *Ātman*; (b) again, as, it is the substratum of the conjunction which brings about the cognition of pleasure etc., like the *Ātman*; and (c) also because, it supervises over all the sense-organs, like the *Ātman*.[256]

(6) It does not possess any specific quality namely, colour, taste, smell, touch, viscidity (*sneha*), natural fluidity (*sāṃsiddhika-dravatva*), knowledge, pleasure, pain, desire, aversion (*dveṣa*), effort, merit and

Mahā-bhūtas', as explained above, and the other—'not made up of any of the *Mahābhūtas*.' In the latter sense, it is certainly not applicable to the *Manas*, which is eternal; and hence, Uddyotakara says that *Manas* is neither *bhautika* (made up of *Mahābhūtas*) nor non-*bhautika* (not made up of *Mahābhūtas*)—*Vide* NV., I. i. 4, p. 38. But Uddyotakara himself admits the former interpretation and holds that *Manas* is non-*bhautika*—*Vide* NV., III. i. 31, p. 374. Therefore, there seems to be no justification in the remark of Prof. Jadunātha Sinha that "this objection of Uddyotakara is based on a mis-conception of the meaning of the word" etc.—Indian Psychology: Perception, p. 19 (1934).

251 NMJ., *MS*. Fol. 4*b*.

252 PPBhā., p. 89; KV., p. 182; Kandalī., p. 93.

253 VS., V. ii. 13; PPBhā., p. 21.

254 PPBhā., p. 21; VU., V. ii. 13.

255 PPBhā., p. 89.

256 NV., I. i. 4, p. 38.

demerit, mental faculty (*bhāvanā*) and sound.[257]

(7) It, being a form of matter and a sense-organ,[258] has no consciousness.[259] And moreover, if it had consciousness, then there would have been two conscious elements in a single organism, which would have made the production of knowledge impossible and would have thereby upset the entire worldly usages.[260]

(8) It is a cause of the empirical world by coming in contact with a particular *Ātman* in a particular organism and helping the experiencing of pleasure and pain.[261] Hence, it is also called a cause of bondage.[262]

(9) Its contact with a particular *Ātman* is said to have no beginning.[263]

(10) It is a common cause of all sorts of cognitions.[264]

(11) It enlightens all sorts of objects without being endowed with any of their specific qualities.[265]

(12) It is, of course, a substance, as it possesses qualities and motion.[266]

II

ALL-PERVASIVENESS OF *MANAS* DISCUSSED AND REFUTED

It has been said above that cognitions of the external objects do not take place when the *Manas* is not in contact with the external sense-organs. But this

[257] PPBhā., p. 95.
[258] NM., p. 498.
[259] NM., p. 498; NMJ., *MS*. Fol. 4*b*.
[260] NM., p. 498.
[261] NV., III. ii. 67, p. 442; NM., p. 499.
[262] NM., p. 499.
[263] NM., p. 499.
[264] NBhā., I. i. 16.
[265] NBhā., I. i. 4.
[266] PPBhā., p. 89; NM., p. 498.

is not accepted by the followers of Kumārila Bhaṭṭa[267] according to whom *Manas*, being ubiquitous in nature, cannot but always remain in contact with the sense-organs, and in support of it, they put forth the following arguments:

Manas is ubiquitous; (1) as, it is a substance having no touch for ever; like *Ākāça*; again, (2) as, it is a substance which does not ever possess any specific quality; like *Kāla* and *Dik*: also (3) because, it, being an eternal substance, does not produce any other substance by its contacts with other substances; like *Ākāça*; and lastly, (4) because, it is a substrate of the conjunction which is the non-material cause of cognition.[268]

The Naiyāyikas take an easy course to refute these arguments. They hold that all these arguments presuppose that the *Manas* is a substance on the ground of its being an instrument of an action (*kriyā*) in the form of cognising colour, etc. But as a non-substance, in the form of a conjunction due to efforts and *adṛṣṭa*, is found to be an instrument of an action, the arguments of the Mīmāṃsakas are beset with the *svarūpāsiddhi* type of fallacy, and hence, they are rejected as untenable.[269]

The Mīmāṃsakas next put forth another argument in support of their view. They hold that *Manas*, being a sense-organ, is a substance; for, it is a substance alone which can be a sense-organ. Now, *Manas*, having been proved to be a substance, can also be inferred to be all-pervasive on the grounds given above.

But, as an all-pervasive substance cannot be a sense-organ without a limitation (*upādhi*), it is essential, hold the Naiyāyikas, that the *Manas* also, like the *Ākāça*, should have a limitation. As to what that limitation is, there are three possible alternatives: one—a certain

267 Bodhanī, p. 96.
268 KP., Stavaka III. verse 1, pp. 346-47; Bodhanī, p. 96.
269 Bodhanī, p. 96; KPP., p. 347.

fixed part of the organism, like the ear-cavity as in the case of *Ākāça*, the other—the entire organism, and the third—any unfixed part of the body. But all these alternatives lead to absurdities; as for example, if the first alternative be accepted, these cognitions would appear only in that particular part of the organism; and if, that part be, somehow, injured or destroyed, no cognition of any kind would ever take place. But this is against the reality; for, cognition is felt everywhere in the body, in succession. Therefore, if the second alternative be accepted, then one particular cognition, for instance, would have been experienced throughout the entire organism at one particular time, and there would have been no justification for cognitions like 'I have pain in my leg, or in my head,' etc. The third also would lead to similar difficulties.[270]

To this the Mīmāṃsakas point out that due to the operation of the non-material cause, the difficulty pointed out above would not arise, and the cognitions would be felt even in different parts of the organism. Hence, there is nothing to prevent the entire organism from being the required limitation.[271]

It would not be out of place to make it clear here that the non-material cause may produce the effects of the all-pervasive substance within its own limitations, or it should *necessarily* produce such effects within the same limitation, or it may produce such effects within its own limitations *alone*. In the first case, no pleasure and pain would have ever been produced beyond the limitation of the non-material cause; in the second case, as the non-material cause *must* produce an effect, it would be possible for the contact of the atomic *Manas* also to produce pleasure etc., within its own limit and also beyond that, as there is nothing to prevent it; while, in the last case, pleasure etc. would have appeared in

[270] Bodhanī, p. 96.
[271] KP., Stavaka III. verse 1, p. 348.

atomic parts alone.[272]

If it be said here, continues the Mīmāṃsakas, that the experience of pleasure and pain etc. in a little or more space of the organism does not depend upon the non-material cause, but on the instrumental one, in the form of the contact of the sandal-paste (*candana*); like the production of sound through the instrumentality of air, then it may be possible even if the *Manas* be accepted to be all-pervasive. It cannot be held that the experience of pleasure etc. would be possible even where there is no sandal-paste-contact; as, it is the non-material cause which does operate in the case of the effects of the all-pervasive substances, like the sound produced by the contact of the drum and the *Ākāça*; for, the fact is that the non-material cause has to depend upon the sandal-paste-contact, in the particular part of the organism where the pleasure due to the sandal-paste-contact is experienced. This shows that the non-material cause does not operate independently. Hence, even if the entire organism be accepted to be the required limitation, the experience of pleasure and pain would be felt in definite parts of the organism due to the help of the instrumental cause; so that, there is no difficulty in holding *Manas* to be all-pervasive in character.[273]

To this the Naiyāyikas reply that according to a logical convention, a particular attribute, an effect of an all-pervading substance, does not occupy a less limited space than its non-material cause; so that, when the *Manas* is all-pervasive, then the contact of it with the individual self, the non-material cause of pleasure etc., would have pervaded over the entire body, and the experience of pleasure etc. would have been felt within the limits of the entire organism. Hence, if the pleasure, which is felt in the foot, be due to the non-material

[272] KPP., Stavaka III. verse 1, p. 349.
[273] KPP., Stavaka III. verse 1, p. 349.

cause, which, in the present case, has been accepted to pervade the entire organism, then that pleasure would have, certainly, pervaded over the whole of the organism; for, the instrumental cause merely leads its own operation to affect larger space. It is, therefore, that a man, feeling too hot in the summer, when dips into water, feels pleasure throughout the whole body.[274] Having these difficulties in mind, the Naiyāyikas reject the above-mentioned view as absurd.[275]

It has been maintained above that the non-simultaneity of cognition is the most important reason to reject the all-pervasiveness of *Manas*. To this the Mīmāṃsakas urge that the non-simultaneity of cognition is possible even if the *Manas* be regarded as ubiquitous, due to the influence of *adrsta* which also has been recognised as a cause of cognition.[276]

But the inclusion of *adṛṣṭa* to help the present case, hold the Naiyāyikas, is not quite justifiable; for, the non-simultaneity of cognition, being the sure proof for the existence of *Manas*, would then become an accidental one (*anyathāsiddha*), and there would remain no strong reason to support the existence of *Manas*; and all the arguments adduced above in support of the all-pervasiveness of *Manas* would have been frustrated with the fallacy of *āçrayāsiddhi*.[277] Hence, the influence of *adṛṣṭa* should not be accepted in this case even by the Mīmāṃsakas.

Again, the Mīmāṃsakas hold that as *Manas* is an instrument (*karaṇa*), and as such, it is endowed with the nature of producing cognitions in succession, like all other instruments, there would be no simultaneity of cognition, even if *Manas* were accepted to be all-pervasive. To this, the Naiyāyikas reply that if the

[274] KPP., Stavaka III. verse 1, p. 349.
[275] Bodhanī, p. 97.
[276] KP., Stavaka III. verse 1, p. 350.
[277] KP., Stavaka III. verse 1, p. 350; Bodhanī, pp. 96-97.

non-simultaneity of cognition were dependent upon there being an instrument, then as other instruments, like the external sense-organs, are present, there would have been no need of another category, called *Manas*.[278]

To this, again, the Mīmāṃsakas point out that as, there are five external sense-organs, and as, each of them would produce its own cognition, the possibility of simultaneous cognitions would ever remain. Hence, it is better to have one instrument in the form of *Manas* alone to explain the succession in our cognitions.[279]

To this, again, the Naiyāyikas point out that the presence of the *Manas* would, no doubt, prevent the simultaneity of cognitions in the manner stated above, but when all the external sense-organs would be, simultaneously, in touch with the all-pervading *Manas*, then either there would be no cognition at all, or if there appears to be any cognition, at all, it would be a sort of joint-cognition consisting of the cognitions of colour, taste, smell, touch and sound, like the variegated colour (*citrarūpa*), and so on. But such a peculiar cognition would be entirely against the record of human experience. Hence, the view-point of the Mīmāmsakas is rejected as untenable.[280]

But the various instances, such as, when a man is eating a big bread, he experiences a sort of joint-cognition produced by the various attributes belonging to the bread,[281] or when a teacher is seen reading, walking, holding a water-pot, looking at the path, hearing the sounds coming out of the forest, being frightened, looking out for the signs of ferocious animals and remembering his place of destination[282]—all these appearing, as if, taking place simultaneously, show that a sort

[278] KP., Stavaka III. verse 1, pp. 351-52.
[279] Ibid. pp. 352-53; Bodhanī, pp. 97-98.
[280] KP., Stavaka III. verse 1, p. 353; Bodhanī, pp. 97-98.
[281] Bodhanī, p. 98.
[282] NBhā., III. ii. 57, p. 632.

of joint-cognition does really exist. To this, it may be pointed out that, if closely observed, it would be quite obvious that in all such cases there is succession, but due to the swift motion of the *Manas*, the intervals of time are not taken into account, like the swift brandishing of a fire-brand (*alātacakra*). In fact, there appears to be a mistaken notion of simultaneity of cognitions. Moreover, the Naiyāyikas add that when there is the *Ātman-Manas*—sense-organ—and object-contact, the cognition that is produced is of only one object alone, and not of all the objects taken together. Hence, the view of the production of a joint-cognition is rejected as impossible.[283]

The Mīmāṃsakas, further, continue that in the cases cited above, the succession is neither due to the absence of the contact of the ubiquitous *Manas* with all the sense-organs at one and the same time, nor to the successive nature of the instrumental *Manas*, but to the absence of a desire to know (*bubhutsā*) all. Hence, the all-pervasive nature of the *Manas* remains unaffected.[284]

The Naiyāyikas reject the above argument on the ground that no such peculiarity is associated with the desire to know (*bubhutsā*), which would prevent the production of cognition when its necessary cause is present, in its absence. The absence of cognition is, in reality, due to the absence of the necessary conditions required to produce the effects. What the desire to know does is to make the cognition, produced by its own ordinary causes, capable of creating a lasting impression.[285]

To this, again, the Mīmāṃsakas reply that if the desire to know were not the cause of the production of successive cognitions, then the cognition would have taken place both as regards the desired and the undesired

283 KP., Stavaka III. verse 1, p. 353.
284 Ibid.
285 KP., Stavaka III. verse 1, p. 354.

objects. But, as a matter of fact, when a man is hearing a sweet song with great attention, he does not get the cognition of other objects, which are, of course, not desired although quite close to him, simultaneously. Similarly, when a man has opened his eyes to look upon a jar, he does not perceive the cloth, which although lies quite within the range of his perception, as it is not desired. In all these cases, simultaneous cognitions would have taken place if the desire to know were not a necessary condition of cognition. In fact, the desire to know removes the *Manas* from other undesired sense-organs, and joins it with that sense-organ alone which cognises the desired object; so that, indirectly *bubhutsā* also is helpful to the non-production of simultaneity of cognition. On these grounds, the Mīmāṃsakas think that the *bubhutsā* can explain the succession in cognition, even if the *Manas* be all-pervading.

To this, again, the Naiyāyikas reply that the *Manas* being all-pervading and its activity being of the nature of contact, there can be no succession. If that activity, on the other hand, be considered to be something of the nature of motion, then there would be difficulty in accepting the all-pervasiveness of it; for, there can be no motion in an all-pervading substance. Again, if the activity be of the type of a quality, then it being eternal, there can be no succession. If it be non-eternal, then, being a quality of an all-pervading substance, it would be *vyāpta* of the conjunction, which is the non-material cause of the non-all-pervading substance; as for instance, the sound, which is non-eternal and is a quality of the *Ākāça*, is found to possess, for its non-material cause, the conjunction belonging to the non-all-pervading substance like the drum and the rest. From this, it is clear, conclude the Naiyāyikas, that we must have a substance which is non-all-pervading and is the substrate of the conjunction which is the non-material cause of cognitions. If the Mīmāṃsakas are ready to believe in such a non-all-pervading substance, then let the *Manas* itself be that substance, as, this is a simpler assumption. Thus, it is asserted that the *Manas* is atomic and not ubiquitous.[286]

It is clear from the above that so far the only argument upon which the entire discussion is based is the non-production of the simultaneity of cognition, which cannot be explained unless the *Manas* is accepted to be atomic. Now, another argument also may be adduced against the all-pervasiveness of the *Manas*. The *Ātman* is, undoubtedly, all-pervading, and now, if *Manas* also be regarded as such, then *Manas* and the *Ātman* both being all-pervading, there would be no contact between the two; for, such a contact should have produced a dimension larger than the dimension of the all-pervading substances; but this is not possible. Hence, there being no contact, cognition and the rest would not have been produced; for, all the psychic products are produced when they have the *Ātman* and the *Manas*-contact as their non-material cause. We cannot deny the causality of such a contact and have in its place, the *Ātman* and the objects of cognition-contact as the non-material cause; for, in that case, the cognitions would have taken place only in place where the objects existed; as all the attributes existing in space are never to be separated from their non-material cause. Nor can we hold that the *Ātman* and the external sense-organ-contact is the non-material cause of the psychic products; for, in that case, at least there would not have been the production of the cognition of sound; as, the *Ātman*, which is all-pervading, cannot come in contact with the organ of hearing, which is nothing but the all-pervading *Ākāça*. But as a matter of fact, we know that neither the cognition takes place outside the organism, nor is there the non-production

[286] KP., Stavaka III. verse 1, pp. 350-57; Bodhanī, pp. 97-99; KPP., pp. 350-57.

of the apprehension of sound. Hence, it is concluded that in cases of psychic products the *Ātman* and *Manas*-contact alone is the non-material cause. But there can be no contact between the *Ātman* and the *Manas* unless one of them is non-*vibhu*. And the *Ātman*, being accepted as all-pervasive, the *Manas* alone can be non-ubiquitous. Again, as the *Manas* has been proved to be eternal, it will have to be admitted that it is also atomic.[287]

III

NON-SIMULTANEITY OF COGNITION DISCUSSED AND PROVED

Against the non-production of the simultaneity of cognitions it is urged that in our daily experience we find that several cognitions take place simultaneously; for instance, a single teacher, while passing through a forest, reads, walks, holds a water-pot in his hand, looks at the path, hears the sounds produced in the forest, becomes afraid and desires to find out the marks of the ferocious animals, and remembers the place of destination. All these activities are found to be simultaneous; for, no order, of whatsoever kind, is noticed in the above case.[288]

To this the answer is that as, in the case of the whirling fire-brand, the existing succession of the various movements of fire is not observed and the whole thing presents a kind of continuous circular motion, due to the swiftness of the movement; so, although there are several separate activities and their cognitions, yet on account of the extreme rapid motion of the *Manas*, there appears to be simultaneity of cognitions. Similarly, the apparent simultaneity in the act of piercing through a hundred lotus-petals can be

[287] Kandalī., p. 93.
[288] NS and NBhā., III. ii. 57.

easily explained on the ground of the extreme rapidity of the action.[259]

Again, it may be asked: if the *Manas* be atomic, how can the various movements in the body of a small house-lizard etc. be explained, when it is rent asunder into two or three parts; for, the *Manas*, being atomic, cannot exist in more than one place? To this the answer is that in that case the various movements are due to the production of an effort occupying the entire body just before cutting the body into parts; or, to the causality of *adṛṣṭa* which forces other *Manas* to produce movements in those parts;[290] or, to the impression of the previous activities left behind even after the activities have stopped to function.

Annam Bhatta gives another reason in support of the atomic nature of the *Manas*. He says that the *Ātman* being ubiquitous, if the *Manas* also be accepted as such, then the result will be that both, being all-pervasive, would not come in contact with each other, and as such, there would not be any cognition of whatsoever kind. If they, on the other hand, come in contact, at all, then their contact also would be eternal. That is to say, there would be no separation between the two ever; so that, there would be no state in our life in which we would be free from cognitions. There would be no sound sleep either. But both the alternatives are quite against the reality. We can neither deny the existence of cognition, nor that of the *suṣupti*. In order to be consistent with the reality, it is essential to hold that there does take place the contact between the *Ātman* and the *Manas*, and also that the contact is not eternal; so that, when the *Manas* enters the *purītat*, it becomes separated from the *Ātman*, and *suṣupti* (wherein there exists no cognition of any kind) takes place. This necessitates the

[289] Vyomavatī, p. 426.
[290] KV., p. 155; KVBhā., p. 181.

Manas to be atomic.[291]

There are two points in the above argument which create some difficulty: one—that the contact of the *Ātman* and the *Manas* alone is the real cause of cognition, and the other—that the *Manas* becomes separated from the *Ātman* during *suṣupti* when the former enters the *purītat*.

Both these points are inter-related. The *Ātman* being ubiquitous remains ever in contact with all the substances having limited form. The *Manas*, having a limited form, ever remains in contact with the *Ātman*. This being a fact, the cause of cognition, namely, the *Ātman* and the *Manas*-contact, being ever present, there should have been always some cognition or other, and that there should have been no *suṣupti* ever. Again, it is wrong to think that the *Manas* becomes separated from the *Ātman*, when the former enters the *purītat*; as if, the *Ātman*, in spite of its all-pervasive character, were absent from the *purītat*. Again, the state of *suṣupti* cannot be denied; so that, we have to admit that the cause of cognition is really absent when the *Manas* enters the *purītat*. It has been seen above that the contact of the *Manas* with the *Ātman* cannot be absent even from the *purītat*; so that, it is essential to hold that the *Ātman* and the *Manas*-contact alone is not the cause of cognition.

Udayana puts it in just a different way. He says that cognitions take place only when the *Manas* is in contact with the external sense-organs; so that, during *suṣupti* when the *Manas* enters the *purītat*, although the *Ātman-Manas*-contact is present there, yet, as the *Manas* is not in contact with any of the external sense-organs, no cognition ever takes place. In the dreaming state, however, although the *Manas* is not directly in contact with any of the external sense-organs, yet cognitions do take place even then, as the previous impressions

[291] TPP., pp. 13-14.

(*saṃskāras*) are aroused, and through the help of the remembrance of those previous deeds, dream-cognitions do appear. Regarding the arousing of the previous impressions, it is said that the continuity of activities of the external sense-organs, though dull, is even then present, and through its help cognitions take place. Even, if it be denied, then we should say that, at least, the hot touch etc. of the organism are cognised through the sense-organ of touch, and which arouses the impressions, which in their turn, cause dream-cognitions. But, when even the contact of the organ of touch is done away with and the *Manas* enters the *purītat* then no cognition ever takes place.[292] It is, therefore, that the tactile organ (*tvak*) and *Manas*-contact is assumed to be the general cause of cognition. This sense-organ is absent from the *purītat*, and hence, when the *Manas* enters into it, its contact with the tactile organ ceases. Hence, there is no cognition in the *suṣupti* state.[293]

The above argument makes it clear that the state of *suṣupti* is possible, even if it is held that the *Manas* is eternal and has limited form, and the *Ātman* is ubiquitous, and that they remain in contact with each other in the *purītat* also. Now, in spite of the fact that the *Manas* is ever in contact with the *Ātman*, the statement—"*ātmā manasā saṃyujyate*" etc. presupposes that the *Ātman* was not in contact with the *Manas* before, and that it has now come to join it. This apparent contradiction is removed when it becomes known that although the *Manas* is ever in contact with the *Ātman*, yet the former, which is in contact with the particular sense-organ, which, in its turn, is in contact with a particular object, is not always in contact with the *Ātman*. That is, there is an extra-conjunction with the *Ātman* to produce cognition, just as, in spite of the natural connection between the *Ātman* and an organism, within which the *Ātman*

[292] KP., pp. 344-46, 357-58; Bodhanī, pp. 96-99.
[293] NSM, on Kārikā 57.

becomes limited, there is another fresh conjunction between the two to produce experiences of pleasure and pain; for which the organism itself is produced and the *Ātman* is put within a limitation.[204] In other words, the natural contact with an ubiquitous substance does not produce any *bhoga*. Hence, for the justification of the existence of the empirical world, it is essential to believe in the production of another fruitful contact between *Ātman* and the *Manas* which alone would explain the experiences of pleasure and pain. Cognition is also a particular kind of experience; so that, it is essential that there should be another *cognition-productive-contact* which would explain the line of the Bhāṣya—"*Ātmā manasā saṃyujyate*" etc. This contact is not always present; hence, it also explains the possibility of *suṣupti*.

Raghunātha Çiromaṇi holds that the *Manas* is a *bhūta* which does not inhere in anything. Raghudeva adds that it is that *asamaveta bhūta* which is atomic according to the old logicians and of the size and form of *truṭi*, according to the Neo-Naiyāyikas. Such a *truṭi* is, undoubtedly, eternal.

An objection may be raised against the above view: If the *Manas* be of the size of a *truṭi*, then when it, along with the organ of touch, is in contact with a jar, for instance, then there would have been several cognitions simultaneously. Again, in that case, the *Manas* also should possess *mahat* dimension; and as such, when it is in contact with the eye-sight, at the same time it would have been also in contact with several sense-organs, which, again, would have produced several cognitions simultaneously. But all these have just been shown to be untenable.

The Neo-Naiyāyikas continue here that even according to those who hold that the *Manas* is atomic, when there is the eye-sight and the *Manas*-contact, there

[204] NS and NBhā., III. ii. 86.

does exist the contact of the organ of touch also; but its non-cognition is believed to be due to a particular kind of *adṛṣṭa*. In the same manner, add the Neo-Naiyāyikas, *adṛṣṭa* would determine the non-simultaneity of cognitions in this case also.[295]

IV

NUMBER OF MANAS IN EACH ORGANISM

It has been proved above that the *Manas* cannot be ubiquitous. It must be atomic and the cognition brought about by it should be in succession. This necessitates not only that there are as many *Manāṃsi* as there are individuals in the universe, but also proves that there is only one *Manas* in each organism. Together with the cognitions taking place in one particular organism, it is found that there are cognitions in other organisms also, which would not have been possible had the cause of these cognitions, namely, the *Manas*, were not many and present separately in each organism. The *Manas* connected with a particular body cannot function outside that body.[296] Another reason to believe in the plurality of the *Manas* is that the generality, called *Manastva*, which depends upon the diversity of the *Manas*, would not have been proved otherwise.[297]

Those arguments, which have been adduced above to prove that the *Manas* is atomic, may also be put forth here to show that each organism has only one *Manas*. Çrīdhara summarises these arguments thus—There is only one *Manas* with each body; because, there exists the non-simultaneity of efforts and cognitions. For, if there were several *Manāṃsi* in one organism, there would have been several contacts of the *Ātman* and the *Manas*; and accordingly, the same man would

[295] Raghudeva's com. on PTNR, p. 10.
[296] NS, III. ii. 26-28; KV. p. 154; NV. III. ii. 67, p. 442.
[297] Kandalī., p. 90.

have been found having several cognitions and putting forth several efforts at one and the same time. But actually, no simultaneity is found in cognitions etc. Hence, there is only one *Manas* in each organism.[298]

V

MANAS AND MOTION

It has been proved above that the existence of *Manas* is necessary for the production of pleasure, pain and other cognitions. These are possible only when the *Manas* comes in contact with the individual self or the external sense-organs. This, again, is not possible unless there is motion in the *Manas*.[299]

It may be asked here: what is the cause of this motion in the *Manas*? It has been said that the first motion imparted to it, in the beginning of the creation, was due to some *adṛṣṭa*.[300] And later on, the motion is always produced by human efforts. In other words, it is through the instrumentality of efforts due to desire and aversion that the contact between the *Ātman* and the *Manas* takes place which produces motion at later stages. This is inferred from the fact that during the waking state, in accordance with our desires, the cognition of the external objects takes place through the instrumentality of the organs of sight and others; so that, when a man desires to perceive colour, he looks upon it; when he desires to have the taste, he has it, and so on. These experiences are not possible without the contact of the internal sense-organ. Hence, it is inferred that through the efforts due to desire and aversion, motion is produced in the *Manas*. When a man gets up from his sleep, motion is produced in his *Manas* by the *Ātman* and the *Manas*-contact proceeding

298 VS., III. ii. 3; PPBhā., p. 89; Kandalī., p. 92.
299 VS., V. ii. 15 and the commentaries.
300 VS., V. ii. 13.

from the efforts belonging to the *Ātman* which is preceded by the fact that the organism is living. This motion of the *Manas* is only to connect it with other sense-organs. This refers to the motion of *Manas* within the physical organism.

The other two kinds of external motion, namely, *apasarpaṇa* and *upasarpaṇa* belonging to the *Manas*, are produced from the *Ātman* and the *Manas*-contact proceeding from the *adṛṣṭa*. Thus, when the merit and the demerit, which are the auxiliaries of one's life, being fully experienced, are exhausted, or become ineffective due to their mutual suppression; there being no more auxiliaries of life, namely, merit and demerit, and also there being the absence of efforts due to these, the vital-air (*prāṇavāyu*) stops to function and the body falls down as dead. Then the merit and the demerit, which would produce experience in the next new body, come into force; as, there is nothing to check its force. Then through the auxiliary of this fresh set of merit and demerit, which is entirely different from that which regulated the experiences of the previous body, and from the *Ātman* and the *Manas*-contact, a motion is produced in the *Manas*, known as *apasarpaṇa*, having the *Ātman* and the *Manas*-contact as the non-material cause; while the fresh set of merit and demerit as its instrumental cause.

After leaving the previous body, the *Manas*, at once, comes into contact with a fresh subtle body known as the *ātivāhika*, produced by a fresh set of merit and demerit for it. Through that subtle body, the *Manas* enters heaven or hell and comes in contact with the body, which is produced there in accordance with the result of that man's previous deeds. It is in this latter body that the *Manas* causes the *Ātman* to experience pleasure and pain in heaven or hell. As the *Manas* is atomic, it is not possible for it to come in contact with that body which will cause the *Ātman* to experience pleasure and pain in heaven or hell, without actually going out. Again, the *Manas*, alone, without the help of any organism, cannot go out to such a distance; for, the *Manas*, without an organism cannot have any motion except during the state that follows immediately after the final universal dissolution (*mahāpralaya*). Hence, the existence of a very subtle and imperceptible body quite close to the dead body, produced out of *paramāṇus* through the usual process of *dvyaṇuka* and the rest has to be assumed.

This body is produced out of *aṇus* which have been moved by *adṛṣṭa*. As it leads the *Manas* to heaven, hell, etc. after leaving the dead body, it is called *ātivāhika* body. The motion which brings the *Manas* in contact with this *ātivāhika*-body is called *upasarpaṇa*.[301]

It appears from the above that *Manas* does not go out of the physical organism as long as the latter is in a living state. But it may be pointed out here that the visual organ, for instance, goes out of the physical organism with which it is connected and brings about the cognition of colour, only when it is attended by the *Manas*. This shows that the going out of the sense-organ must be regarded as the movement of the *Manas*; for, it is possible, only when the sense-organ is occupied by the *Manas*. This leads us to conclude that the motion of the *Manas* is not limited within the physical organism only.[302]

To this, it may be pointed out that it is not correct to hold such a view; for, the *Manas* cannot leave the physical organism and go out, as long as the particular organism is said to be living. If it goes out at all, the organism is sure to fall down as dead, due to its own inherent weight. In other words, when the *Manas* comes in contact with the *Ātman* in a particular

[301] PPBhā., pp. 308-11 along with Kandalī; VS. v. ii. 17 KV., p. 155.

[302] Tāt., I. i. 4; p. 145; NV., III. ii. 26, p. 425; NP., I. i. 4, pl. 632-633 (Bibl. Edition).

organism, their contact produces two kinds of efforts: one—that which retains the body and prevents it from falling down as dead, and the other—that which impels the body. If, now, the *Manas* goes out, the cause of the retaining of the body being absent, the retaining effort would not be produced, which would certainly lead to the downfall of the organism.[303]

Against this view, it is held by the opponents of the Nyāya-Vaiçeṣika that as, the *Manas* possesses the swiftest possible motion, it is quite possible for it to go out and get the impression of the external objects and return to the organism again, to continue the production of the retaining effort; so that, the body will not fall down as dead.[304] If it be, again, pointed out that, after all, the *Manas*, when goes out, would certainly remain out for a few moments at least; so that, during those moments, the retaining effort cannot be produced and the organism would certainly fall down. In order to remove this difficulty, it is suggested by the opponent that the *Manas* would, therefore, leave the organism after producing the desired effort which would continue to preserve the body from falling down during its absence.[305]

The latter suggestion of the opponent is also not quite free from difficulties. It is true that the retaining effort, thus produced, would keep up the body, but only for three moments; for, an effort must come to an end in the third moment;[306] so that, if the *Manas* would come back within three moments, no harm would be done to the organism. But it may be, again, asked: what should be the aim of the *Manas* in going out? The only aim of *Manas* which is to help the *Ātman* in experiencing pleasure and pain, cannot be

[303] NS. and NBhā., III. ii. 28.
[304] NS. and NBhā., III. ii. 29.
[305] NS. and NBhā., III. ii. 29.
[306] NSM., verse 27.

realised in any way by its going out. Even, if there be the *Ātman-Manas*-contact, outside the physical organism, no cognition of any type can be produced there; for, cognition, being a form of *bhoga*, must be experienced in the *bhogāyatana*, that is, the organism. Again, if it were ever possible for the contact of the *Manas* with the *Ātman*, outside the physical organism, to produce cognition etc., then there would have been no need of the physical organism at all and accordingly, there should have been no production of it.[307] Nor is it at all necessary for it to go out for helping the external sense-organs to cognise their respective objects. Again, there is no proof to show that any harm is done without its going out. Hence, it is concluded that the *Manas* does not go out of the physical organism as long as it is living.

Whatever has been said so far as regards the impossibility of the *Manas's* going out of the particular organism seems to be meant for ordinary people. For, it is a fact that the *yogins* do send their *Manas* to their desired places, which certainly goes out of the organism and returns to it after finishing its business there. This also is due to *adṛṣṭa* alone.[308] On this very basis, perhaps, some hold that our *Manas* also seems to go out swiftly to distant places and return back in time; for, just after a contemplation about certain distant places, it is found that the images of those places appear before our mind. But, if closely observed, it would be clear that the *Manas* does not actually go out even in these cases. What happens is that the past memories become revived and images appear thereafter.

It has been proved above that the *Manas* does not

[307] NS. and NBhā., III. ii. 30; *Vide*—Umesha Mishra-Smṛti theory according to Nyāya-Vaiçeṣika, K. P. Pathaka Com. Vol., pp. 183-84.

[308] PPBhā., p. 309; Kandalī., p. 311.

go out of its particular organism, and consequently, does not come in contact with other organisms and *Ātmans*. But it is a fact that the *Manas* does experience pleasure and pain to be experienced in other organisms even without coming in contact with them; just as, in the case of *kāyavyūha*,[309] wherein a single *Manas* experiences pleasures and pains to be experienced in those different organisms which are assumed therein, without coming in direct contact with them. Hence, it is assumed that even on other occasions, the *Manas* should experience the feelings belonging to other organisms and *Ātmans*.[310]

Nyāya and Vaiçeṣika, following the common-sense-view and accordingly, labouring under certain limitations, have to take their shelter under the mysterious *adṛṣṭa*, as usual. They hold that all such peculiar phenomena are regulated by certain *adṛṣṭas*, which being present in the case of *kāyavyūha*, help the experiencing of pleasures and pains to be experienced in other bodies, while the same being absent on other occasions, do not help such experiences.[311]

It may be urged at this stage that the ordinary causes of motion, namely, weight,[312] fluidity,[313] and elasticity (*sthitisthāpaka*)[314] by virtue of which a thing is restored to its previous state,[315] being not found with *Manas*, how can there be any motion in it? Simply because, it has limited form, there can be no motion in it.[316]

[309] It refers to that Yogic powers by which one assumes different bodies according to the nature of one's past merits and demerits which have not been exhausted as yet.—TBhāNP., pp. 154-55, Reprint from 'the Pandit.' (1901).

[310] TPP., *MS*. Fol. 5*a*, NV., III. ii. 67, p. 442.

[311] Ibid.

[312] PPBhā., p. 290.

[313] PPBhā., p. 290.

[314] Vyom., p. 636; KV., p. 157; Kandalī., p. 272.

[315] PPBhā., p. 267.

[316] KV., p. 157.

Regarding the velocity (*vega*) associated with it, it may be pointed out that as it comes to the *Manas* after motion has been produced in the latter, it also cannot be the required cause.[317] To this, it may be said, in reply, that even in the absence of these ordinary causes,[318] motion is produced in the *Manas* for the first time after the dissolution, due to the contact of the *Ātman* having *adṛṣṭa*[319] as in the case of *Manas* causing fresh cognitions after sound-sleep (*suṣupti*);[320] and in other cases, it is due to the contact of the *Ātman* possessing efforts.[321]

VI

PROCESS OF MENTAL ACTIVITY

The last point about *Manas* is as regards its process of functioning. *Manas* has to come in contact within its own organism with which it has acquired its connection through the merits and the demerits of the past deeds with the external sense-organs and the individual self. As regards the former, it is said that when the *Manas* is put into motion by a desire to know something, or by contemplation (*praṇidhāna*), or by *adṛṣṭa*, an effort is produced, which, in its turn, produces a motion in the sensory nerve (*manovahānāḍī*) which is an object of sense-perception. This motion causes velocity in that nerve, and the *Manas*, then, being forced to move by the contact of the nerve which possesses touch and velocity, comes in contact with that external sense-organ through which the desired object is to be cognised.[322] Then only the external sense-organ is able to get the impression of the external object. A sort of stamp seems to have been placed on the sense-organ,

[317] KV., 157.
[318] Setu., p. 423.
[319] VS., V. ii. 13.
[320] Setu., p. 423.
[321] KV., p. 157; Setu., p. 423.
[322] VU., V. ii. 14; KR., p. 43.

which is transmitted to the *Ātman* through the *Manas*. Then there is the particular cognition. The process of the *Ātman* and *Manas*-contact also seems to be the same as that of the *Manas* and external sense-organ-contact as given above.

As regards the *Ātman* and the *Manas*-contact, beside what has been said above in the previous section,[323] it should be added here that the empirical world, whose existence depends upon the merits and the demerits accruing from the deeds of the past, has no beginning. The genesis of merits and demerits entirely depends upon the contact of *Manas* with the individual self. Hence, it is presupposed that their contact also has no beginning. Again, it is only through the help of a physical organism that their contact bears any fruit as a result of the merits and demerits of the past. Therefore, it is concluded that the contact of these three also has been coming down since eternity. Then, regarding the question: which *Manas* and which organism should combine together and bring about fresh contacts with the individual self for the purpose of experiencing fruits of the past deeds, the only answer is that there is *adṛṣṭa*, which itself through the help of Divine Will, determines their different combinations, of course, on the basis of their past deeds.[324]

It will not be out of place to remark here that the *Manas*, being eternal, ever remains with the *Ātman*, even during the state of final emancipation. It is only the presence of *Manas* that one individual self is differentiated from the other, during the *Mokṣa*, and thus, establishes the plurality of individual selves.[325] Hence, the only change that takes place, with every individual birth, whether here or hereafter, is as regards the organism.

[323] *Vide Supra*, pp. 148-50.

[324] NV., III. ii. 67, p. 442; Tāt., p. 582; KP., Stavaka I. verse 4, p. 34; III. verse 1, pp. 359-60; Bodhanī, pp. 99-100.

[325] VV., III. ii. 21; ÇS., p. 366.

CHAPTER IV

MATTER AND ETERNITY—UBIQUITOUS

INTRODUCTORY

OF the eternal forms of matter, the atomic ones have been dealt with, in almost every aspect, in the preceding chapter. The ubiquitous ones may now be taken up. But before doing so, it would not be out of place to point out how these are inseparably connected with the world outside, as the necessary conditions of the creative process.

It has already been made clear that according to the theory of Origination, advocated by Nyāya-Vaiçesika, fresh products come into being in succession, out of the causal material, after the period of Cosmic Rest is over. The sequence of phenomena observed in creation implies the existence of a factor which is technically known as Time or *Kāla*. It is held to be a substance, supersensuous, pervasive and eternal in character. It is not subjective—a mental construction (*buddhinirmāṇa*), as the *yogin* believes, nor a Specific Power (*çaktiviçesa*) associated with the Supreme Lord, as the *Āgamas* (*Çaiva*, *Çākta* and *Vaiṣṇava*) affirm, but is objective and substantial in nature, in so far as it is the substrate of a number of qualities. That it is eternal is evident from the fact that it lies behind all worldly processes, creative as well as destructive, which involve succession. The very fact presupposes its all-pervading character as well. It is for this reason that it has been regarded as a necessary precondition, in Nyāya-Vaiçeṣika, of every kind of action.

Along with the creation, the necessity of having a support for the created objects naturally arises.

Objects having limited dimension only cannot be thought of in relation to a substance of wider extension which may be said to hold them within it, and this latter substance, again, is similarly related to another of still greater extension, and so on, till we come to an ultimate substance with infinite extension holding within itself all the limited and partially extended objects of the Universe in common. This substance, technically known as *Ākāça* or Space, is necessarily a continum and is, therefore, eternal. Our common experience expressed in judgments like '*iha pakṣī*' ('here is a bird') etc. testifies to the logical necessity of assuming a universal *ādhara* of this kind.[1]

In the classical works, however, we meet with an additional argument—and this is, in fact, the more commonly recognised line of reasoning in favour of those works—for the establishment of *Ākāça*, conceived, however, not as *Space* as a logical factor, but as physical space with sound as its property. This aspect of *Ākāça* will be discussed at greater length in the following chapter.

The last principle, which is inseparably connected with the cosmic order, refers to the relative position involved therein. In other words, it is a fact of common experience that two separate objects, having limited dimension, cannot simultaneously occupy the same space. They must remain in separate spaces.[2] But these objects are related to one another, as is evident from the notions of proximity, distance, and so on, which presupposes the existence of a substance called *Dik*. The grounds on which its existence is inferred, namely, the sense of relative spacial positions, are not covered by any other substance recognised in the system.

It has been already said that the objective world

[1] Vyom., p. 155; Kandalī, p. 22. Also cf. VP., kāṇḍa 3, verse 4; Mañjūṣā, pp. 200-201 along with Kuñjikā, pp. 202-204.

[2] NLV., p. 34.

can be split up into conscious (*cetana*) and non-conscious (*jaḍa*) elements, and as some other schools under Indian Realism have included all the above mentioned three principles under matter, as opposed to *cetana*, and also as the definition of matter, given in the previous chapter, holds good of these forms, there seems to be no inconsistency in classifying them as forms of matter.

Of these three, *Ākāça* represents the *bhautika* form, while the other two are non-*bhautikas*. In the following pages, we have followed in our treatment the order given in the table of classification before.

A

BHAUTIKA MATTER

I

ĀKĀÇA

1. *Defined and existence proved*

Reference has already been made to *Ākāça* as pure space with extension as its property. We may proceed now to discuss its physical aspect in which it is conceived as a ubiquitous substance with sound as its quality. It will be shown in the following pages that sound is a quality and not a substance as some systems believe and that it must inhere in a substance which must be different, as shown below, from the other substances, viz., earth, water, *tejas*, air, *Kāla*, *Dik*, *Ātman*, and *Manas*. This is termed *Ākāça*, which has been, therefore, defined as that wherein there exists no absolute negation of sound.[3] It is not an object of sense perception, nor is it amenable from its very nature to purely mental perception. Its existence is, therefore, only an inference with sound[4] as its probans.

[3] LU., p. 34.

[4] Generally, a definition is based on the most important

II

NATURE OF SOUND DISCUSSED

It may be enquired here: what is the nature of sound, which is said to be a quality of *Ākāça*?

The Mīmāṃsakas of the Bhaṭṭa School do not admit that sound is a quality. According to them it is a substance;[5] for following reasons:

1. It is cognisable directly through the sense-organ (through the relation of simple contract, viz., *saṃyoga*),[6] like a pot.[7] That is, the auditory sense-organ—a substance itself—cognises sound through mere contact (*sākṣādindriyasambandha*), which, in its turn, is possible only between two substances. Hence, sound is concluded to be a substance. As regards the possible doubt whether the ear-cavity (e.g., the auditory sense-organ) can cognise a substance or not, it is said that it does apprehend a substance, as it is partless, like the *Manas*.[8]

2. It possesses qualities, such as, number, velocity[9] etc. which are apprehended as qualities of sound. Had these been not the qualities of sound, they would not have been cognised through the auditory sense-organ.[10] But, that these are cognised through the

differentiating characteristic of the object defined, and accordingly, possession of sound is the probans in the present case. NV., III. i. 72, p. 397.

[5] NP., *MS*. p. 930; NLV., p. 665; MNSā., p. 185; TR., pp. 133, 143; Bodhanī, pp. 75-76; NM., p. 229; PP., p. 105; PD., p. 39; GBha., pp. 20-21; PSPM., p. 94; KM., p. 53; HIL., p. 109.

[6] The sense-organ referred to here is the auditory sense-organ which apprehends a substance, as it is a partless sense-organ, like the *Manas*—*Çrotrañca dravyagrāhakaṃ niravayavendriyattvānmanovat*—NLV., p. 665.

[7] *Çabdo dravyaṃ sākṣādindriyasambandhavedyatvāt*—Ibid.

[8] *Çrotrañca dravyagrāhakaṃ, niravayavendriyatvāt, manovat*—Ibid.

[9] As is expressed in the judgment like—'sound travelled a long distance through velocity'—Kaṇṭha., p. 666.

[10] *Açabdadharmāṇāṃ çrotrāvedyatvenāgrahaṇāt*—NLV., p. 75.

auditory sense-organ is a fact where no two different opinions exist.

3. It is all-pervasive,[11] which is proved by the fact that the same sound which is heard at present at one particular place was heard even before in other places and will be recognised to be the same even in future. This shows that the same sound exists in all the three times at every place. This, again, is possible only when sound is eternal and all-pervasive. That substance alone can be all-pervasive is also a fact which cannot be denied by Nyāya-Vaiçeṣika. Hence, it is concluded that sound is a substance.

Besides, the Schools of Mādhva[12] and Vyākaraṇa[13] also hold a similar view.

But Nyāya-Vaiçeṣika, not agreeing with the view put forth above, enquires as regards the first argument whether the probans—*sākṣādindriyasambandhavedyatva* (cognisable through a direct contact of the sense-organ)—is asserted through the method of elimination having all the possible categories into consideration or a single one? In the former case, it is said that as the non-substantive nature of the sound is proved by the same method, the probans is not a sound one. In the latter case, the possibility of sound being regarded as motion, generality, quiddity etc. not being rejected, the probans is beset with the fallacy of *asiddha*.[14]

Again, admitting for the sake of argument that sound is a substance, it may be pointed out that then it must be either tangible or non-tangible. In the former

[11] *Vibhutvācca dravyam*—PD., p. 39.

[12] PPP. of Laugākṣi Bhāskara, p. 11, Quoted in NK., p. 790 Ft. Note (second edition).

[13] Mañjūṣā, p. 218.

[14] *Sākṣādindriyasambandhavedyatvaṃ hi yāvatprasaktapāriçeṣyādvā niççīyate ekadeçapāriçeṣyādvā? nādyaḥ, tata evādravyatvanirūpaṇena lingagrāhakamānabādhāt; netaraḥ, karmatvāderapratiṣedhe saṃyuktasamavāyādivedyatvaçaṅkāyāṃ hetorasiddhatāpattiḥ*—NLV., pp. 667-68.

case, it ought to have been cognised through the tactile organ, while, in the latter case, it would become supersensuous. But, that it is neither apprehended through the tactual organ nor is supersensuous is a fact of everyday experience.[15] Thus, the position of the Mīmāṃsakas becomes untenable.

It may be further pointed out that the argument—*çrotra* can apprehend a substance—is also untenable; as there is the possibility of a counter-syllogism in the form that *çrotra*, being an external sense-organ of ours, is not capable of cognising an eternal substance, like the ocular organ.[16]

As regards the second argument put forth above, it may be said that, in fact, sound does not possess any quality of its own. The so-called qualities, associated with it, really belong to air[17] which is its vehicle,[18] and are apprehended through the tactile organ (*tvak*) pervading over the ear-cavity. The qualities of air are erroneously transferred to sound; just as the qualities of body etc. are wrongly attributed to the *Ātman*, as expressed in judgments—'I am of fair complexion,' 'I am blind,' etc.[19]

As for the third argument of the Mīmāṃsakas, it is said, in reply, that if sound be accepted as all-pervasive, then there would be no contact between a sound and the auditory sense-organ which also is all-pervasive though under limitation, and two or more all-pervasive substances cannot have mutual contact. Again, without any such contact, the fact of auditory

[15] Kaṇṭha., pp. 667-68.

[16] *Çrotraṃ ca na nityadravyagrāhakaṃ ayogibahirindriyatvāt cakṣurvaditi satpratipakṣaṃ dvitīyamanumānam*—NLV., p. 668.

[17] TC; Çabda-khaṇḍa, published in 'the Pandit,' Vol. VI, p. 282, Col. 2 (old series).

[18] Umesha Mishra—Physical theory of sound, Allahabad University Studies, Vol. II, p. 286.

[19] NLV., p. 669.

cognition would remain unexplained. Hence, sound cannot be all-pervasive.

It is thus clear that sound cannot be a substance.[20] It may be, similarly, shown that it cannot be placed under any of the categories beginning with motion (*karman*). Sound cannot be conceived as motion on account of certain characteristics peculiar to motion and absent in it. It is differentiated from generality (*sāmānya*), inherence and quiddity (*antyaviçeṣa*) on the ground that it possesses generality which is not possessed by any of these three categories.[21] Nor can it be identified with negation (*abhāva*) for being positive in character.[22]

Its character as a quality is inferred from the fact that it possesses the generality which is apprehended through an external sense-organ other than the visual[23] and that it is cognised through a single external sense-organ excluding the organ of touch.[24] Again, that it is a specific one is proved by the fact that it is apprehended

[20] (i) A further argument against the position of the Mīmāṃsakas concerning the character of sound is furnished in the Vaiçeṣika Sūtra—*Ekadravyatvānna dravyam*—II. ii. 24. This argument presupposes that it inheres in *Ākāça*. But as *Ākāça* is admitted to be a single substance (*ekadravya*), continuous and homogeneous in nature, it is evident that sound which resides in it must be non-substantial, as no substance is known to inhere in a partless substance.

(ii) Motion indeed inheres in a partless substance, but sound is not motion from which it may be easily distinguished, through possession of several characteristics, such as, not being an object of cognition through the visual organ (*acākṣuṣatvāt çabdasya*)—VS., II. ii. 24, productivity of another sound and non-existence in substances having colour and touch—*Çabdācchabdasya niṣpattiḥ; çabdastu na rūpidravyeṣu vartate; çabdaḥ sparçavatāmaguṇaḥ*—VBhā., II. ii. 24.

[21] VV., II. ii. 24.

[22] Setu., p. 317.

[23] *Çabdo guṇaçcakṣurgrahaṇāyogyabahirindriyagrāhyajātimattvāt*—NMuktā., pp. 84-85 (Vindhyeçvarī Pd.'s edition, Benares).

[24] PP., p. 145.

through a single external sense-organ.[25]

Now, it may be enquired: What is that substance in which sound as a specific quality inheres? To this it is said that it has already been shown that sound must inhere in a substance. Among the substances, again, those which possess touch, namely, earth, water, *tejas* and air, cannot be the required substance; for:

1. Sound, being cognisable through direct perception, is not a product of the quality of the material cause of its substrate, while the qualities of earth, water, *tejas* and air, which possess touch, are produced out of the respective qualities of the material cause of their substrata;

2. sound, being cognisable through direct perception, is not found along with its substratum as long as the latter exists, like the qualities of substances having touch; and

3. it is apprehended in places other than its substrate (*āçraya*); that is, it is heard when it reaches the tympanum far away from the place of its origin, say, the lute.[26]

It may be pointed out here that in spite of the above mentioned reasons, the possibility of air being the required substratum still remains. To guard against this, it is said that the auditory sense-organ, being an external one, cognises only one object, namely, sound. If, now, sound were a quality of air, then the auditory organ also should be an airy one, which would lead to several absurdities.[27] Hence, sound is not a quality of

[25] PPBhā., p. 95; Vyom. points out that this definition of a specific quality is too narrow, as it does not cover specific qualities like viscidity (*sneha*) and fluidity. Hence, its author suggests that it is that which is qualified by a specific quality inherent in it and which differentiates its substratum from the latter's homogeneous class—*svasamavetaviçeṣaviçiṣṭatve sati svāçrayaikajātīya-vyavacchedakatvāt*—p. 432.

[26] PPBhā., p. 58; KV., pp. 106-107.

[27] KV., pp. 107-108.

air and the other three substances having touch.

Again, as sound is a specific quality, it cannot have *Dik*, *Kāla* and *Manas* for its substrates; for, these do not possess any specific quality[28] at all.

Cognisable qualities are apprehended either through external sense-organs or through the internal one. The qualities of *Ātman* are cognised by the latter alone, and as sound is experienced by the external sense-organ, it cannot belong to the *Ātman*. Again, the attributes of one *Ātman* are never cognised by any other man, excluding the *yogins*, of course, and as they are always apprehended along with the egoistic notion (*ahaṃkāra*) as it is found in judgments expressed in forms like 'I am happy,' 'I am feeling pain,' etc., sound cannot belong to it.[29]

Hence, after the method of elimination, the existence of a substance is inferred which alone can be the substrate of sound. Such a substance is named *Ākāça*.[30]

III

VARIOUS OTHER VIEWS REGARDING SOUND

An old Mīmāṃsaka thinks that, no doubt, sound is a quality of *Ākāça*, but it is eternal and all-pervading and is only manifested.[31] According to this view, the air waves, set in motion by a forcible contact or impulsion, move forward until they reach the tympanum and manifest there the sound already subsisting in the ear-cavity—a limited *Ākāça*.[32] Sound is held to be eternal, according to this view, because its substrate is eternal and it's being the quality of *Ākāça* wherein

[28] PPBhā., p. 58.

[29] PPBhā., p. 58 along with Kandalī.

[30] Ibid.

[31] NBhā., II. ii. 13 along with NV. and Tāt.

[32] Tāt. II. ii. 13, pp. 441, 445.

alone it inheres, like the all-pervasiveness of *Ākāça*.[33]

According to a view, attributed to the Sāṅkhya School,[34] sound does not inhere in *Ākāça* alone but in all the five gross *bhūtas* and their modifications, such as, a cow, a jar etc., each of which is an aggregate product of the subtle *bhūtas* produced out of the five *tanmātras*. It remains in these *bhūtas* along with and in the same manner as odour, colour etc., and is likewise manifested[35] by the forcible contact of a particular *bhūta*,[36] as for instance, the forcible contact of a stick with a drum[37]. Regarding the process of manifestation, it is said that the auditory sense-organ, being a modification of *ahaṃkāra*, is more extensive (*vyāpaka*) and pervades over the substrate of sound also; so that, the sound becomes manifested in its substratum after producing a change in it.[38]

Another view that sound is of the nature of the three *guṇas* is also attributed to Sāṅkhya.[39]

Again, the view—that it is produced out of the disturbance caused in the basic elemental substances, that it has no substratum and that it is produced and destroyed—is attributed to the Buddhists.[40]

That sound is a product of subtle sound—*pudgalas* and when it is produced, it travels upto the ear-cavity where it is apprehended, is associated with the Jainas.[41]

A certain school of thought associated with the name of Svātantras thinks that as sound is produced

[33] NV., II. ii. 13, p. 280.
[34] Tāt., II. ii. 13, p. 441.
[35] NBhā., II. ii. 13.
[36] NV., II. ii. 13, p. 280.
[37] Tāt., II. ii. 13, p. 441.
[38] Tāt., p. 441.
[39] ÇV., adhi. 6, verse 319, p. 811.
[40] NBhā., II. ii. 13; Tāt., p. 442.
[41] NM., pp. 215-17; ÇV., adhi. 6, verse 319, p. 811.

in earthly substances like drum, lute etc., it inheres in earth alone.[42]

The Tāntric school holds that the ultimate principle of the Universe is God *Çiva*, and as *Çabda* inheres in Him, it is His quality.

The Vaiyākaraṇas are of opinion that the word or sound which is heard is the manifestation of different letters which constitute it. Such letters have no succession and are eternal.[43]

Sound is sometimes identified with air; so that, the manifestation of sound is really that of air itself.[44] Some, again, while explaining the process of its production, hold that it is a form of vibration produced, in the eternal vacuum known as *Ākāça*, by the Will of God[45].

Some consider that like other kinds of *paramāṇus*, there are atoms of sound also. These, because of their various inherent capacities which become manifest by efforts, produce various effects in form of sounds, just as small pieces of cloud group together and appear before us as cloud in the sky.[46]

Others hold that consciousness itself appears as sound. In other words, the inner consciousness, existing in the form of subtle *vāk*, manifests itself as sound.[47]

Some, again, identify sound with the universe itself in its manifold appearances.[48]

[42] Dinakarī and Rāma. on NMuktā., under verse 44, p. 370, SC., quoted in NK., p. 788; PTNR., p. 7; PTVP., pp. 84-85; KVBhā., p. 129.

[43] Mañjūṣā, p. 183.

[44] Çukla-yajuḥ-Prātiçākhya I. vii. 9; Ubbaṭa on Sūtra 1$\frac{1}{3}$, *ibid*; VP., I. 108-110; Mañjūṣā, p. 184; CK. on SR., chap. I., verses 1-4., PP., p. 163.

[45] Kuñjikā on Mañjūṣā, p. 184.

[46] VP., I. 11.-112; Mañjūṣā, pp. 184-85.

[47] VP., I. 108, 113-116.

[48] VP., I. 119, Tai. Saṃ. 6.4. 7.3. Quoted in the Ft.N. of the Mahābhāṣya, pp. 805-806; Puṇyarāja on VP., I. 119, 121, 130-33.

A particular section of Neo-Nyāya thinks that sound is an attribute of God[49] (*Īçvara*). The Vaidic view, supported by Kumārila, is that sound is an attribute of *Dik*.[50]

These are the various views propounded from time to time about sound.

IV

ATTRIBUTES OF ĀKĀÇA

It, being a *bhautika* form of matter, has the characteristic of being the main material principle of a sense-organ (*indriyaprakṛtatva*) and is endowed with such specific quality as is apprehended by the auditory sense-organ.[51]

Its specific quality, namely, sound, is non-eternal and is produced without pervading the whole of the object.[52] It is inactive and is not corporal.[53] It is devoid of colour, taste, touch and odour;[54] hence, it is not directly perceived. It is one.[55] It is eternal,[56] and all-pervading, which is due to the fact that it is different from the *Manas*, and does not possess tangibility.[57] It has neither displacement (*avyūha*), nor obstructiveness (*aviṣṭambha*).[58] That is, it does not offer obstruction to

[49] PTN., pp. 3-10; Dinakarī, Rāma. and Prabhā on NMuktā., verse 44, NK. p. 819.

[50] ÇV., verses 150-54; NM., p. 226; PRM., p. 26; GBha., pp. 19-20.

[51] PPBhā., p. 22; PRM, p. 26.

[52] PPBhā., p. 25.

[53] VS., V. ii. 21.

[54] NS., II. ii. 36; VS., II. i. 5; NV., III. i. 28, 72.

[55] VS., II. i. 29.

[56] But Candrakānta in his VBhā. says that in fact, *Ākāça* is non-eternal but it is regarded eternal for the sake of the worldly usage, *vide* I. i. 5. This appears to be influenced by Sāṅkhya view; for, in Nyāya-Vaiçeṣika, *Ākāça* is ever eternal.

[57] NV., IV. ii. 22; Āloka, on TC., Pratyakṣa, *MS*. Fol. 50*a*-50*b*; Setu., p. 320.

[58] NS., IV. ii. 22.

things passing through it, like a piece of wood putting an obstruction in the way of the flow of water. This is due to its being partless. As it has no tangibility, it does not counteract that quality of the thing which causes its motion[59].

The very idea is found in the Vaiçeṣika Sūtra where it is said that *niṣkramaṇa*, meaning, the movement of the substance having touch, and *praveçana* are the marks of *Ākāça*.[60] But almost all the commentators of the *Sūtra* are of opinion that this is the view of the *Sāṅkhya* and that the view is mentioned here in the form of a question, and accordingly, they explain this and the following three *Sūtras*. Varadarāja, on the other hand, explains this *Sūtra* in favour of Nyāya-Vaiçeṣika. He says that the existence of *Ākāça* is to be inferred with the help of the probans,—*niṣkramaṇa* and *praveçana*, as given by the Sūtrakāra.[61] No doubt, this view of *Ākāça* does not appear to be quite in keeping with the spirit of the later Vaiçeṣikas, yet there is no reason to disbelieve Varadarāja, who is certainly earlier than even the author of the Upaskāra. Even in recent times, Candrakānta Tarkālaṅkāra took up the same sense.

Although some hold that this gross *Ākāça* is the product of a subtler *Ākāça* and thereby show that it may possess parts and be non-eternal, yet this view does not truly represent the Nyāya-Vaiçeṣika viewpoint,[62] and hence, should be rejected.

It possesses a sort of motion in the beginning of the creation.[63]

[59] NBhā., on ibid.

[60] VS., II. i. 20.

[61] TR., p. 137.

[62] VVV., p. 10.

[63] *Ākāçamapi dravyaṃ dravyāntaraiḥ pṛthivyāntaraiḥ pṛthivyādibhiḥ saṃhanyamānaṃ kriyāvadeva bhavatyādisarge*—VBhā., I. i. 15.

V

SOME OF THE ABOVE MENTIONED ATTRIBUTES DISCUSSED

As the differentiating characteristic of *Ākāça*, namely, sound is proved to be without any diversity, the substratum of it is held to be only one.[64] Vyomavatī, however, makes note of an objection that as the varieties of sound cannot be denied, we should accept more than one substrate of sound; for, if, even without the diversity of the cause, it were possible to explain the diversity of the effect, then there should not have been four kinds of *paramāṇus*; that is, it would have been possible to produce all the various kinds of effects, namely, earth, water, etc. from only one kind of *paramāṇu*. This view is rejected on the ground that the varieties of sound are not due to the diversity of the substratum, but to the diversity of auxiliaries (*sahakāris*). Hence, the loudest form of sound is not due to the particular form of *Ākāça*, but to the most forcible contact (*abhighāta*) which is the auxiliary cause of sound; and similarly, from a less forcible contact we produce a light (dull) sound. This proves that *Ākāça* is one.[65]

Regarding the absence of colour in *Ākāça*, it is said that if it has no colour, how can the expressions, like '*nīlaṃ nabhaḥ*' ('The sky is blue') etc., be justified? To this it is said that truly speaking, it is not the *Ākāça* but the lustre of sapphire (*indranīlamaṇi*) belonging to the mountain *Sumeru* which appears to be blue. If it were the blueness belonging to *Ākāça*, then the blue colour would have been cognised quite close to us also. The non-appearance of it cannot be due to the influence of the lustre of the sun; for, then it would have been much more effective upon *Ākāça*, which is far off from us. Hence, no doubt should be

[64] VS., II. i. 29-30; PPBhā., p. 58.
[65] Vyom., pp. 329-30.

raised regarding the colourlessness of it.[66]

Against the argument that *Ākāça* is not an object of direct perception, as it has no colour, it is argued that had *Ākāça* been not an object of direct perception, then the expressions, like '*iha pakṣī*,' ('Here is a bird') '*iha pakṣī na*' ('Here is no bird') etc., would not have been possible. Hence, it is concluded that the substrate of the term *iha* which is no other than *Ākāça*, is perceptible.[67] It cannot refer to light (*āloka*), as some would perhaps like to think; for, the expression *iha pakṣī* is used even when there is no light. Some, again, understand that *iha* refers to the *absence of mūrta*. Others, on the other hand, hold that it refers to *Dik*.

These are some of the different views on this point; and perhaps due to these difficulties, some are of opinion that the substratum of *iha*, which is no other than *Ākāça* is perceptible, although it has no colour. It is perhaps, therefore, that they hold that colour is necessary for perception of objects other than *Ākāça*.[68]

VI

OBJECTIONS AGAINST THE EXISTENCE AND NATURE OF ĀKĀÇA

Raghunātha Çiromaṇi is of opinion that *Içvara* is the material cause of sound. In that case, there is no need of having *Ākāça*, as a separate entity.[69] Nāgeça also holds a similar view. He says that *Içvara*, under certain limitations (*upādhis*), appears as *Ākāça*.[70]

[66] Setu., p. 315.

[67] This view is attributed to the Mīmāṃsakas *vide* PRM., p. 26; KVP., p. 224.

[68] Setu., pp. 315-316.

[69] PTN., pp. 3-9.

[70] Mañjūṣā, p. 201.

Çeṣa Çārṅgadhara notes that according to Ānandajñāna, *Ākāça* is *anirvacanīya.* As it is one, there can be no *Ākāçatva-jāti.* It is not proved to be the substratum of sound; for, we cannot talk of sound as its *dharma*, when the *dharmin* itself is not proved. Moreover, as sound is not accepted by Ānandajñāna to be a quality of *Ākāça*, there is nothing to prove the existence of the latter according to him.[71]

B

NON-BHAUTIKA MATTER

Coming to the ubiquitous forms of non-*bhautika* matter, it is found that they are two in number, namely, *Kāla* and *Dik*. Here in the present section both of these are dealt with in the order followed before.

I

KĀLA

1. *Defined and existence proved*

Besides what has been said above in the previous section about the necessity of believing in the existence of a principle termed time or *kāla*, and its rational definition, it may be pointed out that in the classical works we find that the necessity to have a substance like time is to explain the more common notions of the relations of priority and posteriority, of simultaneity and succession, of late and soon,[72] and of the various usages of *kṣaṇa*,[73] *lava*,[74] *nimeṣa*,[75] *kāṣṭhā*,[76] *kalā*,[77] *muhūrta*,[78]

[71] LVM, pp. 38-39; Tarkasaṅgraha, pp. 44-47.
[72] Vyom., p. 349.
[73] *Vide* supra, pp. 127-28, Ft.-note, No. 213.
[74] It is equal to two *kṣaṇas*—Vyom., p. 349.
[75] This is equal to two *lavas*—Ibid.
[76] *Kāṣṭhā*=15 *nimeṣas*—Ibid.
[77] *Kalā*=30 kāṣṭhās—Vyom., p. 350.
[78] *Muhūrta*=30 *Kalās*—Ibid.

watch (*yāma*), day and night, fortnight, month, season (*ṛtu*), year, solstice (*ayana*), *yuga*, *kalpa*, *manvantara*, *pralaya* and *mahāpralaya*.[79] These notions[80] are not found to be associated with the other substances, namely, earth, water, *tejas*, air, *Ākāça*, *Dik*, *Ātman* and *Manas*. Nor can we have any doubt about the reality of the above mentioned notions. Hence, that to which these notions are attributed is termed as *Kāla* or time.

The notions of priority and posteriority in relation to time are based on the movements of the sun (*ādityaparivartanāni*). In other words, that object which possesses larger number of contacts with the movements of the sun is called *para*, while that which has smaller number of contacts is termed *apara*.[81] This necessitates the contact of the object and the movements of the sun. But what sort of contact is possible here? As the two objects between which the contact is established are far away from each other, there can be no contact, called *saṃyoga*. Nor can there be *saṃyuktasamavāya* as the sun and the object do not possess any contact. This very reasoning removes the possibility of *saṃyukta-samavetasamavāya* also. Again, as the movement of the sun inheres in the sun alone there can be no *samavāya* between the object and the movement of the sun. This also rejects the possibility of *samavetasamavāya*. Hence, none of the categories of earth, water, *tejas* and air can be the connecting link between the two; for, neither that which is connected with the object is connected with the sun, nor *vice versa*. The view—that a particular kind of *tejas* belonging to the sun may act as the connecting link—is not sound; for, such a *tejas* would not be able to come in

[79] PPBhā., p. 63.

[80] The notions of the relations of priority and posteriority etc. meant here should be distinguished from those which relate to *Dik*. PPBhā., pp. 164-67.

[81] *Janmanaḥ prabhṛtyekasyādityaparivartanāni bhūyāṃsīti paratvam, anyasya cālpīyāṃsītyaparatvam*-Vyom., p. 343.

contact with the objects lying in the dark depths of the earth. In order to connect all the objects of the universe with the movements of the sun, it is essential to have an all-pervading substance.[82] This rejects the possibility of *Manas* also.

Amongst the all-pervading substances, *Ākāça* cannot form the desired link; for, it cannot transmit the attribute of an object with which the former is connected by the relation of *saṃyuktasamavāya* to another. If it were so, then when one particular drum is beaten, sound ought to have been produced in all the drums,[83] which is not the case. Hence, *Ākāça* cannot connect the movements of the sun with other objects (*ākāçasya kriyopanāyakatve'yamatiprasaṅgaḥ*).[84] Similarly, *Ātman* also, not being capable of transmitting the attribute of one object to another, cannot be the connecting link; for, otherwise the colour of one particular object found at one particular place should have been transmitted to another place through the same relation of *saṃyukta-saṃyukta-samavāya*.[85] Therefore, *Ātman* also cannot serve the purpose.

After eliminating these, they believe in the existence of a category termed *Kāla* or time, which through the relation of *saṃyukta-saṃyukta-samavāya* links the

[82] *Na ca sūryagatiḥ sākṣātpiṇḍasambaddhā, nāpi saṃyuktasamavāyaḥ sambhavati piṇḍasūryayoḥ saṃyogābhāvāt......pṛthivyādiṣu yatpiṇḍaprāptaṃ tanna sūryasambaddhaṃ, yatsūryasambaddhaṃ tanna piṇḍaprāptamityaprāptiḥ kiñcit sauraṃ tejaḥ piṇḍasūryobhayasambaddhamastīti cenna; kvacitpiṇḍe tathā bhāve'pi bhūnikhātādau tadabhāvena vyabhicāraḥ. Evñcaitādṛçamekaṃ dravyaṃ svīkāryaṃ yat yāvatpiṇḍasūryasambaddham*—KVBhā., p. 137.

[83] *Na ākāçasya svapratyāsattimātreṇa saṃyukta-samavāyinaṃ dharmamanyatra saṃkrāmayitumasamarthatvāt. Tathātve caikatra bheryāmabhihatāyāṃ sarvabherīṣu çabdotpattiprasaṅgāt*—KV., p. 115.

[84] KVBhā., p. 138.

[85] *Ātmano'pi dravyāntaradharmeṣu dravyāntarāvacchedāya svapratyāsattyatiriktasannikarṣāpekṣitatvāt. Anyathā vārāṇasīsthitena nīlena pāṭaliputrasthitasya sphaṭikamaṇeruparañjanaprasaṅgāt*—KV., pp. 115-16; KVBhā., p. 139.

movements of the sun with each and every object of the universe. The difficulty felt in the case of *Ākāça* and *Ātman* is not at all present here; for, it is the very nature of *Kāla* to do so, due to which it is said to be *kriyāmātropanāyaka*, while *Ākāça* and *Ātman* are not so.[86]

It may be urged here that if the notions of simultaneity and the rest depend upon the movements of the sun, why is not then the movement itself accepted to act as the cause of these notions? The reply is that it is not possible; for, these are not possible from the movements of the sun alone, nor are the objects of the universe expressed in terms of the movements of the sun alone.[87] Again, as to the view—let motion (*kriyā*) itself be the *Kāla*, it is said, if it were so, then there would have been no notions of simultaneity and the rest; for, a *kriyā* is known as *kriyā* and not as a notion (*pratīti*) or *Kāla*.[88]

2. *Attributes of Kāla*

Having thus proved the existence of *Kāla* as a separate category, we now proceed to consider some of the more important qualities of it.

The very nature of *Kāla*, as has been made clear above, shows that it must be all-pervasive.[89] This alone makes the notions of priority and posteriority etc. common to all people of all the countries possible. This is further supported by the fact that time is said to be the instrumental cause (*nimittakāraṇa*) of each and every product.[90] From this it also follows that it is

[86] KV., p. 115; KVBhā., p. 138; VU., II. ii. 6., p. 99; KR., p. 32.

[87] *Ādityaparivartanamevāstu kiṃ kāleneti cenna; yugapadādipratyayānumeyatvāt. Na cādityaparivartanādeva yugapadādipratyayāḥ sambhavantīti. Ekasminnevādityaparivartane sarveṣāmanutpādāt, vyapadeçābhāvācca*—Vyom., p. 343.

[88] Ibid.

[89] PPBhā., p. 63.

[90] VS., III. ii. 2, 9; VII. i. 25; NS. and NBhā., II. i. 23.

eternal and is a substance.[91]

Kāla is the instrumental cause (i.e. the substrate—*ādhāramātra*) of motion. The judgments expressed in the form—'Going at present' etc. refer to time as a substrate of motion.[92] It is also the support (*āçraya*) of the worlds.[93] It is, therefore, said to be the cause of the production, existence and destruction of every product, as these are all expressed in terms of time.[94]

It is supersensuous[95] and has no specific quality.[96]

It is an auxiliary (*upanāyaka*) of motion (*kriyā*) alone.[97]

As it is all-pervasive and connects the objects of the universe with the movements of the sun, it is said to be only one. The various notions of time are due to certain limitations (*upādhis*) in the form of *kriyā* which consists of a series of movements (*kṣaṇas*) of which some are past, some are present, while some are still to come. It is, therefore, that the three divisions of time are attributed to *kriyā* also. Thus, for instance, since the placing of the cooking-pot on the hearth for cooking food and upto the time of its taking off from the hearth, the *kriyā* expressed by the term '*pacati*,' is called '*present*' and so is the time limited by that *kriyā*. The series of *parispandas* past with reference to

[91] PPBhā., p. 64.

[92] *Nimittakāraṇatvenādhāramātraṃ karmaṇaḥ kālo na tu samavāyī*—VU., on VS., V. ii. 26. *Idānīṃ gacchatītyādipratītistu idānīṃ ravītītyādipratītivāt kālikasambandhāvacchinnādhārādheyabhāvamavagāhate na tu samavāyasambandhāvacchinnamiti*—VV. on VS., V. ii. 26. But VBhā., holds that it refers to the non-material cause—*Kālopyasamavāyikāraṇaṃ karmasviti*—Ibid.

[93] BhāP., verse 45.

[94] PPBhā., p. 63.

[95] KV., p. 40; Kandalī., p. 64., VU., VIII. i. 22.

[96] KV., p. 40.

[97] *Na tāttvikaḥ kālasya bhedo varttamānādiḥ, kintvasannapyasau vyavahārasiddhaye kena cidupādhinā kalpyate. Kaḥ punarasāvupādhiḥ, kriyeti brūmaḥ* etc. NM., pp. 139-40; KV., pp. 120-21; Setu., p. 335.

the accomplished result expressed as '*apākṣīt*' (cooked), denotes past action and the time limited by it is known as '*past*'. Similarly, the *kriyā* which will take place with reference to a result not begun and which is expressed by the term '*pakṣyati*' (will cook) is known as future action and the time limited by it is expressed as '*future*.'

Some, however, are of opinion that these divisions of time are, in fact, present in the very nature of time and are not due to any limitation.[98]

Again, it itself establishes limitations (*upādhis*) which are constant. Thus, when one thing is present in time with reference to another thing, then the latter also is present with reference to the former.[99]

The use of priority and posteriority due to *Kāla* is common to all. That is, that which is present for one is present for all people living at that moment, unlike the *Dik* according to which, on the other hand, that which is the east for some, becomes west for others living at that very period of time.[100]

3. *Present time discussed*

There is a view that of the three divisions of time, that which is known as present has no existence at all. What we find, for instance, in the case of a fruit falling down from a tree, refers either to the past or to the future.[101] In other words, when the fruit leaves the stalk and is falling down, then the space, which has been already covered by the fruit, is called the fallen area of the space and the time referring to it is called '*past*;' while the space, which is still to be

[98] KVBhā., p. 144.
[99] VU., II. ii. 10.
[100] *Api cāyaṃ vyavahāro yadi kālakṛtaḥ syāt sarvasādhāraṇaḥ syāt. Tathā ca yathā vartamānaḥ sarvān prati vartamānaḥ, tathā prācī sarvān prati prācī syāt; na caivaṃ kasyacidapekṣayā pratīcītvāt*—KVBhā., p. 147.
[101] NS., II. i. 40.

covered before reaching the ground, is called the area of space which is still to be fallen through, and the time which refers to it is called '*future*.' There is no other space left with reference to which the time will be called '*present*.' On this ground, the existence of *present* time is denied.[102]

To this the *Nyāya-Vaiçeṣika* says that if there were no present time, then there would have been neither the past nor the future; for, both these depend upon the present itself.[103] In other words, time is not denoted in the terms of space, but it is manifested by *kriyā*;[104] so that, when the action of falling down stops, then that time is called '*past*;' while that time at which the action of falling will be produced is called '*future*;' and the time when the action of falling is cognised to be going on is called '*present*.' If, on the other hand, the opponent does not cognise the action of falling as going on, then with reference to what would he say that the action of falling has ceased, or is going to be stopped? On the other hand, when we say that 'the time has fallen,' we mean that the action of falling down has ceased, and when we say that 'the time is to fall,' what is meant is that the action of falling down is to take place. In both the cases, the object falling is devoid of *kriyā*. Again, when it is said that the object is falling down, then the object falling is really connected with *kriyā*. This sort of connection does not exist in the above mentioned two cases. Hence, what the present time does is to connect the object falling and the action of falling down. The other two divisions of time depend upon this present time without which the other two would not exist.[105] The exact implication of

[102] NBhā., II. i. 40.

[103] NS., II. i. 41.

[104] We should know that the word *kriyā* here stands for a general *kriyā* and not merely for *spanda*-Bhāṣyacandra, p. 300.

[105] NBhā., II. i. 41.

the term '*past*' is that the connection of the object with the action of falling down is over; and that of the '*future*' is that the connection of the object with the action is still to come. In both the cases, it is the action of falling down which is the point to determine the past and the future; so that, time, in fact, is ever '*present*.' The notions, like 'it has fallen down,' 'it is falling down,' and 'it will fall down,' are connected with the action of falling down, and hence, they appear only in the action and never in the result. This makes it clear that it is the *kriyā* (action) which manifests time and not the space (*adhvā*).[106]

Moreover, the present time is the indicator of the existence of things, as is clear from the expressions 'a substance exists,' 'an attribute exists,' 'motion exists' etc. where the term '*exists*' denotes the present time. So says the author of Nyāyasūtra—'In the absence of present time nothing is cognised, as no perception is possible.'[107] In other words, perception is due to the sense-organ and object—contact; and that which is not present cannot be in contact with the sense-organ. The opponent does not believe in anything which is present or existing; so that, the cause of perception, the object of perception, and the cognition through perception itself, nothing can exist. Thus, perception being denied, all the other proofs of right cognition, namely, inference etc. would also be denied. This leads the opponent to deny practically everything of this universe,[108] which, of course, is simply impossible to accept.

4. *Direct perceptibility of Kāla discussed*

Some are of opinion that *Kāla* is an object of direct perception; for, it is found as a qualification (*viçeṣaṇa*) of the notions of *kārya*. The notions of

[106] NV., p. 254.
[107] NS., II. i. 43; VP., kāṇḍa i, verse 37.
[108] NBhā., II. i. 43.

succession, simultaneity, soon, and the rest, do not depend upon *kārya* alone.[109]

To this it is asked: how would *Kāla* which has no colour be an object of perception through eyes? How can even the colour itself which is colourless be an object of perception through eyes? How can the *paramāṇus*, having no colour, be an object of perception through eyes? That is to say, the possession of colour is not the only cause of perception through eyes. Hence, both, the perception and the non-perception of a thing depend upon the worldly belief (*pratīti*); so that, we should try to find out the belief about the perception of *Kāla* through eyes and not the cause of perception in the form of possession of colour and the rest.[110]

It is further argued that if you hold that the convention—that which possesses colour can be perceived through eyes—is applicable to substances alone and not to the qualities, then it should be pointed out that it is not applicable to substances even; for, if it were so, then the *paramāṇus* which possess colour should be perceived through eyes, which is not the fact. Hence, the convention ought to be understood in the sense that that which is perceived through our eyes possesses colour. To this it is said that this is not the Divine injunction which cannot be transgressed. We cannot decide the perceptibility and otherwise of anything on the basis of utterance merely. Truly speaking, the perceptibility of a thing means its being an object of cognition through the sense-organ and it is found in the case of *Kāla*; so that, although it does not possess any colour, yet its perceptibility cannot be denied. Hence, there is nothing to deny that *Kāla* is perceived through eyes.[111]

[109] NM., Āhnika 2, p. 136.
[110] NM., Āhnika, 2, p. 136.
[111] NM., pp. 136-137.

Now, it may be further urged that if it be so; then why is not *Kāla* perceived through eyes independent of anything else without the qualification of a notion of a *kriyā*, like a jar? To this the answer is that it is the very nature of it and should not be questioned. It is known as a qualification (*viçeṣaṇa*) of some substance having colour and not like a stick which is known independent of anything else. On the other hand, there is no perception of *Ākāça* and the rest even as a qualification (*viçeṣaṇa*), and so it is not an object of perception which is not due to its not possessing colour. If it be said that the perception of the *viçeṣaṇa* even is possible only when it possesses colour, like a stick used as a *viçeṣaṇa* (adjective) of a man, as in the expression *daṇḍī puruṣaḥ*, which possesses colour; and *Kāla* as a *viçeṣaṇa* does not possess any colour; so that, it cannot be perceived.

But this argument is denied on the ground that a *viçeṣaṇa* even when does not possess any colour is perceived through eyes; for instance, generality (*sāmānya*) and the rest. Regarding the view that such a rule is applicable to substance alone, it has already been said that that which is an object of cognition through the organ of sight is really visual (*cākṣuṣa*) whether it possesses colour or not and whether it is a substance or not. Thus, when we speak of a piece of gold that it is a weighty substance, the weight becomes an object of perception and is not an object of inference through the act of falling. That is, that which is cognised through the organ of sight, whether it is known as a *viçeṣaṇa* or as independent of everything else, is an object of perception. Hence, *Kāla* is perceived and not inferred.[112]

Jayadeva Miçra, however, says that although the various forms of *Kāla*, like *prahara* and the rest, are all supersensuous, yet being of the nature of the

[112] NM., p. 137.

movement of the sun, cognition through the *jñānalakṣaṇā*[113] (*upanītabhāna*), as regards *kṣaṇa* even, is possible. *Kāla*, even on account of its being present, although is cognised through the *jñānalakṣaṇā*, yet is perceived through the sense-organ of sight.[114] Bhagiratha Ṭhakkura says—although *Kāla* is not an object of perception through eyes, yet it is apprehended through the *jñānalakṣaṇā*, and as such, we should see whether it is cognised through all the sense-organs.[115] This view is attributed to the followers of Prabhākara Miçra.[116]

5. *Some other views regarding Kāla*

Some astronomers and astrologers are of opinion that the notions of priority and posteriority and the rest are due to *parispanda* (movement). This *parispanda* cannot be that of any human being. It is that of the planets and the stars. Hence, it is the *parispanda* itself which is known as *Kāla*. All the notions regarding the various *upādhis* of *Kāla* are explained by this very *parispanda*.[117] But as the notions referred to above are possible even in the absence of the planets and the stars we cannot accept the above mentioned view.[118]

Kāla is not an object of *pratyakṣa* like a pot etc. The notions of late and soon and the rest which depend upon *kārya* alone cannot be the probans for proving the existence of *Kāla*; for, like smoke and fire no generalisation (*vyāpti*) is found to exist between the

[113] It is one of the three kinds of *alaukikasannikarṣa* between the organs of sense and the objects of perception, where the connecting link is supplied by *jñāna*. As, when a man mistakes a piece of rope for a snake, the cognition he had of snakes serves as the connecting link between the object of sense and the thing perceived, there being no real contact of the organ of vision with a snake in this case.

[114] Āloka on CM-Pratyakṣa, *MS.* Fol. 4b.

[115] KVPA., *Ms.*, Fol. 52*a*; KPP, Vol. I., p. 281.

[116] NK., p. 233.

[117] NM., Vol. I., p. 138.

[118] Ibid, pp. 138-139.

notions of late and soon etc. and *Kāla*. It is not of the nature of the *parispanda* of planets and stars. The notions of *muhūrta*, *yāma*, *ahorātra* and the rest are all imaginary and through these fictitious notions the worldly usage is carried on. There is no possibility of the usage of past, present, and future even if *Kāla* be something which is one, eternal, and all-pervading. Hence, there is no entity as *Kāla*.[119]

It is further urged: let the notions proving the existence of *Kāla* be due to the circumstances peculiar to each case; so that, there is no need of believing in the existence of *Kāla*.

To this it is said that it is not possible; for, in the absence of *Kāla* nothing can be produced. That is to say, no doubt, there can neither be the production of *Ākāça* which has an absolute existence, nor that of man's horn which is absolutely non-existent, but that of something which has no previous existence; and now, if there be no *Kāla* the word '*prak*' (previous) would have no meaning; and as such, the word '*prāk*' as a qualification of the term '*abhāva*,' as it is in the word *prāgabhāva*, being non-existent, there would be no peculiarity which would make it an object of production as distinguished from *Ākāça* and man's horn; and thus there would be no production at all.[120]

There are some who do not hold *Kāla* as a separate entity; for, they say that the notions on which the existence of it is based are found with *Dik* also; hence, they are not true probans of *Kāla*. But this view is also rejected being the utterance of those who are unfamiliar with the limitations of conventions.[121]

It is very difficult to speak of *Kāla* as a power or a force in order to establish *dravyatva* in it[122] without

[119] NM., Vol. I. Āhnika, 2, p. 136.
[120] Kandalī., pp. 64-65.
[121] NML., pp. 40-43.
[122] Hindu Realism, p. 54.

accepting a sort of motion in it, which, again, is not possible in an all-pervading substance as *Kāla* is.

Çivāditya and Candrakānta Tarkālaṅkāra are of opinion that *Kāla* has not got any independent existence. It is included under *Ākāça* along with *Dik*.[123]

Raghunātha Çiromaṇi, on the other hand, includes it under *Içvara*.[124] It must be remembered in this connection that even then the *kṣaṇa* which is merely a form of time has been accepted as an independent entity.[125]

Veṇīdatta, however, rejects the view of Raghunātha Çiromaṇi and says that the notions which are formed due to *Kāla* are not possible to be explained by *Içvara*; for, *Içvara* being one cannot explain the differences in notions as have been found above. We cannot hold that due to certain limitations present in *Içvara* the differences in notions can be explained; for, if it be so, then let the differences of the all-pervading *Jīvātmans*, namely, 'this is Çaitra,' 'this is Maitra,' and so on, be also explained by the same limitations and do away with the plurality of the *Jīvātmans*; for, with the help of the limitations a single conscious being can explain all the differences found in beings. Hence, the above mentioned view is untenable. Moreover, there is the Çruti also to prove the separate existence of *Kāla*—"*Sa eṣa saṃvatsaraḥ*."[126]

II
DIK

It has already been shown in the previous section that the notion of *Dik*, as denoting a relative position, accompanies the very idea of creation, like the notion of time. The logical necessity to believe in the

[123] SP., p. 17. Tarkālaṅkārabhāṣyaparīkṣā, pp. 331-34; NML., p. 93.

[124] PTN., pp. 1-3.

[125] Ibid., pp. 58-61.

[126] PMV., pp. 1-3.

existence of such a category has been made clear above and now, a fuller treatment of the same is attempted here in the present section.

1. *Existence proved*

The existence of an object, not capable of being cognised through any one of the external sense-organs, remains ever in doubt. *Dik*, like time etc., being supersensuous is inferred through the notions of east, west and the rest.[127] In other words, the existence of *Dik* is proved by the relative positions of the various finite (*mūrta*) objects of the universe, which is not possible to be explained otherwise.[128] In the classical works the existence of *Dik* has been proved on the basis of the relative position of the objects with reference to the contacts of the sun. That is, a particular object, being nearer to the rising sun, is said to be in the east with reference to some other object lying at some other place and not close to the rising sun. Similarly, some other object is said to be in the west as it is nearer to the setting sun. Such common and wide spread notions are not possible unless some all-pervasive substance is believed to bring about such contacts between the sun and the objects concerned. Hence, that which brings about this connection is called *Dik*.[129] The reason why the contact between the sun and the finite objects of the universe is not brought about by other all-pervasive substances, namely, *Ākāça* and *Ātman* is that none of these is capable of transmitting the

[127] PPBhā., p. 66.

[128] *Mūrtadravyamavadhiṃ kṛtvā mūrteṣveva dravyeṣvetasmādidaṃ pūrveṇa dakṣiṇena......iti daça pratyayā yato bhavanti sā digiti; anyanimittāsambhavāt*—PPBhā., pp. 66-67; Kandalī, p. 67.

[129] *Etadapekṣayedaṃ pūrvametasya hi sannihitādimādityasaṃyogāvacchinnamityarthaḥ. Etadapekṣayedaṃ paççimamityasyatu sannihitacaramādityasaṃyogāvacchinnamityarthaḥ. Na codayācalādiṣu vartamānaḥ prathamacaramādityasaṃyogo ghaṭādau vinā sambandhaṃ viçiṣṭapratītijananasamarthaḥ. Na ca sākṣātsambandhaḥ samavāyādilakṣaṇastenāstīti saṃyuktasaṃyuktasamavāyaghaṭakatayā diksiddhiḥ*—KVBhā., p. 147.

dharma of one to the other. Likewise, *Kāla* also cannot help us here; for, its function has been limited to *kriyā* (movement) alone. And moreover, there is much difference in their notions; for instance, as regards *Dik* that which is the east for one may be the west for others and so on, while regarding *Kāla*, that which is present for one is present for all living persons and not future or past.[130]

2. *Dik defined*

Such a *Dik* has been defined, accordingly, as that from which the notions of the various directions are produced with reference to a particular finite (*mūrta*) object as the basis of our judgment;[131] or as that which is the substratum of *mahattva* not co-existing with a specific quality and that which is not the substratum of the conjunction which is the non-material cause of priority and posteriority produced by the *apekṣābuddhi* regarding the vibration (*spandaviṣayakāpekṣābuddhi*); or as that which is different from *Kāla*, is formless, and is the substratum of the conjunction not co-existing with a specific quality, and so on.[132] Again, it is defined as a substance from which, with reference to two simultaneously existing objects having fixed direction and place, such notions, as—this (which is the substratum of a large number of *saṃyuktasaṃyogas*) is prior to that object (which is the substratum of a smaller number of *saṃyuktasaṃyogas*), and again, this (which is the substratum of a smaller number of *saṃyuktasaṃyogas*) is posterior to that (which is the substratum of a larger number of the *saṃyuktasaṃyogas*), arise.[133] Candrakānta elucidates the above with the help

[130] Ibid., pp. 147-48.

[131] PPBhā., p. 66.

[132] KR., pp. 33-34.

[133] VU., under VS., II. ii. 10. Here 'priority' means distance, and 'posteriority' nearness. Priority and posteriority due to *Dik* bring to us the notions about directions.

of a definite illustration. Thus, he says that the man living on the Himālayas, for instance, considers the Pāriyātra as prior (*para*), meaning, distant, having the Vindhyā as the limit, but having the Pāriyātra as the limit, the Vindhyā as posterior (*apara*), that is, nearer. The reason is that the conjunctions existing between the Himālayas and the Vindhyā are smaller in number than those existing between the Himālayas and the Pāriyātra. That which makes these conjunctions possible is named *Dik*.[134]

3. *Attributes of Dik*

It is really one, but for the sake of the usages of the *çruti*, *smṛti* and the worldly people, as is clear from the following expressions—"one should not sleep with his head facing the west;" "one desirous of long life should take his food facing the east;" and "go to the east," etc.[135] it is divided into ten. All these are due to the various conjunctions of the sun moving round the conventional mountain Meru. These are presided over by the ten *lokapālas*. The ten *Diks* are : *māhendrī* (east), *vaiçvānarī* (south-east), *yāmyā* (south), *nairṛtī* (south-west), *vāruṇī* (west), *vāyavyā* (north-west), *kauberī* (north), *aiçānī* (north-east), *brāhmī* (above), and *nāgī* (below).[136]

These various names are not conventional (*pāribhāṣika*) but significant. Thus, *prācī* is so called because the sun appears first in that direction; that which the sun touches downwards is called *avācī* (south); that which the sun touches last is called *pratīcī* (west); and that where the sun reaches high is called *udīcī* (north). Similarly, we have *prāgavācī* (south-east), *avākpratīcī* (south-west), *pratyagudīcī* (north-west), and *udakprācī* (north-east). Having the sun as the limit, the face of

[134] KVBhā, pp. 147-148; KV, p. 123.

[135] Kandalī., pp. 68-69.

[136] PPBhā., p. 67. It has been also called *nāgīya*—NM, Vol. I. Āhnika 2, p. 140.

the earth is downwards (*adhaḥ*), while having the face of the earth as the limit, the place where planets and stars exist is upwards (*ūrdhva*).[137] Others give another kind of explanation of the nomenclature of these directions. Thus, the *Dik* which is in close proximity to the rising mountain is called *prācī* (east); that which is separated from the rising mountain by something intervening is called (*pratīcī*). In other words, having the rising mountain as the limit that which has got smaller number of *saṃyuktasaṃyogas* is called the east (*prācī*); while that which has larger number of *saṃyuktasaṃyogas* is called the west (*pratīcī*);[138] that which lies on the left of the man facing the east is called the north (*udīcī*), and that which lies towards the right of the man facing the east is called the south (*dakṣiṇa*). That which is the substratum of the conjunction produced by the *kriyā* which is the non-material cause of *gurutva* is called downwards (*adhaḥ*), while that which is the substratum of the conjunction produced by the *agnikriyā* (movement of the *tejas*) produced by the conjunction of the *Ātman* possessing *adṛṣṭa* is called upwards (*ūrdhva*[139]). Vyomavatī holds that the particular position (*dikpradeça*) with which the sun comes in contact at the time of rising is called the east; when the sun comes in contact with another particular position (*dikpradeça*) at the midday it is the south; while that with which the sun comes in contact in the afternoon is called the west, and so on.[140]

Çivāditya believes in the existence of eleven divisions of *Dik*. To the above mentioned ten he adds *raudrī*, meaning the position between above and below, which is generally known as the *antarīkṣa*.[141]

[137] KV., pp. 125-126.

[138] Bhagiratha Ṭhakkura's Jalada quoted in KV, Ft.-note, p. 126.

[139] KV., pp. 125-126.

[140] P. 359.

[141] SP., p. 17; Setu, p. 357.

It is all-pervasive.[142] The notions of distance, nearness and the rest are not possible to be found everywhere without there being an all-pervasive cause. It is a substance,[143] as it possesses qualities and is not dependent upon anything else.[144] It establishes conjunctions.[145] It also establishes *upādhis* in the form of the movement of the sun,[146] which are not constant; for, that which is the east in relation to a person becomes sometimes the west in relation to the same person.[147]

It is eternal,[148] as it has no cause to produce it.[149] It does not possess any movement as it is not *mūrta*.[150]

A movement produced here and there makes *Dik* appear as if it were the material cause of it, which it is not. As regards its appearing as the substratum of a movement, it should be taken in the sense in which a jar is said to be the substratum of curd or the forest of the roaring of a lion, and so on. It is not a material cause of anything.[151] Although Candrakānta calls it the non-material cause,[152] yet it is, in fact, the instrumental cause of every product.[153] It does not possess any specific quality.[154] It is not a *bhūta*.[155]

It is a supersensuous substance.[156] There was a view that *Dik* is an object of visual direct perception. The grounds are the same as adduced in the case of

142 PPBhā., p. 67.
143 VS., II. ii. 11.
144 Vyom., p. 359.
145 VU., II. ii. 10.
146 KVBhā., p. 65.
147 VU., II. ii. 10.
148 VS., II. ii. 11.
149 Kandalī., p. 18.
150 VS., and VU., V. ii. 21.
151 Ibid., V. ii. 25.
152 Ibid.
153 *Sarvotpattimatāṃ nimittakāraṇam*—PPBhā., p. 25.
154 KV., p. 40.
155 Ibid.
156 VU., VIII. i. 12.

Kāla.[157] But this is not in keeping with the traditional view of the school.

The consideration of the limitations of *Dik* is operative only with reference to things having limited forms. Hence, the all-pervasive substances are beyond the influence of time and space.[158]

4. *Some other views regarding Dik and their refutation*

Raghunātha Çiromaṇi is of opinion that like *Ākāça* and *Kāla*, *Dik* also is not different from *Içvara* as there is no proof to show its separate existence. The various notions explained by *Dik* are also explained by *Içvara*,[159] through His *upādhis*.[160]

Veṇīdatta rejects this view in support of the traditional view of the school. He says that the notions like 'there is a jar in the east' etc. cannot be explained by denying the separate existence of *Dik*. The various conditions imposed upon *Içvara* cannot explain all the different notions of *Dik*; for, if it were so, then the expressions like 'I am Caitra,' 'He is Maitra,' and others, also can be had from a single *Içvara*, and that there is no need in believing in the plurality of the *Jīvātmans*. And moreover, in the presence of *çrutis* like '*Imā diçaḥ*' etc. how can we deny the very existence of it?[161] Even the followers of the Neo-Nyāya school support the traditional view.[162]

There is the Vaidika view that *Dik* is the auditory organ. This has been also accepted by the Mīmāṃsakas.[163] But this also has been rejected. Jayanta calls it an act of great self-conceit (*āhopuruṣikā*). He adds that the auditory organ cannot but be the *Ākāça* which

[157] NM., pp. 137-139.
[158] PPBhā., p. 66.
[159] PTN., pp. 1-2.
[160] Raghudeva on Ibid.
[161] PM., pp. 1-3.
[162] Prabhā on NSM., p. 380.
[163] ÇV., Çabdādhikaraṇa., p. 151.

is a *bhūta* and is one of the main material principles of a sense-organ, while *Dik* is neither of these. If it were on account of its having the common characteristic of all-pervasiveness, then even *Kāla* and *Ātman* may be said to be identical with *Ākāça*. As regards the *Āgama*—'May your eyes go back to the sun; the sense-organ of hearing to *Dik*, and so on,' which is quoted in support of the Vaidika view, it may be said that it is not due to the presence of any real relation between these that they are so mentioned; for, if it were so, then the vital air (*prāṇa*) would not have been said to go back to the *antarīkṣa* in the same *mantra*; hence, the view is rejected.[164]

Later on, Candrakānta says that according to the Ācārya, *Kāla* and *Dik* are not different from *Ākāça*.[165] The apparent difference is due to their specific functions. The reason adduced is that efforts are made in the sūtras to differentiate *Ākāça* from all other substances, but no such effort is made to make any such differentiation between *Kāla* and *Dik* and the rest of the substances. This shows that the very treatment of *Ākāça* includes the treatment of *Kāla* and *Dik* also. Hence, it appears that the author of the Vaiçeṣika-sūtra does not consider these as three distinct substances.

This view has not been accepted by later writers. As regards the argument of Raghunātha, it may be said, in reply, that if his view be accepted, then what is the need of having two other sūtras[166] through which Kanāda proves the existence of *Kāla* and *Dik* as two distinct substances. We have separate sūtras to prove different qualities belonging to each of these two substances.[167] Moreover, even Gautama attaches equal

[164] NM., Āhnika 3, p. 226.
[165] VBhā., II. i. 27; II. ii. 14.
[166] VS., II. ii. 6, 10.
[167] VS., II. ii. 6, 7, 8, 9, 10-16.

importance to all these three in his work.[168] Hence, we cannot agree with Raghunātha Çiromaṇi on this point.

5. *Difference and similarity between Ākāça, Kāla and Dik*

Although the main difference between these has already been pointed out in the introductory section of *Ākāça*, yet those points of differences, which are mentioned in the classical works on the subject, are given here.

Of these three, *Ākāça* alone is one of the *mahābhūtas*. It alone possesses a specific quality, and it alone is in possession of the nature of the principle of a sense-organ. The quality of this alone is cognised through one of the external sense-organs directly.[169]

As for *Kāla* and *Dik*, we know that apparently almost all the points are common and it is perhaps due to this that some do not make any distinction between these two. But it should be borne in mind that there are some fundamental points of difference which establish their separate existence. Thus, *Kāla* or its divisions are determined merely by the limitation (*upādhi*) of *kriyā* (*kriyāmātropādhinibandhana*). In the case of *Dik*, on the other hand, they are determined by the limitation of *mūrta* (*mūrtamātropādhinibandhana*). Again, *Kāla* is called *niyatopādhyunnāyakaḥ*, while *Dik* is called *aniyatopādhyunnāyikā*. In other words, the notions of time are constant, while those of *Dik* are changing.[170]

In spite of these differences, the common points between these are: all-pervasiveness, possession of the highest possible dimension, and being the common substratum of everything having limited form.[171]

[168] NS., II. i. 22.

[169] PPBhā., p. 22; Helārāja on VP., Kāṇḍa 3, section 6, verse 4, p. 159.

[170] TS., quoted by Bodas and Athalye in their notes on TD., pp. 132-133. VU, II. ii. 10, pp. 103-104.

[171] PPBhā., p. 22.

CHAPTER V

MATTER AND MOTION

I

NECESSITY OF MOTION FOR THE PSYCHIC AND NON-PSYCHIC CHANGES

BOTH for the production and the destruction of the phenomenal world the existence of motion is necessary. *Paramāṇus* out of which the non-eternal objects of the universe are produced, alone cannot do anything. During the dissolution period (*pralaya*) these *paramāṇus* remain separate,[1] and in order that they may combine together so as to form products, such as, *dvyaṇuka* and the rest, we must have motion produced in them. As the world is without any beginning, we cannot be sure whether the production of the universe precedes its destruction or follows it; so that, even when the cosmic order is in existence we must have motion to destroy the produced things and ultimately, the world itself. In any case, without motion there can be neither production nor destruction of the material world. Not only for the cosmic order but even for the objective aspect of the psychic world, the existence of motion is indespensable. It is a fact that the various psychic products, namely, pleasure, pain, desire, consciousness etc., are mainly due to the contact of the *Manas* with the *Ātman*, which contact is possible through the motion of the former alone. Therefore, whether it be the psychic production or the extramental one, presence of motion is necessary.

[1] PPbhā, p. 48.

II

RELATION OF MOTION WITH MATTER

As regards the relation of motion with matter it may be said that these are two distinct categories. But motion is not independent like matter. Matter can exist even without motion, while the latter must have a substance to inhere in. Matter is the very substratum of motion.[2] It is through matter alone that the existence of motion is known. But for the products of matter we have to depend upon motion also. It is the motion which brings about the conjunctions between *paramānus* and the various later products of the world.

As to the question whether motion is intrinsic or extrinsic in matter, it may be said, in reply, that there are two kinds of motions: one which brings about the conjunctions between *paramāṇus* so as to form various products, and ultimately, the world itself; and the other which only marks the time-limit during the dissolution period and does not produce any conjunction or disjunction. In both the cases, the motion is not intrinsic in matter. It comes from without. As regards the latter kind of motion we know that before an object is destroyed a kind of shock (*saṅkṣobha*) is given to that object and then the object is destroyed. The same shock produces velocity (*vega*) in the *paramāṇus* of that object through the production of motion (*karman*) in them. Hence, even when the object is destroyed there follows a series of motions in the *paramāṇus*, which motions possess degrees in the form of slow (*manda*), more slow (*mandatara*), and most slow (*mandatama*). Thus, during the dissolution period there are both the velocity and the motion.[3]

By the way, it may be asked: if there is a sort of

[2] VS., I. i. 17.
[3] Bodhanī, p. 91; Setu, p. 286.

motion during the Cosmic Rest, the mutual conjunction of the *paramāṇus* should not be denied; and accordingly, there should be the production of *dvyaṇuka* and the rest, and ultimately, of the cosmic order itself.

To this it is said that although there is a motion, yet that motion does not produce that conjunction which brings about the desired effects, namely, *dvyaṇuka* and the rest. In other words, the motion at that time produces the conjunction called *pracaya* (grouping-conjunction) and not productive-conjunction; so that, the motion can utmost group the *paramāṇus* into different classes, but is unable to produce conjunctions productive of effects.

Again, it may be asked here: if the motion is non-productive, then what is the use of believing in its existence? In reply, it is said that the only need of such a motion at that time is to mark the time-limit; that is, to show that the Cosmic Rest exists for such and such period.[4] To explain the above point a counter-question may be put here: What is the use of the series of breaths when a man has fallen in sound sleep; for, no activity befitting a living man is produced at that time ? The only answer that is given to this query is that the series of breaths of that time are to mark that so much time of the sleeping man's span of life has been exhausted in sleeping and so much is now left to be experienced. In other words, the vibration of the life at that time is only to keep an accurate account of the span of a man's period of life.[5]

Under such circumstances, it is just necessary to have some such motion which will lead to the productive-conjunctions between the *paramāṇus* after the the Cosmic Rest is over. This is the former kind of motion referred to above. This also comes from without according to *Nyāya-Vaiçeṣika*. Motion, accord-

[4] KP, Vol. I, p. 333.
[5] Bodhanī, pp. 91-92.

ing to this joint system, can be had only through the agency of a conscious being; so that, when the world is produced, for all the worldly purposes, we do get a conscious agent to produce motion, but how can a motion be had just after the Cosmic Rest is over to produce *dvyaṇuka* etc.? No human being is present at that time. *Jīvas* are, no doubt, present even there, but as they are insensate at that time, no motion can be produced by them. Hence, under the circumstances, we have to believe in the causality of a superhuman power and also the cumulative *adṛṣṭa* of the *Jīvas* to produce motion in the *paramāṇus*; so that, during the Cosmic Rest, just when the time for fructification of the past deeds is reached, through the help of the Divine Will and the *adṛṣṭa* of the *Jīvas*, a sort of motion is produced in the *paramāṇus*. This motion, in its turn, brings about the necessary conjuctions for the production of the universe.

Such is the necessity of motion in relation to matter. Accordingly, motion is defined as that which is the non-material cause of the conjunctions and disjunctions without depending upon anything else; which does not possess any quality and which has only one substance for its substratum.[6]

III

CHARACTERISTICS OF MOTION

There is only one kind of motion at a time in one substance.[7] If there inhere two different and contrary motions simultaneously in one substance, then those two motions, being mutually contraries, will counteract each other and will not produce either conjunction or disjunction in any definite direction; so that, the

[6] VS. I. i. 17.

[7] VU, II. ii. 21; VS., I. i. 17; PPBhā, p. 290 along with Kandalī; KR, p. 152.

very definition of motion (*karman*), namely, the character of being the independent cause of conjunctions and disjunctions, will be frustrated. If, on the other hand, these two actions be not mutually contraries, then, as only one of the two motions would be sufficient to produce a particular conjunction and disjunction in any definite direction, there would be no need for believing in the other motion at all. Similarly, one and the same motion cannot remain in more than one substance; for, when one substance moves through the agency of one motion that very motion cannot make other substance move as well[8].

Motion exists only for a few moments. So, when it is produced in a finite (*mūrta*) substance,[9] then there is the disjunction followed by the destruction of the previous conjunctions; then there is the subsequent conjunction; and then there is the destruction of the motion itself.[10]

It belongs only to such substances as have limited forms.[11] It does not possess any quality.[12] It is destroyed by its own effect, namely, conjunction, but not by disjunction; for, in that case, there would not be any subsequent conjunction.[13] It produces effects, namely, conjunctions and disjunctions inherent in its own substratum and also in the substratum of others.[14]

It does not produce effects of its own class. That is, a motion never produces another motion.[15] If motion were to produce another motion, then it would

[8] KR, p. 153; Kandalī, p. 290; PSAH, Ch. II, pp. 129-130, where Dr. Seal wrongly attributes the above explanation to Praçastapāda.

[9] VU, II. i. 21.

[10] NK, p. 205 (third edition).

[11] PPBhā, p. 290; VU, II. i. 21.

[12] VS, I. i. 17; PPBhā, p. 290.

[13] VS, I. i. 14; PPBhā, p. 290 along with Kandalī.

[14] PPBhā, p. 290.

[15] VS, I. i. 11; PPBhā, p. 290.

do so just after its own production, like sound; so that, the previous motion alone have had produced disjunctions with all the combined substances, then with whom the second motion will produce disjunction; for, a disjunction is always preceded by a conjunction and there is no possibility of there being another conjunction; and if no disjunction is produced, then the very definition of motion is falsified. We cannot, in order to get over the above difficulty, hold that it would produce motion at a later time; for, there should be no delay in the production of the effect if the thing which is to produce the effect has capability to do so; for, there is nothing to depend upon, which alone can delay the production. If it be held that the production takes place simultaneously with the destruction of the previous conjunction, even then there remains the impossibility of producing the disjunction. The same will hold good in the case of the production at the moment when the subsequent conjunction takes place. There is no possibility of the production after the production of the subsequent production; for, then the very motion is destroyed. Hence, no motion can produce another motion.[16]

Again, if a motion produces another motion, then when a man moves there should not be the stoppage of his motion; for, every motion will go on producing another motion of its own type *ad infinitum*. If it be held that the movement of the man would come to an end when the desire to move further and the effort to that effect are stopped, then we should say that the cause of the subsequent motions is the desire and the effort and not the motion itself.[17]

It does not produce any substance. That is, although a motion produces conjunctions which, in their turn, produce a substance, so that, indirectly a motion

[16] VU, 1. i. 11.
[17] Kandalī, p. 291.

does produce a substance, yet a motion is never regarded to be the cause of a substance.[18] The reason is that at the time of the production of a substance motion does not exist. It disappears just after the production of the subsequent conjunction.[19]

It always produces an effect marking a particular direction.[20] It is perceived through two external sense-organs, namely, organs of sight and touch, except in the case of *Manas* where it is only inferred.[21]

It possesses the attributes of *Sattā* (the summum genus); non-eternity; the character of having a substance as its material cause; the character of being an effect and a cause; generality and quiddity in common with a substance and an attribute.[22] It has a quality as its non-material cause in common with a substance and a quality.[23] It is a cause of velocity[24] as well as that of elasticity (*sthitisthāpaka*).[25] A single motion for instance, going upward, is a product of several causes, namely, weight, effort, and conjunction.

IV

VARIETIES OF MOTION

It has been said above that motion produces effects marking a particular direction. The same thing is explained through the help of its various divisions, namely, upward motion (*utkṣepaṇa*), downward motion (*apakṣepaṇa*), contraction (*ākuñcana*), expansion (*prasāraṇa*), and motion in general (*gamana*). Now, these divisions can be easily classed under two broad

[18] VS, I. i. 21; VU. on ibid.; PPBhā, p. 290.
[19] Kandalī, p. 291.
[20] PPBhā, p. 290.
[21] KR, p. 152.
[22] VS, I. i. 8, 18.
[23] VS, I. i. 19.
[24] VS, I. i. 20.
[25] VU, I. i. 20.

heads: (1) motion in one particular definite direction, and (2) motion in uncertain different directions. Under the former head, we may have *utkṣepaṇa*, *apakṣepaṇa*, *ākuñcana* (motion towards one particular direction by contracting an extended thing), and *prasāraṇa* (motion towards one particular direction by expanding a contracted object). Under the latter head, we can have only one, namely, *gamana*. This includes all other sorts of motions not included under the aforesaid four varieties. In order to make the sense of these terms quite clear I would like to explain each of them here in detail. Thus:—

1. Upward motion (*utkṣepaṇa*) is that kind of motion which brings about the conjunction of the constituent parts of an organism, for instance, hand and the rest, and things connected with the organism, as for instance, *musala* (a particular kind of very thick stick generally used for removing husks from grains) with parts above and disjunction of these with the parts below. This is due to weight, effort, and conjunctions.[26]

2. Downward motion (*apakṣepana*) is that kind of motion which produces conjunction of the parts of an organism and things connected with them with parts below and disjunction with parts above.[27]

3. Contraction (*ākuñcana*) is that kind of motion by which the upper parts of an extended substance are disjoined with those parts with which they were connected before and are combined with the parts at the bottom; so that, the substance becomes curved.[28]

4. Expansion (*prasāraṇa*) is that kind of motion by which the upper parts of a substance become disjoined with the parts of the same substance at the bottom and become connected with the upper parts with which they were disconnected before; so that, the object

[26] PPBhā, p. 291 along with Kandalī.
[27] PPBhā, p. 291.
[28] PPBhā, p. 291.

becomes straight.[29]

Under the second broad head, namely, *gamana*, meaning 'motion' in general, which is the cause of conjunctions and disjunctions between parts of different uncertain directions, they include revolving (*bhramaṇa*), purging (*recana*), fluidity (*syanda*), vibration (*spanda*), upward flaming (*ūrdhvajvalana*), and oblique or transversal motion (*tīryaggamana*). In all these cases of motions, we find that there is no certainty of any one definite direction. We may include other similar forms of motions under this head.

As to the question: when the term '*gamana*' is a synonym for motion in general, what is the use of having a separate heading under *gamana*? it is said that if *gamana* be not used separately, then under motion (*gamana*) only those particular kinds of motions mentioned above would have been included. But in reality, we find that *bhramaṇa*, *recana*, and the rest are also used in the sense of *gamana*, which would have been otherwise. That is, the use of the term *gamana* would have gone against the worldly usage in that case. Hence, in order to keep up the harmony between the motions and the actual reality, the term *gamana* has been separately used as a distinct head.[30]

V

CAUSES OF MOTION

Motion is produced by weight (*gurutva*), effort (*prayatna*), and conjunction (*saṃyoga*).[31] Praçastapāda adds fluidity (*dravatva*) to the above.[32] Motion due to conjunction is produced by forcible contact[33] or by

[29] PPBhā, p. 292.
[30] PPBhā, p. 366, Kandalī, p. 297.
[31] VS, I. i. 29.
[32] P. 290.
[33] VS, V. i. 3.

impulsion (*nodana*).[34] *Adṛṣṭa* is also considered to be its cause.[35] *Saṃskāra* also produces motion.[36]

An effort is made here to show how each of the above mentioned causes operates so as to produce motion in substances having limited forms:

1. Weight (*gurutva*)--one of the causes of motion, is defined as the cause of the falling motion (*patana-karman*) of water and earth. It is inferred through the falling motion, as it is supersensuous. Vallabha holds that it is perceived while operating downwards.[37] It is neutralised by conjunction, effort, and *saṃskāra*.

As it belongs to water and earth,[38] it will cause motion only in these. Its influence is neutralised by conjunction, effort, and *saṃskāra*. Hence, in the case of watery and earthly objects, when none of the counteracting forces, namely, conjunction, effort, and *samskāra*, is operating its influence over weight, then weight causes downward motion in these. This is called the falling motion of the object. As for instance, in the case of *musala*, in the absence of the hand-contact which is the counter-acting agency of the weight, the downward motion is due to weight. In the same way, in the case of an organism in the absence of effort which counteracts the influence of weight, the falling down is due to weight. In the like manner, in the case of an arrow when thrown out, it falls down in the way without reaching the goal, in the absence of velocity (one of the *saṃskāras*), the falling is due to weight alone.[39] This applies to all the cases of falling down.[40] Now, in all these cases, motion in the *musala*, body and the arrow is due to

[34] VS, V. i. 10.
[35] VS, V. i. 15.
[36] VS, V. i. 17.
[37] NLV, p. 69; PD, p. 14; VU, IV. i. 10.
[38] PPBhā, p. 263.
[39] VS, V. i. 7.
[40] VU, on ibid.

weight alone.

It should be noted down here that the first initiative falling motion is due to weight alone, while the second and the subsequent falling motions are joint products of weight and velocity (*vega*). The first motion towards falling down is produced by weight, but later on, it gives rise to velocity; so that, in subsequent motions, both velocity and weight are found. Here, we have the joint causality, but in other places, each of these two has been found to be productive of motion separately and independently.[41]

It is clear from the above statement that weight causes motion only when there is no velocity, which is one of the counteracting forces for the operation of weight in producing first motion in a substance which, in its turn, leads to its fall. In this case, no doubt, weight is the cause of motion, but only that of the first falling motion (*ādyapatanakarman*). This motion produces velocity which helps the weight to produce joint effects in the form of the subsequent motions, till the falling object reaches the ground.

Now, it may be urged here: velocity being one of the counteracting forces of weight, how can there be any joint effect at all? According to the rule, as soon as velocity appears it should counteract the operation of weight. This may be further explained with the help of two instances. Thus, when an arrow is thrown into the air towards any direction it is accompanied by velocity which really is its conveyance, but there is also weight in it. Now, it is also certain that the independent operation of weight causes falling motion (*patanakarman*); so that, in the case of a flying arrow we will have to infer that although the weight is present there, yet it has not got its independent operation. That is, its influence is counteracted by velocity which alone is causing motion in the

[41] PPBhā, pp. 304-305, along with Kandalī.

arrow. This velocity when exhausted, the weight predominates and causes the downfall of the arrow. This is how velocity is counteracting the operation of weight and does not help the production of a joint effect.

Again, in the case of an object or an organism where there is no velocity and the rest to counteract the operations of its weight, it is really the weight alone which causes the falling motion there. But this weight is the cause only so far as the first falling motion is concerned; because, in the subsequent falling motions the weight is helped by velocity which was produced by the first falling motion itself; so that, here also, we find velocity helping the weight, instead of, as a rule, counteracting it, of course, in the cause. This is a clear case of mutual help with a view to produce a joint effect. Even in the second instance itself, we find apparently contradictory statements. We stick to the rule that there should not be velocity etc. in the case of the first falling motion, although they may be present in the subsequent falling motions.

How to reconcile these two apparently contradictory views? The facts are as stated above. Praçastapāda is quite clear. But Çrīdhara appears to have felt some difficulty; hence, he has tried to give reasons to defend Praçastapāda. But his reasons do not give us ample satisfaction; for, although both weight (*gurutva*) and velocity (*vega*) are found productive of motion elsewhere separately, yet one may counteract the other. When they are independent and separate both produce motion; but when found in one place, velocity counteracts the force of weight and performs its function alone. There is no difficulty in this and perhaps almost all the later writers hold weight as the cause of the first falling motion alone, while velocity that of the subsequent motions alone.[12] There

[12] TR, p. 146; TD on TS, p. 20; Viçvakarman's com. on **TBhā**, p. 126

is nothing in the Vaiçeṣika sutra itself to support the view of Praçastapāda.

Dr. B.N. Seal, on the other hand, says—"Praçastapāda seems to have thought that some *saṃskāras* (e.g. the *vega* of an arrow or other projectile) suspend the action of gravity; other *saṃskāras* (e.g. in the case of a falling body) coalesce with gravity to produce a single resultant motion. The later commentators from Çridhara downwards certainly interpret the Vaiçeṣika sūtras in this sense."[43]

2. Effort (*prayatna*) is also a cause of motion. It is of two kinds—one which proceeds from life (*jīvana*) and the other that proceeds from desire and hatred. Of these, the former, namely, that which proceeds from life is that which is the cause of the movement of the vital-airs, namely, *prāṇa* and *apāna*, while a man is sleeping, and which leads the internal sense-organ to come in contact with the external sense-organs at the time of awakening.[44] In other words, the activities of vital-airs, in a sleeping man, are due to effort. This effort cannot be caused by desire and hatred. It is only due to the life present in a man. Life, on the other hand, has been explained as the contact of the *Ātman* with the *Manas* and an organism depending upon merit and demerit; so that, effort proceeding from life is produced from the *Ātman* and the *Manas* contact depending upon merit and demerit.[45] The other is the cause of the activities which are capable of leading to the desired and of removing the undesired. This also keeps up the body steady. That the body being heavy does not fall down is due to our effort proceeding from desire. This second kind of effort is produced from the *Ātman* and the *Manas* contact helped by the desire or by hatred.[46]

[43] PSAH, p. 142.
[44] PPBhā, p. 263.
[45] Kandalī, p. 263.
[46] PPBhā, p. 263 along with Kandalī.

Such an effort produces motion. When a man, desirous of performing such acts as sacrifice, study, giving, cultivation of land etc., wants to throw up his hand, or throw it down, then an effort is produced in the *Ātman* limited by the part of the body called hand, and then from the *Ātman* and the hand contact helped by that effort and weight motion is produced in the hand; and also in the like manner, in all other parts of the body, such as, leg and the rest and consequently, in the body itself.[47] This motion has got the parts of the body or the body itself as its material cause, the *Ātman* (possessing effort) and the hand contact as the non-material cause, while the effort itself as the instrumental cause.[48] We should remember that effort alone without the aid of weight cannot produce either the upward or the downward motion; so that, we have to admit here the causality of weight as well.

Again, in the same manner, effort produces motion in things connected with the parts of the body, or the body itself. Thus, when a man, having a *musala* in his hand, desires to throw up the *musala* with the help of the hand, an effort is produced in the *Ātman*. With the help of that effort as the instrumental cause and the *Ātman* and the hand contact as the non-material cause, an upward motion is produced in the hand and simultaneously with the help of the same effort, from the hand and the *musala* contact, a motion is produced even in the *musala* itself.[49]

Similarly, we have downward motion of hand and *musala*. Thus, when the *musala* has been thrown up, the desire to throw it up ceases, and another desire to throw it down is produced followed by an

[47] VS, V. i. I., PPBhā, p. 297.

[48] VU, V. i. I. This motion is called *ceṣṭā*, as it is said—"*Ātmajanyā bhavedicchā icchajānyā bhavetkṛtiḥ; kṛtijanyā bhaveccesṭā tajjanyaiva kriyā bhavet*"—Quoted in VV, v. i. I.

[49] PPBhā, pp. 297-298.

effort. With the help of this effort as the instrumental cause and the *Ātman* and the *Manas* contact as well as the hand and *musala* contact as the respective non-material causes, there are simultaneously downward motions in hand as well as in the *musala*.[50]

The motion of the *musala* produces forcible conjunction between a wooden mortar (*ulūkhala*) and the *musala,* which, in its turn, is the cause of the upward motion of the *musala* with the help of the velocity belonging to it, without being preceded by any effort. Here, the velocity is the instrumental cause and the *musala* is the material cause.

This upward motion of the *musala*, in its turn, with the help of the forcible contact produces velocity in the *musala*. With the help of this velocity, again, the *musala* and the hand contact, without depending upon any effort, produces an upward motion in the hand also.

As to the question—that the previous velocity produced in the *musala* by the downward motion being now destroyed by the forcible contact, how can the upward motion of the *musala*, without depending upon any effort, produce another velocity as explained above?[51] it is said that although the previous velocity is destroyed, yet the *musala* and the mortar contact is capable of producing a forcible (*paṭu*) motion productive of velocity.[52] Here, the upward motion in the hand and the *musala* is successive. It appears simultaneous only because of the swiftness of the two motions.[53] It may also be possible to regard the previous velocity itself so strong that even by the forcible contact it may not be destroyed and there would be then no need of having another velocity. Thus, simultaneously with the

[50] PPBhā, p. 298.
[51] Kandalī, p. 290.
[52] PPBhā, p. 298.
[53] Kandalī, p. 300.

production of the upward motion in the *musala,* by the forcible contact with the help of the velocity, without depending upon effort, another motion is produced, even in the hand with the help of the same velocity, from the *musala* and the hand contact without depending upon an effort.[54] Here is the simultaneity of production in the case of the upward motion.[55]

It is clear from the above that the upward motion is produced both by the presence and the absence of an effort.

3. Conjunction (*Saṃyoga*)—As regards conjunction as the cause of motion we know that it depends upon something else than its own substratum to produce it.[56] This produces motion either through forcible contact or impulsion, the two forms of conjunction. The former produces sound when two things between which conjunction takes place come together; while the latter does not produce any sound at all. Impulsion is a form of conjunction, because, it is the cause of that motion which produces the non-disjunction of the impeller from the impelled; and it is only by means of the conjunction in the form of impulsion (*nodana*) that the impeller impels the impelled.[57]

This impulsion is helped by weight, fluidity, velocity and effort operating either collectively or individually. It produces motion in all the four *mahābhūtas.*[58] As for example, we find that in the case of muddy earth when a small piece of stone is gently put upon mud, it gradually sinks down together with the mud. Here, in this case, the contact of the piece of stone with the mud brought about by the weight of the stone is of

[54] PPBhā, p. 298.
[55] Kandalī, p. 300.
[56] PPBhā, p. 139.
[57] PPBhā, pp. 303-304 along with Kandalī.
[58] Ibid.

the type of impulsion (*nodana*). When again, the piece of stone strikes against the mud with effort from a distance, then also the conjunction between the piece of stone and the mud is of the type of impulsion brought about by weight, effort and velocity. Again, when the mud is struck by water, then the conjunction which is of the type of impulsion is brought about by all together, namely, weight, fluidity, effort and velocity.[59]

The forcible contact (*abhighāta*), in the like manner, is that type of conjunction which is brought about by velocity and which is the cause of motion which causes disjunction.[60] In other words, it is the cause of that motion which causes disjunction between that object which strikes against another object and *vice versa*.[61] This also produces motion in all the four *mahābhūtas*. As for instance, when a stone or similar another object falls upon a hard substance, it produces motion which is due to *abhighāta*; so that, when the muddy earth is either impelled or struck by the feet, the conjunction thus produced is known as *saṃyukta-saṃyoga* depending upon impulsion or forcible contact, individually or collectively. It also produces motion in earth etc. which are neither impelled, nor struck.[62]

4. Fluidity (*dravatva*)—Coming to the fluidity as the cause of motion we find that it is the cause of the motion of flowing.[63] It belongs to earth, water and fire. It is natural in water alone, while it is extrinsic to earth and fire. There should be no doubt about the natural fluidity belonging to water; for, in the case of solidified water, like snow, ice, hailstone, etc., the fluidity belonging to the watery *paramāṇus* constituting these solids is counteracted by the mutual

[59] Kandalī, p. 304.
[60] PPBhā, p. 304.
[61] Kandalī, p. 305.
[62] PPBhā, p. 304.
[63] VS, V. i. 4.

conjunction of the *paramāṇus* of water brought about by non-physical fire (*divyena tejasā*).[64] This we infer from the counteraction of the fluidity of salt by the contact of the non-physical fire. That these solids, like salt etc., are watery substances is known from the fact of their melting on other occasions. The melting of ice, snow, etc. is due to the contact of the earthly (e.g. physical) *tejas*, as it is in the case of gold.[65]

The extrinsic fluidity belonging to earth and *tejas* is produced by the contact of *tejas*. For instance, in the case of butter, lac, honey, and the rest, a motion is produced by the contact of the *tejas* helped by velocity in the *paramāṇus* which constitute them. This motion produces disjunction after destroying the conjunction productive of the substance; so that, the effect being destroyed, fluidity is produced in the *paramāṇus* alone through the help of the conjunction of the *tejas*. Then again, through the instrumentality of the *adṛṣṭa* of persons concerned and the conjunction of the *Ātman* and the *paramāṇus*, a motion is produced in those very *paramāṇus* which brings about the effect through the process of *dvyaṇuka* and the rest. Then fluidity is also produced in the effects along with other qualities.[66]

The downward flowing of water in the form of current from a certain place is also due to fluidity. Sometimes, the fluidity of water and some of its constituents is checked by their contact with barriers, such as, high banks, on all sides; and that of those constituents which are not in direct touch with the banks is checked by the *saṃyukta-saṃyoga*. When that check is even very slightly destroyed, then although the fluidity of water as a whole does not operate, being kept in check from all sides of the bank, yet the fluidity of the constituent parts which are in direct

[64] PPBhā, pp. 264-265.
[65] Kandalī, p. 266.
[66] PPBhā, p. 265.

touch with the bank as well as that of the other parts consequently, begin to operate as there is no check now.[67] As the opening is very small, the fluidity of the constituent parts in direct touch alone first operates and subsequently, that of other parts. But even when they move out one after another, they come out conjoined together. Though while moving, these parts do not appear to have moved from their respective places, yet they do so in such a manner as to remain in contact with one another. But this does not mean that they have their previous contacts undisturbed; for, we find that the collocation has changed.[68] Thus, the previous substance being destroyed on account of the destruction of the previous combinations, the collocated particles produce a substance having a long dimension. In that product the fluidity is also produced. So, when the constituent parts move out in close adherence to one another, a sort of motion is also produced in the whole which is known as *flowing*. In this way, through the fluidity of the constituent parts motion is produced in the whole.[69] The same thing may be said regarding the drops of water falling from the clouds and combining together so as to form one connected elongated substance. The flowing of such a substance is due to fluidity.[70]

5. Impression (*saṃskāra*)—is also a cause of motion. Although it is of three kinds, yet only two, namely, *vega* and *sthitisthāpaka* (elasticity), are required here. The former is produced by motion with the help of impulsion, forcible contact and other causes, in all the five kinds of substances possessing limited forms, namely, earth, water, fire, air, and *Manas*.[71] Motion alone cannot produce velocity, as is

[67] Ibid., pp. 305-306.
[68] Kandalī, p. 307.
[69] PPBhā, p. 306.
[70] VU, V. ii. 4.
[71] Kandalī, p. 267.

clear from the fact that velocity is not found in slow motion where there is neither implusion nor forcible contact.

It is the cause of series of motions in one particular direction. It is counteracted by a particular kind of conjunction of a tangible substance. It is, sometimes, preceded by a similar attribute belonging to the constituent parts of the substance.[72] In other words, generally velocity is produced by motion, but sometimes it is also produced by the velocity itself belonging to the constituent parts of the substance in which it is found; as for instance, the velocity found in water as a whole is due to the velocity found in the cause of water, that is, the constituent parts of water which produce water.[73]

Regarding *sthitisthāpaka* (elasticity) we know that it exists in tangible substances of which the constituent parts are very closely combined together. It brings back the substance—its own substratum—to its original position, if that substance had changed its position otherwise, on some other occasion. We find its effects in bow, branch of a tree, horn, tooth, bone, thread, cloth and the rest, all of which are products of some animate and inanimate objects which are subject to contraction and expansion.[74]

The best example of motion produced by impression (*saṃskāra*) is found in the discharge of an arrow and the movement of a wheel etc. In the case of the discharge of an arrow the process is as follows: The man who is strong and has got regular practice in the art of archery, firmly takes up the bow with his left hand; and then taking the arrow with his right hand and applying it to the string of the bow, holds the string along with the arrow with his fist and desires to

[72] PPBhā, pp. 266-267.
[73] Kandalī, p. 268.
[74] PPBhā, p. 267.

stretch the bow along with the string and the arrow. This is followed by an effort on his part. Through the *Ātman* and the hand contact aided by the effort a motion, in the form of drawing, is produced in the hand; simultaneously with that motion another motion is produced in the arrow as well as in the string of the bow from the hand, string of the bow and arrow contact aided by the very effort; and simultaneously with this, again, through the hand, string of the bow and arrow-contact qualified by the said effort two motions are produced in the two ends of the bow from the contact of the string of the bow and the ends of the bow.[75] In this way, the bow being stretched as far as the ear, there springs up an idea within the man who is stringing the bow that the string cannot be stretched further than this. This idea destroys the effort which had been put forth for stretching the bow. Then there, again, appears a desire to leave the arrow as well as the string. Then follows an effort. Aided by this effort through the contact of the *Ātman* and the fingers, a motion is produced in the fingers which produces disjunction between string of the bow and the finger.[76] From this disjunction is produced the destruction of the conjunction between arrow, string and finger. This being destroyed, there being no obstacle, the *saṃskāra* of the type of elasticity, present in the bow, brings the bow, which had been turned into a circular shape, to its original form. Then aided by this very elasticity through the contact of the bow and the string a motion is produced in the string as well as the arrow. This motion through the instrumentality of its own cause, namely, the contact of the bow and the string, produces velocity in the string. Aided by the velocity, the arrow and the string contact produces impulsion on account of the combined movement of the arrow which

[75] PPBhā, p. 301.
[76] Kandalī, p. 303.

is impelled and the string which is the impeller.[77] From this impulsion there is the first motion in the arrow, which aided by impulsion produces velocity in it (e.g. arrow). From that velocity through the help of that impulsion follow series of motions which continue to appear until the arrow is disconnected with the string. The disjunction thus caused leads to the stoppage of the impulsion. Then there appear series of motions due to the velocity present in the arrow, which continue until the arrow falls down to the ground. This fall of the arrow is due to the exhaustion of the velocity which has counteracted the operation of weight; so that, after the disappearance of the velocity, the weight begins to operate and causes the downfall of the arrow.[78]

A question is raised here: Since the moment the arrow is disconnected with the string and till it falls down to the ground there appears several motions, one after the other; but how does a man come to know of it? Why is not a single motion assumed to accomplish it?[79]

The answer to this is that the existence of several motions is assumed as there are several conjunctions since the arrow is disconnected with the string and till it falls down to the ground. During this interval, namely, between the impulsion and the falling down of the arrow on the ground there is only one *saṃskāra*;[80] and it is only when a motion is aided by impulsion or by forcible contact, that it produces a *saṃskāra*, and never by itself alone; for, there is no velocity. During the interval, on the other hand, there is neither impulsion, nor forcible contact; so that, there is only one *saṃskāra* which is produced by the motion of the arrow aided by the arrow and the string contact; and it is this

[77] Kandalī, p. 303.
[78] PPBhā, p. 302; NBhā, III. ii. 42.
[79] Kandalī, p. 303.
[80] PPBhā, p. 302.

saṃskāra alone which accompanies the arrow till the latter falls down; and as the efficiency of the *saṃskāra* to produce further effects is diminishing, the consequent effects become weaker and weaker.[81]

It is to be noted here that the above view is held mainly by the Vaiçeṣikas. The Naiyāyikas, on the other hand, consider that like the series of motions there are also the series of *saṃskāras*.[82] This view is rejected by the Vaiçeṣikas on the single ground of *gaurava*.[83] Although this view is not found in the Nyāyabhāṣya where only a series of motions is mentioned,[84] yet it is found in the Nyāya-Vārtika.[85] Accepting the Nyāya-view, Dr. B. N. Seal says—"it will be seen that the Nyāya view is adequate to explain acceleration, which it logically implies."[86]

Similarly, in the case of a pot-maker's wheel, we know that the first motion is produced in the wheel as a whole due to the contact of the stick, and the subsequent motions are produced from the motion which is due to either impulsion or forcible contact and also due to *saṃskāra*. Thus, the first motion in the part of the wheel which is in contact with the stick proceeds from velocity through the contact of the stick with other parts of the wheel; the subsequent motions of the part which is in contact with a stick are due to *saṃskāra* and impulsion; while motions of other parts are due to *saṃskāra* and *saṃyukta-saṃyoga*; and when the stick is removed, the motion found in the wheel as well as in its parts is due to *saṃskāra* alone.[87]

6. *Adṛṣṭa*. Lastly, we come to *adṛṣṭa* which is also one of the causes of motion. But what is

[81] Kandalī, p. 303.
[82] VU., v. i. 17.
[83] Ibid.
[84] NS, III. ii. 42.
[85] PSAH, p. 137.
[86] Ibid.
[87] Kandalī, p. 307.

adṛṣṭa itself? Literally, it means that which is not seen. That is, it is an unseen force which is mainly due to the deeds performed by a man. These deeds may be due to merit, or demerit, or both. It is even identified with *dharma* and *adharma*. However, such motions which cannot be explained through ordinary causes mentioned above are attributed to this *adṛṣṭa*. Hence, we find that the causality of *adṛṣṭa* is assumed in producing motion in the following cases:

(*a*) The motion found in jewels, needle etc.[88] Thus, when anything is stolen away and the thief is not caught, the man, learned in the art of catching thief, performs some rites in a vessel or a pot, made of some jewel or metal, filled with water. The vessel then is placed on the ground and some one is asked to hold the top of the vessel firmly with his right hand. The artist then repeats some *mantras*, through the force of which the vessel held by the third person, moves towards the direction in which the stolen property is kept. When the vessel reaches the exact place where the property is lying, it stops. Now, in this case, the motion of the vessel is not due to any effort. It is assumed to be either due to the good luck of the real master of the property or the misfortune of the thief. Here, the vessel is the material cause of the motion, the contact of the vessel with the *Ātman* of the thief having *adṛṣṭa* as the non-material cause, and the demerit of the thief as the instrumental cause.[89]

Similarly, the case of the motion of the needle or any piece of iron towards the magnet is also attributed to *adṛṣṭa*. Again, the motion found in grass while moving towards the grass-magnet (*tṛṇakānta*) is also attributed to *adṛṣṭa*. In these cases, needle and grass are the material causes, the conjunction with the *Ātman* of the person possessing *adṛṣṭa* and is affected

[88] VS., v. i. 15; PPBhā, p. 309; Kandalī, p. 311.
[89] VU. and VV., V. i. 15.

for good or for bad by that motion of the needle, the grass etc. are the non-material causes, and his very *adṛṣṭa* is the instrumental cause.[90]

(*b*) Earthquake etc., which are neither caused by impulsion, nor by forcible striking, are said to be caused by *adṛṣṭa*.[91] So, it is said that if a motion in earth alone be of some particular consequence as in the case of earthquake, then it is caused by *adṛṣṭa*; so that, the earth is the material cause, the conjunction of the *Ātman* possessing *adṛṣṭa* of a person whose pleasure or pain is produced by the earthquake is the non-material cause, while *adṛṣṭa* is the instrumental cause. This is true of all the motions found under the earth and which are not due to impulsion and forcible contact.[92]

(*c*) Again, the motion of water within the trees is also attributed to *adṛṣṭa*.[93] Thus, when water is poured into the basin round a tree and it moves into the tree through the roots, the motion is not caused by impulsion, or by forcible contact, or by the sun's rays. Hence, it is attributed to *adṛṣṭa* alone. Here also, water is the material cause, the conjunction of the *Ātman*, possessing *adṛṣṭa* of persons who are to get pleasure or pain from the growth of the leaves, branches, flowers etc., of the tree, is the non-material cause, while *adṛṣṭa* itself is the instrumental cause. This motion of water causes the growth of the tree.[94]

(*d*) Other cases where *adṛṣṭa* is the cause of motion are found in the first upward flaming of fire, the first oblique or transversal movement of air, the first motion imparted to the *paramāṇus* after the Cosmic Rest and the first motion imparted to the *Manas*.[95]

[90] VU. and VV., v. i.15.

[91] VS., V. ii. 2.

[92] VU, on ibid.; Candrakānta explains *adṛṣṭaiḥ* as *ābhyantar-airvastubhiççaladbhiḥ*.

[93] VS, V. ii. 7.

[94] VU, V. ii. 7.

[95] VS, V. ii. 13.

(*c*) Again, we find that *adṛṣṭa* is the cause of the two well-known motions of the *Manas*, namely, *apasarpaṇa* and *upasarpaṇa*. Conjunctions of what is eaten and drunk and conjunctions of other effects are also attributed to this *adṛṣṭa*.[96]

The *apasarpaṇa* and the *upasarpaṇa* are produced by the *Ātman* and the *Manas* contact helped by *adṛṣṭa*. The process is as follows: When the merit and the demerit, helping the existence of the body in the living state, become exhausted and do not produce any more effect due to the experience (*bhoga*) or to their mutual predominance, or to their mutual counteraction, the effort proceeding from the living also having ceased to exist; the functioning of the vital-airs having also stopped, the present body falls down as dead. Then, again, another set of merits and demerits through which the particular *Jivātaman* is to experience pleasure and pain in the next body, comes to function. In other words, the particular set of merits and demerits meant for the experience of pleasure and pain in another body, being checked to function in this body by the set of merits and demerits meant for the experience of pleasure and pain in this very body, finding the present body dead and the set of its merits and demerits exhausted, becomes operative; for, there is nothing to counteract its force now. Then, this fresh set of merits and demerits, aided by the *Ātman* and the *Manas* contact, produces a motion called *apasarpaṇa* which causes the disjunction between the dead body and the *Manas*. Here, the *Ātman* and the *Manas* contact is the non-material cause, the *Manas* is the material cause and the fresh set of merits and demerits which is now operative is the instrumental cause.

Then, this *Manas*, which has left the dead body and has come out, becomes connected with another subtler body called *ātivāhikaçarīra* which has been formed

[96] VS, V. ii. 17.

by the non-operating fresh set of merits and demerits.

The *Manas* thus connected with the subtler body goes either to heaven or to hell. After going there the *Manas* leaves this *ātivāhika* body and enters into another body which is formed in accordance with the past deeds of the person whose *Manas* is moving. This body is meant for the experience of pleasure and pain according to the past deeds either in heaven or in hell. To come in contact with this body the *Manas* must have a motion. Such a motion is known as *apasarpaṇa*.

As to the necessity of having an organism, however subtle it may be, it is said that while moving from place to place *Manas* must have an organism; for, there can be no motion in the *Manas* which is not in any organism, except during the state that immediately follows the Universal Destruction (*mahāpralaya*); so that, it is necessary to assume the existence of an organism, which remains quite close to the dead body. It is produced out of *paramāṇus* and *dvyaṇukas* etc. moved by the *adṛṣṭa*. This body is very subtle and supersensuous. As it leads the *Manas* to heaven and hell, it is known as the *ātivāhikaçarīra*.[97]

The motion of the *Manas*, to enter the fresh body produced either in heaven or in hell for the experience of pleasure and pain, is known as *upasarpaṇa*.[98]

Similarly, the motion found in the *Manas* on other occasions is also due to *adṛṣṭa*. Thus, the motion of the *Manas* of the *yogins* with the help of which the *Manas* goes out of the body to its destination and comes back to its own organism and so on, is due to *adṛṣṭa* alone.[99]

As regards the motion due to *adṛṣṭa*, it should be pointed out that the systems of Nyāya and Vaiçeṣika, following very closely the common-sense view, have

[97] Kandalī, p. 310.

[98] Ibid., p. 311.

[99] PPBhā, p. 309 along with Kandalī, p. 311.

to confine themselves within certain limitations. Hence, sometimes, even in such cases, where one can easily, with a little insight, find out some definite cause of the motion, as for instance, in earthquake etc., these systems pretend to remain ignorant of the reality and attribute the causality to some unseen force (*adṛṣṭa*).

Besides these, there are certain other kinds of motions which are attributed to one of these causes. Thus, for instance, the cloud in the sky is a collection of water-drops moved towards the sky through the rays of the sun helped by the contact of air.[100]

Now, these causes sometimes operate separately, independent of any other cause and sometimes, they join together to produce one joint effect.

[100] VS, V. ii. 5-6 along with VU.

CHAPTER VI

MATTER AND CAUSALITY

I

INTRODUCTION

NYĀYA and Vaiçeṣika systems being realistic in nature take the things of the universe as they appear to us in reality. In the universe, at every moment, we find that certain things are produced, while others are destroyed; so that, production and destruction are constantly going on. Not only the constituents of the universe are affected by the Law of Change but also the universe itself.

Now, a question is raised: How does this production, or the destruction take place? In other words, whether production, or destruction is brought about by chance, or through some agency? This is a question which every school of thought had to face since the very dawn of reasoning in India. This very question in a different form is found in the Upaniṣads. Thus, the Çvetāçvatara Upaniṣad notes several views advanced at that time in answer to the question: What is the cause of the origin of the universe, its existence and its destruction (*pralaya*)? Those views are summarised in the following çruti:—

Kālaḥ svabhāvo niyatiryadṛcchā
bhūtāni yoniḥ puruṣa iti cintyā;
Saṃyoga eṣāṃ na tvātmabhāvā-
dātmāpyanīçaḥ sukhaduḥkhahetoḥ[1].

Here, we have got *Kāla*, *Svabhāva*, *Niyati*, *Yadṛcchā*,

[1] Çu, I. 2.

Bhūtas, *Puruṣa*, and *Jīvātman* representing the several views advanced in explaining the origin of the empirical world. These are, undoubtedly, very old views. Even coming to the Nyāya-Sūtras,[2] we find some more views enumerated there. Thus, it is said there that some are of opinion that both the universal and the individual productions are from *abhāva*—void[3]. This naturally refers to the Çūnyavādin school of the Buddhists. Again, further it is said that some hold that *Içvara* is the cause of the universe[4]. This is the same as is in the Çvetāçvatara Upaniṣad given above and in the Mahābhārata[5] of which a reference is made by Vācaspati Miçra I in his Tātparyaṭīkā[6]. This view appears to have a wider circulation. It finds its place in the Mahābodhijātaka[7] and also in the Buddhacarita of Açvaghoṣa.[8] In these Buddhist works this view is referred to as held by '*others*'; so that, we should not mistake it for the Buddhist view. Then, again, Gautama refers to the view of some who hold that positive things are produced without any cause (*animittataḥ*[9]). This *nirnimittavāda* is most likely the *svabhāvavāda* of the Çvetāçvatara referred to above. This is also found mentioned in the Suçruta,[10] the Buddhacarita of Açvaghoṣa[11] and also in the Gommaṭasāra of Ācārya Nemicandra.[12] Gautama mentions some other views. Thus, he says that some hold that everything of the universe is non-eternal; for, everything is

[2] IV. i. 14-43.
[3] NS., IV. i. 14.
[4] NS., IV. i. 19.
[5] Vana-Parva, xxx, 28.
[6] pp. 604-605.
[7] *Issaro savvalokassa sace kappeti jīvitaṃ* etc.,—Jātak, Vol. V.
[8] IX. 53.
[9] NS., IV. i. 22.
[10] Çārīrasthāna, I. 11.
[11] IX. 52.
[12] Verse 883.

produced and destroyed. That is, nothing exists before the production and also after the destruction. Hence, everything is non-eternal.[13] Similarly, there is another view that everything is eternal; for, the five *bhūtas*, which constitute the objective world are eternal.[14] Hence, there is no need of any cause or effect. In this way, we find that there have been several views about the origin of the world and which can very well apply to all cases of individual productions.

Of these, some do accept some sort of causality, while others reject it entirely. Almost all the views which reject the principle of causality are very closely related. There appears to be a kind of gradation between some of these views. Thus, Çaṅkarānanda says[15] that the upholders of the *Kālavāda* think that there is a great *gaurava* in holding *paramāṇu* to be the ultimate cause; hence, *Kāla* is accepted to be the required cause. By *Kāla* Çaṅkarācārya understands the cause of the change of every *bhūta*.[16] Some take it in the sense of *Içvara*.[17] Again, as *Kāla* cannot do anything without the immanent nature of a thing; it is replaced by *Svabhāvavāda*. The latter, again, is of no use without the *niyati*. By *niyati* Çaṅkara means *karman* of the type of merit and demerit (*aviṣamapuṇyapāpalakṣaṇaṃ karma*). Ḍalhaṇa in his commentary on the Suçruta identifies it with merit and demerit themselves (*pūrvajanmārjitau dharmādharmau niyatiḥ*). It is to be noted down here that *niyati* used in the sense of *adṛṣṭa* is not objected to by the orthodox schools; hence, it appears that here it has been used in the sense of mere *chance* in some form or other, and therefore, it is objectionable. *Yadṛcchā* is used in the sense of mere coincidence (*ākasmikaprāptiḥ*).

[13] NS., IV. i. 25.
[14] Ibid., IV. i. 29.
[15] Çvetāçvataropaniṣaddīpikā, I. 1.
[16] *Sarvabhūtānāṃ vipariṇāmahetuḥ*—ÇBhā. on Çvetā. I. 1.
[17] Ḍalhaṇa's Comm. on Suçruta.

In later times, these various views have come to represent in some form or other the view point of the Cārvākas regarding the theory of causality. But it should not be forgotten that none of these accepts the Law of Causality, as it is understood by the orthodox schools.

It is clear from the above that the problem of Causality is very important in Indian thought. Since every school of thought had to face it in its own way, it became very controversial. The difference does not exist between the orthodox and the heterodox schools alone, but even amongst the orthodox schools themselves there is hardly any agreement on this point.

The following are the points on which the controversy is based: What is the relation between the cause and the effect? Is the effect absolutely identical with the cause, or is different from it? Is the effect produced out of something which is real and eternal, or is created from the void? What is the process of production of the effect? Is it merely the manifestation of that which existed before, or is a real and fresh production? All these questions are independently upheld mainly by the four most important schools of thought, namely, Nyāya-Vaiçeṣika, Sāṅkhya, Vedānta and Buddhist of the Mādhyamika school. The view point of each of these schools is represented distinctly by the well-known theories of Indian philosophy, namely, *Ārambhavāda*, *Pariṇāmavāda*, *Vivartavāda* and *Çūnyavāda* respectively. Of these, the *Pariṇāmavāda* represents the view point of Sāṅkhya; the *Vivartavāda* stands for the Çaṅkara-Vedānta; the view point of the Buddhist is found under the *Çūnyavāda*, while the joint-system of Nyāya and Vaiçeṣika is represented by the *Ārambhavāda*. These four theories although associated with the above mentioned four schools, yet represent almost all the schools of Indian thought in some form or other. It is certain that all these theories assume the principle of causality.

1. Thus, according to the *Pariṇāmavāda* there is

the primordial cause called *Mūlā-Prakṛti*. This constitute the equilibrium of the three *guṇas—Sattva*, *Rajas* and *Tamas*. The peculiar nature of *Rajas* makes the *Prakṛti* ever-changing.[18] Hence, *Prakṛti* is self-moved (*svataḥpariṇāminī*). Motion in the form of *Rajas* is inherent in it by nature and does not come to it from without.

By *pariṇāma* we mean disappearance of one *dharma* followed by the appearance of another *dharma* in the same *dharmin*.[19] Although, in reality, there is only one kind of *pariṇāma*, yet due to the distinction between *dharma* and *dharmin* there appear to be three kinds of *pariṇāmas*, namely, *dharma*, *lakṣaṇa* and *avasthā*. The meaning of *pariṇāma* given above is the definition of *dharma-pariṇāma*. The *lakṣaṇapariṇāma* is the name of the change of *lakṣaṇa*, meaning, time. That is to say, the change, from future to present and thence to past, is due to the *lakṣaṇapariṇāma*. In this case, the change is with reference to the *dharma*. As for instance, all the *dharmas* of the type of cow, horse, jar, cloth etc., are mutations of the *dharmin* in the form of *pṛthvī* etc. This is the example of the *dharmapariṇāma*. Again, when the change of the very *dharma* takes place in regard to time, that is, from future to present and thence to past, it is called *lakṣaṇapariṇāma*. Again, when, with reference to the *dharmas* which have come to exist in the present time, say the existing cow, for instance, we speak of their states (*avasthās*), such as, *bālya*, *kaumāra*, *yauvana*, *bārdhakya*, or old and new states of a jar etc., it refers to the *avasthāpariṇāma*. In this way, constantly the *guṇas* are changing[20].

According to this theory, there is a primordial cause which unfolds itself and manifests effects. This school

[18] SK., verse 13.

[19] *Avasthitasya dravyasya pūrvadharmanivṛttau dharmāntarotpattiḥ pariṇāmaḥ*—YBhā., III. 13.

[20] TV., on YBhā., III. 13, p. 204.

of thought believes in the *Satkāryavāda*, according to which the entire universe exists in the *Prakṛti* as its aspect, even before the causal operation. The true relation between the cause and the effect, according to this school, is that the effect is a *dharma*, an aspect of the cause, and constitutes a mode (*vikāra*) of it. In other words, the various effects known as *vikṛtis* are the various modifications of the primary *Prakṛti* itself. In fact, the relation is that of absolute identity in difference (*bhedasahiṣṇu atyantābheda*) as opposed to the absolute difference in identity (*abhedasahiṣṇu atyanta-bheda*) of Nyāya and Vaiçeṣika. Hence, the difference between the two effects is that of collocation alone. The *Prakṛti* is the Unmanifest, while the effects are the manifestations of the same Unmanifest. There is no fresh production, in fact, under this head. Everything exists in the cause potentially. But we should not forget that the effects are as much real as the cause itself.

2. The theory of *Vivarta* is associated with the school of Çaṅkara Vedānta. As has been said before, Vedānta in its empirical aspect is also a realistic school, and as such, cannot neglect to give an account of the phenomena of the world. That there is a constant change going on in the phenomenal world cannot be denied. And it is one of the important functions of this school also to give some account of the endless series of events and effects. No doubt, the theories of *Pariṇāma* or *Ārambha* cannot help the Empirical school of Vedānta to explain the nature of the principle of causality as applied to the external world. Even allowing a sort of reality to the external world according to Çaṅkara-Vedānta, it is not of the same type as we have with Nyāya-Vaiçeṣika, or Sāṅkhya. There is a vast difference between the notion of reality of this empirical school and that of all other schools; so that, it is quite evident that the nature of the Law of Causality will also be of a different type. In Nyāya-Vaiçeṣika, the

cause is a permanent, unchanging entity in the form of *paramāṇus* but not self-sufficient, while the effect is real, although it is destructible. According to Sāṅkhya, the cause is the Unmanifest *Prakṛti,* which is permanent and eternal[21], while the effects are merely the manifestations of *Prakṛti*, and as such, are as much real as the cause itself. According to the empirical school of Vedānta, at least, the nature of the effects is entirely different. About the nature of the cause we shall soon see what it is. At present we can only say that it is not as it is with the other schools. There is only one reality, namely, *Brahman*, and the entire universe, which is merely an imposition upon that unchanging reality, is really a false appearance, unreal (*anirvacanīya*), and hence, illusory. Just as, water is the only permanent entity, while waves, bubbles, ripples etc., are merely so many appearances having no reality of their own. Similarly, the Çruti says that the only truth is clay, while all the modifications are but illusory forms and names imposed upon that single truth through speech only. (*Vācārambhaṇaṃ vikāro nāmadheyaṃ mṛttiketyeva satyaṃ etc.*). This is known as the theory of *vivarta*.

As regards the nature of cause itself, there are different views even in the Çaṅkara school. Thus, says Appaya Dīkṣita, in his Siddhānta leça[22], that according to the followers of the author of the Saṅkṣepa-Çārīraka, the pure *Brahman* is the cause of the world. This is clear from the meaning of the Vedānta Sūtra[23] '*Yanmāpyasya yataḥ*' which means that the *Brahman* is that from which as a form of cause, the production etc., of the

[21] I am not quite sure whether *Prakṛti*, although *pariṇāminī* by its very nature, is self-sufficient in manifesting its effects. Is it possible that *Prakṛti* would continue to manifest effects, even if *Puruṣa*—the consciousness—be removed? If not, should we not say that it is also not self-sufficient like the *paramāṇus* of Nyāya-Vaiçeṣika?

[22] Pp. 57-78.

[23] I. i. 2.

world take place[24]. Hence, it is said that *Ākāça* comes out of *Brahman*[25], where the pure *Brahman* is meant as the cause (*upādāna*). Again, the followers of the Vivaraṇa think that *Brahman* in the form of *Içvara*, under the influence of *Māyā*, is the cause of the universe. Hence, they say that under the Sūtras[26] '*Antastaddharmopadeçāt*,' '*Sarvatra prasiddhopadeçāt*' etc., *Brahman*, as *Içvara*, is described. Others again, hold, they say, that the world is the *pariṇāma* of *Māyā* which belongs to *Içvara*, while *Içvara* himself is the *upādāna-kāraṇa* (efficient cause). This is said of the external world. While as regards the *antaḥkaraṇa* etc., of the individual beings, it is said that the causality belongs to both the *Içvarāçritamāyā* and the *Jīvāçritāvidyā*. In other words, in the case of the *antaḥkaraṇa* etc., the *Jīva* associated with the *Avidyā* is the *upādāna*. This view undoubtedly takes *Māyā* as different from *Avidyā*. Some, again, hold that *Jīva* alone is the *upādāna-kāraṇa*. There is also a view that *Māyā* alone is the cause of the universe. Again, the author of the Padārthatattvanirṇaya thinks that both the *Brahman* and the *Māyā* or the *Avidyā* are together the cause of the universe; *Brahman* as the cause through the *vivartamānatā*, while *Avidyā* through the *pariṇamamānatā*. Vācaspati Miçra I is of opinion that *Brahman* is the *upādāna-kāraṇa* influenced by *Māyā* associated with *Jīva*. *Māyā* is only the *sahakāri* (auxiliary). Prakāçānanda is, however, of opinion that *Māyā* alone is the *upādāna-kāraṇa* of this phenomenal world[27]. These are some of the views about the origin of this phenomenal world according to the followers of the Empirical school of Çaṅkara-Vedānta. Apart from these differences in the view point, it is clear that there is no difference between

[24] *Yataḥ kāraṇādasya jagato janmādi, tat Brahma.*
[25] *Ātmana ākāçassambhūtaḥ*, etc.
[26] BS., I. i. 20; I. ii. I.
[27] VSM., p. 38. For further details on the subject vide VPS., pp. 204-209; 224-225.

Brahman and the universe which may be said to be the so-called effect, though illusory in nature, of *Brahman*, pure or impure.

3. Now, coming to the *Çūnyavāda*, we find that it is associated with the Mādhyamika school of the Buddhist thought. It not only denies the external reality of the world but also dispenses with the necessity of recognising the existence of ideas (*vijñāna*). All traces of phenomenal experience, both objective and subjective, are effaced, and what is left behind is the Serene Depth of an Infinite Void. It is called *Çūnya* in the sense that it is eternally free from everything with which our subjective or objective consciousness is acquainted. It is above the world, beyond the world, and even permeating the world, though not defiled by it, as its abiding background. It is neither positive, nor even negative (as the word might seem to apply); nor both simultaneously, nor other than both; so that, it is undefinable and in a sense has no 'character' (*lakṣaṇa*). This school of thought explains the whole paraphernalia of cosmic experience from the stand-point of this *Çūnya* with the aid of *Avidyā*.

4. The *Ārambhavāda* is the theory which is advocated by Nyāya and Vaiçeṣika. According to this joint-system, which stands for common sense, there is an absolute difference between a cause and its effect, although both are bound together by a mysterious tie of relationship; so that, as long as the effect exists, it inheres in its cause and even when it does not exist, that is, before its production and after its destruction, its non-existence in both the cases, technically called, *prāgabhāva* and *dhvaṃça*, also is attributed to the same cause. Why is it so, is not known even to the Naiyāyikas and the Vaiçeṣikas themselves. They would, naturally, say that it is in the very nature of the cause and the effect to be so related. This difficulty is perhaps due to their not believing in the *Satkāryavāda* and

labouring under limitations.

According to them, the *paramāṇus* of the four *mahābhūtas* are eternal. It is out of these *paramāṇus* alone, as the material cause, that the individual products and consequently, the entire universe are produced. Hence, these are recognised as the ultimate material cause of the external sensible world.

As the effects are quite fresh and distinct from their cause and as they are produced after a particular kind of *Ārambhaka-saṃyoga*, the view-point is known as the *Ārambhakavāda*.

This theory of Origination gives us an opportunity to discuss the problem of causality. We have seen above that this school of thought believes in the existence of eternal *paramāṇus*, which combine together and produce effects. It may be asked here: how do these *paramāṇus* combine? This combination is not by chance but is due to some efficient cause. During the state of *pralaya*, or otherwise, these *paramāṇus* first remain without any productive motion. Then, as soon as the cumulative *adṛṣṭa* of the *Jīvas* matures for fructification, the Will of God, which is eternal, becomes as it were creative, and immediately, productive motion is produced in the *paramāṇus* which group themselves round the *Manas* and form organisms, one for each *Jīva*. The initiation of motion in the *Manas* and the *paramāṇus* is attributed to *adṛṣṭa* quickened by the Divine Will. In this way, all other effects of this world and consequently, the world itself are produced. All this is due to the Law of Causality. Thus, from the very beginning of the universe there is the necessity of this Law. It is, in fact, at the very root of the theory of Origination. No event can be properly explained without the Law of causation.

II

CONSERVATION OF MATTER AND WEIGHT

It is clear from the above that the whole process of the theory of Causality is nothing but a process of change. Now, it may be asked here: while undergoing change from cause to effect, and *vice versa*, is any part of the changing object lost? It has been made clear above that there is one permanent ultimate element in the form of *paramāṇu* which never changes, although in certain case, their qualities change according to the Vaiçeṣikas. The products of these *paramāṇus* change; so that, in the course of this change, the *paramāṇus*, as such, remain without undergoing any change. Not only this, but even the number of the *paramāṇus* constituting the cause also remains the same. In fact, it is due to this, that we can say that in this world 'nothing is created and nothing is destroyed.' Although the effect is entirely different from the cause and is not merely the grouping of the constituent parts, yet essentially, there is neither any addition to, nor any deduction from the number of *paramāṇus* constituting the effects. Hence, if a certain product be reduced to its constituent *paramāṇus*, we shall find exactly the same number of *paramāṇus* out of which that product had formed. That is to say, the ultimate matter, as such, remains the same throughout the entire process of change. This is what is known as the *Conservation of matter*. This also explains that the *Conservation of weight* is also possible according to Nyāya-Vaiçeṣika[28]. That is to say, the weight of the constituent parts is equal to the weight of the effect produced out of those constituent parts.

[28] We find that Uddyotakara and some others hold that the weight of the effect (*avayavin*) increases from that of the cause—NV., p. 236. But this seems to be a partial view, as has been made clear before.

III

CAUSE DEFINED

Having thus established the necessity of the Law of Causality, it may be asked: what should we exactly understand by the term cause? Cause has been defined as that which invariably precedes an effect and is not connected with it too remotely. In order to be a cause it must precede an effect. But all the antecedents do not necessarily represent the cause. For instance, the potmaker's ass or bullock that brings the clay out of which the potmaker makes the pot, precedes the effect, but it is not a cause of the pot, as neither of these is an invariable antecedent of the effect; for, even if the clay be brought on a cart it can produce the pot. Hence, the attribute *invariable* is essential. Again, all that precedes an effect invariably should not necessarily be the cause; for instance, the potmaker's father, the colour of the stick, the generality known as *daṇḍatva* all these although precede the effect in the form of a pot invariably, yet none of these is recognised as a cause of the pot. The reason is that all these are too remotely connected with the effect. The pot can be produced even without these. Hence, they are not the cause.

IV

ANYATHĀSIDDHA

It may be now asked: What is the meaning of 'connected too remotely'? Under what conditions an antecedent is said to be connected too remotely? The invariable antecedents which are not at all necessary for the production of the effect but are invariably connected with the effect too remotely are known as *anyathāsiddhas*. There are several varieties of it. Gaṅgeça Upādhyāya mentions three varieties:

1. Things that are connected with the cause

through inherence are, therefore, antecedents to the effect through it; as for instance, the colour of the thread and the generality *tantutva* which being inherent in the thread, are invariable antecedents to the effect—cloth, but are not causes of the cloth.

2. Things that are antecedents to a cause and are therefore, antecedents to the effect, such as, the father of the potmaker, who is an antecedent to the potmaker and consequently, to the pot itself; or, as *Ākāça* which is an antecedent to a pot, because it is a cause of the word *ghaṭa* which always precedes the object *ghaṭa*; but these are not the causes; for, even without these the pot can be produced.

3. Lastly, all other concomitants of a cause that are not connected with it through inherence, such as, the *prāgabhāva* of the colour which is not the cause of smell, although it is concomitant of several earthly things.

These are only *anyathāsiddhas* and not the causes. Later writers mention five such varieties. Thus, according to Viçvanātha an *anyathāsiddha*[29] is—

1. That due to which the antecedence of the cause takes place. As for instance, it is due to the generality called *daṇḍatva* that the antecedence of the stick, which is the cause of the pot, takes place; hence, *daṇḍatva* is one of the *anyathāsiddhas*.

2. That which precedes the effect not independently but through the cause itself. As for instance, the colour of the stick. The colour alone does not precede the effect, namely, pot, independently, but it does so only through the stick which is the cause of the pot. The stick must have some colour or other.

3. That which is known to be an antecedent to an effect only because it chanced to be an antecedent to something else; as for instance, *Ākāça* in relation to a pot; because, the object pot is preceded by the word (sound) pot, which is preceded by *Ākāça* as the material

[29] BhāP., verses 19-22.

cause of sound; so that, *Ākāça* is known to precede the object, pot, only because, it precedes the sound pot.

4. That which is an antecedent to an effect, only because, it is an antecedent to the cause of that effect; as for instance, the father of the potmaker, who is an antecedent to the pot, only because, he is an antecedent to the cause of the pot, namely, the potmaker.

5. Lastly, that which is other than that which alone is capable of producing the effect. As for instance, the ass who brings the clay for making the pot.

The last variety alone can include all other varieties under it; hence, this variety has been recognised as the most important of all the other four varieties mentioned above.

V

LAW OF CAUSALITY AND THE CĀRVĀKAS

It has been already said above that the Cārvākas do not believe in the Law of causality. This is quite evident from the fact that they do not believe in any means of right cognition except *pratyakṣa*. And causality cannot be proved through *pratyakṣa;* for, even when the *dharmin*, as such, is perceived doubt may remain as to its causal character. The Cārvāka continues that the argument, 'that through the absence of the auxiliary of the cognition based on the method of agreement and difference the causal relation is established,' is not acceptable; for, the very argument is applicable to the *vyabhicārī*, that is, to disprove the causality. Not being connected too remotely and being an invariable antecedent to the effect are also full of doubts, and as such, cannot ascertain the causality. As for inference, it is said that the Cārvākas have no faith in its validity as a means of right cognition. They further add that sometimes *asiddhi* is found in the course of proving the causality; and the *anvayin* being unknown cannot remain there; so that, difference (*vyatireka*) also cannot be ascertained. And consequently, there is no possibility for the *kevalavyatirekin*. To the Cārvākas, who believe in the *asatkhyāti* (non-existence) of an object, not rightly cognised, there is no difficulty on the ground that the object of denial is 'unknown.[30]

Vardhamāna Upādhyāya says that the cognitions expressed in the forms that—'this takes place after this,' 'in the absence of this,' 'this does not take place,' etc., show that the theory of causality is proved through the direct perception itself[31]. He, continuing further, says that the first alternative is not good; as its object is imaginary. In other words, if the Cārvākas do not believe in the theory of causality, how is it that they use the words which are meant to result in the genesis of conviction in others (*parapratipattiphalakavacana*)? A Cārvāka is sure to commit contradictions; for, the more he attempts to reject causality, the more is he put into troubles[32].

It may be further urged: if the effect does not depend upon anything, that is, if causality be denied, then there is the possibility of the production or creation being perpetual. If production were denied, then there would be no production even afterwards; for, there is no difference between the two states. The alternative *svasmāt* (from itself) is untenable; for, the effect before its production is itself non-existent, and therefore, incapable of production itself. The relation of cause and effect is one of invariableness in priority and posteriority. One single object cannot be both an antecedent and a consequent; for, this (sequence) is possible only where there is difference[33]. It is impossible to think of identity between the cause and the effect;

[30] KPP., p. 33; PWSS., Vol. II. p. 182.
[31] KPP., p. 34.
[32] Ibid.
[33] KP., pp. 42-43.

for, the view that one who is desirous of having a cloth not only takes cloth but also the threads which existed before the production of the cloth along with it, is quite contradictory to the usage of the world.[34]

If unreal (*anupākhya*) be believed to be the cause of production, then even before the production, the effect should have existed which would have made the production perpetual.[35]

It may be, however, urged that the term *akasmāt*, in the expression '*akasmādeva bhavati*', is not meant merely to deny the cause or production, nor does it mean the affirmation of the effect being its own cause, or being caused by something unreal, but shows that the product is by nature associated with a fixed *Kāla*, just as, it is naturally associated with a fixed *Deça*.

The Naiyāyikas reject the above view; because, they hold that the denial of a limit in time, or of fixedness of limit in time, both would be subversive of *kādācitkatva* which does not consist merely in the existence at a succeeding moment but in such existence which is accompanied by prior-non-existence. In case the limit in time is admitted, this upper or prior limit itself becomes the cause.[36]

To this the Cārvākas say—let prior-non-existence (*prāgabhāva*) itself be the limit sought. But the Naiyāyikas do not accept this; for, other positive things also exist along with the prior-non-existence. If they, hold the Naiyāyikas, do not exist, it would not be possible to know the non-existence itself. Hence, the effect does not possess the prior-non-existence alone as its limit, because of there being no difference between this and the *prākkālaniyatatva*.[37] If the prior-non-existence,

[34] KPP., on Ibid., p. 43.

[35] KP., p. 43.

[36] Ibid., pp. 44-45; Pandit Gopinātha Kavirāja's English translation—PWSS., Vol. II, pp. 183-84.

[37] Bodhanī, p. 9.

independent of anything else be the limit, then in that case, the effect, as being due to that limit, would exist even before.[38]

Again, the Cārvākas hold—let there be any number of limits, but they are not required here. This non-requirement explains the meaning of the term *svabhāva*. To this the Naiyāyikas reply: what is the meaning of the expression 'they are not required'? Does it mean that the limits are not invariable (*niyata*)? Or that though they are invariable, yet they are not helpful? That is, the stick etc., although invariably precede the pot, yet they are not at all helpful in producing it.[39] In the first case, there being no determinant (*niyāmaka*), smoke could have an ass also as its limit, just as it has fire as its limit. In the second case, what is the use of another helper, because the meaning of dependence (*apekṣā*) is nothing but invariable character and this is of the nature of cause? It should be, however, known that the theory of *svabhāva*, when used in this sense, is accepted by the Naiyāyikas.

Again, the Cārvākas hold that this theory of *svabhāva* is like the restriction of the *svabhāva* of the eternal things, like *çabdāçrayatva* for the *Ākāça*, *Ātmatva* for the *Ātman* etc. It is not proper to say, why should not the nature of everything be accidental, just as the nature of *Ākāça*, namely, *Ākāçatva* is accidental? To this, again, the Naiyāyikas reply that the above view is untenable; for, the word *svabhāva* would lose its significance, if it were common to all. One thing cannot possess several *svabhāvas*, because, this would then lead to contradictions.

Again, the Cārvākas reply that in the same way, in the present case also, there would be contradiction by

[38] KP., p. 46; Çaṅkara Miçra, however, explains this saying that if the prior-non-existence alone be the limit, then the effect will depend upon it alone for its production; so that, the *kādācitkatva* which is being felt would be subverted—Āmoda, Ms. Fol. 6*a*.

[39] Ibid., Fol. 7*a*.

admitting *kādācitkatva* as the *svabhāva* of a thing which is eternal; so that, the solution is the same. To this the Naiyāyikas rejoin that the solution is not the same; for, there would be self-contradiction if the effect were accepted to be without any fixed or unfixed limit. If a fixed limit is assumed, then really the doctrine of causality is accepted.[40] In this way, the Naiyāyikas reject the theory of *svabhāva* as advocated by the Cārvākas.

But it is found that this doctrine in a certain sense has to be admitted by all thinkers at some stage. It is well-known that a product, as for instance, jar, inheres in its material cause, namely, clay, according to the Naiyāyikas. But, it may be asked why does not the jar, for instance, inhere in the threads? In plain language, why is the effect produced from one kind of cause rather than from another? What is the inner meaning of *upādāna-niyama* which is a fact of general experience? The Naiyāyika's analysis, acute as it is, fails to provide the right solution to this question. Another example may be taken by way of illustration. In Nyāya-Vaiçeṣika, universals (*sāmānya*) are declared to be eternal and omnipresent. But how is it that they are not manifested always and everywhere? Of course, there are certain conditions which determine and limit this manifestation. A universal, for example, in so far as it inheres in a composite, is revealed by the peculiar collocation of the parts (*ākṛti*) constituting that composite. In other words, as Nyāya-sūtra expressly states, the relation between a particular universal and a particular collocation is one of *vyaṅgya-vyañjakabhāva*. Now, the question arises: what determines this *vyaṅgya-vyañjakabhāva*? To be plain, how is one universal manifested through one collocation and not through another? Why does not *kambugrīvādimatva* reveal *gotva* instead of *ghaṭatva*? What is the root of the corres-

[40] KP., pp. 42-51.

pondence between a *jāti* and an *ākṛti*? The Naiyāyikas cannot furnish an adequate rational answer to these questions. The only answer, if answer it could be called, is to fall back upon the nature of the thing about which no further question is permissible. So says the author of Kandalī[41]—that this is the nature of the cause in the form of threads that in the thing produced out of these threads only the generality of cloth, namely, *paṭatva*, inheres and no other generality. This is the *mahimā* of a lump of clay that in the thing produced out of this, *ghaṭatva* alone inheres and nothing else, and so on.[42] The causality may be attributed to nature, or to *mahimā*, or to anything else, but they are all the same. It is really the *svabhāva* which is the only solution for explaining these cases. This makes it clear that what the Nyāya-Vaiçeṣika understands by *svabhāva*, while rejecting the view, is something like *ākasmika* or chance, which cannot be explained through the doctrine of causality.

Thus, after all it can be said that the theory of causality must be admitted, in some form or other, to explain the phenomena of the world. It may be called by any name, say, *svabhāva*, *çakti*, *mahimā*, *hetu*, or *kāraṇa*, but the fact is there. It may also be pointed out that even those who do not accept the theory apparently, as for instance, the *Cārvākas*, have, in some form or other, to accept something in place of cause, although it may not be spoken of by the name of cause.

So, we find that while refuting the doctrine of the so-called non-causality, the Nyāya-sūtra says—what the opponent suggests that the production of positive things is from *animitta*[43] itself proves that there is a cause to produce the positive effects; for, from whatever a thing is produced is called its *nimitta* (cause); so that, the *animitta* itself becomes the cause of positive produc-

[41] PWSS., Vol. II. pp. 189-191.
[42] Kandalī, p. 317.
[43] *Animittato bhāvotpattiḥ*—NS., IV. i. 22.

tion. Hence, it is wrong to hold that a product is uncaused.[44]

We may add some more reasons to show the necessity of accepting the doctrine of causality. We find that even when clay, water, the potmaker and the thread are present, there is no production of the jar; even when soil, water, air, sun and the rest are present, there is no germination of the sprout. Hence, we are led to assume that there is something the absence of which prevents the production of an effect. In order to have the effects, like a jar, or a sprout, we should believe in the presence of a stick, or seed, which is a fact supported by experience. If there were no law of causality, why should there be any *pravṛtti* and *nivṛiti* in the universe? But that these things exist cannot be gainsaid. People do take steps to perform certain action which they like, and also to abstain from performing certain activities which they hate. These steps do show that there is the law of causality working in the mind of people; for otherwise, there would have been no activity of whatsoever kind. We are fully aware of the dictum—*prayojanamanuddiçya na mando'pi pravartate*. The world would have been desireless without causation. It is really the cognition of attaining good by doing certain things that we perform those activities and knowing that such activities will only lead to hatred, we abstain from them. Now, had there been no Principle of Causation, how could one have faith in all these?[45] There would have been no law and order of whatsoever kind in the world, had there been no causation.

Further, the Vaiçeṣika sūtra says—had there been no relation of cause and effect, then even from the absence of effect, we could have found the absence of cause as well. But we find that it is not the case.[46]

[44] NS., IV. i. 23 along with NBhā.
[45] VU., I. ii. 1.
[46] VS., I. ii. 2. along with VU.

Therefore, we assume that there is the Doctrine of Causality.

VI

DIVISIONS OF CAUSE

Such a cause is of three kinds: *Samavāyi*, *Asamavāyi* and *Nimitta*.

1. *Samavāyi-kāraṇa* (material-cause) has been defined as that wherein the effect is produced through the relation of inherence. As for instance, the cloth is produced in the threads, that is, out of the threads wherein the cloth exists through the relation of inherence (*samavāya*); so that, the threads are the material cause of the cloth; or the cloth itself is the material cause of the colour of the same cloth; which again, inheres in the very cloth after it is produced. It may be asked here: Why does the cloth inhere in the thread which is the material cause and not in the shuttle (*turī*) etc., which are also apparently equally connected with the cloth? The answer is that as there is no relation of inherence between the cloth and the shuttle, the former does not inhere in the shuttle but in the threads.

This leads us to talk of the nature of the *relation* (*sambandha*) itself. It has been defined as that which is one and is different from those two in which it subsists but has got those two objects as its substrata.[47] Such a *sambandha* is of two kinds: *saṃyoga* and *samavāya*. The former means a sort of contact between two positive objects. It is separable. The latter, on the other hand, is that relation which exists between two *ayutasiddhas* which stand to each other in the relation of the container and the contained. This relation is the cause of the notion that such and such a

[47] TBhā., p. 84.

thing inheres in this.[48] The *ayutasiddhas* are those two objects between which the relation is that if one wants to exist, it can do so only having the other as its substratum; as for example, the pairs, like part and whole, attribute and substance, *kriyā* and substance, genus and species, quiddity (*viçeṣa*) and eternal substance, are all *ayutasiddhas*. That is, whole, *guṇin*, *kriyāvān*, *vyakti*, *and nityadravya* can exist only having parts, attributes, *kriyā*, *jāti*, and *viçeṣa* as their substrata respectively. They cannot exist in any other thing[49].

This relation consists in the mutual dependence or inseparableness of such things of limited extension as are distinctly known to be different from each other. This *samavāya*, according to the Vaiçeṣikas, is supersensuous and is known only through inference. Thus, just as we find that the notion 'there is curd in this big jar' is due to there being some sort of relation between curd and the big jar; so, there are notions like 'cloth is in these threads,' 'mat is in these reeds,' 'the attribute and motion are in this substance,' '*sattā* (the summum genus) is in these substances,' 'there is *dravyatva* in this substance,' 'there is *guṇatva* in this *guṇa* (quality),' 'there is *karmatva* in this *karman*,' 'there are quiddities in these eternal substances,' and so on, where there exist such relations. Now, this relation is not *saṃyoga* (a mere separable contact); for, the *sambandhins* (the connected things) are *ayutasiddhas*; this relation is not possible to be brought about by the motion of any of the members thus related; it is not found to disappear by the disjunction of the related members; and also because it is found to exist only between the container and the contained. All these conditions are not found in the case of *saṃyoga*. It is altogether a different kind of relation.

This is different from *dravya* and the rest of the

[48] VS., VII. ii. 2; PPBhā., p. 324.
[49] TBhā., pp. 15-16.

categories; for, like *bhāva* (*sattā*) its nature is altogether different. That is, as in the case of the summum genus, we find that while bringing about the notions of itself in regard to its substitutes—*dravya*, *guṇa* and *karman*—it differs from its substrates and even from one another. So also in the case of inherence, as regards the five categories, namely, *dravya*, *guṇa*, *karman*, *sāmānya*, and *viçeṣa*, the notion that 'it exists here' differentiates it from the above mentioned five categories. It is only one. Even if it is one, there will be no difficulty in the restriction of container and contained due to the *vyangya-vyañjaka-çaktibheda*[50]. In other words, although there is only one inherence, yet the inherence belonging to *dravyatva* subsists in *dravya* alone, and not in *karman* or *guṇa*. Similarly, the inherence of *guṇatva* subsists in *guṇa* alone, and not in *dravya* or *karman*. This is determined by the methods of *anvaya* (agreement) and *vyatireka* (difference). Just as we find that the curd subsists in a big jar and not that the big jar subsists in the curd although there is no difference as far as the *saṃyoga* is concerned. A substance manifests *dravyatva* alone and not *karmatva* or *guṇatva*. These are known through *saṃvit* or appealing to the nature of things alone;[51] so that, the cloth is produced in the threads and not that the threads are produced in the cloth.[52]

Thus, after all, we find that there exists the relation of inherence between two things, because the nature of such pairs demands it so. Hence, the relation of cause and effect, which is that of inherence, and accordingly, is so intimately connected, is only through the nature of objects thus connected. It is a peculiar bond of affinity and not identity (*tādātmya*) which keeps the cause and the effect together, although they are absolutely different things. Really, it is a mystery which

[50] PPBhā., along with Kandalī, pp. 326-328; VU., VII. ii. 26.
[51] Vide—*Saṃvideva hi bhagavatī vastūpagame naḥ çaraṇam.*
[52] VU., VII. ii. 26.

the Naiyāyikas alone can solve, or it may be simply called their weakness. It is the very nature of *Ārambhavāda* that such relation between the cause and the effect has to be assumed. Perhaps the Naiyāyikas could not do anything otherwise.

2. The non-material cause (*asamavāyikāraṇa*) is that which inheres in the material cause and is capable of producing the effect. For instance, the non-material cause of a cloth is that which inheres in the material cause of the cloth, namely, threads, and is also productive of the cloth. Such a cause is nothing but the conjunction existing between the threads themselves. It is found that the above definition of the non-material cause does not satisfy all the cases; for instance, we know that the colour of the cloth is an effect of which the cloth itself is the material cause. The non-material cause, in that case, should be some such quality which inheres in the cloth and is productive of the colour of the cloth also. But there is nothing like it. Hence, the definition given above is a bit modified, and which then comes to mean that the non-material cause should be that which inheres either in its own material cause, or in the material cause of its own material cause. As in the case of the colour of the cloth, we know that the non-material cause of it is not found inhering in its own material cause, namely, the cloth, but in the material cause of the cloth, namely, threads. That is, the colour of the threads is the non-material cause of the colour of the cloth[53].

3. Instrumental Cause (*nimittakāraṇa*)—But even in the presence of these two causes, no effect is produced. Hence, the Naiyāyikas believe in the existence of a third kind of cause, named instrumental (*nimitta*). It is that cause which is other than the material and the non-material causes and is a cause in the true sense of the term. As for example, a stick is the instrumental cause

[53] TBhā., pp. 20-22.

of the jar.[54]

Of these three kinds of causes that which is the most efficient one is called the *karaṇa*[55].

Of these three kinds of causes, the first two are always extraordinary or uncommon (*asādhāraṇa*) causes, while the third is of two kinds: *sādhāraṇa* and *asādhāraṇa*. Under the former head we generally include the following eight: *Īçvara*, *jñāna*, *icchā* and *kṛti* of *Īçvara*, *Dik*, *Kāla*, *adṛṣṭa* and *prāgabhāva*. The *asādhāraṇa*—instrumental cause is innumerable[56].

VII

SOME CHARACTERISTICS OF CAUSES

1. *Cause in general*

(1) All the three varieties of causes are meant for positive (*bhāva*) things alone. As for the non-existing things (*abhāva*), there is only one cause and that is the instrumental; for, there can be no relation of inherence between the non-existing things; so that, neither the material cause, nor the non-material cause can be connected with non-existences (*abhāvās*)[57].

(2) In every case of the production of existing things (*bhāva*) all these three causes operate together. Even when any one of these is absent, there is no production.

(3) The theory of causality has no beginning. It is presumed to be valid like the *vījāṅkuranyāya*.[58]

(4) The validity of an inference is based on a valid generalisation, which in its turn, is possible through the doctrine of causality alone.[59]

[54] TBhā., pp. 20-22

[55] Ibid, p. 23.

[56] NK., p. 226, third edition.

[57] TBhā., p. 22.

[58] KP., Stavaka 1, verse 6.

[59] Kandalī, p. 207.

2. *Cause in particular*

(1) *Samavāyi-kāraṇa*

Only substance can be the material cause; because, effects like substance, quality and motion (*karman*) are produced in a substance alone through the relation of inherence.[60] But sometimes a substance also is an instrumental cause due to conjunction[61]. As for instance, in the case of the production of cloth, the threads are the instrumental cause also; for, the conjunction of the shuttle and the threads is also a cause of the cloth, and through that conjunction, the shuttle and the threads are also the instrumental cause of the cloth[62].

(2) *Asamavāyi-kāraṇa*

(*a*) Only qualities and motions can be the non-material causes[63].

(*b*) Of qualities, again, only the following can be the non-material cause: colour, taste, smell, non-hot-touch, number, dimension, one separateness (*ekapṛthaktva*), smoothness and sound[64]. But the *viçeṣaguṇas* of the *Ātman*, namely, intellect, pleasure, pain, desire, hatred, effort, merit and demerit, and *bhāvanā* are not the non-material causes of anything[65].

(*c*) The nature of the non-material cause shows that it is a sort of limitation (*niyāmaka*) for the existence of effects.[66]

(*d*) Every product is destroyed by the destruction of the non-material cause.

[60] VS., and VU., X. ii. 1; BhāP., verse 23.
[61] *Saṃyogādvā*—VS., X. ii. 2.
[62] VU., X. ii. 2.
[63] VS., X. ii. 3-4.
[64] PPBhā., p. 101.
[65] NMuktā., on verse 23.
[66] NK., p. 103 (second edition).

(3) *Nimitta-kāraṇa*

(*a*) All the specific qualities of *Içvara* are the instrumental causes.[67]

(*b*) It is the only cause of non-existing things (*abhāva*).

(*c*) It is the only cause separable from the effect.

We find that in certain cases of qualities there is a sort of overlapping of the non-material and the instrumental causes; for instance, conjunction, disjunction, hot-touch, weight, fluidity and velocity[68].

VIII

PLURALITY OF CAUSES DISCUSSED

Now, it is enquired here: whether one kind of effect is produced from one kind of cause or from more. The Cārvākas, as we have seen before, do not believe in the causality. But some others of almost the same type come forward and say that, in reality, we do not see that one kind of effect is produced from one kind of cause alone; for, it is found that one fire which is a particular kind of product is produced from different causes, namely, grass, *araṇi* (a piece of wood of the *samī* tree used for kindling fire by attrition), and also a particular kind of jewel (*maṇi*).

This view is rejected by the Naiyāyikas who hold that it is wrong to think that there are several different causes to produce a single effect. In the example cited above, no doubt, there are three causes, but at the same time, the effect, namely, fire is not one but three. In other words, the fire produced by grass is different from the fire produced out of either *araṇi* or jewel, and so on.[69] Again, if fire were produced from different causes,

[67] VS., X. ii. 7.

[68] PPBhā., p. 102.

[69] KP., Stavaka 1, verse 6; Nyāyakaustubha, Pratyakṣa, p. 26.

then the inference of fire from smoke would not have been possible.[70]

The subversion of the causal rule regarding the particular cause is easier than that of the classwise. If there be no restriction of the class of the cause, then there would be no restriction about the class of the effect as well; for, there is the absence of *hetu*. If it be said that the determination of the class of the effect, even if produced from a different class, will be according to the *svabhāva* itself, then it may be asked: Is it the *svabhāva* of the effect that the determination of the particular class of effect is made, or is it that of the cause that the different classes of effects are determined, although there is only one class of cause? The first alternative is untenable[71]. If a fixed class of effect be not due to a fixed class of cause, and if it be due to the very nature of things that a particular class of effect is produced from any class of cause, then it will have to become an effect of all the classes. In other words, if a jar is produced from the cause of the cloth, then the jar would belong to the class of cloth; or, if the same jar be produced from the cause of fire, then the jar would be classed under the class of fire; similarly, the jar would have to be included in all the possible classes of effects. In the same manner, it will have to be assumed that the effect different from the jar, if produced from the cause producing the jar, would become of the class of the jar; so that, all the troubles would arise if it be assumed that it is in the very nature of the effect that of whatever class the cause may be, the effect would be the same. Even the second alternative is untenable. That is, if, on the other hand, it be held that it is in the very nature of the cause itself that in spite of all the differences of the causes, the effect would always be a fixed one, even then the diffi-

[70] KKH., p. 16.
[71] Bodhanī on KP., p. 12.

culties would be the same. Thus, if the implements (*sāmagrī*) producing a jar be of the nature of producing a cloth, then that *sāmagrī* would be productive of the class of cloth, and so on[72].

If this be the fact, then it may be asked: Why is there one class of product, namely, fire from so many causes, namely, grass, *araṇi* and jewel? We cannot believe in the existence of a category called *çakti* belonging to the grass, *araṇi*, and jewel due to which alone there may be assumed only one kind of effect called fire; for, in that case, we cannot infer the existence of a particular cause from the knowledge of an effect anywhere. Another difficulty in holding the theory of *çakti* would lead us to assume that a particular effect would be produced from any kind of cause, only if that cause were to possess that class of *çakti*.[73] It may be said here by the opponent that the above mentioned difficulty can be overcome by assuming the existence of a *çakti* favourable to produce one kind of effect in causes of different class where it is found that even in the absence of the required cause an effect of one particular class is produced from a different cause and not in any other place. But this is not possible, hold the Naiyāyikas. It is asked here: whether such a *çakti* is assumed to belong to the *nimitta* or to the *adṛṣṭa*? By the former we understand that the presence of which alone denotes the presence of another thing; but such a *nimitta* is not found here. The grass, the *araṇi* and the jewel, which are found here, are not *nimittas*; for, in their absence, we do not find the absence of the effect. Nor can we depend upon the method of agreement (*anvaya*) alone to believe in the existence of *çakti*; for, in that case, an ass, or similar other things, may also possess such a *çakti* and be the cause of fire. Hence, the existence of *çakti* should be

[72] KPP., pp. 56-58; Bodhanī, pp. 12-13.
[73] KPP., pp. 56-58; Bodhanī, pp. 12-13.

assumed in those which are seen through *nimittas*[74].

Again, the Buddhists urge here that the *çakti* may not explain the point, but there is a subtle kind of *jāti* in the form of *kurvadrūpatva* which in spite of the grosser form of difference existing between the grass, the *araṇi* and the jewel, determines that the effect is of one kind only. This view, like the previous one, is rejected by the Naiyāyikas on the ground that the so-called subtle *jāti* may be present even in non-fire and from which smoke may be produced.

It is, again, urged by the opponent that the difference and the identity of the class of effect depend upon the difference and the identity of the material cause and not upon the *nimitta* and the non-material causes. Grass and the rest are the instrumental causes; so that, there is no harm if grass and the rest belong to different classes; for, it would not affect the product at all.

To this, again, the Naiyāyikas reply that if this be the fact, that is, in spite of the difference of the class of the instrumental and the non-material causes, the effect becomes of the same class, then the instrumental and the non-material causes should not be called causes at all.

Now, in order to defend the causality of the instrumental and the non-material causes, it is held that the causality of these depends upon the agreement (*anvaya*) with the effect. But this also is rejected by the Naiyāyikas who hold that their causality is not merely a case of agreement (*anvaya*) with the effect, but only when they are present, the effect takes place and not otherwise; and thus, the method of difference (*vyatireka*) also comes in. Again, in order to determine the class of effect, it does not depend upon the material cause alone, but upon the whole *sāmagrī*; otherwise, there would be no difference between substance, quality and motion having the same material cause. We cannot hold that this rule applies to the substances which are products

[74] KP., pp. 58-59; Bodhanī, p. 13.

and not to *paramāṇus*; for, we find that curd is produced from *paramāṇus* of milk and not by milk itself. It is verified by the common-sense belief also that milk is now destroyed and curd is now produced[75].

Now, in the absence of the theory of *çakti*, we find that the rule, 'that with reference to a particular class of effect there should be the cause in the form of *svabhāva* belonging to a particular class,' is also frustrated. Hence, the fact that there should be one particular individual cause for each effect is to be accepted as final; so that, the fire produced from the grass through the help of fanning (*phūtkāra*) is different from the fire which is kindled from the rubbing of the *araṇi* and the fire which is produced out of the reflection of the sun falling upon a particular kind of jewel[76].

Regarding the view—let there be only one particular cause or a class of particular cause for an effect and there should be no diversity in the cause, it is said that the *vaicitrya* of the cause is inferred from the *vaicitrya* of the effect, which we cannot avoid; but the *vaicitrya* does not form any part of the cause; so that, in order to explain the *vaicitrya* of the effect, we have to assume the *vaicitrya* of the *kāraṇa-sāmagrī*[77].

On these grounds, we find that the Naiyāyikas do not favour the plurality of causes. They believe that every effect has its own particular kind of cause; and if there is any *vaicitrya* in the effect, it is due to the *vaicitrya* of the *kāraṇa-sāmagrī*.

IX

ÇAKTI AND CAUSE

We know that the Mīmāṃsakas of the Prabhākara school hold *çakti* to be a different category altogether.

[75] KPP., pp. 58-61; Bodhanī, p. 14.
[76] KP., pp. 61-72.
[77] KP., pp. 83-88.

Çakti being supersensuous, its existence is proved through inference. The form of inference is this: fire possesses *çakti* (a particular kind of capacity) favourable to the production of burning. This capacity is not found to be operating when any obstacle, as for instance, the *candrakānta-maṇi*, comes in its way and when the *maṇi* is removed or any other stronger counteracting force, say the *sūryakānta-maṇi*, is brought in, the capacity, again, begins to work. This shows that there is a particular kind of thing which being destroyed, there is no burning, and when it is free from obstacles and is not destroyed, there is the burning. This particular kind of thing or capacity is called *Çakti*. It is different from all other categories.

But the Naiyāyikas do not admit it as a different category. The above mentioned instance is explained by them through the help of *pratibandhakābhāva*, meaning, the absence of the obstacles. Hence, the assumption of *çakti* would only lead to a great *gaurava*, which is not desirable.

But a close observation shows that what the Mīmāṃsakas call *çakti* is really included in the conception of cause according to the Naiyāyikas. Hence, in fact, the notion of *çakti* is accepted by the Naiyāyikas also in some form or other. What they deny, it seems, is its being given a separate place.[78] Thus, they say that the non-existence of the obstacles being a common cause of all the effects, there is no need of assuming the existence of *çakti* as an independent category; and moreover, *çakti* itself is nothing but the cause itself.[79]

[78] KP., Vol. I, pp. 144-157.
[79] TD., on TS., p. 65 along with Nīlakaṇṭhī, p. 188.

X

SATKĀRYAVĀDA REFUTED

We have seen above that Sāṅkhya, upholding the *Satkāryavāda*, holds that an effect is present in the cause potentially even before the causal operation. The necessity of the causal operation is only to manifest that which already existed in the cause. Essentially, there is no difference between a cause and an effect. They are, in a way, identical. Hence, the relation between them is called *bhedasahiṣṇu atyantābheda*, that is, absolute identity having the possibility of separation.

This view is not accepted by Nyāya and Vaiçeṣika. They are of opinion that if the effect really exists in the cause in the form in which it is found in the external world, then there is no need of the causal operation; for, they say, what is there then left at the manifestation or production of which the causal operation ceases? Moreover, it is against our experience to assume the existence of a pot in the form in which it is present in the cause. What we actually see in the clay, before the production of the pot, is not a pot but merely a lump of clay, which, after the causal operation, manifests itself as a pot. In whatever form, say in the form of a particular kind of *çakti*, or a particular kind of manifestation, or a particular kind of collocation of the parts of the object, and so on, the effect be assumed to exist in the cause, we cannot have a real *satkāryavāda*. That is, we cannot find the pre-existence of the effect, as found after the causal operation, in the cause. The effect and the cause cannot be identical in the true sense of the term. As the Naiyāyikas take their stand upon the actual experience of the common people, they cannot understand the theory of *satkārya*[80]

Besides these, there are several other reasons

[80] NM., pp. 492-496.

to support the *asatkāryavāda* of the Naiyāyikas. Thus, the *arthakriyābheda*, meaning, the difference in the use of the cause and the effect, establishes the *asatkāryavāda*. They hold that both the clay and the pot do not serve the self-same purpose, which shows that there is a real difference between them. Similarly, the notion of the cause is different from that of the effect. The *vyapadeça* (naming) also supports the Nyāya view-point. Never the term 'effect' is used for the term 'cause', and also, *vice versa*. Their functions, which are predetermined (*arthakriyāvyavasthā*), also help the theory of *asatkārya*.

It will not be out of place to point out that although the Naiyāyika's view-point is quite in keeping with the spirit of the school and the tradition associated with it, and as such, it may be taken to be quite correct, yet we must know that the view-point of Nyāya-Vaiçesika as regards this point is quite different from that of the Sāṅkhya. The *satkāryavāda* has been quite misunderstood and wrongly interpreted for the sake of criticism. But as already made clear elsewhere, we should not be carried away by the remarks made by Nyāya and Vaiçeṣika on this point. We should not forget that both the view-points are quite correct within their own limitations.

CHAPTER VII

MATTER AND CREATION[1]

I

INTRODUCTION

We have seen above that matter and consequently, the external world itself are very intimately connected with motion and the doctrine of change, which, of course, does not operate by chance. It has to be explained in terms of cause and effect. Every change that takes place in the universe has got a cause behind it, which shows that the doctrine of change operates in perfect harmony with the law of causality. Although it is a fact that Nyāya-Vaiçeṣika does not believe in the doctrine of momentary change (*kṣaṇabhaṅgavāda*) like the Buddhists, yet it is also a matter of everyday experience that the joint system cannot deny the influence of the law of change in the universe. Except the eternal forms of matter, all the material products of the universe undergo gradual change. There are the four kinds of ultimate particles of matter, namely, the *paramāṇus* of earth, water, air and *tejas*, which are put into motion through the instrumentality of the Divine Will and the cumulative *adṛṣṭa* of the *Jīvas* and which result in various changes in the forms of *dvyaṇukas*, *tryaṇukas* etc. Again, these products do not remain in the same form for more than a few moments, after which, they

[1] The term '*creation*,' as a synonym for *sṛṣṭi*, cannot be correctly used in any of the orthodox systems. But as there is no other suitable word in the language and as its use is so very common in this very sense, the use of the term has been retained here also.

may either go on producing new forms in addition to the already existing constituents of the universe, or be destroyed and reduced back to the ultimate forms again. Thus, the law of change helps both the creation and the destruction of the material products of the universe. Beside the everyday production and destruction of the material products of the universe, there are the universal creation and the universal dissolution also. In other words, there comes a time when every product is destroyed and reduced back to its ultimate cause, the *paramāṇus*. This period of time is known as the period of Cosmic Rest. After this period is over, again, out of those very *paramāṇus*, a fresh creation takes place. This process has got neither any beginning nor any end. It continues *ad infinitum*.

But there are some (e.g., the Mīmāṃsakas) who do not believe in this process. They think that there can be no universal destruction and consequently, there is no possibility of any fresh creation after it. The following will make the position of both the schools clear.

II

OBJECTIONS AGAINST THE REALITY OF COSMIC REST (PRALAYA) AND THEIR REFUTATION

1. The Mīmāṃsakas urge that every set of day and night is found, necessarily, to be preceded by another set of day and night, and that there is nothing to deny the continuity of such a tradition either in the past or in the future. This shows that there exists a sort of causality between the infinite sets of days and nights. Hence, it is presumed that there would not be any occasion for the cessation of the universal activities, and consequently, there is no *pralaya* at all.

To this it is said, in reply, that the above argument is entirely wrong, as it is based on a false assumption.

There does not exist any causal relation between the various sets of days and nights; so that, it is not at all necessary that one set of day and night should precede another. It does so, however, because of the fact that there exists the universe (*bhava*). In other words, day and night are not causally related, but it appears to be so, due to the nature of the universe itself.

2. Again, it is urged by the Mīmāṃsakas that the existence of a being is full of activities (*karman*) and accordingly, there is no time in one's life when he can be said to be free from any action. This necessitates that, as every action is bound to bear its fruit, there would not be any time in future which would remain without bearing any fruit; so that, when one set of past actions is experienced and consequently, becomes exhausted, then another set of actions comes in for fruition, and so on. Hence, it is impossible to think of the cessation of actions and their fructification ever even in the case of a single individual. This is true of every individual. Such being the case, there cannot be a simultaneous cessation of the functioning of all the modes (*vṛttis*) of *adṛṣṭas* leading to *pralaya*.

Against this, it may be pointed out that the above view is, again, based on a false assumption, and hence, it is untenable. It is a common experience of every day that during the dreamless sleep (*suṣupti*) the function of all the modes do actually cease simultaneously. Similar is the case with the general dissolution. Hence, there is nothing to prevent the state of Cosmic Rest.

3. The next argument adduced against the reality of *pralaya* is that during the dissolution period there being no existence of any Brāhmaṇa, Kṣattriya, Vaiçya and Çūdra, how would the caste distinction be determined when the universe would, again, come to exist? That the caste distinction is a fact cannot be denied. Nor would it be reasonable to believe in the production of a Brāhmaṇa from non-Brāhmaṇa, and so on. Hence, in order to maintain the link undisturbed, it is

necessary to deny the existence of *pralaya.*

Against this argument of the Mīmāṃsakas, the Naiyāyikas point out that the tradition of caste system would be maintained as it is done in other cases. In other words, although it is a fact that apparently a scorpion is produced from a scorpion, for instance, yet it was first produced from cow-dung. Again, likewise, a *taṇḍulīyaka* (a particular kind of grass) is, at present, produced out of another *taṇḍulīyaka*, yet it was first produced from the seed of it. Similarly, in other cases also, namely, milk, curd, ghee, oil, etc., the first product was not from that out of which they are generally produced. So is the case with human beings, lower creatures, Brāhmanas, Ksattriyas etc. That is, although these are at present found to be produced from their own homogeneous class, yet, in the very beginning of the creation after the Cosmic Rest was over, they were all produced out of the ultimate forms of matter under the influence of their respective *adṛṣṭas* accruing from the deeds of the past ages.

4. Again, it is held that if there were a *pralaya*, then all the previous usages and traditions of the empirical world would have been lost and that there would have remained no one to start such traditions again, after the Cosmic Rest.

To this it is said, in reply, that in order to give a start to the old usages and traditions, *Içvara* Himself appears at the end of *pralaya* and through His *Māyā* performs all the necessary activities required to maintain the old connecting link[2].

In this way, the Naiyāyikas refute all the possible objections of the Mīmāṃsakas against the real existence of *pralaya*. Beside these, there are several direct proofs to show that as there is a gradual deterioration in every phase of human life, it is inferred that some day or other, the gradual degeneration would certainly end in

[2] *Vide* BS., I. iii. 30 along with ÇBhā. on the same.

the absolute cessation of the modes (*vṛttis*) of *adṛṣṭas* of the beings of the universe leading to *pralaya*. That there is such an obvious decay in the universe is clear from the following:

1. First of all, there used to be mental creations (*mānasī sṛṣṭi*); then from the fusion of the male and the female for the purpose of producing a son as a part of religious duties; and later on, simply to satisfy one's sexual desires although on right lines. But now, no consideration of any kind exists even in such productions.

2. First of all, *saṃskāra* used to be performed in *caru* and the rest; then in the fields etc.; then in the womb of the mother; and now, after the birth of the child, and that too, only based on worldly usage.

3. Regarding the *Veda*, we know that first of all, people used to study the thousand *çākhās* of it; later on, separately; then one out of the six *aṅgas*; and now, anyone of the *çākhās* alone; and that also partly.

4. Coming to the means of livelihood (*vṛtti*), we find that Brāhmaṇas used to live upon *ṛta*, meaning, the act of picking up grains; then upon food brought to them without asking for it; then upon food begged for; then upon the act of ploughing the field; then upon trade; then upon some art; then upon the protection of cow and the rest; but now, they depend upon service (*sevā*).

5. Again, first of all, Brāhmaṇas used to receive guests with great difficulties; later on, they themselves became guests of Kṣattriyas; then those of Vaiçyas; and now, they eat food supplied by Çūdras. It is further found that at present some people have begun to eat food from the hands of sweepers and other members of the depressed class (*antyajas*).

6. Again, first of all, they used to eat the remainder (*çeṣa*) of the rites and sacrifices (*yajña*); then that which used to remain after feeding the guests; then that which used to remain after feeding the servants; and now,

they live upon that which is got out of pure selfish motive.

7. Again, the *Dharma* is said to have possessed four feet or limbs, namely, *tapas*, *jñāna*, *yajña*, and *dāna* in the beginning of the creation, but gradually, the first three feet disappeared; and now, only one, that is, *dāna*, remains. But that one also is ever trembling on account of the various diseases, which it possesses, in the form of gambling etc., loss of faith, and so on.

In this way, in every phase of life there is a distinct gradual decay, which shows that, some day or other, there is bound to be some sort of stoppage of the worldly activities for a certain period. And it is, therefore, that the Lord Himself has said—I shall manifest Myself when virtue (*dharma*) is entirely weakened and vice (*adharma*) prevails upon in every *yuga*[3].

Besides, there are Çrutis, like '*dhātā yathāpūrvamakalpayat*' etc., to support the existence of *pralaya*, which leaves no doubt about the existence of it. Such a *pralaya* is of two kinds—*khaṇḍapralaya* and *mahāpralaya*, according to the Naiyāyikas. The former is also called *avāntarapralaya*. In the former type of *pralaya*, all the produced substances alone are destroyed, while in the latter, all the positive products (*bhāvakārya*) are destroyed[4]. It is believed that after *mahāpralaya* there is no creation[5].

III

PROCESS OF PRALAYA

It is held that at the end of every hundred years, according to the measure of *Brahmā*[6], there comes the

[3] KPP., pp. 314-329.
Also *Vide—Yadā yadā hi dharmasya glānirbhavati bhārata, Abhyutthānamadharmasya tadātmānaṃ sṛjāmyaham*—BG., IV. 7.

[4] TD., p. 10.

[5] Padārthamālā of Jayarāma, quoted by NK., p. 528, 2nd edition.

[6] One day of *Brahmā* is equal to one year of human beings. The table of the measure of time followed here is given below:

2 kṣaṇas = 1 lava;

time for the relief of the then existing *Brahmā*. At that time, there arises a desir, in the mind of *Maheçvara*, the Lord of the entire universe, to destroy the entire production of all the living beings who are tired of births and deaths for the purpose of rest at night. Just after the desire to do so, the modes (*vṛtti*) of the *adṛṣṭas* of all the living beings, which are the causes of the production and the existence of organisms, sense-organs and all other *mahābhūtas*, are stopped and motions are produced from the conjunctions belonging to the *Ātmans* and the *paramāṇus* helped by the Divine Will. These motions are followed by the disjunctions produced between the ultimate particles out of which organisms and sense-organs etc. are produced, leading to the destruction of the conjunctions existing between them. Thus, every product, including the four *mahābhūtas*, is destroyed and reduced to its respective ultimate particles. This is the universal state of rest known as *pralaya*.

During this state of destruction, the ultimate particles of matter remain disconnected and are not capable of producing any effect. Not only the *paramāṇus* but all other eternal substances, including the *Ātmans* together with merit and demerit, remain during the *pralaya*. Udayana adds that qualities, like colour and the rest, which are produced out of the chemical action, also exist then in the form of the limitations

2 lavas=1 nimeṣa;
18 nimeṣas=1 kāṣṭhā;
30 kāṣṭhās=1 kalā;
30 kalās=1 muhūrta;
30 muhūrtas=1 ahorātra;
15 ahorātras=1 pakṣa;
2 pakṣas=1 māsa;
2 māsas=1 ṛtu;
3 ṛtus=1 ayana;
2 ayanas=1 year;
1 year=1 ahorātra of gods.—Kandalī and KV.

(*upādhis*) of *Kāla;* and motions produced by the velocity caused by the destruction of the *mahābhūtas* also exist during this dissolution period. The existence of these during this period is necessary to mark the time-limit of it and to make the subsequent production of the constituents of the world possible[7]. Besides, the prior-non-existence (*prāgabhāva*) also remains during this period[8]. This state of universal rest continues for one hundred years, according to the measure of *Brahmā*[9] This is the description of the *Khaṇḍapralaya*[10].

IV

CAUSE AND AIM OF CREATION

After *pralaya*, naturally, creation (*sṛṣṭi*) takes place. But before a description of it is given, it may be asked: why should there be any creation at all, and if there be any, what is the cause of it?

In answer to this, it is needless to say that all the orthodox schools of Indian thought believe in the beginninglessness of creation. That is, every creation is necessarily preceded by another. Thus, when a being takes birth, he cannot remain without any action even for a single moment[11]. Produced beings are always thinking, desiring and doing deeds. All these thoughts, desires and deeds must result in some effect. There is no thought, desire and deed which do not bear their requisite fruit. The fructification of desires and deeds is possible in a day's time, or in a year's time, or in one life, or in several lives. Without the experience of the fruits of these there is no freedom. These, when performed, remain in the form of 'something'

[7] KV., pp. 92-93.
[8] Setu, p. 286.
[9] KV., p. 93.
[10] NK., p. 528, Ft. N. (Second edition).
[11] BG., III. 5.

unseen till the time of their fructification; and during this period, this 'something' is known as *adṛṣṭa.* Without the experience of the fruits of these desires and deeds, there is no escape. The very aim of human life and the end of all the *Darçanas* would remain unrealised and would be frustrated without the experience of the results of these. Therefore, until the whole of the treasure of the fruits of the past desires and deeds is not exhausted, there will be series of productions, both individual and universal. Hence, the only aim of creation is to have the experience (*bhoga*) of the past thoughts, desires and deeds; and through it, the final realisation of the highest aim of human life is achieved. This is the secret of the *Law of Karman.*

As regards the next point—what is the cause of it? the answer is almost the same. That is, the cause of creation is really the activities of the past lives. But this is only the instrumental cause. As for the material cause, we know that after the previous production of the world, the objects of the world are completely destroyed in course of time, and are reduced to the four kinds of *paramāṇus.* Then with the help of the Divine Will quickened by the *adṛṣṭas* a kind of productive motion is produced in those *paramāṇus*, which gradually, produce all the objects of the world, and subsequently, the universe itself.

V

ADṚṢṬI AND CREATION

We have been referring to *adṛṣṭa* all along, but what is it, and how is it connected with the theory of creation are the questions before us. The very word *adṛṣṭa* signifies that it is something which is not seen. But then, how is it assumed to exist at all? In answer to this, it is said that there are the feelings of pleasure and pain, like and dislike, and so on, in the world which cannot be denied. Now, it may be asked: to what are all these due? They cannot be attributed to any external thing; for, if it were so, then the same external thing, which gives pleasure to a man at one particular time, should not cause pain to the same man at any other time; and also, the same external thing should give pleasure to all others equally. But such is not the fact. Hence, the cause of these should be searched within and not without. The *Ātman*, which is the seat of these feelings, is also the material cause of these, but not the instrumental one; for, if it were the requisite cause, then the *Ātman* being eternal, the effect ought to have been ever present, which is not the fact. Again, if *Ātman* were the only cause to produce these feelings of pleasure and pain, then it may be enquired: why should it ever like to produce pain? Why should not there be pleasure always? There is nothing in the very nature of the *Ātman* to determine this. Hence, the presence of a determining factor to help the *Ātman* is very necessary. It is also neither possible nor proper to assume *Paramātman* to be the determining factor of these feelings; for, it would lead us to admit that *Paramātman* is partial, which, again, is not correct. Hence, in the absence of any such known factor, the orthodox schools believe in the existence of an unseen force, which the Naiyāyikas call *dharmādharma* (merit and demerit) and the Vaiçeṣikas *adṛṣṭa*[12]. It is this unseen force which, like an auxiliary, helps the adequate fructification of the deeds of the past.

It would not be out of place here to point out that the experiences of pleasure and pain cannot take place in the *Ātman* unless it becomes limited within a gross organism (*bhogāyatana*). Again, all sorts of experiences cannot be experienced in all sorts of organisms. In other words, the form of organisms also has to be determined according to the nature of the experiences to be

[12] NK., p. 8 (Second edition).

gone through[13]. All these are done under the influence of *adṛṣṭa* alone. This is not only true of living organisms, but also of everything else; for, all the inorganic constituents of the universe have been created simply to meet with the demands of the organic creation. Hence, it may be said that every constituent of the universe, whether organic or inorganic, has to remain and function under the direct or the indirect influence of *adṛṣṭa*. There are, however, the Cārvākas, the Indian Materialists, who do not subscribe to the above mentioned view. They do not believe in the *law of Karman*. They consider that everything, whether organic or inorganic, is produced out of the peculiar collocations of the particles of matter through chance[14].

Now, coming to the details of the creation of human organisms, it may be pointed out that the process is almost the same as it is in the case of inorganic matter. Creation cannot take place out of one; so that, there must be two particles to produce a thing. Again, those two particles should not be of the same substance. Hence, the fusion of semen and blood is necessary to produce a human organism. When such a fusion takes place in the uterus under the influence of *adṛṣṭa* of the parents to experience pleasure and pain through an issue and that of the would-be issue to have the experience of pleasure and pain through those parents, then that fusion becomes the seed of a human organism in the uterus. That there exists such an influence is clear from the fact that every union of a male and a female does not produce such a seed[15]. This seed also is, after all, produced out of the ultimate particles of matter moved through the *adṛṣṭa* itself. Now, when such a seed is sown, then it, along with the food and drink taken by the mother of the would-be child,

[13] NS., III. ii. 60 and NBhā. on the same.
[14] NBhā., III. ii. 61.
[15] NS. and NBhā., III. ii. 65.

undergoes chemical changes. The chemical process present in the uterus turns such food and drink into a fine, subtle and liquid substance which helps the gradual growth of the seed till it develops into such aggregates as cell, mass, foetus, foetus embryo, arteries, head, feet, etc. and subsequently, the organism along with the sense—organs. All these developments take place in the womb itself through the instrumentality of the *adṛṣṭa* of the parents and the child in the womb[16].

It has been said that the production, both the individual and the universal, is meant for the experience of pleasure and pain. Now, a question may be raised here: how does a particular *Ātman* come in contact with a particular organism in order to have its adequate and predetermined experience (*bhoga*)?

The only answer that can be given from the Nyāya-Vaiçeṣika point of view is that it is, again, the *adṛṣṭa*, accruing from the past deeds, which determines all these things. In other words, it is the very operation of the *Law of Karman* that the contact of these two particular things are brought about. Every production of an organism is really with reference to the *bhoga* of a particular *Ātman*. Hence, if that *Ātman* be not connected with that organism, the production of that organism would be useless, which is impossible under the *Law of Karman* and the *Nature of Uniformity*. Such particular contacts can only explain the diversity of *bhoga* also which is a fact not admitting any denial.

Moreover, because the organism is produced by *adṛṣṭa* and its contact with a particular *Ātman* is also due to *adṛṣṭa*, it is held that when the realisation of *Ātman* takes place and the particular *adṛṣṭa* connected with the particular *Ātman* limited by a particular organism becomes exhausted, the organism also falls down as dead. Had it been due to the *bhūtas* alone, then as the *bhūtas* are

[16] NS. and NBhā., III. ii. 62-64.

always present, there would have been no possibility for the absence of an organism, and consequently, there would have been no *mokṣa*[17]. The same reason which explains the possibility of the contact of a particular organism with a particular *Ātman* for *bhoga*, also, explains the contact of a particular *Manas* with a particular body and a particular *Ātman*. This is all that can be said about the individual production.

VI

PROCESS OF CREATION

Coming to the universal creation, it is held that after the expiry of the hundred years of Cosmic Rest, the accumulative *adṛṣṭas* of the *Jīvas* come to operate through the Divine Will for the creation of beings and objects suited to their needs for the purpose of reaping the fruits of their past deeds. Through the help of these *adṛṣṭas* conjunctions are produced between the *Ātmans* and *paramāṇus*. These conjunctions produce motion in the ultimate particles of air which then join together so as to form *dvyaṇuka*, *trasareṇu*, and consequently, the final (*mahān*) air which remains vibrating in the sky. It possesses continuous and strong vibration; because, (1) it is the first product, (2) there is intense velocity in it,[18] and (3) no other substance, which would have put obstacles in its way, has been, as yet, produced[19]. After this, in the very *mahān-vāyu*, which is of the sort of a substratum due to its being an obstacle of weight on account of the possession of velocity and touch[20], a big reservoir of water, from the watery *paramāṇus* through the usual process, is produced

[17] NS. and NBhā., III. ii. 66-67.
[18] Vyom., p. 300.
[19] KV., p. 94.
[20] KV., p. 94.

which remains flowing due to the velocity of air.[21] After this, in the same manner, from the *paramāṇus* of earth is produced the big[22] earth which exists in a solid form. After the production of earth, in that very reservoir of water, a big heap of fire (*tejas*) is produced from the *paramāṇus* of *tejas*, which not being overpowered by anything else remains luminous. In this way, the four *mahābhūtas* are produced one after the other. This being done, through the Divine Will (*saṅkalpa*), a big cosmic egg is produced out of the *paramāṇus* of fire assisted by the ultimate particles of earth. In that big egg *Brahmā*, the grand-father of the entire universe and having four lotus like faces is produced together with all the worlds, and is engaged by the Divine Will in the production of living beings. Being endowed with intellect, dispassion, and other extraordinary powers, *Brahmā*, knowing the time of fructification of the past deeds of beings, begins to create first, his mental productions (*ayonijas*), such as, *Prajāpatis*, *Manus*, several groups of *devas*, *ṛṣis* and *pitṛs*[23]; and next, out of his mouth, arms, thigh and feet are produced the four castes—*Brāhmaṇa*, *Kṣattriya*, *Vaiçya*, and *Çūdra* respectively, and also other living beings of all grades high and low. Having produced these, *Brahmā* connects them with adequate degree of *dharma*, *jñāna*, *vairāgya* and *aiçvarya* according to their past deeds. He also adds to them the proper degree of *adharma*, *ajñāna*, *avairāgya*, and *anaiçvarya*, and the result of these, namely, pleasure, pain, and the rest[24]. It is thus how the production of this objective world takes place.

[21] KV., p. 94.

[22] It is called 'big,' because, it is the first earthly product and there has been no digging of it in any way—Setu, p. 288.

[23] By '*Gaṇas*' Udayana also means '*Kūṣamāṇḍas*'—KV., p. 96.

[24] PPBhā., pp. 48-49; and KV., p. 96.

VII

CLASSIFICATION OF SṚṢṬI

The entire creation may be divided into two broad heads: *yonija* and *ayonija*. The former includes such living beings as are produced out of the fusion of the male and the female. The latter may be, again, subdivided into *Mānasika* and non-*Mānasika*. Under the former, we include the *Mānasika* sons of *Brahmā*, and under the latter, we have the production of the other worldly living beings and food, drink, and so forth suited to them. These productions also are due to the influence of *adṛṣṭa*.

VIII

THE LAW OF KARMAN AND ITS FUNCTIONING

We have heard enough of the *Law of Karman*. Now, it may be asked: what does it mean and how is it regulated? In answer to this, it may be said that the law means that our activities (*karmans*) are performed according to certain regular laws and not haphazardly. All our activities, both psychic and physical, are performed with certain end in view. For each and every action, there is enough responsibility. Almost all of them are predetermined. These activities may be good or bad. Those which are good, that is, which tend towards the realisation of the highest good, are called meritorious (*dhārmika*), and those which are bad are called demeritorious (*adhārmika*); so that, when they are performed, they leave behind some impressions which remain unseen and are known as *adṛṣṭa*, or *dharmādharma*, or *puṇyapāpa*, or *apūrva*, and so on. After this, whenever these impressions get anything to arouse them, they appear, again, in some form or other, not necessarily, in their previous forms, and are experienced then as the result of the previous deeds or thoughts.

This sort of fructification of the impressions of the past deeds may be possible in a year's time or more, and may extend to several lives even. Hence, the impressions of the deeds of one life may continue for several lives. Now, it may be asked: Are we to experience the result of all our activities? But, before giving a direct answer to this question, it is better to know more about our activities with a view to find out whether it is essential to experience the result of all our activities or not.

Nescience (*avidya*)[25] is considered to be without any beginning. The *Law of Karman* is the manifestation of this very nescience. Under its influence due to the effects of the meritorious and the demeritorious deeds, the *Jīvātman*[26], passing through various births and deaths, imposes upon itself the qualities of *kartṛtva* and *bhoktṛtva*. In fact, it is due to these very attributes that there appear to be two *Ātmans*; so that, the chains of births and deaths, the experience of the dualistic nature of the self, the distinction between name and form, all these continue until the *avidyā* or its manifestation, namely, the *Law of Karman* is entirely annihilated.

It is all due to the differences of *karman* under the influence of the three *guṇas*, namely, *Sattva*, *Rajas* and *Tamas*, that there are obvious differences in the result. Thus, the *Jīvātman* under the influence of the *Tamas* aspect of the *avidyā* enters the body of lower creatures, such as, birds, deer, elephants etc. (*adhovṛtti*), and acts according to the nature of the organism into which it takes its abode, and finally, attains such *loka* where suffering alone prevails. If the *Rajas* prevails, then the *Jīvātman* enters such organisms

[25] It is of the nature of the harmonious state of the three *guṇas*. It manifests itself in the form of subtle and gross bodies and is the same as *ajñāna*.

[26] The *pratibimba* of the *Paramātman* falling upon the *Prakṛti* is called the *Jīvātman*.

as occupy the intermediate stage, namely, the organisms of *vidyādhara*, *yakṣa*, *rākṣasa*, *manuṣya* etc. (*madhyavṛtti*), and finally, goes to the *loka* where both pleasure and pain are found in equal proportion. If, on the other hand, the *Sattva* predominates, then the *Jīvātman* enters the organism of *ṛṣis*, gods etc. (*ūrdhvavṛtti*), and thereby, obtains the *svargaloka* and the *maharloka*[27]. The difference in *karman* not only produces difference in the organism, but also in the *Jīvātmans* themselves; otherwise, there is no difference between one *Jīvātman* and the other.

Although there is only one kind of *karman*, yet due to the difference in the time of the experience of it, it is divided into *Sañcita*, *Sañcīyamāna*, or *Kriyamāṇa* and *Prārabdha*. By *Sañcita* we mean that kind of *karman* which is still kept in store and whose fructification (*bhoga*) has not yet begun. By *Sañcīyamāna* we mean that kind of *karman* which is being done every day in the course of the experiencing of the deeds of the *Prārabdha-karman*. And by *Prārabdha* is meant that *karman* for the experience of whose fruit the particular organism has been assumed at the present time and is being regulated.

One must exhaust the *bhoga* of these three kinds of *karmans* before the highest aim is attained. About the order of *bhoga*, it is held that it takes place in the order in which its experience has begun, or in which each action has taken place, or according to the force (*bala*) of each activity. In other words, the *Prārabdha-karman*, for the experience of which the particular organism is assumed, is experienced first, and then comes the turn of the *Sañcitakarman*, at the end of which, the *bhoga* of the third form of *karman* begins. All these may be just possible in one or more births. Sometimes the *Prārabdha* itself occupies more than one birth. It is also quite possible that after the *bhoga* of the

[27] Also *vide* BG., XIV. 18-19.

Prārabdha is exhausted, the *Sañcita-karmans* come up for being experienced in the order in which they had been performed. It is also quite possible that the order of *Sañcita-karmans* may be overlooked, and in accordance with the strength of the *Sañcita*, the *bhoga* may take place. That is, the *karman* which is very forcible and vivid will come up first for being experienced, and then the less forcible, and so on. Some are of opinion that this sort of change in the order of *bhoga* is possible even in the *Prārabdha-karman*; so that, although usually the deeds of the previous births bear fruit in this birth and those of this birth in the next, yet if the deeds are very forcible, then they will bear fruit in this very life by changing the order of the experiencing of the *Prārabdha-karman*. Whatever may be the order, it is a fact that the *bhoga* of each and every kind of *karman* must be exhausted before the highest aim is realised.

Of these three kinds of *karmans*, the *Sañcita* and the *Sañcīyamāna* can be exhausted either by their actual experience, or even without it[28], in which case, these can be exhausted by the *tattvajñāna* also[29].

This is how our activities are exhausted, partly, by *bhoga* and partly, by the true knowledge. It is also clear from the above that only for the sake of exhausting the *bhoga* of our own desires and deeds, we have to take birth after birth which necessitates the existence of *Saṃsāra* till final emancipation is attained.

[28] Vyom., p. 644.

[29] *Vide-Jñānāgniḥ sarvakarmāṇi bhasmasāt kurute tathā*—BG. IV. 37.

CHAPTER VIII

MATTER, LIFE AND CONSCIOUSNESS

I

INTRODUCTORY

Due to the initiation of motion the earthly ultimate particles group together and form different earthly products. These products may be classed under two broad heads, namely, organic and inorganic. That class of product which is the substrate of such activities as tend towards the attainment of what is favourable and liked and also which cause abstinence from objects which are unwholesome and disliked is called organic. It is also the substratum of sense-organs and is the receptacle of the experiences of pleasure and pain through the sense-organ and object contact. It is through this kind of material product that life and consciousness find their manifestation. There is growth and healing of the wounds in this very form of the organism. The inorganic form of matter, on the other hand, is that which does not possess any of these attributes. It is technically called *viṣaya* in Nyāya-Vaiçeṣika. It is, therefore, called *jaḍa*. In spite of these vital differences between these two types of material products, as far as their production is concerned, the process is the same in both the cases. In other words, both the types of products are ultimately produced out of the ultimate particles of matter according to the usual process of creation. But then, it may be asked here—how, when and why does life (*jīvana*) come to be connected with one sort of product and not with the other?

II

THE MATERIALISTIC VIEW-POINT

The Cārvākas, representing the Indian Materialistic view-point, do not appear to differ much from what has been said above. They hold that there are only four kinds of elements (*tattvas*), namely, earth, water, *tejas* and air[1]. Physical organism, sense-organ and inorganic matter (*viṣaya*) are all produced out of these[2]. But as regards the details of the process of production, we are not sure what they actually hold. On the basis of their explanation of the actual facts of the universe, however, it can be assumed that according to the Materialists the production is due to certain collocations of these four types of matter.

According to the Materialists, life and consciousness are practically the same. They are recognised to be the products of matter. The vital difference between the two sorts of products, which is quite obvious from their very nature, is however, due to the manifestation, or otherwise, of consciousness. This manifestation, which is spontaneous, takes place only in certain collocations of the ultimate particles of matter or their products, and not in all[3]. This assumption of the Cārvākas is supported by their everyday experiences. Thus, it is found that although no intoxicating property is present in each and every constituent of a particular preparation, say a wine, yet when all those particles come to be grouped together spontaneously in a particular form, the intoxicating property becomes manifested

[1] *Pṛthivyaptejo vāyuriti tattvāni*—Bhāskara on BS., III. iii. 53; ST., p. 8.

[2] *Tatsamudāye çarīrendriyaviṣayasamjñā*—Bhāskara on BS., III. iii. 53.

[3] Daçaçlokī of Çaṅkarācārya, verse 1; Siddhāntabindu, p. 116; Nyāyaratnāvalī, pp. 116-17; Nārāyaṇī, pp. 116-17 (chowkhamba edition).

therein[4]. In the like manner, the particular type of colour present in a cloth, called variegated colour (*citrarūpa*), although does not belong to each and every constituent of that cloth, namely, the threads, yet when those threads are arranged in a particular collocation, the peculiar colour finds its manifestation therein. Illustrations of this sort can be easily multiplied[5]. Similarly, although the various particles of matter, forming a particular collocation, do not severally[6] possess life or consciousness, yet when those particles group together so as to form a particular physical organism, life and consciousness find their place in it[7]. Hence, it is concluded that life and consciousness are spontaneous products of matter. Their appearance is just like the variations in the form of opening and closing of the petals of a lotus flower, and is not due to any cause[8].

The Materialistic position as stated above leads us to consider another more important question—whether consciousness belongs to matter or non-matter, that is, the individual self. In answer to this, the Materialists hold that as there is activity (*pravṛtti*) and inactivity (*nivṛtti*) in a physical organism, desire, hatred and consequently, consciousness also belong to it[9]. The presence of activity shows that there is desire in the organism for the fulfilment of which the physical organism performs certain activities. The absence of activity, in the like manner, indicates that as there is hatred in the physical organism, there is no activity in it. Again, there can be neither any desire nor any hatred without

[4] *Madaçaktivadvijñām*—Bṛhaspati-sūtra, quoted in Çaṅkara. on BS., III. iii. 53; Bodhanī, p. 44; Bhāskara on BS., III. iii. 53; ST., pp. 7-8.

[5] ST., pp. 7-8.

[6] There seems to have been a view that consciousness belongs to each and every *paramāṇu*—ST., p. 7.

[7] *Vide supra*, p. 277, Ft.n. 3.

[8] NS. and NBhā., III, i. 19.

[9] NBhā., III. ii. 35-36.

consciousness. Hence, it is presumed that like activity and inactivity, a physical organism possesses desire, hatred and consciousness also. Thus, consciousness (*caitanya*) belongs to matter; and it is, therefore, that *Puruṣa* or *Ātman* has been defined by the Materialists as an organism possessing consciousness (*Caitanyaviçiṣṭaṃ çarīramātmā*[10], or *Caitanyaviçiṣṭaḥ kāyaḥ puruṣaḥ*[11]).

Again, that consciousness is the function of the physical organism is proved by the joint methods of Agreement and Difference (*anvaya* and *vyatireka*). It is found by observation, and which has been never contradicted, that there exists some necessary connection between matter and consciousness, due to which alone consciousness is manifested through the physical organism only. Besides, that there is such an intimate relation between matter and consciousness is further proved by the fact that the Indian Medical Science believes that if some particular food and drink be prepared with the help of some herb, as for instance, *brāhmīghṛta* or *brāhmībūṭī*, and be used, then consciousness (that is, the intellectual power) develops. Even in ordinary cases it is found that if good and substantial food and drink are always used, then the consciousness becomes more keen and sharp, and in the absence of such food and drink it becomes dull. It is, therefore, that butter (*ghṛta*) has been identified with the life itself (*āyurvai ghṛtam*[12].)

Further, this very view of the Cārvākas is also supported by the universal experience as expressed in judgments like, 'I am fat,' 'I am thin,' and so on.

[10] PHṛ. on Sūtra 8.

[11] Çaṅkara on BS., III. iii. 53; Madhusūdana, Nīlakaṇṭha, Dhanapati and Çrīdhara in their comm. on BG., XVI. ii; Advaitabrahmasiddhi of Sadānanda, chapter II, p. 99 (Cal. Uni. publication).

[12] KP. Stavaka I., Kārikā 15, p. 173; Bodhanī on *ibid.* p. 44; NM., p. 439.

There is no doubt that the term 'I' used in the above expressions and which is identified with the individual self (*Ātman*), refers to the physical organism and not to any other element[13]. Again, the Cārvākas of this school have got also a *çruti* to support their view-point, which runs as—'*Sa vā eṣa puruṣo'nnarasamayaḥ*[14].' This school of the Cārvākas is known as *dehātmavāda*.

It appears from this that according to this school of the *Cārvākas*, life (*jīvana*) and consciousness (*cetanā*) are practically the same, and both originate from matter. But a close study of the views of all the schools of the Cārvākas, namely, *Indriyātmavāda*, *Prāṇātmavāda*, and *Ātma-Manovāda*, shows that according to the *Ātma-Manovāda*, at least, life (*jīvana*) is considered to be different from consciousness. They recognise *prāṇa* (the life function) as different from *Manas* to which consciousness is attributed[15].

III

REFUTATION OF THE MATERIALISTIC VIEW

But the above view is untenable according to the orthodox schools. The Nyāya-Vaiçeṣika rejects all the above arguments and asserts that consciousness does not belong to matter.

Thus, the Naiyāyikas hold that the particular kind of collocation of the parts of clay which is the mark of activity is found in a jar produced out of that clay but no desire is attributed to it; and consequently, no consciousness belongs to the jar. Hence, it is concluded that consciousness does not belong to matter[16].

If really consciousness had belonged to the *paramāṇus*, then it ought to have been assumed that there

[13] ST., p. 6; VSS., p. 7. (Vāṇīvilas Press-edition); Advaitabrahmasiddhi of Sadānanda., p. 98.

[14] Tai. Up., II. i. 1.

[15] VSS., pp. 74-76; ST.—Ātmasiddhi, pp. 12-14.

[16] NBhā., III., ii. 36.

are as many consciousnesses as there are *paramāṇus* in a single body, which is not the fact, and is not supported by any valid means of reasoning. Moreover, there would have appeared counteractions in a single body at every moment which would have either resulted in the upsetting of the functions of the body, or in the cessation of all possible activities of the body[17].

Consciousness cannot belong to the grouping or the collocation of matter; for, such collocations are always changing; so that, a particular impression (*saṃskāra*) of a particular act performed by a particular group passes away along with that group of *paramāṇus*. Hence, remembrance (*smaraṇa*) also would not be possible at all; for, in the case of remembrance it is essential that only that thing can remember anything if that thing itself had done or seen the act to be remembered, and no one else. Again, if, for instance, any act is done by the foot or hand and if that foot or that hand is cut off, there would have been no remembrance of that deed which was done by the foot or the hand. If some money is given to a person by the right hand as debt, and if by chance that right hand is cut off, the man, whose right hand it was, should not remember the giving of the debt, and the debt should not have been repaid; for, the so-called person who had given the debt is dead, and there is no one else responsible for that debt.

We cannot hold that like the transmission of the fragrance of musk from one thing to another due to contact, the impression of the action performed by one group of *paramāṇus* can be transmitted to another group of *paramāṇus* to make remembrance quite possible; for, if that be the fact, then whatever is experienced by the mother should also have been experienced by the child in the womb of that mother; so that, it is not at all right to think that consciousness is an attribute of matter[18].

[17] NBhā, III. ii. 37.
[18] KP. Stavaka I, Kārikā. 15.

As regards the argument that the sharpness or the dullness of the consciousness depends upon the use of good or bad food and drink, it is said that the reasoning is unsound; for, the keenness or the dullness of the consciousness is known from the apprehension of things. In other words, consciousness is nothing but the apprehension of things itself. This apprehension of things is due to the keenness of the sense-organs, which in their turn, are helped by organism[19]. Hence, consciousness is not at all causally related to matter. This very fact shows that what the *brāhmīghṛta* or the *brāhmībūṭī* does is to make the sense-organs keen, and has nothing to do with the consciousness itself[20].

As regards the instance of variegated colour (*citrarūpa*), it is said that *citrarūpa* means collocation of several colours, which, again, is produced out of the collocation of several threads possessing several different colours. Although that *citrarūpa* is not found in each thread, yet when the threads out of which the cloth is produced are collected, then we do see the *citrarūpa* in the collected threads and express it in the form of the judgment that these threads are of variegated colour. Even if it be held that *citra* is not a collection of several colours but a different colour altogether, that also is produced in the composite out of the colours belonging to the cause; but such is not the case with consciousness; for, it, belonging to the living organism, is not produced out of the collection of the consciousness belonging to the constituent parts of the organism; so that, consciousness cannot be proved to be causally related to matter, or to be a quality of matter.

As regards the production of the red colour of the betel leaves, it is said that the red colour in some indistinct form is found in each of the constituents of betel, but consciousness is not at all found in the

[19] NS., I. i. 11.
[20] NM., p. 440.

paramāṇus constituting the organism. Hence, the argument of the Materialists does not sound well.[21]

Moreover, the Cārvakās establish causality, if at all, merely on the basis of the joint methods of Agreement and Difference which the Naiyāyikas do not consider to be a safe reasoning for establishing causality. For example, that sound is caused by *Ākāça* is accepted by all, but this causality cannot be established through the joint methods of Agreement and Difference, as it is not possible to have the absence of *Ākāça* ever[22].

The support of experience is rejected on the ground that 'I' can never be used for organism. It is used for something which is within the organism. This may be supported by the expressions like—'This is my body' (*mama idaṃ çarīraṃ*) etc. This clearly shows that 'body' (*çarīra*) is different from 'my' (*mama*) which is used for something else than the body, or matter[23].

As regards the support of the *çruti* it is enough to say that the context has been misunderstood due to which body and the *Ātman* are wrongly identified.

In this way, the view-point of the Materialists is rejected, and *cetanā* is proved to be the quality of non-matter.

IV

LIFE, PRĀṆA AND CONSCIOUSNESS

Having refuted the view that life and consciousness are products of matter, an attempt is made to show that they are not identical as supposed by the Materialists.

According to Nyāya and Vaiçeṣika, life (*jīvanaṃ*) means the contact of the *Manas* with the *Ātman* which has become connected with a particular organism as a

[21] ST.—Ātmasiddhi, pp. 11-12.
[22] TBhā., p. 14.
[23] ST., p. 9.

result of the past deeds (*prārabdha-karman*) the fructification of which has begun[24]. In other words, life—meaning the state of living—is that period during which a particular *Ātman* remains in contact with a particular organism due to the influence of *adṛṣṭa*, for the purpose of *bhoga* and with a particular *Manas*, of course, to help the *bhoga*. This contact under the influence of one's own past deeds takes place in the very womb of the mother. This really is the birth of the child.

Prāna, on the other hand, is the function of life. It is through *prāna* that we know the existence of life in an organism. Even when a man is in sound sleep (*suṣupti*), it is the *prāṇa* which distinguishes the sleeping man from a dead man in whom there is no life and consequently, no *prāṇa*. There is a sort of indirect causality between life (*jīvanaṃ*) and *prāṇa*. In other words, when a particular *Ātman* comes in contact with a particular body and a particular *Manas*, it is known as birth, and life begins since then[25]. This *jīvana* produces a sort of effort, which subsists in the *Ātman*, with the help of *adṛṣṭa* and the contact of a particular *Ātman* and a particular *Mānas* within the limitation of a particular organism. This effort is known as *jīvanayoniprayatna*. Its function is to put a stimulus to the functioning of life through the vital airs (*prāṇa*, *apāna*, and the rest) during the state of *suṣupti* and also to bring about the contact of the *antaḥkaraṇa* with other sense-organs during the waking state[26]. This effort continues as long as the life exists, and is supersensuous. It is, consequently, inferred from the functions of *prāṇa* etc.[27]

By the way, it should be remembered that the modern school of Nyāya does not believe in the existence of this kind of effort. They say that the

[24] NBhā., III. ii. 26-27.
[25] Kandalī, p. 263.
[26] PPBhā. along with the Kandalī, p. 263.
[27] VU., V. ii. 16.

function of *prāṇa* etc. is either due to the living (*jīvana*) itself, or to the *adṛṣṭa* influenced by the living (*jīvana*); so that, there is no proof to believe in the existence of such an effort[28].

This *prāṇa* manifests itself in several forms according to its different locations and different functions[29]. Thus, *prāṇa* is the outgoing and incoming breath. It locates in the heart. *Apāna* is that which causes ejection. The third is *samāna*. It causes assimilation. The fourth *vyāna* causes distribution of the essence of the food to the various *nāḍis*, while the fifth *udāna* causes things to be taken up or out.[30]

Both life and its function (*prāṇa*) are quite distinct from consciousness which is a quality of the *Ātman*. It is manifested by the contact of the *Manas* with the *Ātman*. Consciousness is not at all identical with life or *prāṇa* although they co-exist. We have seen above that it is not a quality of matter. What matter can do for consciousness is, that matter gives an opportunity for the manifestation of it.

V

SPONTANEITY OF LIFE REFUTED

The next question which comes before us is: whether life comes out of another life, or there is the spontaneous generation of life?

This question, like the previous one, can be answered in various ways. But here also, I confine myself to the view-points of the Materialists and the Nyāya-Vaiçeṣika. The Materialists believe that life is produced out of matter alone, and hence, it is not at all necessary to hold that there should be an antecedent

[28] Dinakarī on NMuktā., *Guṇa* section, on kārikā 152, p. 836 Mylapore Ed.

[29] NMuktā, p. 361.

[30] Dinakarī on NMuktā, on kārikā 44, p. 361.

life. We find, they continue, that during the rainy season in a very short time small worms and insects are found moving in curd and some other substances. It is obvious that these worms are produced from no other cause than the constituent parts of the curd. Similarly, in rice, and in almost every decomposed substances, insects and worms are produced. There never existed any life in the rice so as to attribute causality of the production of the present life of the insects to it. Hence, it is obvious that in all these cases life is spontaneous[31].

It may be asked here: if this be the only point of view of the Cārvākas what would they say in the case of the production of living beings from another living beings? We see that a child having life is produced from a mother having life, where it is clear that a life has got an antecedent life. To this, the Cārvākas, to be consistent in their thought, would say that although we see that a child having life comes out of a mother having life, yet the life or the consciousness present in the child is not due to the consciousness or life of the mother but to matter alone. When the child's body is fully developed, then the life generates there spontaneously, as in the instances cited above.

The Naiyāyikas, on the other hand, hold that although we find that life is produced from life as in the case of every production of living beings and also we find that life generates even from things having no life, for instance, scorpion is found to come out of cow-dung; frogs are produced from mud; worms and insects are found to generate in the rice, and so on, yet we cannot say that life is produced from matter. Whether it is produced from a living being, or apparently from a non-living being, everywhere life is due to the contact of the *Ātman*, endowed with *adrsta*, on the point of fruition, with an organism. The *Ātman* being all-pervading exists

[31] NM., p. 440.

everywhere and there is no end or a fixed type of *karman* to be fructified; so that, the *Jīvas*, in order to reap the fruits of the deeds of their previous lives, come in contact with any substance under the influence of *adṛṣṭa* and make it their home for a particular set of *bhoga*. This also makes it clear that even here the plurality of causes is not possible according to Nyāya-Vaiçeṣika[32]. We can only say that what matter does in the production of life is to help its manifestation and nothing else[33]. This is the only relation between life and matter. The harmonious working between the two is determined by *adṛṣṭa*.

This explanation is true of the *yonija* type of organism as well as of a particular section of *ayonija*. But what about the life in the case of the mental (*mānasika*) production? We have seen before that the mental production is also possible only under the influence of *adṛṣṭa*; so that, the same explanation holds good in this case as well.

It will not be out of place to say here that all the forms of mental activities recognised in the western psychology, namely, voluntary action, voluntary action as deliberate choice, motive, feeling of effort, action against the will, habit, interest, attention, and others[34], are all connected with life through the *Ātman*. These are due to various causes, namely, *adṛṣṭa*, contact of the *Ātman* and the *Manas* under the influence of previous deeds, and the bodily help is, of course, indispensable.

[32] KP., Stavaka 2, Kārikā 2, p. 305. NM., Āhnika 7, p. 440.

[33] Sir Oliver Lodge—Beyond Physics, p. 29.

[34] Elements of Psychology by Margaret Drummond and S. H. Mellone, Chapter V., pp. 102-145.

CHAPTER IX

NON-ETERNAL FORMS OF MATTER

INTRODUCTORY

THE eternal forms of matter, in almost all their possible aspects, have been dealt with in previous chapters. Now, here an attempt is made to consider the nature of the non-eternal forms of matter in detail. These forms are : air (*vāyu*), water (*iala*), earth (*pṛthivī*) and *tejas*. All of these possess intermediary dimension (*madhyama-parimāṇa*) and are, therefore, destructible. Each of these is ultimately produced out of its ultimate particles, called *paramāṇus*. The process of the production of these forms of matter has already been given in great detail in previous chapters. Hence, each of these four non-eternal froms of matter, as it appears to us after production, is taken here, in the order in which each has been produced, for further consideration. The following treatment of these forms of matter is based on their distinctive features which have been also clearly mentioned before.

I

AIR (VĀYU)

1. *Existence of air proved*

It has already been said above[1] that after the Cosmic Rest is over, motion is produced in the ultimate particles of air which then join together so as to form airy-

[1] *Vide Supra*, p. 270.

products. Hence, the products of air are considered to be the first material products. Those who think that direct perception is possible only through the organ of sight cannot believe in the existence of air directly. Hence, it is necessary to prove its existence through inference before proceeding further. The following are the probans for the existence of air: touch (*sparça*), sound (*çabda*), upholding (*dhṛti*), and quivering (*kampa*). Thus, it is found that there is a particular type of touch which is non-chemical (*apākaja*) and moderate, that is, neither hot nor cold. This touch, being a quality, must inhere in a substance. The substance required here cannot be earth; for the touch, belonging to it, is chemical (*pākaja*); nor can it be water which has cold touch. It also cannot be *tejas*, as the latter possesses hot touch. Substances like *Ākāça*, *Kāla*, *Dik*, *Ātman* and *Manas* do not possess any touch. Hence, that which possesses the particular type of non-chemical and moderate touch is known as air (*vāyu*). Or the form of inference may be as follows: the particular type of touch which is felt, being a quality, must inhere in some substance, like the touch of earth etc. Earth, water and *tejas* cannot be the required substance; for, the touch of these is always associated with colour, while the particular type of touch is not so. Again, the substances, like *Ākāça*, *Kāla*, *Dik*, *Ātman* and *Manas* not possessing any touch, cannot be the required substance. Hence, through the method of elimination, that which remains is proved to be the substratum of the particular kind of touch. Such a substance is air[2].

In the like manner, sound proves the existence of air. Thus, the sound produced in the *Ākāça* due to the contact of cloud etc. must be due to some instrumental cause. In the absence of any other possible substance having touch, air is assumed to be the required

[2] VU. on VS., II. i. 9.

instrumental cause of that sound[3]. Or the form may be as follows: in the absence of the striking of a substance possessing colour, the series of sound produced in the leaves etc., is due to the striking of a substance possessing velocity and touch; because, it is a series of sound related to a substance the parts of which are indivisible (*avibhajyamānāvayavadravyasambandhiçabdasantānatvāt*), like the series of sound produced from the drum due to the striking of the stick. The absence of the striking of the substance possessing colour is known by the non-perception of what is capable of perception. Such a substance is different from the eight other substances, namely, earth, water, *tejas*, *Ākāça*, *Kāla*, *Dik*, *Ātman* and *Manas* and possesses touch and velocity. This is air[4].

Similarly, a particular upholding (*dhṛtiviçeṣa*) also proves the existence of air. Thus, the upholding of straw, grass, cotton, cloud, air-ships and the rest in the sky is due to the conjunction with a substance having touch and velocity; because, it is the steadiness of a substance which is not presided over by a conscious being[5], like the steadiness of grass, wood, boat etc. in the current of a river. In the case of the upholding of poison etc. caused by thought, no doubt, it is the human agency presiding over it. Same is the case with the steadiness of a bird, the trunk of a tree etc.

Quivering (*kampa*), also, proves the existence of air. Thus, the motion in grass etc., without the striking of the substance possessing colour, is due to the striking of the substance possessing touch and velocity, like the motion not produced by the contact of the *Ātman* possessing weight and effort like the motion of the cane-forest being struck by the waves of a river. The

[3] KR., p. 22.
[4] VU. on VS., II. i. 9.
[5] By conscious being here we mean other than God.

word 'weight' implies conjunction of the *Ātman* qualified by *adṛsta*, fluidity and *saṃskāra*; hence, the motion not produced by these is the probans of air[6].

2. *Definition*

Such an air has been defined as the substratum of touch and the absolute absence of colour[7]. Çaṅkara Miçra defines it in several ways. He says—air is that which is the substratum of the generality which has the common substratum with touch but not with colour; or, it is that which possesses the generality which is directly pervaded by the generality called *dravyatva* and which is supersensuous; or, it is that which has the generality which does not subsist in things having colour and which exists in a composite; or, it is that which possesses the generality which has a common substratum along with a specific quality but not with colour and consciousness; and so on[8]. All these definitions are more or less based on the specific characteristics of air.

3. *Characteristics*

It possesses a peculiar type of touch called non-chemical (*apākaja*) and is neither hot nor cold (*anuṣṇā-çīta*). This particular nature of touch distinguishes it from *tejas*, water and earth.

It possesses the qualities of number, dimension, separateness and velocity. As air is non-visible, these qualities also are supersensuous. That they belong to air is proved from the fact that without these airy particles could not have produced airy products. Besides, it may be pointed out that without disjunction there is no possibility of destroying the conjunction, so that, the airy products would not have been destroyed

6 VU., II. i. 9; KR., p. 22.
7 LU., p. 33.
8 KR., p. 21; VU. on VS., II. i. 4.

without disjunction. Hence, it is necessary to believe in the existence of disjunction in air. Again, had there been no priority and posteriority in air, then the difference between the large and the small number of conjunctions belonging to air would not have been determined, and the limitedness of the dimension also would not have been explained. The presence of velocity in it is inferred from the presence of motion in straw, grass etc. This motion is, no doubt, due to the contact of air with the straw, but it is possible simply because air possesses velocity; for, the conjunction of a substance without velocity is not capable of producing any motion.[9]

Its motion is transversal (*tīryak*). It keeps the clouds at rest in the sky and also moves them from place to place. It causes the showering of rains, checks the force of weight and does not let the weighty substance fall down. That it helps the air-ships and similar other things to fly in the sky[10] is proved from the fact that the contact of a substance having touch is essential to keep things in the sky; and such a substance is no other than air[11].

Air is said to be the instrumental cause of all the *taijasa* products even including gold etc. It is, therefore, that a lamp-light burns only when there is air to help it and not otherwise[12].

It is never at rest[13]. The collision of a particular current of air with another, due to which there is upward motion, is the mark of its plurality[14]. As it has neither manifested nor unmanifested colour, it is not perceived through the organ of sight[15].

[9] VS., V. i. 14; PPBhā., p. 44; KU., p. 80; Kandalī, p. 45.
[10] PPBhā., p. 47; KU., pp. 85-86; Kandalī, p. 45.
[11] KR., p. 22.
[12] KP., pp. 81-82; KPP. and Makaranda. pp. 81-82.
[13] VBhā., II. i. 9.
[14] VS., II. i. 11-14.
[15] KR., p. 21; Nyāyasāra of Mādhavadeva, p. 44.

4. *Perceptibility of air discussed*

The question of the perceptibility of air is a much vexed one. Some are of opinion that it is perceived, while others think that its perception (*pratyakṣa*) is impossible, because it has neither manifested nor unmanifested colour. The supporters of the former view think that the experiences expressed in the forms—'air blows,' 'air is cold,' 'air is hot,' etc., show that air is perceived through the instrumentality of touch sensation[16]. Now, as to the apparent difficulty presented by the Sūtra laying down the conditions of perception, that is, a substance is perceived, because it possesses magnitude, is composed of more than one substance and has a particular kind of colour[17], it is suggested that these conditions should be applied either separately (*vyasta*) or collectively (*samasta*). It is, therefore, that *Ātman* is perceived, because it possesses magnitude; air is perceived, as it has magnitude and is composed of more than one substance; while in the case of those substances which are cognised through the organs of sight and touch all the three conditions are required. Hence, there should not be any difficulty in the direct perceptibility of air[18].

To this it is urged by those who do not believe in the direct perceptibility of air that wherever there is the tactile perception, there exists the activity of the organ of sight also; hence, along with the touch sensation of air, its qualities, like number etc., should have been perceived through the organ of sight. But it is not so. Hence, it is concluded that here in the case of air the perception is limited to touch alone, as it is found in the case of the heat belonging to water. That is, as the hot touch

[16] Vyom., p. 272.

[17] *Mahattvādanekadravyavatvāt rūpaviçeṣācca dravyaṃ pratyakṣam*—VS., IV. i. 6.

[18] Vyom., p. 272.

of the boiling water is felt, but its substratum, namely, fire, is not perceived, similarly, the touch of air is felt, but its substratum, namely, air, is not perceived.[19]

To this, again, it is pointed out that the analogy is not a sound one; for, in the case of the heat of the boiling water, the colour being unmanifest, the touch alone can be perceived. But it is not the same with air. As regards the non-perception of the qualities of air, it may be pointed out that the perception of the qualities of that substance whose perception is due to its possessing colour, is possible, while it is not the case with air, where the perception is due to conditions other than the possession of colour. As it is found with the *Ātman* which is perceived through the *Manas* even without having any colour; and it is, therefore, that its qualities, like number etc., are non-perceptible[20]. Therefore, air, even without having any colour, is directly perceived. Moreover, holds the author of the Vyomavatī, there can be no inference through the probans—touch, to prove the existence of air; for their is neither any generalisation (*vyāpti*) nor its remembrance. Nor can there be any *parāmarça* to that effect[21].

Others prove the perception of air even through inference; because, they believe that adherence to inference is possible for the sake of others even when the man making the inference has got the direct perception of it. The form of inference is as follows :[22]

(1) Air which is the substratum of touch being experienced by us is an object of direct perception through our organ of touch;

(2) because, it is the substratum of touch being experienced by us, and which is other than the unmani-

[19] Vyom., p. 272-73.

[20] Vyom., p. 273.

[21] *Rūpaṃ vināpi vāyoḥ spārçanena pratyakṣatvāt*-Vyom., p. 273; *Idānīṃ pratyakṣeṇa vāyusadbhāve vyavasthāpite* etc. Vyom., p. 274.

[22] Vyom., p. 274.

fested colour;

(3). whatever is, being other than the unmanifested colour, an object of touch being experienced by us, is an object of perception through our sense-organ of touch, as is the case with jar and others;

(4) so is the case with air which, being other than the unmanifested colour, is an object of touch being experienced by us;

(5) therefore, air is an object of perception through the organ of touch.

Now, it is argued here that in this way all the supersensuous things would become perceptible through *prameyatva* as their probans. But this is not correct, says the author of the Vyomavatī; for, it is frustrated by the cognition of others expressed in the form—'we do not possess the cognition of *paramāṇu* and the rest, for instance. And the use of inference is quite justified for convincing them even when one is in possession of the cognition through perception. This is possible in the case of air and not in the case of *paramāṇus*. If *paramāṇus* become an object of our perception, then they would not remain *paramāṇus* any more[23].

Similarly, Raghunātha Çiromaṇi says that possession of touch alone is the cause of having the touch perception of a substance[24], and that there is no need in believing in the presence of manifested colour as well; for, in that case, there is a great *gaurava*[25]. Koṇḍa Bhaṭṭa also supports this and adds that the perceptibility of air is proved also through the judgment expressed in the form —'I touch air'; otherwise, there would not be the touch perception of a jar and the rest; but a jar, for instance, would be inferred, while only its colour would be perceived through the organ of sight[26].

[23] Vyom., p. 274; Setu, pp. 263-64.
[24] PTN., p. 41.
[25] CM., Pratyakṣa, p. 730. Bibl. Ed.
[26] TPP., *Ms.* Fol. 2b.

Others do not quite agree with the above view. They hold that if perception be due to manifested touch, then lustre (*prabhā*) would become non-perceptible; and in that case, when a bird is flying in the sky at the perception of the colour of lustre, there would not be the cognition of its conjunction and disjunction. We cannot say that the conjunction and disjunction are inferred from the non-perception of the previous point in space (*deça*) and the perception of the consequent point in space; for, *deça* being *mānasika* its cognition will take place from *upanītabhāna*. Hence, the manifestation of colour itself is the cause of direct perception. This being absent in air, it is non-perceptible.

Others hold that if manifested colour be the cause of perception, then the lustre and the bilious substance of the eyes also would be perceptible. If this be accepted as favourable, then the cognition of number etc. belonging to air will have to be accepted as perceptible, which is not desired. Similarly, if manifested colour be held to be the cause of perception, then the heat of the summer and the rest, being *vyāpya* of the perceptible number etc., will have to be accepted as perceptible; so that, it is assumed that both colour and touch are the causes of perception. Hence, in the absence of colour, air is non-perceptible[27]. Gangeça Upādhyāya adds that both are necessary in every case of perception through external sense-organs[28].

It is held that even in the case of perception through the tactile organ the presence of manifested colour is essential. It is due to this that lustre (*prabhā*), even air, etc., are not perceived through it[29]. But is it possible? For, if we do not get the cognition of air through the tactile organ, how can even the inference of it be pos-

[27] Setu., pp. 264-67.

[28] CM., Pratyakṣa pp. 730-38; Nyāyakaustubha, pp. 103-110; Jalada of Bhagīratha, *Ms*. Fol. 36b.

[29] PRM., *Ms*. Fol. 7b.

sible? The cognition through tactile organ alone is the probans to prove its existence.

The question may be approached from a different point of view also. We know that according to Nyāya-Vaiçeṣika inherence is only one. But due to its relation with all the qualities separately, we speak of *sparça-samavāya*, *rūpa-samavāya*, and so on. Now, the point is: if there be only one inherence (*samavāya*), then where there is the *rūpa-samavāya*, there is the *sparça-samavāya* also, and *vice versa*; so that, that there is the *sparça-samavāya* in air is not objected to by any school, and consequently, there should be the *rūpa-samavāya* also in it. This being accepted, we will have to say that just as due to the presence of *sparça-samavāya* in it there is *sparça* in it, so there should be *rūpa* also in it, as there is now the *rūpa-samavāya* also in it. To this they say that although there is the *rūpa-samavāya* in air, yet there can be no notion (*pratīti*) of the presence of *rūpa* in it.[30]

To this, again, it is said that when there is the *rūpa-samavāya*, then how can there be the absence of colour? For, is it possible to hold that the relation, namely, inherence, is there, but the related (*sambandhin*) is not there? There is the relation of *vyāpya-vyāpakabhāva* between *sambandha* and *sambandhin*. To this the reply is that it is not so; because, the *sambandha*, only when qualified, leads to the presence of the particular *sambandhin*. That is, when the *samavāya* is qualified by *rūpa* (*rūpanirūpitatvaviçiṣṭa*), only then it leads to the presence of *rūpa* in air. But as it is not the case with air, we cannot say that there is colour in it.[31]

Kaṇāda says that although there is the *magnitude* in air, yet due to the absence of *rūpa-saṃskāra*, it is not perceptible.[32] The Upaskāra understands by the term

[30] NMuktā., on verse II; Āloka, *Ms.* Fol. 101a.
[31] NMuktā., on verse II, p. 32.
[32] VS., IV. i. 7.

rūpasaṃskāra, the *samavāya* of colour, the manifestation of colour, and the non-suppression of colour; so that, although there is the *sparça-samavāya*, which is identical with the *rūpasamavāya*, in air, yet the inherence is not qualified by colour, as there is the absolute absence of colour. Thus, by *rūpasaṃskāra* here we mean *rūpa-samavāya*. The Vṛttikāra explains the term, *rūpasaṃskāra* as '*rūpaṃ ca rūpasaṃskāraçca*' of which, one *rūpa* is dropped; so that, it means that due to the mere absence of colour air is not perceived.[33]

Candrakānta, on the other hand, suggests that the sense of the author of the *Sūtra* is that in air although there is colour, but as the *saṃskāra* of that colour is not present in it, the visual perception of it does not take place.[34]

Some, again, suggest that the notion 'air possesses colour' is not due to mere *inherence*, but to a different *adhikaraṇatā* limited by the *samavāya-sambandha*. This particular kind of *adhikaraṇatā* is not present in air. Hence, the notion 'air possesses colour' is not correct.[35]

It is due to these difficulties that the modern school of Nyāya believes in the plurality of inherence; so that, only *sparça-samavāya* is present in air just as only *rūpa-samavāya* is present in fire, and so on. Hence, when the inherence of colour is absent from air, the colour also naturally is absent[36].

It may be suggested here that regarding the notion of direct perception (*pratyakṣa*), which has been defined as the cognition produced out of the contact of the object and the sense-organ,[37] there are two different possible interpretations. One school appears to hold

[33] VU., IV. i. 7.
[34] VBhā, IV. i. 6.
[35] Nyāyakaustubha—Pratyakṣa, pp. 127-28.
[36] Nyāyakaustubha—Pratyakṣa, p. 128.
[37] NS., I. i. 4.

that direct perception is that cognition which is produced out of the contact of the organ of sight and the object possessing colour. This school of thought can in no way recognise the cognitions arrived at through the contact of the other four sense-organs with their respective objects as cases of direct perception.

There is another school of thought which holds that just as the cognition, produced out of the contact of the organ of sight and the object having colour, is called direct perception (*pratyakṣa*), so every cognition produced from the direct contact of the other sense-organs with their respective objects should be called cases of direct perception. Thus, we have five different kinds of external direct perceptions, namely, visual, (*cākṣuṣa*), gustatory (*rāsana*), auditory (*çrāvaṇa*), odorous (*ghrāṇaja*) and tactile (*spārçana*), and one internal, namely, mental (*mānasika*). By '*akṣa*' in the word *pratyakṣa*, they mean all the sense-organs, while others mean only 'eye.'

It appears that if in the very beginning of any discussion on perceptibility of anything, the meaning of the term *akṣa* be clearly explained, then much of the confusion would be very easily removed. The truth is only one and that also must be common for all.

Mallinātha, in his commentary on the Tārkikarakṣā, says—"*Svamate vāyoh spārçanatve 'pi Vaiçeṣikobhūtvā āha apratyakṣasyeti.*"[38] From this it may be understood that the view is that like visual perception there are other kinds of perceptions also due to the contact of the objects and the other four external sense-organs. But the Vaiçeṣika holds that perception is only visual, and not gustatory etc.

5. *Identity of air with earth*

It appears that there was a view that air is identical

[38] p. 136.

with a particular division of earth.[39] But this view is wrong; for, if it were so, then air must have possessed manifested colour like earth; because, the contact of fire productive of manifested touch also produces manifested colour.[40]

6. *Division and sub-divisions of air*

Such an air is divided into eternal[41] as *paramāṇus* and non-eternal representing the class of airy products. This latter is subdivided into organism, sense-organ, inorganic mass, and vital air (*prāṇa*).[42] The modern school of Nyāya, however, does not believe in the fourth sub-division.[43]

(1) *Organic air*

The airy organism is only *ayonija*, and hence, it is not produced out of the fusion of the male and the female as is in the case of the earthly one. Such an organism is produced from the airy *paramāṇus* which are also helped by *adṛṣṭa*. Their mutual contact is the non-material cause, while the *paramāṇus* of earth and the rest are the instrumental causes.

Such an organism exists in *Vāyuloka*. Now, the question is: As such a body does not possess the tongue etc., there is no possibility of speech; in the absence of hands and feet, there is no possibility of eating and walking; and in the absence of peculiar kind of collocations, it cannot be the substratum of any sense-organ; so that, how can the airy organism be used for the

[39] DSS., *Ms.* Fol. 85-86.
[40] DP., *Ms.* Fol. 60a.
[41] Candrakānta here remarks that although air, like *Ākāça*, is really non-eternal, yet for the sake of the worldly usage it is recognised as eternal. This is clear from the fact that air exists in intermediate *sargas* as well as in *Pralaya*-VBhā., I. i. 5; VVV., pp. 6; 13.
[42] PPBhā., p. 44; SP., p. 15; KR, p. 22.
[43] NK., p. 737 (third edition).

experience of pleasure and pain? The Vyomavatī further suggests that as it is ever in motion the airy body cannot be a means of the experience of pleasure and pain[44]. Without such an experience there is no use of an organism.

To this the reply may be given tnat the airy body is made capable of being used as a means of experiencing pleasure and pain through the contact of the earthly particles in the form of its auxiliaries. Udayana distinctly says that not only earthly *paramāṇus* are present in the airy organism, but there are the *paramāṇus* of other *bhūtas* also.[45]

(2) *Airy sense-organ*

It is a fact that touch is felt. As such, it must have an instrument to bring about the cognition of it and also because, it is an activity (*kriyā*), it must be preceded by an instrument (*karaṇa*), as it is in the act of a cut. This *karaṇa* must be airy; for, out of the five specific qualities, namely, colour, taste, smell, touch, and hearing, the touch is always felt by the tactile sense-organ alone, as it is in the case of the air of a fan. Hence, it is concluded that the tactile sense-organ is airy.

Now, it is asked: whether any and every kind of air can produce the tactile sense-organ or not? The answer is—no; only those airy *parāmāṇus*, which are not suppressed by the *paramāṇus* of any other *bhūtas* can be productive of the tactile organ. In other words, the airy *paramāṇus*, with the help of *adṛṣṭa* either alone without the least contact or mixture of the *paramāṇus* of other *bhūtas*, or if at all there is any contact of the airy *paramāṇus* with the *paramāṇus* of other *bhūtas*, it is a very slight one, produce the sense-organ of touch.[46]

[44] p. 271.
[45] KU., p. 81; Kandalī, p. 45.
[46] Vyom., p. 271.

Çrīdhara calls such a production a specific one (*viçiṣṭotpāda*).[47] It is, therefore, that when a particular part of the tactile organ is destroyed or overpowered by any disease of the type of leprosy etc., there is no feeling of touch in that part. In other words, that portion of the organ is overpowered by the influence of non-airy substance; hence, that part does not act as a sense-organ of touch.[48]

The place of location of the airy sense-organ is throughout the body.[49] Jayanta says that by the tactile organ we should not mean the external skin on the body alone but those layers of skin (*tvak*) also, which pervade the entire body, both in and out. It is due to this that cooling and burning touch sensations are felt even in the hearts of heart.[50]

(*a*) *Bhautika nature of the organs of sense discussed*

By the way, we find that this view of the Nyāya-Vaiçeṣika has provoked the anger of the Sāṅkhya School which thinks that the sense-organs are produced from the *Prakṛti* and not from the *bhūtas*. Now, we find that the sense-organs possess partly the characteristics of *bhūta* and partly that of the *Prakṛti*. Thus, the organ of sight, for instance, is found to cognise colour etc., when the black pupil of it is not destroyed, and when it is destroyed, there is no cognition of colour etc. This establishes its *bhautika* nature. Again, we find that the pupil cognises its object without coming in contact with that object and not when that object is brought in close touch with the sense-organ of sight. This is its non-*bhautika* characteristic. An object cannot both be *bhautika* and non-*bhautika*. Hence, in the absence of the distinguishing factor we find a doubt regarding the

[47] Kandalī, p. 45.
[48] KU., p. 82; Vyom., p. 271.
[49] PPBhā., p. 44.
[50] NM., p. 477.

true nature of the sense-organ in general[51].

On this the Sāṅkhya holds that because things having magnitude and atomic dimension are perceived through the sense-organ, it is inferred that it is non-*bhautika*[52]. In other words, we find that the organ of sight perceives things of very big size, as for instance, mountain, ocean, and so on, and at the same time, it perceives things of quite a smaller dimension, as for instance, the seed of a banyan tree, which goes against the *bhautika* nature of it; for, a *bhautika* object can perceive things of its own size, while a non-*bhautika*, being all-pervading in nature, can perceive things of any dimension[53].

The Naiyāyikas reject the above argument saying that merely because the organ of sight perceives things both of big and small dimensions, the non-*bhautika* nature of it cannot be proved; for, these two dimensions are cognised due to the contact of the dimensions themselves with the rays coming out of the eyes[54], as we find in the case of the rays of the lamp and the object. The particular kind of rays and object contact is to be inferred from the obstruction; that is, the rays of the organ of sight do not illumine things which are obstructed by wall and the rest; just as, it is the case with the lamp-rays.[55]

Again, the opponent refutes the argument of the Naiyāyikas on the ground that the rays and object contact cannot be a case of inference. It should be a case of perception; for, *tejas* is tangible and possesses colour; because, perception takes place due to the possession of magnitude and colour and also to the subsistence in several substances. Hence, the contact should be a

[51] NS. and NBhā., III. i. 32.
[52] NS., III. i. 33.
[53] NBhā., III. i. 33.
[54] NS., III. i. 34.
[55] NBhā., III. i. 34.

case of perception and not inference; so that, the fact is that had there been rays in the organ of sight, then they would have been perceived, but as they are not perceived but only inferred, it is concluded that no such rays exist in the visual organ[56].

This, again, is rejected by the Naiyāyikas on the ground that the non-perception of the rays, whose presence is inferred by the obstruction not allowing the contact (*sannikarṣapratiṣedhenāvaraṇena liṅgenānumīyamānasya*), does not prove the absence of the rays; just as the non-perception of the other side of the moon or the lower part of the earth does not prove their non-existence[57].

We know, on the other hand, that the construction of the sense-organs (*vyūha*) is due to the influence of *adṛṣṭa* and is meant for the experience of pleasure and pain of the *Jīvas*. In the case of the organ of sight, to give effect to the very aim of *bhoga*, the existence of rays has been assumed. That is, the material cause of the visual organ is *tejas*, one of the *bhūtas*; so that, the effect of it, namely, the sense-organ of sight, is also *bhautika*. In the same manner, we know that all the other external sense-organ shave got some or other *bhūtas* as their material cause. Hence, all of them are *bhautikas*.

There is another reason to prove that the external sense-organs are *bhautikas* and it is this: obstruction is the nature of *bhūtas* alone. If there be an obstruction between a sense-organ and its object of cognition, then there would not be the cognition of that object through that sense-organ. This is found with all the external sense-organs; hence they are all *bhautikas*. A non-*bhautika* object is never obstructed. But we must know that the objects whose activities are not stopped by any obstruction are not all non-*bhautikas*; for, in the very

56 NBhā., III. i. 1 35.
57 NBhā., III. i. 36.

case of the visual organ, we find that there are certain objects like glass etc., which do not put any obstruction in the way of the rays of the organ of sight. But this cannot prove the non-*bhautikatva* of the sense-organ; for, non-obstruction is equally an attribute of both *bhautika* and non-*bhautika*; as we find in the case of the rays of the lamp which illumine things in whose way stand glass etc., and there is no obstruction of the heat of the cooking fire operating upon things placed on hearth. That fire is *bhautika* cannot be objected to. As for the non-perception of the rays of the organ of sight, we find that it is possible due to certain causes, as it is in the case of the fall of meteor during the mid-day; because, it is suppressed by the stronger light of the sun; so that, in spite of the cause of perception being present in the case of the rays of the organ of sight, due to the non-manifestation of colour and touch the *tejas* of the eyes is not perceived but only inferred. Hence, the sense-organs are *bhautika* and not non-*bhautika*[58].

Those who think that there can be no non-obstruction of what is purely *bhautika* are wrong; because, as a matter of fact, there is no obstruction of the rays of the sun, of the objects lying behind a piece of rock-crystal (*sphaṭika*) and of things which are to be burnt[59]. In other words, in spite of the fact that the organ of sight is *bhautika*, there is no obstruction in its way caused by substances, like glass etc. Now, against the view that all *bhautika* objects must have obstruction and that there is no exception to this rule, the author of the Nyāya-Sūtra points out instances to refute it. It is held according to the Nyāya-Vaiçeṣika that—

(i) There is no obstruction of the rays of the sun; for instance, the rays of the sun enter the jar not being obstructed by the wall of the jar and come

[58] NS. and NBhā., III. i. 39-44.
[59] NBhā., III. i. 48.

in contact with the water therein and make it hot. The hot touch of the rays of the sun suppresses the cold touch of the water of the jar.

(ii) The obstruction is not caused by the crystal; that is, when anything is lying behind the crystal, the light of the lamp pierces through the crystal and comes in contact with the thing lying behind the crystal, and illumines it; so that, it is wrong to hold that *bhautika* substance, like the light of the lamp, is obstructed.

(iii) Again, lastly, there is no obstruction in the way of the roasting of anything; that is, when anything is roasted in a pan and heat is applied to the pan for roasting, the heat of the fire is not obstructed by the surface of the pan. The heat passes through the pan and comes in contact with the grains to be roasted and makes them hot. This shows that the heat which is *bhautika* has not always got obstruction in its way to function[60]. Therefore, we conclude that the sense-organs are *bhautikas*, and that the *mahābhūtas* are the main material principles of these sense-organs.

Against the argument that the organ of sight cognises an object without coming in contact with the object; for, we find that when the rays of the organ of sight are obstructed by a glass even then the cognition of things beyond the glass takes place[61]; so that, the sense-organs are non-*bhautikas*[62], it is said that when we find that the objects lying behind the wall are not perceived by the organ of sight, how can we assume that the organ of sight cognises things even without coming in contact with them[63]? In the case of glass, we know that the sight is not obstructed; so that, even there the

[60] NBhā., III. i. 48; Kandalī, pp. 23-24.
[61] NS., III. i. 45.
[62] NBhā., III. i. 45.
[63] NBhā., III. i. 46.

cognition of colour etc., takes place after the sense-organ has come in contact with the object[64].

3. *Inorganic air*

The inorganic air is the substratum of the manifested touch sensation, which is denoted by quivering, upholding (*dhṛti*), sound and touch[65].

4. *Vital air (prāṇa)*

It is that which is the cause of the movement of the liquid substance and other various elements within the body, such as, the carrying of blood, semen, the internal fire, bile, phlegm, and so on. It is in these aspects that vital air is differentiated from the inorganic air. Although there is only one kind of air within the body, yet due to its different functions it is subdivided into five :—*prāṇa*, *apāna*, *samāna*, *udāna*, and *vyāna*.

Prāṇa is that which comes out of the mouth and nostrils and goes in; *apāna* is that which causes ejection of dirts of the body; *samāna* is that which carries the internal fire for the digestion of the food etc., in the body from place to place; *udāna* is that which causes the things to move upward; while *vyāna* is that which takes the essence of the food etc. to all the parts of the body through the various veins (*nāḍis*)[66].

Some, again, add five more varieties to the above mentioned five. They are: *nāga*, *kūrma*, *kṛkara*, *devadatta*, and *dhanañjaya*[67]. But as the functions of these are served by the above mentioned five alone, this set is not recognised. *Tāntrikas*, on the other hand, believe in 49 kinds of air.

Some hold that motionless air is another subdivision. But it is not so. It is not different from the

[64] NS. and NBhā., III. i. 47.
[65] PPBhā, p. 44.
[66] KU., pp. 88-89; Kandalī, p. 48.
[67] VSS., p. 61 (Vāṇīvilās Press Ed.).

mere collection of airy *paramāṇus*[68], but even then it is difficult to think of air as motionless.

II

WATER

1. *Definition of water*

Water has been defined as that which naturally possesses cold touch[69]; or, that which possesses the generality which belongs to hail, snow, ice, but does not belong to any other substance, such as earth, etc.[70] Besides, the general definitions given by Çaṅkara Miçra are all more or less the enumeration of the various specific qualities of water[71]. Thus, it has been defined as that which possesses the *upādhi* which separates one substance from the other; or, that which exists in that which possesses non-illuminating (white) colour; or, that which does not possess a common substratum with other than pure white colour, and which possesses the colour which is not due to chemical action and is non-illuminating[72].

Candrakānta refers to that kind of water which is produced by the combination of the two kinds of gases. It is, no doubt, an artificial one and does not stand, according to him, in the way of the existence of natural water as dealt with in this section[73]. This view is, undoubtedly, based on the influence of the Western science.

2. *Qualities of water*

Water possesses the qualities of colour, taste, touch,

[68] SP., p. 16.
[69] VS., II. ii. 5.
[70] LU., p. 30.
[71] KR., pp. 12-13.
[72] Setu., p. 239.
[73] VBhā., I. i. 5.

natural fluidity, viscidity, number, dimension, separateness, conjunction, disjunction, priority and posteriority, weight and velocity[74]. Of these, colour, taste, touch, natural fluidity and viscidity are peculiar qualities of water which differentiate it from all other substances. A brief account of these qualities are given below :

(1). *Colour*

Non-illuminating whiteness is its natural colour. However heat may be applied to water, its colour will remain unchanged[75]. This is not the case with earth which by the application of heat changes its[76] colour. Whatever other colour is seen in water, as in the waters of the Yamunā, or various juice-waters, it is all due to the mixture or the influence of earthly particles.

(2). *Taste*

Similarly, the taste of water is only sweet (*madhura*). We find that if heat is applied to sweet earthly things, like milk and sugar, the sweet taste is removed; while in the case of water, however heat is applied to it, its sweetness remains unchanged. Whatever other taste is found in water, as saltish taste in the sea-water, lemon-taste in lemon-juice, and so on, it is due to the mixture of earthly particles with it; and consequently, the non-sweet taste apparently found in water belongs to earth, otherwise we cannot explain the sweet taste of the rain waters showered by clouds. Generally, when we drink water the sweet taste of it is not found. The reason is that it is destroyed or suppressed by the influence of earthly or firy substances present in the mouth. For this reason it is believed that in order to bring out the real taste of water, we should first take

[74] PPBhā., p. 35.
[75] KU., p. 67; KUP., p. 267.
[76] KU., p. 67.

in astringent substance, like the fruit of the yellow myrobalan tree, before drinking water. As regards the experience of bitter (*tikta*) taste of water after chewing the fruit of cucumber, it is held through experiment that it does not belong to the juice or water of cucumber fruit, but to the fruit itself which is an earthly substance; it may also be possible that when the cucumber fruit is eaten, it manifests the bilious nature present at the tip of the tongue; so that, the bitter taste may be due to the manifestation of the bilious nature of the tip of the tongue[77].

(3). *Touch*

Coming to the touch of water we find that it is naturally cold. It is just possible that sometimes due to the influence of fire the cold touch of water is suppressed, but when that influence is removed, again, the water becomes cold.[78] But what about the cold touch found in the sandal-wood which is undisputedly earthly? It is not the cold touch of the water which is used in the rubbing of it; because, even without rubbing it with the help of water, there is that touch sensation; and also when it is rubbed, the cold touch which is found in the sandal-wood is far more cooling than that of the water which is used in rubbing it. The answer is that in the former case, the cold touch belongs to the watery particles present in the sandal-wood; and in the latter case, it is said that as it is found after rubbing also, it really belongs to water. It has been enhanced by coming in contact with the parts of sandal-wood.[79] Lakṣmīpati says that the hot touch belonging to water is only conditional, just as in a fine crystal the red colour is due to the presence of *japā* flower near it;

[77] KU., pp. 67-68; KUP, pp. 268-269; KUPV, on Ibid; Dravyasārasaṅgraha, *Ms.* Fol. 66.

[78] KU., 68.

[79] KUP., pp. 269-270; KR., pp. 15-16.

and is not natural[80].

The colour, the taste, and the touch of water do not undergo any change due to the chemical action[81]; as the latter does not affect water. Against the view that there is nothing to prevent the peculiar kind of heat contact in water, it is said that if, like earth, here also we believe in the presence of the peculiar heat contact, then the previous colour and touch would have to be assumed to have been destroyed and a fresh colour and touch produced in their place. That is, the non-illuminating colour and the cold touch belonging to water should have been destroyed giving place to another type of colour and hot touch. Then even when the heat contact is removed from water, there would be nothing to remove the hot touch which would have come to belong to water after the chemical action, and consequently, that water would have never become cold; and we should have actually felt hot touch in water even long after the chemical action. It is just possible that the touch may be counteracted and water may be reduced to a touchless substance. But this is against the reality. Hence, we must hold that there is no chemical action in water[82].

(4). *Viscidity*

Viscidity (*sneha*) is also one of the natural qualities of water. It does not belong to anything else.

Some reject it on the ground that just as there is no oil and the rest in water, so there is no viscidity, also, in it. It is not a specific quality of earth; because, it is not found with all the forms of earth. It is, however, found only in certain particular forms of

[80] PV., *Ms.* Fol. 7b.
[81] KR., p. 16.
[82] Prabhā and Mañjūṣā on NMuktā., p. 331, Mylapore Ed.

earth, namely, *ghṛta*, oil, fat, and so on[83].

This is a wrong view, says the Siddhāntin; for, if it were a quality of earth, it ought to have been present in the very *paramāṇus* of earth also; but in the *paramāṇus* of earth there is no other generality except *pṛthivītva*. As for its presence in *ghṛta* etc., it is due to something else, just as in the absence of the natural weight in *tejas*, the presence of weight in gold is said to be due to its mixture with earthly substance. If it were not the quality of water, then sugar, or any other powder, or flour etc., would not have become a lump. This is due to viscidity along with the help of fluidity and not to the fluidity alone. If making a lump be due to fluidity only, then when glass, or gold etc., are melted, then through it sand and the rest should have been also made a lump; but it is not a fact. Hence, viscidity is a natural quality of water alone[84]. We cannot hold that just as there is conditional fluidity in earth, so let there be conditional viscidity also in it; for, no such viscidity is found in earth. The viscidity belonging to *ghṛta* etc. is due to the presence of the watery *paramāṇus* in them as auxiliaries.

(5). *Fluidity*

Natural fluidity is also a quality of water alone. It, together with viscidity, is essential for making a lump of anything. Without the help of both, water alone cannot collect together any powder, flour, and the rest, into a lump. This natural fluidity does not belong to oil or to milk; for, oil and milk are earthly substances. This is proved by oil's being a fuel for earthly fire, and milk's being recognised even in a lump (*jatukṣīrasya ca piṇḍībhave'pi pratyabhijñānāt*)[85].

[83] KU., p. 68 (Vindheswari Prasad's Edition).

[84] KU., p. 69 (Vindheswari Prasad's edition) along with KUP. on Ibid. pp. 270-275 Bibli. Ind. edition. Setu. pp. 239-242.

[85] KU., p. 70 (Vindheswari Prasad's edition); KUP. pp. 276-277 (Bibli. Ind. edition); Setu. p. 241.

What about the natural fluidity in hails, snow, ice, etc.? It is also natural in these cases; but it has been obstructed due to the influence of *adṛṣṭa* helped by the absence of the earthly heat; and hence, it is not obvious in the above mentioned substances.

The view that the solidity (*kāṭhinya*) present in hails etc. is due to the influence of the presence of earthly element in them is wrong; for, if it were so, then when these hails fall to the ground, even then they would have remained unmelted as before; but it is not so. Moreover, when they are melted we do not see any earthly element mixed with them.

3. *Divisions and subdivisions of water*

Water is, as usual, divided into eternal and non-eternal forms. The former is in the form of *paramāṇus*, the details of which have been already given. The latter is in the form of products. This form of water is sub-divided into organic, sense-organ and inorganic.

(1). *Organic water*

Water, also like earth, is productive of organism. A substance must produce a substance in the form of organism, sense organ, and inorganic bodies. Through the joint methods of Agreement and Difference it is proved that if any one of the above mentioned three forms is produced, the other forms also should be produced; so that, if there be no watery organism, then there should not be watery sense-organ in our body as well. But this is not the case. We cannot deny the presence of the watery sense-organ in our body. Hence, it is proved that there is an organism of water also. But of what kind of organism is it? Is it *yonija*, or *ayonija*? We have seen that the former is due to the fusion of the male and the female of the parents and is purely earthly. This is not possible in the case of watery organism. Earthly *paramāṇus* cannot produce watery bodies. Hence, the organic water is only *ayonija*. The reason why such an organism of water is never perceived is that it is found in the *Varuṇaloka* which is far away from here; and there are so many obstacles in the way of its perception.

It is, again, asked: water is naturally fluid; so how can a body formed out of the fluid watery *paramāṇus* be a means of the experiences of pleasure and pain? The answer is that just as the earth is intensely solid, but the body made out of the earthly *paramāṇus* becomes useful for *bhoga* through the peculiar conjunction (*upaṣṭambha*)[86] of the *paramāṇus* of water, so also water, although fluid by nature, yet due to the similar peculiar conjunction[87] of the *paramāṇus* of earth and the rest, turn into an organism which becomes capable of *bhoga*. What is denied is that the organic water can be produced out of the *paramāṇus* of different *bhūtas* used as its material cause, but their mutual assistance is not denied[88]. Koṇḍa Bhaṭṭa says that the organic water is either due to the mixture of the earthly *paramāṇus*, like hails etc. or due to the particular kind of *adṛṣṭa*[89]. The earthly elements stop the fluidity of water and make it fit for *bhoga*[90].

(2). *Watery sense-organ*

It has already been said above that if there is an organic water, there must be a watery sense-organ also. This is also proved through inference; that is, there is the cognition of taste which is a *kriyā*; and as such, it must have a *karaṇa*; for, every *kriyā* necessitates the presence of a *karaṇa*. Such a *karaṇa*, in the case of the cognition of taste, is tongue. Thus, we conclude that *rasanā* is the watery sense-organ. It is further proved

[86] Kandalī, p. 38.
[87] Kandalī, p. 38.
[88] KU., p. 71 (Vindheswari Prasad's edition).
[89] PD., p. 2; PBT., *Ms*. Fol. 21a: TP, *Ms*. Fol. 1b.
[90] Kandalī, p. 38.

that of the various specific qualities of colour, touch, smell etc., it is the taste alone which is invariably cognised by the organ of taste (*rasanā*). This shows that there is some sort of natural affinity between tongue, water and taste. Tongue is made up of mainly watery *paramāṇus* with a very little help of the *paramāṇus* of other *bhūtas*. The *paramāṇus* of other *bhūtas* do not overpower the watery elements; so that, there being the excess of watery *paramāṇus* in the construction of the tongue, it is quite natural that it should cognise the taste which is the specific quality of water.[91]

So has been said by Gautama that a particular sense-organ predominates in a particular element due to its excess; and hence, it is capable of cognising that particular quality of it alone[92]. For instance, the sense-organ of taste although possesses colour, taste and touch, yet it is capable of cognising and manifesting taste alone and not the other two; because, there is the excess (*utkarṣa*) of taste (*rasa*) alone in it[93]. That substance which is distinguished, by having the excess of a particular quality, from others is called *utkṛṣṭa* on account of the manifestation of that quality alone[94]. Hence, although there is no difference as far as the inherence or the *saṃyuktasamavāya* of the above mentioned three qualities are concerned, yet it is the excess of taste (*rasa*) alone which is present in the tongue.[95]

Some, on the other hand, explain that the tongue is capable of apprehending *rasa*, because, it is made up of purely watery *paramāṇus* without the combination of *paramāṇus* of any other *bhūtas*. It is really due to the influence of *adṛṣṭa* that there is an excess in that part of the body alone through which *rasa* is apprehended.

[91] Vyom., p. 246.
[92] NS., III. i. 68.
[93] NBhā., III, i. 68.
[94] NV. on NBhā., III. i. 68.
[95] Tāt., on NV., III. i. 68.

In all these things, *adṛṣṭa* alone is the determining factor[96].

(3). *Inorganic water*

That which is different from organic water and watery sense-organ and is produced out of watery *dvyaṇukas*, *trasareṇus* etc., is the inorganic water; because, it is helpful to us as an object of cognition alone[97]. The forms of inorganic water are all the forms of water used by us and also hails, snow, ice, etc[98].

A question is raised here: Fluidity should not be said to be the natural quality of water; as it is not found in solid forms of inorganic water. This view is wrong; for, due to the influence of non-physical *tejas*, the collection of the various watery *paramāṇus* becomes solid which is known as *saṅghāta*; so that, the fluidity is stopped in certain cases at the very *paramāṇu* stage. Hence, the products of these *paramāṇus* also are without fluidity. In the case of ice, again, the solidity is either due to the physical *tejas* or to the non-physical *tejas*. The case is similar to salt where we find that the fluidity of salt is checked by the contact of *tejas*. That salt is also watery is proved from the fact that like hails etc., its fluidity is seen at some other time. But the saltish taste must be explained as due to the influence of earthly elements. The melting of hails etc. is due to the physical heat contact, as it is in gold etc. The stopping of the fluidity and the starting of it both are due to the influence of non-physical and sometimes that of the physical *teias*[99].

[96] Vyom., pp. 246-47.
[97] Vyom., p. 247.
[98] Kandalī, pp. 265-66.
[99] Ibid.

III

EARTH

1. *Definition of earth*

Earth is defined as that which possesses the absence of the absolute negation of smell[100]. That is, that which has natural smell is called earth. Smell is found in other substances, but it is not natural in them. Its presence in non-earthly substances is due to the mixture of the earthly particles with them.

2. *Qualities of earth*

It possesses colour, taste, smell, touch, number, dimension, separateness, conjunction, disjunction, priority, posteriority, weight, fluidity, velocity and elasticity. Of these, only smell is the quality which differentiates it from all other substances. A brief treatment of these qualities are given below:

(1). *Colour*

All the seven kinds of colour, namely, white, blue or black, yellow, green, gray, red, and *citra* (variegated) naturally belong to earth. As regards the variegated colour, they say that a composite is produced not from one thread alone, but from several threads. Of these threads, some are white, some red, others green and some, again, are blue; so that, out of these threads as the cause, a composite is produced where all these colours join together and produce one effect called variegated colour (*citrarūpa*). These colours cannot counteract one another; because, in that case there would have been no colour in the composite, and consequently, it would not have been perceived. Nor can it be said to be merely a collection of so many colours; for, colour is

100 T.U., p. 18.

vyāpyavṛtti, that is, it pervades over the entire object in which it exists. No one particular non-variegated colour pervades the whole of the particular cloth, for instance; hence, there is no harm in having an independent colour called variegated colour[101]. We should not understand that the word variegated is used in the sense of several colours collected together, but it is altogether an independent word used for an independent colour, like white etc[102].

(2). *Taste*

Taste is of six kinds, namely, sweet, acid (*āmla*) saltish, bitter (*tikta*), hot (*kaṭu*) and pungent (*kaṣāya*). All these belong to earth. These prolong the life, make the body fully developed, strong and healthy[103].

(3). *Smell*

Smell is of two kinds—good and bad.

As to the argument that smell and earth are not co-extensive; for, there are substances, like precious stones, admantine, and even other ordinary stones, where smell is not experienced, it is said that as there is the colour produced by the chemical action in them there exists smell also[104]. Others point out that if such substances are reduced to powder, smell is found in it, and as the composite is produced out of these parts, there is naturally smell in the composite also. That smell is not felt in these is due to the non-manifestation of it[105]. When it is said that earth has both good and bad smell it does not mean that in any one part of an earthly substance both the kinds of smell simultaneously exist;

[101] Kandalī, p. 30; TD., p. 14.
[102] KUP., 205.
[103] PPBhā, p. 105.
[104] KU., p. 47.
[105] Setu, pp. 204-205.

so that, in a single mango fruit, for instance, one portion may be rotten, while the other may be good. Hence, we say that it possesses both the smells; good portion provides good smell and the rotten part gives bad smell. There is no possibility of the smells counteracting each other or producing a variegated smell[106].

(4). *Touch*

Touch of earth is neither hot nor cold, and is produced from chemical action (*pāka*).

These four qualities belong to both the earthly forms eternal and non-eternal. But in both the cases they are non-eternal due to the chemical action, unlike the qualities belonging to the *paramāṇus* of water, *tejas* and air.

(5). *Fluidity*

Fluidity is not natural but conditional in earth.

(6). *Saṃskāra*

There are two kinds of *saṃskāras* in earth, namely, velocity and elasticity.

3. *Division and subdivision of earth*

Such an earth is of two kinds—eternal in the form of *paramāṇus* and non-eternal in the form of products. This latter form of earth consists of parts which are so combined as to serve some useful purpose of our daily life. They are used in forming our bed, seat, and so on[107]. The qualities of both the eternal and the non-eternal forms of earth are non-eternal.

This non-eternal form of earth is, again, subdivided into organic earth, sense-organ, and non-organic earth.[108]

[106] KU., p. 48; TD., p. 7.
[107] PPBhā, p. 27 along with KU. and Kandalī.
[108] Some hold that these three subdivisions belong to the

(1). *Organic earth*

By organic earth we understand an organism produced for the experiences of pleasure and pain by the *Jīvātman* through the influence of the *adṛṣṭa* of persons concerned, and which has come in contact with a particular *Jīvātman* under the influence of the same *adṛṣṭa*. This is the final composite. It is in this body that the consciousness of the *Ātman* becomes manifested and life finds its place. Such an organism is produced from the ultimate particles of earth which form its material cause.

This organism is, again, of two kinds: *Yonija* and *ayonija*. The word *yoni* although generally is used in the sense of a mere cause, yet it is used here in the sense of that cause alone which represents the fusion of the male and the female (*çukra* and *çoṇita*) of the parents. The *ayonija*, however, is not a product of that type. But we should not, therefore, understand that this kind of body is without any cause. The material cause here is the *paramāṇus* and their conjunction is the non-material cause, and merits of a definite type are the instrumental cause. The *ayonija* class of organisms, when produced by the influence of merits, represents the organisms of gods, *ṛṣis*, and others of the *divyaloka*; but when it is produced from the influence of demerits it represents the organisms of lower creatures, insects and those organisms which are meant for experiencing extreme pain in the various hells[109]. The organisms which experience extreme pain in the hell are of the class of *ayonija*, because, it is not possible for the *yonija* class of organisms to bear the intense sufferings of hells.[110] Although the *ayonija* class of organisms is generally watery, *taijasa*,

eternal form of earth, namely, *paramāṇu*;—*anye tvasyāḥ paramāṇulakṣaṇāyāḥ trividha.n kāryaṃ çarīrādirūpamiti manyante*—Vyom., p. 228.

[109] Vyom., p. 229.

[110] KU., p. 56; PBT., *Ms.* Fol. 18b.

and airy, yet the above mentioned forms of *ayonija* organisms are earthly bodies and as such, have earthly *paramāṇus* as their material cause[111].

The *yonija* organism is, again, of two kinds—*jarāyuja*-produced from *jarā*, that is, viviparous, and *aṇḍaja* produced from egg, that is, oviparous. Under the former, we include the organisms of human beings, quadrupeds, wild animals etc., while under the latter, the bodies of snakes, birds, and the rest are included. Udayana says here that the *udbhid* class of organisms, representing trees, plants etc., ought to have been included here, but it appears that Praçastapāda, thinking that this class of organisms possesses a very dull intelligence and also that people in general do not like to think it as an abode of *bhoga*, has not included it here under this class. This shows that Udayana himself is willing to include the class of *udbhijja* under it.[112] Koṇḍa Bhaṭṭa, on the other hand, holds that really speaking there are five kinds of *yonija* organisms, namely :—

(*a*) that which is produced by the earthly *paramāṇus* helped by particular kind of *adṛṣṭa* without the fusion of *çukra* and *çoṇita*, as that of Vaçiṣṭha and others;

(*b*) *Jarāyuja*, as that of human beings and others;

(*c*) *Aṇḍaja*, as that of bird, snake etc;

(*d*) *Svedaja* that which is produced from sweat, as louse, nit, and so on; and

(*e*) *Udbhid*, that which germinates after piercing through the earth, as trees, plants etc[113].

Raghunātha Paṇḍita holds that according to Nyāya there are only two kinds of organisms as pointed out by Praçastapāda, but the Vaiçeṣikas include the *udbhid* class

111 PD., p. 2.

112 KU., pp. 57-58.

113 PD., p. 2; TPP., *Ms*. Fol. 1b.

as well under *yonija*, as held by some[114].

The process of the production of *yonija* organism is described below:

When the semen and ovule mix together in the mother's womb due to the fruition of the parents' *adṛṣṭa*, simultaneously with that there is brought about the contact of the *antaḥkaraṇa*. The fusion produces a sort of substance within the mother's womb; where, due to the force of the contact of the internal *tejas*, a sort of activity is produced in the parts of that substance followed by disjunction leading to the destruction of the substance productive of conjunction. Then through the contact of another *tejas* the previous colour etc. of the *paramāṇus* forming that substance get changed, and fresh colour etc. are produced therein. Thus, we have then before us *paramāṇus* with the chemical products in which motion is produced through the influence of *adṛṣṭa* and the *Ātman-paramāṇu* contact; and then the motion leads the *paramāṇus* to form a body in accordance with the usual process of the formation of *dvyaṇuka*, *trasareṇu*, and the rest[115].

(2). *Pāñcabhautikatva of organism discussed*

Now, a question is raised here: Is an organism made up of the five *bhūtas* or not? We know that the human organism, for instance, is earthly. But our observation shows that the human body is not earthly, but *pāñcabhautika*. In other words, if the human organism be produced out of the earthly *paramāṇus* alone, then it cannot be the substratum of activity, (*ceṣṭā*), of sense-organ, and of pleasure and pain (*artha*), and consequently, the definition of organism given above would not be applied to it. The mutual contact among all these *bhūtas* is not denied. We know that in

[114] PRM., p. 21.
[115] Vyom., p. 230.

the bodies of other *lokas*, namely, *Varuṇa*, *Vāyu*, and *Āditya*, there is the contact of all the other *bhūtas*; because, only then the various bodies can be the source of *bhoga*. Moreover, even in ordinary earthly products, like plates etc., it is found that without the help of other *bhūtas* there can be no production. Again, it is a recognised fact that the qualities found in the product must belong to its cause. We find that a human organism, for instance, possesses smell, wet substance, like juice, *taijasa* element, breathing and openings, which prove that the body is made of all the five elements (*pāñcabhautika*), having the *paramāṇus* of all the four *bhūtas* and the *Ākāça* as its cause[116].

This view is wrong, holds the Nyāya-Vaiçeṣika; because, the arguments adduced above are all doubtful and fallacious. The reasons are: It is said that the presence of the qualities of the five elements may be due to their being the material cause and also otherwise; that is, if the *paramāṇus* of earth be the material cause and those of the other *bhūtas* be the instrumental cause, even then in the product we can have the qualities of all the five *bhūtas*; just as, in the case of the production of a plate, for instance, the earthly *paramāṇus* are the material cause, while the *paramāṇus* of water etc. are the instrumental cause alone; but consequently, the qualities of all the five *bhūtas* are found in it. Hence, it is doubtful whether the *dharmas* of the five *bhūtas* found in a human body, for instance, are due to their being the material cause, or their being the instrumental cause alone except earth which alone is the material cause.

Now, the following are the arguments to support the view that human organism, for instance, has only one *bhūta* as its material cause :

(*a*) If more than one *bhūta* were the material

[116] NS. and NBhā., III. i. 28-30; KU., pp. 58-59.

cause of a human body, then in the effect, namely, in the body itself, there would not have been any smell, or taste, or colour, or touch. In other words, if, for instance, one earthly *paramāṇu* and one watery *paramāṇu* be taken together as the material cause of a human body, then neither smell nor taste can be produced in that body; because, there can be no production of whatever kind from a single *paramāṇu* of any *bhūta*. That is, the first product, namely *dvyaṇuka* must have two *paramāṇus* of the same class for its production; a single *paramāṇu* of earth, or of water, or of *tejas*, or of air alone cannot produce that *dvyaṇuka*. The *dvyaṇuka* requires two *paramāṇus* of the same class for its material cause. If a production be from one *paramāṇu* alone, then there should be a constant production. And as the *dvyaṇuka* is not produced out of three *paramāṇus* or more, it cannot be produced. The same rule applies to the production of the qualities. A single quality, say smell, belonging to a single earthly *paramāṇu* cannot produce smell in the *dvyaṇuka*; nor can a single taste, belonging to a single watery *paramāṇu* produce taste in the *dvyaṇuka*; so that, all the products, consequently, would become smell-less, tasteless, colourless and touchless. This is due to the very nature of the theory of causality. In other words, there is a sort of rule that the specific quality of the material cause is the specific quality of the effect. This rule would be disturbed if a human body were produced having all the five *bhūtas* as its material cause[117].

(*b*) Again, earth possesses the generality called *pṛthvītva*, water has *jalatva*, *tejas* has *tejastva*, and air has *vāyutva*. These are mutually exclusive. Now, if any product be produced out of

117 NS., NBhā., NV., Tāt., III., i. 30.

all these *bhūtas*, then there would be, consequently, all the generalities present in that product. That is, there will be the fallacy of the overlapping of the generalities; so that, there would be no separate generality, like *pṛthvītva*, *jalatva*, *tejastva* and *vāyutva*[118].

(*c*) There is the *śruti* also to support that the human body is earthly. It is said in the *mantra* which is uttered at the time of the death of a person that may your (addressed to the dead person) body be mixed with the earth[119]. So is said of all other *bhūtas* constituting the body.

(*d*) Again, of the five *bhūtas*, some are perceptible and some not. Now, if a body were produced out of these two kinds of elements, then it would not have been perceived through our eyes, like the contact of the non-perceptible air with the perceptible trees[120].

On these grounds, it is established that the human body, is mainly earthly; because, it has for its material cause the earthly *paramāṇus* alone, while the other *bhūtas* are only its instrumental cause. This is the reason why the characteristics of all the *bhūtas* are found in a human organism.

Similarly, as regards the organisms of *Varuṇa*, *Vāyu* and *Āditya lokas*, we should know that the material cause of each is only one kind of *paramāṇu* of the class to which the organism belongs, while the *paramāṇus* of other *bhūtas* help that particular *paramāṇu* to produce that particular organism.

(3). *Earthly sense-organ*

The sense-organ is that which is supersensuous,

[118] Vide the *Jātibādhakakārikā*—KU., p. 33.
[119] MS., III. i. 31.
[120] NMLU., p. 23.

is an instrument of some cognition, is a substance, and possesses a particular location in the body. It is the direct cause of direct perception[121].

Such a sense-organ in the earthly organism is the odorous organ. It is produced out of the earthly *paramāṇus* which are not suppressed by the *paramāṇus* of other *bhūtas*. This is known from the apprehension of smell. That is, it is through the activity of the odorous organ alone that smell, which is the distinguishing quality of earth, is known and not otherwise. No doubt, there also much depends upon the influence of *adṛṣṭa* to adjust it. As it is earthly, it possesses all the qualities possessed by earth with this difference that there is the excess of smell in it. Some are of opinion that in order to guard against the suppression of a particular sense-organ from the influence of other *bhūtas*, it is better not to allow any connection between the parts of that particular sense-organ and the parts of other *bhūtas*. But this is not possible. However, we should not forget that in the earthly sense-organ, for instance, the earthly element alone predominates, while the contact of other *bhūtas*[122] is only subordinate.

(*a*) *Number of sense-organs in a human organism discussed*

Although sense-organs have been proved to be *bhautika*, yet doubts cannot be finally removed unless it is proved that there are five external sense-organs. The ground which leads us to doubt is that we find that the diversity of the sense-organs is generally established on the different locations of these sense-organs. But this is not a safe ground to prove the diversity; a composite, for instance, occupies as many places as there are parts in a body; but, in spite of this, it is only one. Therefore, we find the opponent arguing that there is only one

[121] Vyom., pp. 232-33.
[122] VS., VIII. ii. 5; Vyom., pp. 233-34.

sense-organ. They hold that there is a single organ of touch, called *tvak*, which pervades over the entire organism, and as it touches all the locations of the so-called different sense-organs, it manifests itself as so many different sense-organs. This is also supported by the causal relation existing between the organ of touch and the external cognition in general.

But this is a wrong view; for, if this be the fact, then a blind man, or a deaf man, or a tongueless man, or noseless man all of whom possess the organ of touch, should get the cognitions of colour, of sound, of taste and of smell respectively. But this is against the reality; hence, it is wrong to hold that there is any one single sense-organ.

To this, again, it is pointed out that just as a particular part of the *tvak* alone apprehends the smoke and no other part, so the particular parts of *tvak* alone would apprehend colour etc.; and if any of these parts of *tvak* be destroyed, then that particular object would not be apprehended.

But this very argument of the opponent, says the Naiyāyika, proves the plurality of the sense-organs. And moreover, the various *bhūtas* also help cognitions through the sense-organs as all the locations of sense-organs are *vyāpta* by the *bhūtas*.

Again, if there be only one sense-organ pervading throughout the whole body, then there should be the simultaneity of the contacts of the *Ātman*, the *Manas*, and the sense-organs; so that, the simultaneity of cognitions cannot be denied. But it is not the fact.

There is another difficulty in the way of holding the view that there is a single sense-organ. We know that in every case of perception the sense-organ and the object contact is essential. But now, if there be a single sense-organ, then the apprehension of colour and sound cannot take place. If it be held that certain sense-organs are *prāpyakārī*, while others are *aprāpyakārī*, like the organ of sight, then there would be another difficulty that every colour, whether in front of or behind the walls, would have been cognised, which is, again, against the reality.

Moreover, there being five different kinds of objects in the world, five different exclusive kinds of sense-organs have been assumed to apprehend these respectively. This definite arrangement would not be possible, if there be a single sense-organ.[123]

On these grounds, the existence of five different and mutually exclusive sense-organs is proved.

(4). *Inorganic earth*

The inorganic earthly objects are those which help our experiences of pleasure and pain, and can be perceived through the external sense-organs. It is produced through the usual process of *dvyaṇuka*, *trasareṇu*, etc. Although there are innumerable number of inorganic earthly productions according to their common nature, yet these are subdivided into clay (*mṛt*), stone (*pāṣāṇa*) and *sthāvara*. Under clay, we have the various portions of earth, buildings, bricks, and so on; under stone, we include the various kinds of stones, adamantive, and so on; while under *sthāvara*, we include grass, grains, plants, trees, creepers and *vanaspatis*.[124]

It should be noted down here that by *sthāvara* is meant that which has no independent activity (*ceṣṭā*). Now, in that case, almost the entire class of the inorganic earthly object can be very easily included under *sthāvara* alone, while trees, plants, creepers etc. should not be at all included under it. But because, stone etc., have other characteristic also, they are not spoken of by that name.[125]

But, in any case, it is almost wrong to include trees

[123] NS., III. i. 52-61 along with NBhā.
[124] PPBhā., p. 28.
[125] Kandalī, p. 35.

etc. under *sthāvara* when we know that almost all their activities resemble the activities of living beings. The only difference is that of degree in the manifestation of consciousness.

IV

TEJAS

1. *Definition of tejas*

Tejas is defined as that which is the substratum of colour, which has the common substratum with the absolute absence of *taste*;[126] or, it is that which has the common substratum with colour, but not with weight. The definitions generally given only enumerate the special characteristics of *tejas*.[127]

2. *Qualities of tejas*

It possesses colour, touch, number, dimension, separateness, conjunction, disjunction, priority, posteriority, fluidity, and velocity. Of these, colour and touch are the only distinctive qualities of *tejas*. The colour possessed by it is illuminating (*bhāsvara*); and the touch is hot. These do not naturally belong to any other *bhūta*. The fluidity in *tejas* is unnatural; that is, it is found only when strong heat is applied to it; as in the case of all the metals.[128] The appearance of red, yellow and other colours in *tejas* is due to the presence of earthly or watery substances in it.

The touch of *tejas* is hot. Non-apprehension of hot touch in the moon, the eyes and other *taijasa* objects is due to the non-manifestation of touch. In the case of the touch of gold it is not felt as hot owing to its being overpowered by earthly particles; for, if it were

[126] T.U., p. 31.
[127] KR., pp. 17-18.
[128] Vyom., pp. 255-56.

due to the unmanifestation, then gold would not have been perceived.

Its natural movement is upward.[129] Its colour and touch do not undergo any chemical change; hence, they are eternal in the *paramāṇus*, while non-eternal in the products.[130]

Although there are only two prominent qualities in *tejas*, namely, colour and touch, yet even taste and smell are present there through the relation of *saṃyukta-samavāya*;[131] for, in order to make the *taijasa* objects fit for *bhoga* through the influence of *adṛṣṭa*, earthly elements are combined with *taijasa*[132] ones, as it is in gold and other metals.

The colour and touch of *tejas* are found varying. Thus, in certain objects, it possesses both colour and touch manifested, as in the rays of the sun; in others, the colour is manifested, but touch remains unmanifested, as in the light emitting from the moon, lamp, and so on; sometimes, again, the touch is manifested, but colour is unmanifested, as in the *tejas* present in the boiled water; sometimes, on the other hand, both colour and touch remain unmanifested, as in the eyes.[133] But there seems to be an exception in the case of the cat's eyes where the touch alone is unmanifest, while the colour is manifest; so that, even in dark the colour of cat's eyes is perceived. This also proves that there is really *tejas* present in the eyes.[134] Heat belongs to *tejas*.[135]

129 PPBhā., p. 39.
130 TS., p. 16.
131 PPBhā. p. 39.
132 Kandalī, pp. 40-41.
133 NBhā, III. i. 36.
134 NS. and NBhā., III. i. 44.
135 VS., II. ii. 4.

3. *Divisions and subdivisions of tejas*

Such a *tejas* is of two kinds—eternal existing in the form of *paramāṇus*, and non-eternal existing in the form of products. The latter kind of *tejas* is subdivided into organic *tejas*, *taijasa* sense-organ and inorganic *tejas*.

(1). *Organic tejas*

The necessity of organic *tejas* is meant for *bhoga*. But it being entirely *taijasa* cannot serve the purpose. It may be suggested that really speaking, it is the earthly organism alone which is meant for *bhoga* ordinarily. No doubt, there are deeds which necessitate the *bhoga* in organisms of other elements also, but it is possible only when earthly particles are mixed with them. Hence, in the *taijasa* organisms also the presence of earthly particles has to be admitted to make them fit for *bhoga*. It is not *yonija*; because, *yonija* organisms are earthly alone. Such *taijasa* organisms exist in *Ādityaloka*.

(2). *Taijasa sense-organ*

That which does not apprehend smell, taste, touch and sound but manifests colour alone is the *taijasa* sense-organ. In other words, that which is the uncommon cause of the apprehension of colour is the *taijasa* sense-organ.[136] Such a sense-organ is the organ of sight. Its location is said to be at the tip of the pupil.[137]

Now, it is urged here that heat (*uṣmā*) being *taijasa*, and the relation of *saṃyuktasamavāya* being common, and there being no other particular cause for apprehension, like colour, the eyes being *taijasa* should illuminate heat also.

To this it is said that the eyes are produced from

[136] KUP., pp. 284-85.
[137] PD., p. 3.

the ultimate particles of *tejas* which are not suppressed by the parts of other *bhūtas*; so that, they apprehend colour alone. In other words, there is very little influence of the earthly particles on the ultimate particles of *tejas* when the latter produce the organ of sight without being suppressed by anything else. But what is the proof that such a thing is produced? The proof is supplied by the action of the organ itself. Thus, due to the activity of the organ of sight the apprehension of colour alone takes place and not that of taste, touch, smell and sound. This is not possible unless there is a causal relation between the organ of sight and the apprehension of colour. This particular production is helped by *adṛṣṭa* also; so that, the *paramāṇus* of *tejas*, helped by a particular *adṛṣṭa* along with a very slight combination of the *paramāṇus* of other *bhūtas*, produce the organ of sight That which is *taijasa* must be produced from *taijasa paramāṇus* alone. That there is the *taijasa* element present in the organ of sight is proved from the fact that it apprehends the quality of *tejas* alone which is not possible unless there is some intimate affinity between them.

Such a sense-organ is supersensuous, because of the non-manifestation of colour in it. The explanation of the non-manifestation of colour in the organ of sight is that all the positive objects are produced for the sake of *bhoga*; now, if the colour were manifested, then the eyes would have been apprehended even in the darkness, and there would have been no *bhoga* for the *dṛṣṭa-sattvas*; in order that the *dṛṣṭasattvas* may experience *bhoga*, the *adṛṣṭa* influenced the creator (*prajāpati*) to produce the eyes without manifested colour.

As regards the non-manifestation of hot touch in the organ of sight, it is said that if there were manifested touch in the eyes then, for instance, when a dancing-girl is dancing, or when any pleasant thing is before us, and all the eyes are set upon her, or that particular pleasant object, particularly, in the hot season, the hot rays emitting from our eyes would fall upon the beautiful object and burn it; so that, for helping *bhoga*, the aim of production, *adṛṣṭa* has prevailed upon the creator to make the hot touch of the eyes unmanifested.[138] It is due to this very *adṛṣṭa* that there is no manifested touch in the organ of sight.[139]

(a) *Buddhist view regarding the visual organ*

What has been said above regarding the nature of the visual organ is true of all the orthodox schools of thought. The Buddhists, on the other hand, entirely differ from the view held above. Diṅnāga and others think that the very eye-balls represent the visual organ.[140] They hold that the organ of sight, being a material product, cannot move up to its object of perception at a distance.[141] Accordingly, by the organ of sight, that is, the eye, they mean a material product in the shape of the blue eye-ball—the pupil, which is helped by a particular kind of external matter, that is, light (*āloka*), and depends upon the past deeds preceded by a desire to apprehend an object.[142] In other words, the eye is that material product which wants to make a colour known under the influence of the past deeds.[143] That the eye-ball is itself the organ of sight is further proved by the fact that all the eye-diseases are cured by the

[138] Vyom., p. 257.

[139] NS., NBhā. and NV., III. i. 38; Kandalī. p. 40.

[140] *Adhiṣṭhānādbahirnākṣam*—Diṅnāga's kārikā, quoted by Tāt. on NS., I. i. 4, p. 118.; PRM., p. 21; *Cakṣurgolakam*—Rev. Rāhula's gloss on ADK., I. 23; p. 11.

[141] *Na ca cakṣuṣastenārthena prāptirasti, bhūtaviçeṣasyendriyabhāvāt* —NV., I. i. 4., p. 33.

[142] *Ya evāyam kṛṣṇasāralakṣaṇo bhūtaviçeṣaḥ sa bāhyābhūtaviçeṣaprasādānugṛhītastattṛṣṇāpūrvakakarmāpekṣaḥ cakṣurityucyate* etc. NV., I. i. 4., p. 33; Tāt., p. 116.

[143] *Bhūtaviçeṣaḥ karmāpekṣo rūpañca cakṣāṇaçcakṣurityucyate*—Tāt., p. 117.

treatment of the eye-balls alone.[144]

(b) *Prāpyakāritva of the sense-organs discussed*

The Buddhist idea of the organ of vision creates another serious difficulty. It has been said before that direct perception (*pratyakṣa*) takes place only when there is a contact between a sense-organ and its analogous object.[145] But now, when the eye-ball is said to be the visual organ, and the objects cognised through this sense-organ are found to be lying at a distance, then it is held that direct visual cognitions take place without there being any contact between the organ of sight and the object perceived.; for, no one has ever seen the eye-balls going out of their sockets[146]. Moreover, the capacity to perceive the objects is not found with the eye-balls when they are taken out of their sockets. If it were so, then things should have been perceived even when the eyes are closed[147]. In the same manner, the auditory organ also is found to cognise its analogous object lying at a great distance. Hence, it is concluded by the Buddhists of the Vaibhāṣika School that the sense-organs of sight and hearing cognise their respective objects without coming in contact with them.[148]

The following are the arguments adduced in support of the Buddhist view:[149]

(i) *Sāntaragrahaṇāt*—because, things lying a distance are cognised.

[144] *Taccikitsādiyogataḥ*—Diṅnāga's kārikā, quoted in Tāt., p. 118; PRM., p. 21.

[145] NS., I. i. 4.

[146] NV., I. i. 4., p. 33; (*Aprāptārthānyakṣimanaḥçrotrāṇi*) *trayam-anyathā*—ADK., I. 43. along with Rev. Rāhula's gloss., p. 18.

[147] *Satyapyakṣabahirbhāve na çaktirviṣayekṣaṇe* ।
yadi ca syāttadā paçyedapyunmīlya nimīlanāt ॥
—Quoted in Tāt., p. 118; PRM., p. 22.

[148] ADK. along with Rev. Rāhula's gloss; I. 43, p. 18.

[149] *Sāntaragrahaṇaṃ na syāt prāptau jñāne'dhikasya ca*—Diṅnāga's Kārikā, quoted in Tāt., I. i. 4; p. 118; PRM., p. 21.

(ii) *Pṛthutaragrahaṇāt*—because things of bigger dimension are apprehended. If the eye were to cognise objects after coming in contact with them, then it would have done so with the objects having dimension equal to its own. But it is not so.[150]

(iii) *Digdeçavyapadeçāt*—because, there is the specification of directions in the case of cognitions obtained through the visual organ, in the form that such and such cognitions have taken place in such and such directions. Vardhamāna Upādhyāya, however, explains the above as *viprakṛṣṭadigdeçavyapadeçāt*, that is, the visual cognition is expressed as taking place at a distance from the organ of sight, which would have been expressed as taking place quite close to the visual organ had the latter actually come in contact with the object of perception.[151]

(iv) *Sannikṛṣṭaviprakṛṣṭayostulyakālagrahaṇāt*—because, things lying quite close to and also at a distance both are apprehended simultaneously; as for instance, both the branches of a tree and the moon are perceived simultaneously.

Before any argument, from the Nyāya-Vaiçeṣika point of view, is put forth to refute the arguments of the Buddhists adduced above, it is desirable to point out that the very first assumption that the eye-ball is the visual organ is not admitted by Nyāya-Vaiçeṣika. The orthodox view is that the visual organ is produced out of the ultimate particles of *tejas*. The eye-balls are only the means through which the rays, centred in the *taijasa* particles constituting the organ of sight, go out gradually expanding in wider circles, and come in

[150] *Dvyāçrayo hi saṃyogo'lpameva saṃyoginamanurudhyate na mahāntam. Na jātu rathādisaṃyogā nabho vyaçnuvate, mā bhūt sarvatra rathādīnāṃ tatsaṃyogādīnāñcopalabdhiḥ, tena yāvanmātraṃ rāṣṭravanādergolakena vyāptaṃ tāvanmātrasya grahaṇaprasangaḥ*—Tāt., I. i. 4; p. 117.

[151] NPP. on NP., I. i. 4. pp. 507-508 (Bibli. Ind. edition).

contact with the object of perception. Hence, according to Nyāya-Vaiçeṣika, there is no difficulty for the visual organ to come in contact with its objects before their cognition takes place.

Now, coming to the above mentioned probans, it is found that they are all fallacious for some reason or other, and hence, all are rejected as unsound. Thus, as regards the first probans—*sāntaragrahaṇāt*, it is pointed out that the term-*sāntara* may mean either the apprehension of things which are not reached at, or apprehension together with the intermediary things (*antara*) which may, again, include *Ākāça*, or negation (*abhāva*), or any other object.

The former alternative, when put in a syllogistic form, appears to be identical with the *pratijñā* (the first proposition of the syllogistic reasoning); so that, it cannot act as a probans for proving any conclusion. Hence, it is rejected as unsound. In the case of the latter alternative, if the intermediary (*antara*) be the *Ākāça*, then it being colourless, cannot be the object of apprehension through the visual organ. Again, if it be the negation, then also the eyes cannot perceive it for being alone. Whenever a negation is perceived, it is perceived only as related to something; and never independently. If, therefore, the negation that is meant here be that which is perceived not alone but as pertaining to an object having colour that is perceived by the eye, then the probans cannot conclusively prove that the eye does not get at its object; for, it is then applicable to the organ of touch also;[152] for instance, when the cool touch of water is felt, then the absence of heat also is felt along with it.[153] Hence, it is also rejected as involving the fallacy of *anaikāntika*. The term intermediary cannot include any substance having

[152] NV., I. i. 4; p. 34.
[153] Tāt., I. i. 4; p. 119.

colour, for, in that case, that object would be an obstacle in the way of apprehending things through it. Hence, the argument is rejected as unsound.[154]

Some, however, explain the term—*sāntaragrahaṇa* as the perception of a thing in the form—this is remote from me. But this also cannot prove that the visual organ does not come in contact with its object; for, the idea that the thing is remote from me—is due to some other cause and not to the sense-organ getting or not getting at its object. It is, in fact, having body as the limit, the ideas of remoteness and nearness are determined, and not due to the thing being got at or not got at by the sense-organs. The notion of nearness takes place where the body and the sense-organ both come in contact with the object, and when the sense-organ alone comes in contact with the object, then the idea of remoteness takes place. The perception of the thing as remote, being due to some other cause, cannot be accepted as a proof for the eye not getting at its object.[155]

While refuting the second argument of the Buddhists, it is pointed out that things of varying dimensions are perceived simply by their slight contact with the visual organ, and it is not necessary that the eye should come in contact with the entire dimension of the object perceived.[156] It is, therefore, that the cognition of the dimension of an object is determined by the four kinds of contacts—(*a*)the whole of the sense-organ with the whole of the object; (*b*) the parts of the sense-organ with the entire object ; (*y*) the whole of the sense-organ with the parts of the object; (*x*) and the parts of the sense-organ with the parts of the object.[157] Vācaspatī Miçra says that just as the *tejas*, centred in

[154] NV., I. i. 4; p. 34
[155] NV., I. i. 4; pp. 34-35.
[156] NV., I. i. 4; p. 35.
[157] Tāt., I. i. 4; p. 119.

the wick of a lamp, spreads out gradually in wider circles, and illumines the nearing object of varying size, so the *tejas* centred in the eye comes out and gradually expands in circles as it proceeds further and further and illumines the object of varying size. This is the nature of *tejas*[158].

Regarding the specification of the directions, it is said that here also one's body is assumed to be the limit for determining the directions, and as such, there can be no specification of any direction where the sense-organ and the body both come in contact with the object. Such specifications are possible only where the sense-organ alone comes in contact with the object; so that, the argument adduced by the Buddhists cannot deny the eye getting at its object.[159]

Regarding the argument that both a branch of a tree and the moon are simultaneously cognised, it is said that the very assumption is wrong; as, it is not a fact. No sane person holds that there is a simultaneous apprehension of both the branch of the tree and the moon through the visual organ. The notion is really a case of false knowledge due to the non-apprehension of the difference of the points of time, like the non-apprehension of the difference of the points of time in the piercing through the hundred lotus-petals together. It should always be kept in mind that the *tejas* is so light and its velocity is so great that it becomes really difficult to mark the difference of moments in its movements; as it is the case with the rays of the sun which travel at such a great speed that it appears, as if, they spread over the entire world simultaneously in a single moment.

Some want to justify the possibility of the simul-

[158] *Na caitanniryato vinā pṛthvagratāṃ bhavatīti pṛthvagratā sūcitā. Yathā varttideçe piṇḍitamapi tejaḥ prasarpatprāsādodaraṃ vyāpnoti* etc., Tāt., I. i. 4; pp. 119-20.

[159] NV., I. i. 4; p. 35; Tāt., I. i. 4; p. 120.

taneous apprehension of a branch of a tree and the moon through the visual organ. They say that water and *tejas* are commingling (*saṃsṛṣṭa*) substances; so that, just as any other kind of water commingling with the water of the Ganges becomes Ganges-water, so the solar *tejas* commingling with the ocular *tejas* becomes the *tejas* of the eyes. This being the fact, when the *tejas* emanating from the eyes mixes with the external *tejas* which is simultaneously pervading over all the objects of the world and becomes one, we can say that the *tejas* of the eyes comes in contact with every external *tejas* whether near or remote simultaneously.[160]

But this view is wrong; for in that case the objects hidden behind the wall, or any other obstacle, whether in close proximity, or far away, should be apprehended, which is not the fact.[161]

Again, if a man enters a bit dark room, where there exists a very little contact of *tejas* which is the necessary condition of the conjunction of the eyes, from the outside where there is enough *tejas*, he should at once see all the objects of the room. The condition of the contact of the organ of sight with the objects in the dark room being present, there is nothing to prevent the perception; and if there be no perception, at once, then there should be never. But this is not correct. The external *tejas*, which is quite close to the eye-ball and possesses hot touch, prevents the different kind of (*vijātīya*) contact of the eyes with the objects, in a bit dark room, at once; and after a moment, that external

[160] KU., p. 75; PP., p. 45; TPP of Koṇḍa Bhaṭṭa, *Ms.* Fol. 28a. This view is attributed to Çālikanātha by Vardhamāna in his KUP, p. 288; but Çālikanātha in his Prakaraṇapañcikā attributes this view to some one else saying—'*Samasamayasaṃvedane tu kecit parihārameva ṃ varṇayanti* etc.'—p. 45; while he gives his own view some nine or ten lines below in the very place in that very text, and which we refer to here also.

[161] KU., p. 75.

tejas being removed the contact takes place. It is, therefore, that a man, although unable to perceive the mid-day sun, directly, can perceive it with the help of a screen in the form of a piece of cloth.

Similarly, it is asked: why does not a man, forty years old, having the direct contact of the eyes with the object of perception, perceive the object? The reason is that there is the *tejas* produced from the bilious nature of that age which prevents the real contact of the organ of sight and the object of perception. By the use of glass-pairs (*upanetra*) that bilious *tejas* is removed and through it the organ of sight perceives the external objects of perception.[162]

Çālikanātha Miçra, however, says that the view that both a branch of a tree and the moon can be perceived simultaneously due to the commingling of the *tejas* is correct, if, only, we add to it the influence of *adr̥ṣṭa*. That is, when the rays, emanating from the eyes, mix with the external *tejas* and become one, then only that much of it, which is determined to be the means of apprehension through the influence of *adr̥ṣṭa*, is capable of apprehending things and not all. Hence, we cannot say that every thing is known simultaneously, although there is the simultaneous perception of *Bhauma*, *Dhruva* and others through the influence of *adr̥ṣṭa*.[163]

Moreover, if the organ of sight were *aprāpyakārī*, then there is nothing in the walls and similar other things to put an obstacle in the way of the organ of sight to get at the things behind the walls. And we are sure that the organ of sight does not cognise things which are behind the walls and similar other things. Hence, we conclude that the organ of sight is *prāpyakārī*. Again, had the sense-organ been not *prāpyakārī*, there

[162] TPP. of Koṇḍa Bhaṭṭa., *Ms*. Fol. 28a-29a.
[163] PP., p. 45.

would not have been notions to the effect that a particular thing could not be cognised, as it is at a great distance, while others could be cognised, because they are quite near. But such notions do exist; so that, the sense-organ cannot but be *prāpyakārī*. It is further proved by the fact that the organs of sight and hearing are also sense-organs like others, and as such, should be *prāpyakārī*. If the *prāpyakāritva* of all the sense-organs be doubtful, then we should take the help of some instrument (*karaṇa*) and prove the inference. Thus, for example, an axe, which is an instrument (*karaṇa*) and where the activity (*kriyā*) depends upon the coming together of the axe and the object of cut, and not otherwise. Lastly, it may be said that if the sense-organs, or any other instrument (*karaṇa*), be not *prāpyakārī*, then their products, namely, the cognitions of colour, touch, taste, smell, and hearing etc., should be found everywhere and at all times. But it is not so. Hence, we conclude that all the instruments (*karaṇas*) including the sense-organs are *prāpyakārī*.[164]

These very arguments also disprove the Buddhistic assumption that the eye-balls with a specific attribute represent the organ of sight. Jayanta adds, further, that the view that the existence of a specific capacity (*dharma* or *viçeṣa*) in the eye-ball helps the perception is untenable; for, it may be asked here—if there is such a specific capacity, then what is its support? It cannot remain unsupported; eye-ball cannot be its substratum. Hence, the assumption of the Buddhists is untenable and is rejected.

As regards the medical treatment of the eye-disease in the eye-balls, it is held that it is done for the purifications of the substratum (*ādhāra*), through which the *ādheya* is purified.[165] Hence, it is essential to hold

[164] NV. and Tāt. on NS., I. i. 4; KU., pp. 74-75; TPP., *Ms.* Fol. 28a-29a; PRM., pp. 21-22.

[165] NM., pp. 478-80.

that all the sense-organs apprehend their respective objects after coming in contact with them.

(c). *Number of eyes in an organism discussed*

But even these arguments leave us in dark as to the number of eyes in a man's body. Even in the old school of Nyāya we find two different views. Thus, Vātsyāyana appears to hold that there are two independent eyes, and consequently, two sense-organs of sight. With this assumption he refutes the view—'that, really speaking, there is only one organ of sight extending from one corner to the other but apparently separated into two by the bone of nose,—by saying that if there were only one organ of sight, then when one of the eyes is destroyed or removed the other should also stop functioning, but this is not the fact; the organ of sight of one eyed-man works quite well. Hence, there are two independent eyes.

Against this view of the Bhāṣyakāra, it is said that the above reason falls down on the ground that even if a part of it is destroyed, the remaining part works quite well; as, we find in the case of a tree, where even if one branch of it is cut off, the whole is not destroyed.

Vātsyāyana refutes this argument, again. Thus, he holds—

(i) That if the part is removed the whole does not exist; for, if it exists, then we will have to believe in the eternity of the effect; so that, when the branch is cut off, really speaking the tree does not exist.

(ii) When a man is dead we find in his skull two distinct holes on either side of the bone of the nose on the spots where the two eye-balls exist. This would not have been possible, if there were only one organ of sight.

(iii) And lastly, when one eye is pressed with a finger in the corner, then a single object appears as if it were two distinct objects. This is not possible if there were only one organ of sight; because, when that pressing finger is removed, then, again, that object appears to be only one. In other words, really if there were only one organ of sight extending from one corner to the other, and apparently divided into two, by a nose-bridge upon a river-like flowing substance, then when we press a bit of one of the eye-balls in a corner, then the rays of that particular eye should flow to the other eye through the passage below the nose-bone-bridge, and we should not perceive one single object as two. But this is not the fact; hence, it is assumed that there are two distinct organs of sight.[166]

But it is strange that Uddyotakara does not agree with the above view of Vātsyāyana. On the contrary, he gives arguments in support of the singleness of the organ of sight. Thus, he says—those who hold that there are two organs of sight are wrong; for, there can be no simultaneous contact of the atomic *Manas*, with the two organs of sight. In that case, there should be no difference in the act of perception of a man having two organs of sight from that of another who has only one eye. But this is not the fact; a man perceives more with his two eyes than with a single eye. Moreover, it has been established that there are five sense-organs. Now, if there were two organs of sight, then there is a clear case of contradiction, which is not possible.[167] Vācaspati and Viçvanātha also agree with the interpretation of Uddyotakara. Later writers also hold the same view.[168] Even the Buddhist writer Vasubandhu says that although there are two eyes, yet they represent only one sense-organ. The two eye-balls are meant for making the appearance good[169].

[166] NBhā., III. i. 8-11.
[167] NV., III. i. 7.
[168] PRM., p. 21.
[169] *Jātigocaravijñānasāmānyāt ekadhātutā* ı
Dvitve'pi cakṣurādīnāṃ çobhārthaṃ tu dvayodbhavaḥ ıı
—ADK., I. 19., pp. 8-9.

(3). *Inorganic tejas*

The inorganic *tejas* is of four kinds: *bhauma*—pertaining to earth; *divya*—pertaining to heaven; *audarya*—belonging to one's own body (stomach), and *ākaraja*—produced from mines.

The *bhauma* is produced from the earthly fuel, and due to this, it is differentiated from all other kinds of *tejas*.[170] The *divya* is produced from the fuel in the form of water;[171] as for instance, the solar *tejas*, the lightening *tejas*, the *tejas* of the meteors, and the rest.[172] That *tejas* which exists within the organism and helps the digestion of food and drink and turns these into fine subtle essence is called *audarya*. The change brought about by this *tejas* is the same as that of the chemical action described before. It has the fuel of both kinds: earthly (*bhauma*) and heavenly (*divya*).[173] The last form of *tejas* is that which is produced from mines. It includes all the metals—gold, silver, copper, and so on.

By the way, a question is raised here: how do we know the *taijasatva* of these metals, and particularly, that of gold which is apparently an earthly object? Thus, the Mīmāṃsakas urge that gold is earthly; because, it possesses conditional fluidity, like *ghṛta* etc. It may be suggested then that if it were an earthly substance, then just as in *ghṛta* the application of heat takes away the fluidity of it, so the fluidity of gold also should have been destroyed by the application of heat, which is not the fact. To this it is pointed out by the Mīmāṃsakas that the application of heat affects the fluidity of other substances not that of gold. And moreover, gold is not well-known as a piece of *tejas*.

[170] Vyom., p. 258.

[171] *āpaḥ indhanaṃ yasya*—Vyom., p. 258; and *āpaḥ eva indhanaṃ yasya*—KU., p. 76.

[172] Vyom., p. 258; KU., p. 76.

[173] TPP., *Ms.* Fol. 2*a*.

The Naiyāyikas, against this, hold that it is not earthly. The negative form of inference shows that however extreme the heat is applied to gold, its fluidity is not destroyed. This is not the case with any earthly object; for, no contradictory instance is found.[174] As regards the various kinds of gold and silver dusts used in medicine, it is said that they are possible only when some other substance is mixed with gold, and not otherwise.[175] Moreover, this assumption of the Naiyāyikas is based on the *Āgama* that—'gold is the first product of *Agni*.' The presence of yellow colour and the weight is due to the peculiar kind of conjunction of the earthly *paramāṇus*.[176]

After giving the general view of the Naiyāyikas, Mahādeva, gives his own view. He says—'according to me the application of heat to *ghṛta* which is mixed with water does not destroy the fluidity of *ghṛta*. This shows that the conjunction of the fluid substance other than the earthly is an obstacle in the way of the destruction of the conditional fluidity; so that, in the present case, where the conjunction of the fluid substance, in the form of gold which is *tejas*, exists as an obstacle there is no possibility of the destruction of the fluidity. Thus, the red or yellow colour belonging to gold and the non-perception of the illuminating white colour are all due to the influence of earthly substance mixed with it. It is due to this very suppression of the colour of gold by the influence of eathly *paramāṇus* that gold is not perceived in darkness.[177]

[174] Nyāyakaustubha-Pratyakṣa, pp. 100-101.
[175] KV. p. 78.
[176] Nyāyakaustubha-Pratyakṣa, p. 101.
[177] Nyāyakaustubha-Pratyakṣa, pp. 101-102.

CHAPTER X

CONCLUSION

The idea of matter, as understood by Nyāya and Vaiçeṣika, has been made clear in the preceding pages. Like all other schools of Indian philosophy, these two systems also aim at the realization of the Highest Good (*niḥçreyas*)[1]. This aim is achieved by the true knowledge of each and every object of the universe. Accordingly, Nyāya has classified the positive objects of the universe under sixteen categories—1. means of right cognition (*pramāṇa*); 2. objects of right cognition (*prameya*); 3. doubt (*saṃçaya*); 4. motive (*prayojana*); 5. instance (*dṛṣṭānta*); 6. theory (*siddhānta*); 7. factors of syllogism (*avayava*); 8. hypothetical reasoning (*tarka*); 9. demonstrated truth (*nirṇaya*); 10. discussion (*vāda*); 11. disputation (*jalpa*); 12. wrangling (*vitaṇḍā*); 13. fallacious reason (*hetvābhāsa*); 14. perversion (*chala*); 15. casuistry (*jāti*); and 16. clinchers (*nigrahasthāna*), the true knowledge of which leads to the attainment of the Highest Good. If the nature of these categories is closely observed, it is found that all of them can be easily included under the single category of the objects of right cognition (*prameya*), and for the knowledge of which, again, the knowledge of the means of right cognition (*pramāṇa*) is required; so that, it would have been advantageous to recognise these two categories alone. But in spite of this, that the author of the Sūtra includes all the rest of the categories shows that the necessity of the treatment of the categories of

[1] NS., I. i. 1; VS., I. i. 4.

doubt etc. is to distinguish the Nyāya system from the Upaniṣads[2]. This, again, makes it clear that the objects of knowledge dealt with here are only those which are required in the system within certain limitations. In other words, the treatment of the *Ātman*, for instance, here will be according to the scope of Nyāya; so is the case with the other objects of knowledge.

Again, of the objects of knowledge[3]—*Ātman*, physical organism, sense-organs, things (*artha*), cognition (*buddhi*), *Manas*, activity (*pravṛtti*), defect, (*doṣa*), rebirth (*pretyabhāva*), fruition (*phala*), pain and emancipation (*apavarga*), except the first and the last, all other are subsidiary. The only object of knowledge required for the attainment of the aim is the emancipation with reference to the *Ātman* which is apparently in bondage due to the influence of nescience[4]. In other words, the Highest aim is achieved, ultimately, by the true realization of the nature of the *Ātman*, for which the knowledge of the means of right cognition is also essential[5]. Hence, Nyāya lays more emphasis on the means of cognition. The treatment of the objects of right cognition in Nyāya is only subsidiary.

Coming to the Vaiçeṣika system, we find that it also wants to achieve the Highest Good through the true knowledge of its categories[6], namely, substance, quality, motion, generality, quiddity and inherence, into which the whole universe is classified. Here also, ultimately, the true knowledge of the *Ātman* alone is required for the realization of the Highest Good; for which, again, the right knowledge of the true nature of the rest of the categories is essential. This system, thus, lays more emphasis on the ontological aspect of

[2] NBhā., I. i. 1.
[3] NS., I. i. 9.
[4] NM., pp. 427-28.
[5] NBhā., I. i. 1.
[6] VS., I. i. 4.

the universe. In so doing, it has, sometimes, to go deeper into the nature of its categories.

Both of these systems take into account the common-sense view and the worldly usage in explaining the worldly phenomena. They seldom go beyond the common-sense experience. They take the objects of the universe as they are, and rightly believe in the existence of the close correspondence between the order of our thoughts and the order of the external reality. The existence of the external world is independent of our consciousness, in so far as its existence is prior to the existence of, and is a condition of the possibility of, our mental phenomena[7].

The orthodox view about the nature of the various systems of Indian philosophy is that there exists a sort of synthesis between them. They represent the various phases of one and the same *Truth*. The synthesis is in the ascending order which is corroborated by the actual experiences of our life also. The true knowledge of the objects of the universe being recognised to be the means of achieving the Highest Good, every school has to give its own explanation of the objects of the universe. We begin with the most ordinary form of explanation given by the Indian Materialists. They hold, as has been said even before, that there are only four elements, namely, earth, water, fire and air which constitute the entire universe. Every object is ultimately a product of these elements. *Ākāça* is considered to be that which possesses no obstruction, and perhaps, therefore, includes *Dik* within it. *Ātman* is nothing but an organism, or a sense-organ, or a vital air, or the *Manas*, endowed with the quality of consciousness, which, in its turn, originates from matter. This is the crudest form of explanation given about the phenomenal world.

[7] PWSS., Vol. I. pp. 33-34.

Next, it is found that an attempt is made, for the first time in the history of Indian philosophy, to distinguish between the nature of *Ātman* and that of matter, and to show that these are two independent entities. In fact, it is for the first time that the existence (*sat*) of *Ātman* as an independent entity has been established by Nyāya and Vaiçeṣika. But, if we go a bit deeper, we shall see that this *Ātman* is essentially *jaḍa*, and becomes conscious only when consciousness is produced in it; so that, although its independent existence has been established, yet its nature is not very much different from that of matter. Again, when we look to the nature of the material world, we find that it is classified under eight categories, namely, earth, water, *tejas*, air, *Ākāça*, *Kāla*, *Dik* and *Manas*. The first four categories have got two forms—one eternal and the other non-eternal. The other four are all eternal. Thus, there are, ultimately, eight eternal forms of matter, according to Nyāya and Vaiçeṣika. Beyond these they cannot go.

But as the scientific enquiry always wants to find out unity amidst diversity, it cannot stop with these eternal forms of matter. Hence, when a subtler enquiry into the nature of these is made, it is found that these are no longer incapable of being reduced to subtler forms. They are all non-eternal, and consequently, are reduced to their subtle forms at the next stage represented by Sāṅkhya. The causal analysis of Sāṅkhya leads gradually to *Prakṛti*, which is pure matter and consists of extremely fine composites, called *guṇas*, in a state of equilibrium.

If we study the classification of the elements of Sāṅkhya, we shall find that we are lifted up step by step from the grosser to the subtler elements until we reach a very high level. The *paramāṇus*, which were supposed to be indivisible with Nyāya and Vaiçeṣika, are shown here as products of the five *tanmātrās*, which are, again, the products of the *tamas* aspect of *ahaṅkāra*.[8] *Ākāça*, *Kāla* and *Dik*, which were all-pervading and eternal with Nyāya-Vaiçeṣika, are reduced to one divisible element, namely, *Ākāça*[9], which, in its turn, is a product of the *çabda-tanmātrā*[10]. Similarly, the indivisible atomic *Manas* also is proved to be a product of *ahaṅkāra*[11]. So it is quite obvious that the so-called eternal elements of Nyāya-Vaiçeṣika are reduced to subtler elements in Sāṅkhya[12].

But the scientific enquiry, again, does not stop with the dualism of Sāṅkhya. It is left for the Çaṅkara-Vedānta to resolve the dualism of the former into the unity of the *Supreme Truth*. Here the enquirer realizes his ultimate end, and hence, stops. This is how from the grossest form of matter we start and end in the Absolute Unity.

Leaving the Çaṅkara School of Vedānta for the present, if we look into the Kashmir Çaivaism, we find that both *Prakṛti* and *Puruṣa* of Sāṅkhya are capable of further dissolution. The *Prakṛti* itself is a manifestation under *Māyā* along with her five *kañcukas*[13]. This *Māyā*, again, is ultimately resolved into *Parama Çiva*, through the various other stages represented by *Çuddhavidyā*, *Īçvara*, *Sadāçiva* and *Çakti*[14]. It is the *Parama Çiva-tattva* which possesses within itself the entire universe as its own *svarūpa*[15]. It is at this stage that the final unity is reached and all the enquiry into the nature of the material world stops. Although the so-called entire

[8] TK. on SK., 22.
[9] SS., II. ii. 12.
[10] SK., 22.
[11] SK., 24-25.
[12] Umesha Mishra—Synthetic gradation in Indian philosophy-AUS., Vol. I., pp. 90-94.
[13] Parāpraveçikā, pp. 8-9.
[14] Parāpraveçikā., p. 6.
[15] PrHr., p. 8.

material aspect of the universe merges into *Parama Çiva*, yet it does not lose its existence[16]. All the forms in their own independent nature remain present within Him until He wants to manifest them out of His own Free Will[17]. Besides the dissolution of matter into such a subtle entity, as *Parama Çiva*, the matter itself becomes endowed with the very nature of intelligence, as it is the very nature (*svarūpa*) of *Parama Çiva*[18].

These make it clear that matter, which is devoid of consciousness and is *jaḍa* with the schools of Nyāya, Vaiçeṣika, Mīmāṃsā and Sāṅkhya, not only becomes endowed with intelligence, but also merges itself into *Brahman*, or *Parama Çiva*, and remains no longer distinct from consciousness. (*Caitanya*). This is like a mystery surrounding the conception of matter in Indian thought. We should never forget that Absolute Unity is the final aim of Indian *Darçana* and when that aim is achieved, we think that *Darçana* has achieved its end. This is realized with the systems of Çaṅkara-Vedānta and Kashmir Çaivaism.

This is a very brief reference of the different stages of matter in Indian thought. But as the present thesis is limited in its scope, I have confined myself with the treatment of matter as found in Nyāya and Vaiçeṣika; and by the way, I have touched the other phases of it only to keep myself in harmony with the highest aim of *Darçana* which rightly teaches—

Vācārambhaṇaṃ vikāro nāmadheyaṃ
Mṛttiketyeva satyam.

[16] *Cf. Antaḥsthitivatāmeva ghaṭate bahirātmanā*—Īçvarapratyabhijñā, p. 13.

[17] *Cf. Çrīparamaçivaḥ svātmaikyena sthitaṃ viçvaṃ* etc.—PrHṛ., p. 8.

[18] PrHṛ., p. 8; Tantrasāra., p. 8; Yogarājācārya's Com. on Paramārthasāra., p. 73.

CHAPTER XI

CONCEPTION OF ĀTMAN

INTRODUCTORY

IN the foregoing pages, the idea of matter, according to the systems of Nyāya and Vaiçeṣika, has been dealt with at great length. Besides what has been said in Chapters I[1] and II[2] about the necessity of the treatment of the nature of the conscious element, it is an admitted fact that a thing, in order to be known thoroughly, should not be merely distinguished from objects of its own class, but also from its heterogeneous class. This, again, is possible only when its heterogeneous class also is known in all its aspects. Hence, our knowledge of the conception of matter, as shown in the previous chapters, would remain incomplete unless we also know the conception of non-matter, that is, the *cetana* aspect of the phenomenal world, which is, generally, known as *Ātman*. Therefore, with a view to have the complete knowledge of the idea of matter, an effort is made here to study the nature of the *Ātman* also as given in Nyāya and Vaiçeṣika.

It has already been made clear before that there is a conscious element also in the universe. Its existence is as indispensable as that of the matter itself. Even then, following the traditional line, it is necessary to prove its existence before proceeding further. Nyāya-Vaiçeṣika, representing the Realistic School of thought, believes in the existence of two *Ātmans*—*Jīvātman* and

[1] *Vide Supra*, pp. 51-55.
[2] *Vide Supra*, p. 57.

Paramātman[3]. Hence, both of these are separately treated here under different sections.

A

JĪVĀTMAN

I. Existence of Jīvātman proved

The existence of *Jīvātman* is proved through direct perception (intuition—*pratyakṣa*), inference, and authority. Now, to begin with the first means we know that a certain section of the Naiyāyikas, whom Jayanta designates as *svayūthyāḥ*, holds that the term '*I*' in the expressions—'I am happy,' 'I am sorry,' 'I know' etc., is an object of perception. This '*I*,' naturally, refers to the *Jīvātman* and not to any material object, like body, sense-organ, *Manas* etc. It is clear from the above mentioned expressions that the substratum of happiness, sorrow, desire, cognition etc., is nothing but '*I*.' Now, this is not possible, if '*I*' were taken to mean anything other than the *Jīvātman*, such as body, sense-organ, *Manas* etc.; for, none of these is conscious; while happiness etc. cannot be attributed to a non-conscious agent. Happiness, sorrow etc. show that their substratum must be a conscious and eternal agent.

The opponent may raise an objection here against the implication of the term '*I*' in the above expressions; for, the term '*I*' in the expressions—'I am fat,' 'I am beautiful,' 'I am blind,' 'I am deaf' etc., really refers to either body, or a sense-organ; so that, it is not quite sound to base the decision merely on the implication of the term '*I*.'

To this it may be said in reply that as the objection of the opponent is based on the false identity of the body with the *Ātman*, it has no weight. The substratum of the term '*I*' is *Ātman* alone, while in other cases,

[3] KR., p. 39.

it is due to wrong notion[4] and false imposition.

Çaṅkara Miçra adds that inasmuch as the cognition of the term '*I*' refers to one's own *Ātman*, and as it does not refer to other's *Ātman*, it is concluded that the term '*I*' primarily refers to *Ātman*. If, on the other hand, it were to refer primarily to the body, then the cognition of the term '*I*' should have been produced through the external sense-organs; for, the body is not an object of perception directly through *Manas*, while the cognition, expressed in the form 'I am this,' is produced through the instrumentality of *Manas*; as it is produced even without the operation of the external sense-organs.

As regards the view that if *Ātman* be directly perceived, then it should have colour, it is pointed out in reply, that the necessity of having colour is restricted to the external substances alone. Hence, there is nothing to prevent the intuitive perception of *Ātman*.[5]

Others are of opinion that there are direct *çrutis* to prove the existence of *Ātman*[6]. But as the *çrutis* will not convince the unbelievers like the Buddhists, they adduce inferences to prove the existence of it. So says, Gautama, in his Nyāya-sūtra[7], that desire, hatred, effort, pleasure, pain and consciousness[8] are the various probans to prove the existence of *Ātman*. Kaṇāda adds[9] the vital airs—*prāṇa* and *apāna*, the closing and the opening of the eye-lids, state of living, the movements of *Manas* and the affections (*vikāra*) of the other sense-organs to the above mentioned probans of Gautama.

[4] NM., pp. 429-434; VS., III. ii. 9-14; ĀTV., p. 95; TM., pp. 3-6.

[5] VU., III. ii. 14.

[6] NBhā., I. i. 10; *Vide-Dve brahmaṇī veditarye etc.*

[7] NS., I. i. 10.

[8] Viçvanātha holds that as consciousness, desire and effort are the probans of both the *Ātmans*, pleasure, pain and hatred alone should be taken to be the right probans of the *Jīvātman*—Vṛ. on NS., I. i. 10.

[9] VS., III. ii. 4.

Now, desire, etc., being qualities, cannot exist without a substratum. Then, inasmuch as it is known that the qualities, which belong to the physical organism etc., continue as long as the physical organism etc. exist; and as desire etc. are not found to be so, they cannot be regarded as qualities belonging to the physical organism[10].

Again, it is a fact of common experience that there exists desire, which has been defined as a wish for the attainment of something not already obtained[11]. This desire is produced in a man for the attainment of an object which had been the source of pleasure to him in the past. This necessitates that the substratum of the desire should be that which possesses consciousness and is identical with that which had experienced pleasure from the object of desire in the past. Physical organism, neither being conscious nor being an unchanging element, cannot be the required substratum. Recognition (*pratyabhijñā*) is not possible in physical organism. The organs of sense also cannot be the substratum of desire; for it is not necessary for a single sense-organ to be both the desirer and the experiencer of the past. For instance, when a man perceives a mango fruit and desires it to have, we cannot say that the visual organ which perceives the fruit at present also possesses the experience of the good taste of the fruit. Again, *Manas*, being accepted as a sense-organ and an instrument; cannot be the substrate of desire[12]. Hence, that which is the substratum of desire is *Ātman*. Similarly, hatred etc. also prove the existence of a separate entity, called *Ātman*.

Likewise, consciousness (*jñāna*) also is an indicative of the existence of *Ātman* as an independent entity.

[10] NV., I. i. 10; NM., p. 434.

[11] PPBhā., p. 261.

[12] NBhā., NV. and Tāt., I. i. 10; NM., pp. 434-42, Kandalī., p. 261.

Besides what has been said before regarding the substratum of consciousness[13], it should also be further pointed out that it cannot belong to the *Manas*; because, if the *Manas* be the substratum of consciousness and accordingly be regarded as perceiving colour etc. with the help of some sense-organ which is other than the five external sense-organs, then the difference is only verbal, that is, that other sense-organ would become the *Manas*, while the *Manas* itself, as a substratum of consciousness, would become the *Ātman*. If the *Manas*, however, be believed to be functioning independently and not in co-operation with that another sense-organ, then in the case of an object with a colour, taste etc., the organ of sight etc., being always present, there should be simultaneity of knowledge, which is against the reality. Hence, consciousness does not belong to the *Manas* which is merely an instrument[14].

Again, as from the motion of a chariot the existence of a conscious guiding agent, in the shape of a charioteer, is inferred, so also from the activity and cessation from activity appearing in the physical organism which have the capacity of acquiring the desirable and avoiding the undesirable, the existence of an intelligent guiding agent for the body is inferred. This conscious agent is no other than the *Ātman*.[15]

There are several other grounds for establishing the existence of *Ātman*[16]. Thus—

1. The presence of the variegated functioning of the vital airs in an organism proves the existence of a conscious agent in the organism who acts like the blower of the wind-pipe.

2. From the regular action of the opening and closing of eye-lids, the existence of a conscious agent

[13] *Vide Supra*, pp. 53-55; 280-83.
[14] PPBhā., p. 99; Kandalī., pp. 72-73.
[15] PPBhā., p. 99.
[16] PPBhā., p. 99.

in an organism, who would act like the puller of the pulley, is inferred.

3. From the fact that the wounds of an organism are healed up, we infer the existence of a conscious agent who would be like the master of the house repairing it.

4. From the action of *Manas* towards the contact of the sense-organs apprehending desirable objects, we infer the existence of an agent, who would be like the boy in a corner of the house throwing a ball to another ball stuck in the ground.

5. When we see an object through the organ of sight, and recall the taste of that object (experienced before), we find a certain change appearing in the organ of taste. From this, also, we infer the existence of a single guiding agent of the two activities, like a person looking through many windows[17].

These are some of the proofs adduced to prove the existence of the *Ātman*.

Now, let us examine the same question in a different way. We are aware that the viewpoint of the Indian Materialists represents the feelings of the common class of people. Ordinarily, it is very difficult, if not impossible, to reject their views. The reason is quite simple. However learned one may be, after all, in his every day dealings, he is no better than a true Materialist. Proceeding on this assumption, it is, undoubtedly, very difficult to assert the existence of the world hereafter, the existence of the *Ātman*, and similar other things. In the course of our busy worldly life surrounded by the thickest fog of nescience, it is difficult to see things beyond ourselves; and it is no strange that one is entirely unable to know of the *Ātman* which is so very subtle in nature.

This is the reason why the existence of *Ātman*,

[17] PPBhā., pp. 69-70.

as understood by the orthodox schools, is questioned. But at the same time nobody ever denies that there is an entity which possesses consciousness. And accordingly, even the extremists of the Materialistic school have given some explanation or other of *Ātman*. They do not recognize the existence of *Ātman* as something different from matter, or its product. Within their own limitations, nothing more and better can be expected of them. No worldly man apparently ever thinks that the term '*I*' is not used for body or sense-organs. Even in the expressions 'I am happy,' 'I possess consciousness,' etc., the term '*I*' apparently refers to body, or to the various sense-organs. But all these views fail to satisfy the needs of the Naiyāyikas and the Vaiçeṣikas, and the propounders of other orthodox schools.

It seems to be a recognized fact that the joint system of Nyāya-Vaiçeṣika occupies the first starting place in the realm of Indian Metaphysics. Hence, it appears that the first attempt, to assert the existence of *Ātman* as quite different from matter or its product, was made by Nyāya and Vaiçeṣika. We know that the description of the Supreme Entity from the empirical (*vyāvahārika*)[18] point of view is that it is *Sat*, *Cit*, and *Ānanda*. The last two aspects naturally depend upon the first. If a thing has no existence (*sat*), it is impossible to assert of it anything. Hence, the first and the foremost attempt should be made to prove that there is (*Sat*) a Supreme Entity quite apart from body, sense-organ, vital airs, and the *Manas*. This is done by Nyāya and Vaiçeṣika. We do not know anything of this *Ātman* within the limitations of Nyāya and Vaiçeṣika except that it exists (*Sat*). The attempt to prove the existence of other aspects, namely, *Cit* and *Ānanda*, remains for Sāṅkhya and Vedānta respectively.

[18] From the *pāramārthika* point of view nothing can be said of the Supreme Entity; cf. the Çruti—*yato vāco nivartante aprāpya manasā saha*.

It may be asked here: when it is possible to have the intuitive perception of the *Ātman*, why should an effort be made to prove the same through inference? There are two possible answers to this question—(1) That there is the intuitive perception of it is not accepted by all, and (2) that it is generally seen that those who take delight in argumentation desire to prove a thing through inference even when it is proved through direct perception. So says Çaṅkara Miçra that although sometimes the *Ātman* is really perceived through intuition, yet, like cognition, produced by the flash of lightning, it does not get so much fixity being disregarded by such other conflicting perceptions as 'I am fair,' 'I am lean and thin,' and the like. Here another form of cognition produced by probans which are other than those connected remotely (*anyathāsiddhas*), makes the former cognition itself (that is, the intuitive cognition) quite firm. Moreover, it is necessary to have argumentation (*manana*) about the *Ātman* as taught in the injunction—'the *Ātman* should be heard about, reflected upon,' etc. —which only is a means towards the realization of that which is desirable, namely, the Highest Good. If there be no argumentation about it, then meditation (*nididhyāsana*) would be impossible, and consequently, there would be no direct realization, and no final emancipation (*apavarga*)[19].

II. *Jīvātman defined*

The existence of the individual self having been proved, it is defined as that which is the substratum of consciousness which itself being a product is non-eternal,[20] and also that of the feelings of pleasure, pain etc.[21] within the limitation of a physical organism. Again,

[19] VU., III. ii. 11.
[20] SC., 1; p. 12, quoted by NK., p. 263 (Second edition).
[21] TD., p. 13.

it has been defined by the author of the Upaskāra as that which employs the olfactory and other sense-organs to their respective objects of cognition and that wherein the experiences of the objects of cognition reside.[22] Uddyotakara defines it as one who recognises (*pratisandhātā*)[23].

III. *Qualities of Jīvātman*

Jīvātman possesses consciousness (*jñāna*), pleasure, pain, desire, aversion, effort, merit, demerit, impression (*saṃskāra*), number, dimension, separateness, conjunction and disjunction[24]. A brief treatment of some of the qualities is given below.

1. *Consciousness (buddhi or jñāna)*

Here in Nyāya-Vaiçeṣika, the term consciousness (*jñāna*) is synonymous with intellect (*buddhi*) and apprehension (*upalabdhi*)[25] as against the Sāṅkhya view according to which intellect (*buddhi*) is the first evolute of the unconscious primordial matter (*Prakṛti*) and is an inner instrument;[26] consciousness (*jñāna*) is the function of this intellect[27]; while apprehension (*upalabdhi*) belongs to the non-active *Puruṣa* itself[28].

[22] VU., III. i. 2.
[23] NV., I. i. 10; p. 64.
[24] PPBhā., p. 70.
[25] NS., I. i. 15; PPBhā., p. 171.
[26] SK., 22, 33.
[27] SK., 23.
[28] *Cetanasyākarturupalabdhiriti*—NBhā., I. i. 15. The psychological process involved in the above is explained by Vācaspati Miçra as given below:—*Buddhi* is a modification of the three *guṇas*, which are unconscious entities. Hence, *Buddhi*, which also is unconscious, through the passage (*praṇālī*) made by the sense-organ, comes in contact with the object and becomes itself modified into the form of that object. The *citiçakti*, on the other hand, is unchanging and is of the nature of eternal consciousness. When *Buddhi* comes

Though there are various forms of cognition (*buddhi*), as objects of cognition are innumerable, yet it is classified under two broad heads—right cognition (*vidyā*) and wrong cognition (*avidyā*).[29] The former is subdivided into directly sensuous, inferential, recollective and superhuman (*ārṣa*)[30]. The latter also is subdivided into doubt, perversion (*viparyaya*), indistinct cognition (*anadhyavasāya*) and dream[31].

Of the right cognitions, that cognition which is produced by the contact of the sense-organs with their respective objects is said to be directly sensuous or direct perception[32]. Gautama makes it more clear when he says that direct perception is that cognition which is produced by the contact of the sense-organ with the object, which is not expressible (*avyapadeçyam*), which is not erroneous and which is decisive[33]. The objects of perception is either gross, as a pot, a cow etc., or subtle, as pleasure, pain etc. The perception of gross

into close proximity to this *citiçakti*, it reflects within itself this *citiçakti*, and thereby appears as if it itself were conscious, and becoming modified into the form of the object, it cognises the object; so that, the modification of the *Buddhi* into the form of the object cognised is said to be the cognition (*jñāna*) of that object. The contact of the conscious entity, through reflection, with the *Buddhi* in the shape of the object cognised, is expressed as the function (*vyāpāra*) of the conscious entity (*Ātman or Puruṣa*), and is called the apprehension (*upalabdhi*) of the object by the conscious entity. Just as the moon, being essentially devoid of light, reflects the light of the Sun which is essentially in possession of light, and with this reflected light illumines objects. In the same way, *Buddhi*, though itself unconscious, yet reflects the consciousness of the *Citiçakti* and thereby cognises objects and makes them apprehended—Tāt., I. i. 15, pp. 233-34; Kandalī, pp. 171-72.

29 PPBhā., p. 172.

30 PPBhā., p. 186.

31 PPBhā., p. 172.

32 PPBhā., p. 186.

33 NS., I. i. 4.

objects is through the external sense-organs, while that of the subtle objects is through the internal sense-organ[34] alone. Even in the case of the perception of gross objects, there are two definite stages of perception. For instance, after the operation of the psychological process involved in the act of direct perception, namely, the contact of the sense-organ with the object, followed by the contact of the *Manas* with the sense-organ and lastly, that of the *Manas* with the *Ātman*[35], the first cognition that is produced is said to be free from discrimination. It is, therefore, expressed as *simple apprehension* or *indeterminate cognition* (*nirvikalpajñāna*)[36]. This is followed by the *determinate cognition* which is accompanied by the knowledge of the object along with its qualities. This is technically called *savikalpajñāna*[37].

Against the view that determinate knowledge (*savikalpajñāna*) is the only type of direct perception, it may be pointed out that if the indeterminate form of cognition of an object be not admitted, then inasmuch as there would be no remembrance of the word denoting it, there would not be the determinate cognition of it either. Hence, in order to have the determinate knowledge of an object one must admit the indeterminate knowledge of it also[38].

The auxiliaries for the direct perception of an object are: the presence of magnitude (*mahattva*), possession of several parts, presence of manifested colour aided by merit and demerit. Besides these, the contacts of the *Ātman*, *Manas*, sense-organ and the object are also necessary factors for the direct perception[39].

[34] Kandalī., p. 188.
[35] NBhā., I. i. 4; Kandalī., p. 188.
[36] PPBhā., p. 186; Kandalī., p. 189.
[37] PPBhā., p. 186; Kandalī., p. 189.
[38] Kandalī., p. 189.
[39] PPBhā., p. 186.

The direct perception of colour, taste, smell and touch is caused by the contact of their respective sense-organs with their respective objects, by their inherence in composite substances, and by virtue of their having peculiarities within themselves (*svagataviçeṣāt*)[40]. The perception of sound proceeds from the two-fold contacts, namely, the contact of the *Manas* with the sense-organ wherein the sound inheres, and that of the *Manas* with the *Ātman*. It is cognised through the auditory organ itself[41]. The perception of number, dimension, separateness, conjunction, disjunction, priority, posteriority, viscidity, fluidity, velocity and motion proceeds from their inherence in perceptible substances through the instrumentality of the visual and the tactile sense-organs[42]. The perception of cognition, pleasure, pain, desire, aversion, motive is due to the contact of the *Manas* with the *Ātman*. The perception of the generalities of substance, quality and motion is by means of those sense-organs which perceive their substrates, wherein they inhere[43].

As regards the perception of *yogins* in the ecstatic condition, it is due to the *Manas* aided by the yogic properties that the intuitive perception of one's own self and that of another, of *Ākāça*, *Dik*, *Kāla*, *Paramāṇu*, air, *Manas*, and of the qualities, motions, generalities, quiddities and inherence inhering in them, takes place. In the case of *yogins*, who are not in ecstatic mood, direct perception is possible regarding objects, which are subtle, hidden and removed far off through the four-fold contacts helped by the yogic properties[44].

The next is the inferential cognition which is pro-

[40] PPBhā., p. 186; Kandalī., p. 194.
[41] PPBhā., pp. 186-87; Kandalī., p. 194.
[42] PPBhā., p. 187; Kandalī., p. 194.
[43] PPBhā., p. 187.
[44] PPBhā., p. 187.

duced by the perception of the probans[45]. The *Çabda-pramāṇa* admitted by Nyāya is included under inference[46]. The third form of *vidyā* is remembrance. It is caused by the contact of the *Ātman* and the *Manas* aided by such causes as the perception of an indicative (*liṅga-darçana*), desire for remembering and the associated ideas and the like, and from impression produced by distinct cognition, by repetition and by an impressive regard for the object concerned[47].

Coming to the superhuman (*ārṣa*) type of cognition, it is found that in the case of sages who are responsible for the propounding of the Vedas, it is found that from the contact of the *Ātman* and the *Manas* helped by a particular kind of merit, there appears an intuitional cognition (*prātibhajñāna*), correct in all its details, as regards the supersensuous objects—past, present and future, and also regarding *dharma* etc. mentioned or not mentioned in the scriptures. Generally, such an intuitive perception is found with superhuman beings—sages etc., but sometimes it is also possible with ordinary human beings[48].

Besides these forms of cognition, there is another form of cognition called *siddha-darçana*. This is a sort of direct perception which is acquired by the use of certain ointment applied to the eyes and to the feet and also by the use of pills etc., through which one can directly perceive objects which are very subtle, hidden and removed far off[49].

Of the wrong cognitions (*avidyā*), that wherein a doubt is felt as to the nature of the object on account of its possessing the distinctive characteristics of several

45 PPBhā., p. 200.

46 PPBhā., p. 213.

47 PPBhā., p. 256 Also *Vide*—Umesha Mishra—Smṛti Theory according to Nyāya-Vaiçeṣika—K. P. Pāthaka Commemoration Vol. pp. 177-86.

48 PPBhā., p. 258.

49 PPBhā., p. 258.

objects but not the differentiating characteristics; so that, no decisive knowledge can be had about that object, it is said to be a case of doubtful cognition[50]. A perverse knowledge (*viparyaya*) pertains to direct perception and inference only. As for the former, we find that of the two objects, possessed of distinctive characteristics, it so happens that the real object is not perceived by a person whose sense-organ is affected by bile, phlegm and wind; and then from the impression produced by the previous perception of the object not present before the observer, helped by the contact of the *Manas* with the *Ātman* aided by demerit, there appears a cognition which is quite opposite to the nature of the object present. This is a case of perverse knowledge[51].

Indistinct cognition also appears in regard to direct perception and inference. As for instance, sometimes we find a mere idea, about an object, appearing in the form-'what may this be'? This may be either due to the absent-mindedness of the observer, or to the fact that the observer is desirous of knowing further details about the object itself. This is said to be a case of indistinct knowledge[52].

The last form of wrong cognition is dream. When our sense-organs have ceased to function, and the *Manas* has retired, then through the impressions of the sense-organs certain cognitions are produced during our half-sleeping state. These cognitions are known as dream cognitions[53].

Now, it may be enquired whether these forms of cognition belonging to the *Jīvātman* are eternal or not; for, we find that non-touchability, which is a quality of

[50] PPBhā., pp. 174-75.
[51] PPBhā., p. 177.
[52] PPBhā., p. 182.
[53] PPBhā., pp. 183-84; Also *Vide*—Umesha Mishra—Dream Theory in Indian Thought—Allahabad University Studies, Vol. V. pp. 269-321.

consciousness, is found both in an eternal substance, like the *Ākāça* and also in a non-eternal entity like *karman*; hence, there appears a doubt. To this it is said in reply that—(1) Consciousness is known to everybody as non-eternal, like pleasure and pain. (2) The experiences, expressed as 'I shall know,' 'I know,' 'I have known', refer to all the three divisions of time, which is not possible unless consciousness is non-eternal. (3) Again, it has also been said above that cognition is a product[54]. All these prove that cognition is non-eternal. But by non-eternity of consciousness we should not mistake it for being momentary (*kṣaṇika*).

It is also clear from this that consciousness is not the very nature of *Ātman*. In fact, the *Ātman* is essentially non-conscious (*jaḍa*), but it becomes conscious only when, due to the sense-organ and the object contact, consciousness is produced in it[55]. If consciousness were the very nature of it, then everybody would have become omniscient[56]. By consciousness the Naiyāyikas mean the cognition of an object produced by *Manas*, or the sense-organ and the object contact. Such a consciousness is only occasional in the *Ātman*, although both are inseparably related to each other[57]. This, again, is produced, as is clear from the above, only when the *Ātman* comes to possess an organism, and not otherwise[58].

2. *Pleasure and pain*

Happy experiences, felt in the *Jīvātman* through the contact of the *Ātman* and the *Manas* aided by the results of virtuous deeds, are denoted as pleasure (*sukha*). Affection, happy appearance etc., are its effects. In regard to past objects, it is produced through

[54] NS., I. i. 4; NM., p. 496; Kandalī., p. 73; PRM, p. 34.
[55] NM., pp. 432-33, 512; SPBhā., I. 145.
[56] NM., p. 432.
[57] NM., p. 512.
[58] NK., p. 264, (2nd Edition).

memory; in regard to future objects, it is brought about by volition (*saṅkalpa*); and that which is felt by the wise, even in the absence of such causes as remembrance of objects, desire and volition, is due to their self-knowledge, control over the sense-organs, contentment and specific merits[59]. As it is not a fact that all the feelings of one who has acquired discriminative knowledge (*vivekin*) are naturally of painful nature, we should not consider pleasure to be merely an absence of pain. That persons having true knowledge do possess happy experiences (*anugraha*) within themselves is a fact which admits no denial[60].

Similarly, unhappy experiences felt within one's own self at the presence of undesirable objects through the contact of the *Manas* with the *Ātman*, aided by the results accruing from non-meritorious deeds, are described as pain (*duḥkha*). In case of past objects, it is due to memory, while in case of future objects, it is produced by volition (*saṅkalpa*)[61]. Pain should not be considered as merely an absence of pleasure[62].

Naiyāyikas do not admit pleasure to be a distinct category. But then it should not be considered that they deny the very existence of feelings of pleasure. What they mean is that pure happiness cannot be found in this universe. It is generally mixed up with pain. Hence, pleasure also is a form of pain[63].

3. *Desire* (*icchā*)

It is a sort of wish for the attainment of an object which one has not got[64] and which is expressed in the

[59] PPBhā., p. 259.
[60] Vyom., p. 624.
[61] PPBhā., p. 260.
[62] Vyom., p. 624.
[63] NBhā., I. i. 2, 9.
[64] PPBhā., p. 261.

form—'may this be mine' etc.[65] This is produced out of the contact of the *Manas* with the *Ātman*, through pleasure etc., or through remembrance etc. It is the cause of effort, remembrance, merit and demerit. It has several forms[66].

4. *Aversion (dveṣa)*

It is the feeling which makes one think himself burning or being irritated. It proceeds from the contact of the *Manas* with the *Ātman* through the help of pain or remembrance. It is the cause of effort, remembrance, merit and demerit. It has several forms[67].

5. *Effort (prayatna)*

It is of two kinds—(1) that which proceeds from mere living, and (2) that which proceeds from desire and aversion. The former is that which helps the series of upward and downward breathings in the sleeping man and which brings about the contact of the *Manas* with the external sense-organs during the waking state. This is produced from the contact of the *Manas* with the *Ātman* aided by merits and demerits. The latter kind of effort is, however, produced out of the contact of the *Manas* with the *Ātman* helped by desire, or aversion. It helps the preservation of physical organism and such activities which lead to the attainment of desirable and to the abandoning of the undesirable[68].

6. *Impression (saṃskāra)*

Regarding the process of its production, it may be pointed out that after the usual process of cognition,

[65] Kandali., p. 261.
[66] PPBhā., p. 261.
[67] PPBhā., p. 263.
[68] PPBhā., p. 263.

when the result is obtained, a kind of impression is left behind by that resultant cognition which itself vanishes away afterwards. Such an impression, which is the exact copy of that cognition, has got the *Ātman* as its substratum. Every piece of cognition leaves behind it an impression. But those which are due to (1) intensified (*paṭu*) cognitions, (2) repeated cognitions, and (3) impressive (*ādara*) cognitions produced by special efforts are more vivid and are easily recalled[69].

It is the cause of remembrance and recognition of objects previously seen, or heard, or experienced; and is counteracted by contrary cognition, intoxication and intense pain etc.[70]

7. *Merit and demerit (dharmādharma)*

Merit (*dharma*) is produced in the *Jīvātman* by the contact of the *Manas* with the *Ātman* itself helped by the various means, the purity of thoughts (*bhāvaprasāda*) and the absence of desire to attain any visible result from those means[71]. The means are: faith in *dharma*, harmlessness, benevolence, truthfulness, freedom from desire for undue possession, freedom from lust (*brahmacarya*), purity of intentions, absence of anger, bathing, use of purifying substances, devotion to particular deities, fasting and carefulness towards one's own duty. Besides, the performance of the various religious duties of the four castes and the *āçramas*, as laid down in the *çrutis* and the *smṛtis*, also helps the accruing of merit[72].

The performance of these injunctive deeds cannot be said to be the direct cause of those happy results which appear after a long interval; hence, it is assumed

[69] PPBhā., p. 267. Also *Vide* Umesha Mishra—Smṛti theory according to Nyāya-Vaiçeṣika, K. B. Pāṭhaka Com. Vol. pp. 179-80.

[70] PPBhā., p. 267.

[71] PPBhā., pp. 272-73.

[72] PPBhā., p. 272.

that such deeds when performed leave behind them their impressions in a stagnant form which, when, in course of time, become mature, yield their respective results[73]. These after-effects of our meritorious acts remain unseen for sometime and hence, they are called *adṛṣṭa*.

It brings about happiness, means of happiness (*hita*) and final emancipation to the agent (*kartṛ*). It is supersensuous. It is destructible by the experience of final happiness;[74] so that, it should not be confused with the mental impression[75]. It is also destroyed by true knowledge.[76] It cannot be said to be eternal, as some hold it to be; for, in that case, as there would be no exhaustion of it, and consequently, no end of the worldly experiences of pleasure, there would have been no final emancipation.[77]

Likewise, demerit (*adharma*) is also a quality of the *Ātman*. It is produced by the contact of the *Manas* with the *Ātman* aided by the performance of deeds which are prohibited in the scriptures, and which are contrary to the causes of merit mentioned above; the non-performance of deeds which are enjoined in the scriptures; and carelessness (*pramāda*). It brings about pain, means of pain and sin to the doer (*kartṛ*), that is,

[73] Setu on PPBhā., p. 368.

[74] PPBhā., p. 272. Inasmuch as *dharma* is an effect, it must be destroyed. But it is not destroyed so soon. Sometimes its results are such as can be experienced in thousands of years. Such being the case, if the *dharma* were to be destroyed by its very first result, then there would be nothing left to yield the remaining parts of its results; nor is it possible for *dharma* to be destroyed in parts, as it is an absolute integrity (*eko nirbbhāgaḥ*). It is for these reasons that *dharma* is held to be destructible by the experience of final happiness resulting from it—Kandalī, p. 275.

[75] *Saṃskāro'pi smṛtidvāreṇaivaṃ bharatītyatontyasukhasaṃvijñānavirodhīti*—Vyom., p. 638.

[76] *Samyagvijñānena dharmo vinaçyate*—Kandalī., p. 275.

[77] Kandalī., p. 275.

the *Jīvātman*. It is supersensuous and is destroyed by the experience of the last pain resulting from it[78].

That both merit and demerit belong to the *Jīvātman* is proved by the fact that there must be something on the basis of which the physical organism, for the experience of pleasure and pain by the *Jīvātman*, is to be made. The qualities belonging to the organism themselves cannot be of any use, as the organism itself has not come to exist yet; nor can such qualities of the *Jīvātman*, which come to exist in it after its connection with the organism, namely, consciousness, pleasure, pain, desire, aversion and effort, help the production of the organism. Even the impression (*bhāvanā*) which accompanies the *Jīvātman* from one organism to another, cannot be the required cause; for its capacity becomes known when it gives rise to remembrance, which itself is possible only when the *Jīvātman* has come to possess an organism. Hence, through the method of Residue it is assumed that the qualities which guide the production of physical organism are merit and demerit[79].

Besides, there are also *çrutis* like—*Yāvadātmani dharmādharmau tāvadāyuḥ çarīramindriyāṇi viṣayāçca etc.* as long as the *Jīvātman* possesses merit and demerit, so long there exist span of life (*āyus*), physical organism, sense-organs and other objects for the experiencing of pleasure and pain, for it, to prove that merit and demerit belong to the *Jīvātman*[80].

Some are of opinion that merit is of the nature of *paramāṇu* itself. If it were so, then like *paramāṇus*, merit also would have been eternal, and that there would have been no religious activities etc. to produce any merit. There would have been no death even. But as these are against the actual reality, Nyāya-

[78] PPBhā., p. 280.
[79] Vyom., pp. 638-39.
[80] Vyom., p. 639.

Vaiçeṣika rejects the view as unsound[81].

Likewise, the view that both merit and demerit are the qualities of *paramāṇu* is also rejected as wrong on the ground that inasmuch as *paramāṇus* are like common properties for all, all persons ought to have experienced only one type of pleasure and pain. This, again, is not the fact[82].

Some, again, improving upon the former view, think that some *paramāṇus* possess merit, while others possess demerit; so that, those organisms which are produced out of the meritorious *paramāṇus* are meritorious, and cause the experience of pleasure, while those which are produced from the demeritorious *paramāṇus* help the experiences of pain. To this it is said in reply that if it were so, then as *paramāṇus* are eternal, there would not have been any religious activity in the world; and also there would not have been any death. Hence, this view, also, like the previous one, is rejected as unsound[83].

8. *Plurality of Jīvātmans*

As regards the question—Whether there is only one *Jīvātman* or many, it is pointed out that there are as many *Ātmans* as there are living beings in the universe. The proof for this assumption is the existing differences in the universe[84]. Thus—

(1) It is found that some are in bondage and have to pass from one life to another, while others are free. Had there been only one *Jīvātman*, then together with the liberation of one *Ātman*, all others also should have been liberated.

(2) Similarly, some are happy, while others are unhappy. Some, again, are rich, while others are poor.

[81] Vyom., p. 639.
[82] Vyom., p. 639.
[83] Vyom., 639.
[84] VS., III. ii. 20; KU., pp. 150-51; Kandali., pp. 686-87.

That these and similar other differences do really exist in the universe cannot be denied. Had there been only one *Jīvātman*, how would it be possible to explain these differences?

As to the view that just as in the case of *Ākāça*, although it is only one, yet due to the diversity of its limitations (*upādhis*) in the form of ear-cavity, we have diversity in the sound-experiences; so, in the case of *Ātman*, believing that it is only one, we may explain the diversity of experiences as being due to the diversity of its limitations, in the form of physical organisms, it may be said in reply that the instance cited above is not quite analogous. The diversity of sound experiences might well be explained as due to the sound-comprehending agencies, in the form of ear-cavity and the rest, which have been brought about by the merit and demerit, which are restricted to each individual person. But in the case of *Ātman*, on the other hand, there would be no diversity in the merit and demerit, since all these would belong to one and the same *Ātman*; and as such, there being no diversity in the bodies (which are brought about by the merits and demerits of the *Ātman* ensouling the body), what would be the cause of the diversity of pleasure and pain experienced by different persons; especially, when the *Ātman* is one, the contact of the *Manas* also would be common to all persons?

For one, however, who believes in the plurality of *Ātmans*, though all of them, being omnipresent, would be present in all the bodies, yet their experiences would not be common to all of them; as each of them would experience only such pleasures etc., as would appear in connection with the particular body brought about by the previous deeds of that *Ātman* and not those which belong to other bodies also. Again, the past deeds also stick, in the form of *adṛṣṭa*, to that very *Ātman* in contact with which the particular organism had performed it. Hence, the restriction of body is due to the restriction of the past deeds[85].

The *çrutis* laying down the non-difference of the *Ātmans* must be taken as figurative. Besides, there are direct *çrutis* also to prove the plurality of the *Ātmans*[86].

It has been shown above that every individual being has got one separate *Ātman*, and consequently, there are as many *Ātmans* as there are individuals in the world. To differentiate one *Ātman* from the other, several reasons have been given which are just in keeping with the view-point of the school. But besides these, there is another point also to consider in support of the above view. The Vaiçeṣika-Sūtra—'*Vyavasthāto nānā*'[87] says that the plurality of the *Ātmans* is due to *vyavasthā* (status), which has been explained and illustrated above. Now, this gives rise to several questions, such as—(1) To what is the status (*vyavasthā*) due? (2) How long does the cause of the status operate? That is, does this status influence the *Ātman* only in this world, or even hereafter? (3) How far does this status influence the *Ātman* during the state of *Mokṣa*?

If we just think a bit we find that this status is exclusively due to the result of the past deeds. In other words, it is for the sake of the experience of pleasure and pain of our own deeds of the past life or lives that we come to this world, and also pass from one life to another, in case the experiences of pleasure and pain are not exhausted. The status and the condition of a being are determined by his own deeds. This being the case, as long as the influence of the past deeds lasts, the status (*vyavasthā*) is sure to continue. As for the continuity of the influence of the past deeds, no one can say how long would it last; so that, the

[85] Kandalī., p. 87.
[86] YV., XIX, 46; Kaṭha, V. 13.
[87] VS., III. ii. 20.

vyavasthā not only operates in this world, but also continues hereafter. And it is due to this that some go to heavens, while others enter hell; and even there, all do not experience equal status.

What about the *Ātmans* which are liberated? It is a fact that the *Ātman* becomes liberated only when it has exhausted the experiences of the results of all its past deeds; so that, there being no more influence of the past deeds, the *Ātman* will become free from all the *vyavasthās* which were due to those past deeds. Now, if there be no *vyavasthā*, then it will have to assume, according to the apparent meaning of the *Sūtra*, that there is no plurality of the *Ātmans*. That is, the plurality, which is due to the presence of the *vyavasthā*, will cease, when that *vyavasthā* is removed. In other words, as Candrakānta appears to think,[88] in the state of liberation, there will be only one *Ātman* without having any distinction.

But, is it a fact that when *Ātmans* become free from the influence of the past deeds, there is nothing to differentiate one *Ātman* from another, due to which alone, Candrakānta Tarkālaṅkāra and others think that beyond this empirical world (*vyavahārabhūmi*), the plurality of the *Ātmans* does not exist? The answer is in the negative. We know that according to Nyāya and Vaiçeṣika, the *Manas* is as much eternal as the *Jīvātman*. Their connection also is eternal; so that, when a particular *Ātman* becomes free from the bondage of the universe, even then its eternal companion, the *Manas*, remains with it. The presence of this very *Manas* makes every *Jīvātman* retain its own personality although each of the liberated *Ātmans* may be pure and free from the influence of its past deeds. Hence, even after the

[88] (i) *Vyavahārabhūmikāyāṃ khalu vyavasthāto nānā;* (ii) *Çāstrasāmarthyācca pratipadyāmahe eka evātmā vyavahārabhūmau bhidyate*—VBhā., III. ii. 20-21.

nescience (*mithyājñāna*) is removed, the difference (*bheda*) existing between one *Ātman* and the other is sure to remain as before, even in the state of liberation[89].

9. *Dimension of Jīvātman*

It is all-pervasive and hence, it possesses the highest dimension[90]. If it were not so, then action would not have been produced in the respective objects possessing limited dimension, as a result of conjunction of the *Ātman* carrying its *adṛṣṭa*, inasmuch as *adṛṣṭa* being present in a different substratum is dependent upon proximity (*pratyāsatti*) in order that it may be productive of action; and that proximity is nothing but conjunction of the *Ātman* carrying its *adṛṣṭa*. Likewise, as the body moves on, the production of knowledge, pleasure etc., in particular situations is impossible or incapable of proof except on the ground of the all-pervasiveness of the *Ātman*[91].

It is further suggested that as the effects of *Ātman*, namely, consciousness, happiness, etc., are found everywhere, it is proved that *Ātman* is all-pervasive[92]. We know that both merit and demerit are the qualities of *Ātman*, and if their substratum, namely, *Ātman*, be not all-pervasive, then there would have been no upward motion of the fire, no transversal motion of the air, and no initial motion of the *aṇu* and the *Manas*; for, merit and demerit depend upon the conjunction with their substratum. Being the qualities of the *Ātman*, they cannot produce any motion without the contact of the *Ātman*, just as the effort requires the contact of the *Ātman* to produce activities in the hand. In the

[89] VV., on VS., III. ii. 21; Vyom., p. 410; ÇS., p. 366.

[90] VS., VII. i. 22.

[91] *Yadyātmanaḥ sakalamūrtasaṃyogitvaṃ na bhavettadā teṣu teṣu adṛṣṭavadātmasaṃyogātkriyā notpadyeta, vyadhikaraṇasyādṛṣṭasya pratyāsattyapekṣayā kriyājanakatvāt* etc.—VU., VII. i. 22.

[92] KU., p. 151.

absence of any other cause, *adṛṣṭa* is assumed to be the cause of these[93]. Hence, *Ātman* is all-pervasive.

Again, it is a fact that a *yogin*, having acquired higher powers, constructs various bodies equipped with all the sense-organs, and simultaneously, experiences pleasure and pain in all those bodies. This is possible only when the *Ātman* is all-pervasive[94].

Jīvātman possesses, on these very grounds, the highest dimension. It cannot be atomic; for, in that case, pleasure, pain, desire etc., also would have become supersensuous. Again, it cannot be of the intermediate dimension (*madhyama-parimāṇa*); for, in that case, the *Ātman* would have become non-eternal[95]; which is not possible. Again, no person, who has no feeling of attachment (*rāga*), is found to take birth ever. Possession of such a feeling necessitates previous existence of the *Ātman*, which is not possible, if the *Ātman* were non-eternal[96]. Moreover, there is nothing to prove that *Ātman* has got parts[97].

Again, it is supported by the recognition (*pratyabhijñā*) in the form 'I, who had seen the thing, am also touching that very thing,' and again, 'that very I, who had touched that very thing, am also looking at it.'[98] Its being eternal also shows that there is no beginning of this *Ātman*.

It is also clear from the fact that a few days old baby sometimes smiles, sometimes quivers, and sometimes

[93] *Tathā dharmādharmayorātmaguṇatvāttadāçrayasyāvyāpakatve na syāt agnerūrdhvajvalanaṃ vāyostiryaggamanamaṇumanasostvādyaṃ karmeti tayoḥ svāçrayasaṃyogāpekṣitvāt. Yathā prayatno hastakarmaṇyātmasaṃyogāpekṣastathā dharmādharmāvātmasaṃyogaṃ vinā na karma kuryātāmātmaguṇatvāt* etc. Vyom., p. 411.

[94] NBhā., III. ii. 19; TBhā., pp. 91-92, (S. M. Paranjape's edition); PWSS., Vol. I, pp. 47-58; Vyom., p. 411.

[95] Setu., p. 390.

[96] NS. and NBhā., III. i. 24.

[97] VU., III. ii. 5.

[98] KR., p. 38.

cries out, which activities are only due to the recognitions of the deeds producing joy, fear and grief, of the past life[99]; for, being only a few days old, his smiling etc. cannot be due to his experiences of this life[100].

It is further said that had not the *Ātman* been eternal, one, who is desirous of the other world, would not have been attracted towards its acquirement. Again, the knowledge, that the particular activity will be helpful, which leads the newly born baby to suck the mother's breast, also proves that *Ātman* is eternal[101]. That a person takes birth itself proves that the *Ātman* must have existed even before the particular birth, wherein it had cherished desires for the next birth; for, persons free from longings are never found to be born[102]. The very fact that the *Ātman* is eternal proves that it will exist even when the present body falls down as dead[103]. All these things prove that the *Jīvātman* is all-pervasive.

10. *Other qualities of Jīvātman*

Jīvātman also possesses conjunction and disjunction. This is proved by the production and the destruction of pleasure and pain where the presence of the non-material cause, in the form of conjunction and disjunction respectively, is necessary[104]. It is a substance as it possesses qualities[105]. Because it is all-pervasive, it does not possess any motion[106].

It has no *āçritatva*. That is, it has nothing as its

[99] KR., p. 38.
[100] NBhā. and NVṛ. on NS,, III. i. 18.
[101] NS. and NBhā., III. i. 21.
[102] NS., III., i. 25; KP., p. 167, and Makaranda on the same; ĀTV., pp. 104-105.
[103] NS., IV. i. 10.
[104] Vyom., p. 411; KU., p. 152.
[105] VU., III. ii. 5; VBhā., III. i. 3.
[106] VS., V. ii. 21.

substratum[107]. That it has no cause of its own follows from its being an eternal substance[108]. It possesses the specific qualities,[109] which are neither eternal nor pervasive.[110] It is the agent (*kartṛ*)[111].

IV. Mokṣa and the Possibility of its Achievement

We have talked much about *Mokṣa*, but doubts are felt as regards its possibility. There are several unsurmountable difficulties in its way, some of which are given below:

1. *Ṛṇānubandha*—According to the *çrutis* when a man comes to this world, he owes three debts—(1) to the *Ṛṣis*, (2) to the *Pitṛs*, and (3) to the gods. To clear off the first debt, he has to live as a *brahmacārin* for a certain period. For clearing off the second debt, he has to marry and produce a child, and then pass his days as a householder (*gṛhastha*). Lastly, he has to engage himself in the performance of religious rites and ceremonies, such as *Darçapūrṇamāsa* etc., which sometimes last for even hundred years, to pay off his debt to the gods. All these debts must be cleared off. Now, during the lifetime of a man there is hardly any time even to do these. How can then one think of *Mokṣa*? Hence, the talk about *Mokṣa* is only a pious wish. The view—that since one does not live long enough to do all these things, and then to prepare for *Mokṣa*, he should leave something undone, cannot help him to seek after *Mokṣa*; for, no one is entitled to try for *Mokṣa* unless he has finished all other duties.

[107] Kandalī., p. 16.
[108] Kandalī., p. 18.
[109] Kandalī., p. 24.
[110] KU., p. 38; Kandalī., p. 25.
[111] KR., p. 37.

2. *Kleçānubandha*—The defects—attachment, aversion and ignorance, are so powerful that it is not easy to get rid of them. There are hundreds of instances where these defects have shown their superiority. And without becoming free from these no one can achieve *Mokṣa*. This also is a great obstacle in its way.

3. *Pravṛttyanubandha*—Again, the presence of attachment etc. compels a man to engage his attention towards the worldly activities, which, instead of leading him towards the liberation, entangles him with the worldly aims, which in their turn, help him to take more births and deaths.

4. And lastly, it is a fact that every such activity must end in some result, the experience of which must be exhausted. But as there is no end to the activities it is very doubtful if they will be ever exhausted completely. The view—that the attainment of the true knowledge destroys the activities, is merely a blind faith in the *çrutis*.

On these grounds, it appears that the attainment of *Mokṣa* is merely a pious wish. Now, the Naiyāyikas reject all these views and show that the attainment of final emancipation is quite possible. The following are their arguments :

1. The use of the term '*debt*' in the above case is only secondary. All that has been said in that connection is to show that observance of *brahmacarya*, the producing of children, and the performance of religious rites etc., must be done. Reference to the *jarāmaryavāda* etc., is only recommendatory and is said in praise of *karman*. Regarding the complaint of time, it is said that had there been no possibility of liberation due to the lack of time, then there would have been no mention of the stage of life after the *gṛhasthāçrama*. The real significance of the fourth stage of our life lies in preparing for *Mokṣa*. Even *çrutis* and *smṛtis* support this[112].

[112] Manu., Chap. VI.

2. As regards the presence of defects, it is said that the constant thinking of the contrary of these will naturally make a man free from these. And again, these are not eternal, nor are they products of chance, nor are the means of their destruction unknown. Hence, it is quite easy to get rid of them. Besides, there are so many defects in all these that a man naturally becomes disgusted with the world and is compelled to seek after *Mokṣa*. The constant thinking of the contrary of these defects (*pratipakṣabhāvanā*) is sure to bring freedom from their influences. As for the possible objection that the *Ātman* is never found to be free from the continuous chain of these defects; hence, it is impossible to think that the constant thinking of the contrary of these even will ever bring freedom, it may be pointed out that it is not true; for, every one of us has got the experience that the *Ātman* is completely free from these defects during the state of *suṣupti*.

3. Regarding the *Pravṛttyanubandha*, it should be understood that when the defects, the cause of the bondage, have been removed, the activity (*pravṛtti*) cannot help the continuity of the *saṃsāra*[113].

An objection is raised here: well, the defects being removed there may be no further addition to the performance of deeds and consequently, there would be no further birth for reaping the fruits of fresh deeds. But what about the result of those deeds which have been already hoarded up? Several views are advanced to remove the above objection. Some think that the future being stopped, the gradual experiencing of the fruits of the past deeds will, some day or other, be exhausted. Others hold that through the *yogic* powers all the past deeds will be experienced in the same single body by the help of the *nirmāṇakāya*[114]. The third and the

[113] NS., IV. i. 64.

[114] (i) It is a body or a series of bodies assumed at will by a *Yogin* who has risen above the so called laws of nature and learnt

most important view is that the true knowledge itself will make the past deeds quite ineffective, as heat does to seed, and thus, one can easily become free from the chains of *karman* and secure *Mokṣa*[115].

The fact is this that the result of the *prārabdha-karmans* will be exhausted only by experiencing them, either in the ordinary course, or through the *yogic* powers. The *sañcita* and the *sañcīyamāna*, on the other hand, will become ineffective by the attainment of the true knowledge. In this way, no difficulty is felt towards the achievement of *Mokṣa*.

There being no doubt as regards the possibility of realizing *Mokṣa*, both Gautama and Kaṇāda have said that the true knowledge of the categories will bring the Highest Good, that is, the *Mokṣa*[116]. After the true knowledge has been acquired, the wrong notions about the *Ātman* will disappear followed by the disappearance of the defects. The defects having been removed, there will be no activity (*pravṛtti*) towards the worldly things. In fact, our worldly activities alone compel us to take fresh births; but now, when the cause itself is made ineffective, there would not be any more birth. Again, all our pains are due to our taking birth, but now, when the birth is stopped, why should there remain any pain? That is, a man becomes free from pain, in the long run, after acquiring the true knowledge. In other words, he acquires *Mokṣa* in the true sense of Nyāya and Vaiçeṣika[117].

There are certain other kinds of doubts. For instance, some feel that if there be really the cessation of

to command its secret forces—PWSS., Vol. I., pp. 47-58.

(ii) *Yogī hi yogardhisiddhyā vihitanikhilanijadharmādharmakarmā nirmāya tadupabhogayogyāni teṣu teṣūpapattisthāneṣu tāni tāni sendriyāṇi çarīrāṇi* etc. NM., p. 520.

[115] NM., pp. 513-24.

[116] NS., I. i. 1; VS., I. i. 4.

[117] NS. and NBhā., I. i. 2.

pain in the *Mokṣa*, then everybody would like to become liberated. And if that be the fact, then some day or other, all will become liberated, and the worldly process will certainly stop. To this it is said that the knowing ones being continuously emancipated, there does not become a void (of the *Ātmans*), inasmuch as the number of these *Ātmans*, in the universe, is infinite; if there were an end, or an increase and decrease in their number, then alone could such a void be possible, as in the case of things of limited dimensions. When the *Ātman* is without any limitation, then there is no possibility of such doubts[118].

Again, others feel that the *Ātman* being eternal, there would be no emancipation for one who perceives or realizes this eternal *Ātman*; as being always affected by a longing for pleasure, he would have an attachment to the means of pleasure and aversion to those of pain; and these two, namely, attachment and aversion, would give rise to constant activities and cessations from activities; and these, in their turn, would give rise to merits and demerits which will lead to births and rebirths and consequently, there is no possibility of *Mokṣa*.

To this it is said that it is not so; because, for one who recognizes the eternal *Ātman*, there would come about due dispassion, produced from a recognition of the evils inseparable from the objects of enjoyment; and this dispassion would, in due course, bring about liberation[119].

V. State of Jīvātman during liberation (Mokṣa)

Mokṣa has been defined as the absolute freedom from pain[120], its cause[121] and everything connected with it. In order to achieve this, one has to acquire the

[118] Kandalī., p. 88.
[119] Kandalī., p. 89.
[120] NS., I. i. 22.
[121] Tāt., I. i. 22, p. 238.

true knowledge of the categories laid down by Gautama[122] and Kaṇāda[123], which in gradual process brings about liberation, as has been shown before. As the qualities of *Ātman* are non-eternal, they leave the *Ātman* in the state of liberation. Hence, the *Ātman*, being free from all its qualities, remains in its own natural state during the state of liberation. It was, perhaps, this very aspect of the *Ātman* that led Çrīharṣa to remark that *Ātman*, according to Gautama is a mere slab of stone[124].

It appears that there was an old view that eternal bliss becomes manifested in the *Ātman* during the state of liberation. But Vātsyāyana shows that this view is not tenable for want of sufficient proofs, and hence, he rejects it[125]. The arguments of Vātsyāyana are given below :

He says—what is the cause of the manifestation of the eternal bliss? It also cannot be eternal; for, if it were so, then why should it not be felt during the state of bondage? If both were eternal, then it will also have to be assumed that together with the eternal manifestation of the eternal bliss, even during the state of bondage, there are the simultaneous experiences of pleasure and pain due to the merits and demerits, which, of course, is against the reality.

In order to remove this difficulty, if it be held to be non-eternal, then, again, the cause of it must be found out. Besides the contact of the *Manas* with the *Ātman*, there must be some auxiliary cause also. Merit cannot be this auxiliary cause; for, in that case, it is necessary to find out the cause of this merit also. Nor can it held that the merit produced by the Yogic *Samādhi* is the necessary cause; for, every merit, after producing its requisite result, is destroyed; so that, the

[122] NS., I. i. 1-2.
[123] VS., I. i. 4.
[124] NC., xvii. 74.
[125] NBhā., I. i. 22.

yogic *dharma* also will come to an end at some particular time, and together with it the effect of it, namely, the experience of eternal bliss, will also disappear.

Nor can it be held that although the bliss is eternal, and as such, is equally present both in the state of liberation and that of bondage, yet it is not experienced during the latter state owing to the presence of an organism; for, the presence of organism, which is exclusively helpful to the experience of pleasure and pain, cannot be an obstacle in the way of the experience of eternal bliss.

Therefore, Vātsyāyana thinks that the view is unsound and rejects it.

It is very difficult to say exactly what was the original view of the Naiyāyikas and the Vaiçeṣikas on this point. It is clear from the Nyāya and the Vaiçeṣika Sūtras,[126] and other works of the schools that absolute freedom from pain exists during the state of liberation. In other words, the *Ātman* becomes free from all the qualities which directly or indirectly lead to pain[127]. But we find that there exists some distinction between the viewpoint of the two schools. Mādhavācārya in his Saṅkṣepaçaṅkarajaya[128] says that Çaṅkarācārya being asked by some one, had said that according to the Vaiçeṣikas, the state of the *Ātman* is just like the *Ākāça* and that it is absolutely free from its qualities, while according to the Naiyāyikas, there is also the experience of bliss. Although much doubt is felt regarding the authenticity of this work, yet we cannot entirely overlook this view. Even later on, the author of the Sarvasiddhāntasaṅgraha[129] and Bhāsarvajña[130] clearly support the view

[126] NS., I. i. 22; VS., I. i. 4.

[127] We should remember that pain includes the worldly pleasure also—NBhā., I. i. 2, 9.

[128] XVI. Verses 68-69.

[129] Naiyāyika Pakṣa, Verses 41-42.

[130] Nyāyasāra; Āgama-Parichheda.

of Mādhava. And it is, therefore, that we find an old verse wherein some one expresses his desire to go and pass his days in the fine forest of Bṛndā, as a jackal instead of desiring for the *Mokṣa* of the Vaiçeṣika[131]. It may also be suggested that perhaps it was the Nyāya view which led Vātsyāyana to criticise it in his Bhāṣya.

Considering both these two views it appears that the view—'there is the mainfestation of eternal bliss in the *Mokṣa*' is an old one. The supporters of this view might have thought that even the Gautama-Sūtra does not deny the existence of eternal happiness. What the Sūtra says is that there is the absolute freedom from pain and its cause. But what does it mean except that there is eternal happiness which appears after the pain and its cause are removed? It is quite likely that even in the later centuries, the view got its supporters. But the supporters do not represent the Nyāya-view in general. Bhāsarvajña, one of the supporters, has got his own independent views on several topics which are not accepted by all the Naiyāyikas.

Moreover, it is not quite certain whether the view originally belonged to the Naiyāyikas. Scholars, like Raghunātha Çiromaṇi, Gadādhara Bhaṭṭācārya, Raghūttama, and others attribute this view to old Mīmāṃsakas, while Vācaspati Miçra I, Udayanācārya, and others appear to attribute it to the Vedāntins. There is some confusion between the views of the old Mīmāṃsakas and those of the Naiyāyikas on certain points, and our investigations show that some of the views which originally belonged to the Mīmāṃsakas became associated with the Naiyāyikas so much so that people forgot the original source and came to recognize the Naiyāyikas as their original propounders. This might be also due to the fact that the view-points of these two schools resemble very much.

[131] Vide—*Varaṃ bṛndāvane ramye çṛgālatvaṃ bhajāmyaham* ।
Na punarvaiçeṣikīṃ muktiṃ prārthayāmi kadācana ॥

Hence, as it has been already said, it appears that at no stage, the *Ātman* of the Naiyāyikas possesses any natural happiness or bliss. It is essentially *jaḍa* although owing to the activities of the sense-organs and the *Manas* it comes to possess happiness etc. The only thing which remains with the *Ātman* during the state of liberation is its own *Manas*.

VI. *State of Jīvātman during the Cosmic Rest*

It would not be out of place to point out the difference between the state of liberation and the state of *Ātman* during the dissolution period (*pralaya*). In both the states, the *Ātman*, is undoubtedly, free from pain, but in the former state the cause for the experience of pleasure and pain is absolutely exhausted, while it is not so in the latter case. It is, therefore, that as soon as the Cosmic Rest is over, the *Jīvātman* comes to possess an organism under the influence of merit and demerit[132].

B

PARAMĀTMAN

It has been said above that both the production and the destruction of the individuals and the universe ultimately depend upon the good will of *Maheçvara*[133]. But the very existence of His is doubted by some. Hence, it is necessary to adduce arguments in support of His existence before proceeding further.

I. *Existence proved*

Inference and authority (*Āgama*) are the only means

[132] NM., pp. 507-508.
[133] *Vide Supra*, pp. 258, 264, 270.

of right cognition to prove His existence. But as the Āgamic proof is not accepted by the non-believers, like the Buddhists and others, the Naiyāyikas first adduce several inferential proofs in support of His existence. As for the Vaiçeṣikas, it is very difficult to say whether they actually believed in the existence of the *Paramātman.* Efforts have been made to interpret some of the Vaiçeṣika Sūtras[134], so as to show that the Vaiçeṣikas also, like other orthodox schools, were originally theistic in nature. But the interpretations are very doubtful. One can easily interpret these two Sūtras and see that Kaṇāda did not mean to include *Īçvara* in his Sūtras. And it is, perhaps, one of the reasons why the Vaiçeṣikas have been called half-atheists (*ardhavaināçikas*) by the later orthodox writers. But there is no doubt that the later writers on the Vaiçeṣika Sūtras did introduce the theistic element in their works.

1. *Udayana's view about the existence of God*

It has been said above that the existence of the *Paramātman* is doubtful; hence, proofs are adduced to prove His existence. But Udayanācārya in his famous theistic treatise says that there is hardly any ground for doubt and consequently, any need for investigation regarding His existence; for, every one knows and worships Him in some form or other. Thus, he says that the followers of the Upaniṣads (including the Vedāntins) worship Him as One who is pure (secondless) and enlightened by nature; the followers of Kapila, as the perfected First-Knower (*Ādividvān, Siddhaḥ—Kūṭasthanityaḥ*)[135]; the followers of Patañjali, as the Being who is untouched by the afflic-

[134] VS., I. i. 3; II. i. 18.

[135] For the implication of these epithets *vide* PWSS., Vol. II. pp. 170-173.

tions (*kleças*)[136]; actions (*karman*);[137] their fruits (*vipāka*) in the form of *jātis*, namely, *manusyatva* etc., *āyus* (the contact of the vital air with the organism), and *bhoga* (the experience of pleasure and pain within oneself); and *āçaya* (that which sleeps or remains in the *Ātman* till the time of the fruition of the past deeds, that is, the *adṛṣṭa*), and Who by assuming a '*phantasmal body*' (*nirmāṇa-kāya*)[138] revealed the Veda[139] and imparts grace (in the form of bestowing upon us the reward of heaven and liberation etc.); the followers of *Mahāpaçupati*, as the absolutely Independent One who is undefiled by actions opposed to those enjoined in the Vedas and sanctioned by popular usage, that is, He who is absolutely free from the so-called demeritorious acts; the Çaivas, as *Çiva* (free from the three *guṇas*); the Vaiṣṇavas, as *Puruṣottama*,[140] the Paurāṇikas, as the Supreme Father (lit. the Father of father); the Sacrificialists, as the Presiding Deity of the sacrifice (*yajñapuruṣa*); the Saugatas (that is,

[136] The five kinds of afflictions referred to here are:—*avidyā* (nescience), *asmitā* (egoism), *rāga* (attachment), *dveṣa* (aversion), and *abhiniveça* (love of life as expressed in the form 'would that I were never to cease. May I live on') YS. and YBhā., II. 3-9.

[137] By *karman* is meant here the performance of meritorious deeds in the form of *Açvamedha* etc. which is the cause of *dharma* and the demeritorious deeds in the form of killing a *Brāhmana* etc. which leads to *adharma*.

[138] It is felt that how can God without having an organism, in the absence of any worldly action, be able to start a tradition? For this it is said that He for the purpose of creating the universe manifests His own body merely by His desire or out of the collected *cetana* of the worldly creatures and this body of His is known as the 'phantasmal body.' For the full explanation of this term *vide*—PWSS., Vol. I. pp. 47-58.

[139] *Sampradīyate guruṇā çiṣyāyeti sampradāyo Vedaḥ*—KPP., p. 14; Bodhanī includes the usage of *ghaṭa*, *paṭa*, etc., also. Thus, God has revealed the Veda and has taught the usage of *ghaṭa*, *paṭa*, etc.

[140] *Uttama* means all-knowing and non-worldly.

the Buddhas), as the Omniscient;[141] the Digambaras (one of the Sects of Jaina) as Uncovered;[142] the Mīmāṃsakas, as That which is enjoined (by the Vedas) as the object of worship; the Naiyāyikas, as the Being who is endowed

[141] The term *kṣaṇika-sarvajña* as used by Vardhamāna explaining the term *sarvajña* is really God conceived as such. It is well-known that *sarvajña* is one of the names of the Buddha (*Vide*- Amarakoṣa, I. 13). The word *kṣaṇika* implies that the doctrine was of those Schools of Buddhism which upheld the theory of Universal Flux. The Çūnyavādins are, of course, excluded—PWSS., Vol. II. p. 178.

[142] There is no room for a Supreme God in the Jaina religious philosophy. The Digambaras believe that every soul passes through fourteen stages, (*guṇasthāna*) on its way to final deliverance. The last two are known as *Sayogikevalīguṇasthānaka* and *Ayogikevalīguṇasthānaka* and correspond to *Jīvanmukti* and *Videhamukti*, respectively. The former represents the stage in which the soul gains eternal wisdom, unlimited insight, everlasting happiness and unbounded power, and becomes, as a matter of course, the *Guru* of the entire universe, including the *devas*. The third part of *Çukla-dhyāna* is developed in this stage, the first two having been already perfected in the preceding stage. Though the soul still resides in the body, it reaches every part of the Universe. On this level of spiritual culture the *Jīva* is able to found sects (*Tīrthas*) and thereby, become a *Tīrthaṅkara*, if only he is inclined towards it and preach the truths revealed to him. Such a *Jīva*, viz., a *Tīrthaṅkara*, is the object of human worship. The fourteenth stage, called by the name of *Ayogi-Kevalī*, is the last in the series, and as soon as this is reached, the soul realizes *Nirvāṇa* and becomes a *Siddha*. The *Siddha* and freed soul, together with infinite others of a similar order, dwell for ever, above the *Siddha-Çilā*, descending no more on the lower planes and taking no longer any interest in the affairs of the world. He has a formless existence, and a body which is neither light nor heavy.

The term *Nirāvaraṇa* (uncovered) as used in the text stands for the last two *guṇasthānas*, specially, the fourteenth. All the *ghāṭikarmans*, viz., those which obscure the *jñāna* and *darçana* (*jñanāvaraṇīya* and *darçanāvaraṇīya*) of the soul and those which infatuate it (*Mohanīya* and *antarāya*) disappear in the 12th stage; so that what are generally known as *aghāṭi-karmans* (viz., *Vedanīya*, *Āyus*, *Nāma* and *Gotra*) only remain in the thirteenth. [These *aghāṭikarmans* correspond to a certain extent to the so-called '*prārabdha*' *karmans* which result in *jāti-Nāma* and *Gotra* as named

with all the attributes which befit Him; Cārvākas, as One whose authority is established by the convention of the world;[143] what more—whom even the artisans worship as *Viçvakarman*, the Great Architect, now, although with regard to such a Being, the Lord *Çiva*, whose power is universally recognized, like caste, family,[144] *pravara*,[145] school (*çākhā*) of Veda, family duties etc., there can hardly be any ground for doubt, and consequently, any need for investigation.[146]

A question is raised here: If God is so well-known, then no effort should be made even by the Naiyāyikas to prove His existence according to the dictum—'inference should not be adduced in support of things having either absolute non-existence, as hare's horn, son of a barren woman etc., or being proved beyond all doubts, like the *Paramātman* in the present case; but only in cases where doubt exists.'[147] To this Udayana says that all the discussions and inferences about His existence are of the nature of contemplation (*manana*) which follows *çravana*. His references in the *Çrutis*, *Smṛtis*, *Purānas* etc. represent the stage of *çravaṇa* only; so that, nothing is wrong if in spite of His being so well-known to all, efforts are made to prove His existence through inferences.

here), *Āyus* and *bhoga* (= *Vedanīya*)]. These do not obscure the omniscience of the soul, but help to keep up the body, and as soon as these are exhausted the body falls off. The two kinds of *Mokṣa* (*Sadeha* and *Videha*) are known as *Bhāvamokṣa* and *Drvyamokṣa* respectively—PWSS., Vol. II; pp. 178-179.

143 King etc., or an image with four hands etc.—Bodhanī, p. 4.

144 The word *gotra* means the name of the *Ṛṣi* in whose line one is born, the ancestor being a son or descendant of one of the seven great *Ṛṣis* and the eighth *Agastya*. For a clear understanding of these terms—*gotra* and *pravara*. *Vide* P. V. Kane—JBBRAS (N. S.) Vol. 11., Nos. 1 and 2, 1935, pp. 1-17.

145 Vardhamāna explains it as the *Ṛṣi* chosen by the *Yajamāna* in a sacrifice.

146 KP., Stavaka I, Verse 2 along with the prose portion.

147 NBhā., I. i. 1.

2. *Grounds for doubts*

Udayana notes five kinds of objections against His existence which may possibly be raised by the non-believers, on the following grounds: (1) absence of a supersensuous ground for the existence of life after death; (2) the possibility of otherwise (that is, without admitting God) carrying out the means to another world, namely, sacrifice; (3) the exitsence of proofs demonstrating His non-existence; (4) His unreliable character as a proof or a source of right knowledge even on the assumption of His existence; and (5) absence of proofs proving His existence. Now, these five objections are generally attributed to the Cārvāka, the Buddhist and the Mīmāṃsakas. Udayana has given very clear and lucid answers to all these objections in his Nyāya-Kusumāñjali and Ātmatattvaviveka. Giving even in brief the summary of these answers would unusually enlarge the volume of the book. In fact, answers to these questions exhaust a considerable portion of Nyāya and Vaiçeṣika and may form a separate independent volume altogether. Hence, I do not want to proceed here on that line. I shall give answers to the last objection which requires direct proofs for demonstrating His existence, and then pass on to His other aspects.

3. *Grounds for His existence*

The following are some of the reasons to prove the existence of the *Paramātman* :

(1) The earth being a product, like a pot, must have a doer. A doer must have the direct knowledge of the cause of the product, a desire to produce it, and also an effort to bring about the effect. A human being cannot be such a doer. Therefore, we conclude that there is God who is the creator of this earth.

(2) Again, it is a fact that *paramāṇus* do not possess productive motion during the Cosmic Rest (*Pralaya*).

Without such a motion they cannot join together so as to form effects in the form of *dvyaṇuka*, etc. *Paramāṇus* and *adṛṣṭas*, being non-*cetana*, cannot produce that motion. The *Jīvas*, also, without being in contact with an organiism, which is not possible during the period of dissolution, cannot produce that motion. But motion must be imparted to the *paramāṇus* for grouping together. Hence, it is inferred that there is an Intelligent Agent, that is, *Içvara* who imparts this motion.

(3) Again, the whole universe must have a direct or an indirect support; for, being weighty it does not fall down; like the body of a bird in the sky. Similarly, the whole universe is to be destroyed by the effort of some one; as the universe is a product, like a cloth which is to be destroyed. Now, a human being can neither be a support, nor a destroyer of the universe. Hence, we infer the existence of *Içvara* for these purposes.

(4) The various traditional arts of this universe, such as, the making of pot, cloth,. etc. must have a teacher to teach to others and give a start to the convention. This also is not possible for any human being. Hence, we presume the existence of a supernatural Being who is God.

(5) The authoritativeness of the Veda depends upon the authoritativeness of the cause, that is, its author. This is not possible in other than God.

(6) Again, the Vedas necessitate that they must be produced by an Omniscient Being. That which is not so is not a Veda. It must be said here that the Naiyāyikas believe that the Vedas have got authors, like other authoritative texts. Against the *apauruṣeyatva* of the Mīmāṃsakas, the Naiyāyikas hold that there is no authoritativeness in a work if its author is not known. So says Udayanācārya—when we have proved that words are not immaculate self-sufficient entities, we can regard the Veda as the word of a reliable authority, and hence, an instrument of right cognition. Otherwise, if the

Veda were eternal, it would be open to this suspicion that it may not be reliable; as no one knows when and by whom it was propounded; in ordinary usage, all such words as cannot have their source traced, are regarded as of doubtful veracity[148]. In this way, also it is proved that there is an Omniscient God.

(7) Lastly, the *dvyaṇuka* and the *tryaṇuka*, being substances, possess dimension which, being a quality of an effect, is an effect itself. Neither the dimension of the *paramāṇu* nor that of the *dvyaṇuka* can be its cause; for, the former is the eternal dimension, while the latter is *aṇuparimāṇa*. If these were the causes, then it will have to be admitted that an effect is produced even without a support, and that the *dvyaṇuka* possesses magnitude, which is not possible. Owing to these and similar other difficulties, it is admitted that the dimension of the *dvyaṇuka* and the *tryaṇuka* is produced by number. For the production of the dimension of a *dvyaṇuka*, out of number two we require an *apekṣābuddhi* in order to produce the generality called *dvitva*. No human being is present just after the Cosmic Rest is over; so that, our *apekṣābuddhi* cannot help the production of the dimension of the *dvyaṇuka*. Hence, we infer that there is God whose *apekṣābuddhi* has helped the production of this dimension, and consequently, the production of the entire universe[149].

All these are supported by *çrutis* and *smṛtis*. Besides, there are several other *çrutis* to prove the existence of the *Paramātman*.

II. Definition of Paramātman

Having proved the existence of *Paramātman*, we may proceed with His definition. The authors of Nyāya have

[148] NP., *Ms.* pp. 930-31. *Vide* also Ft. Note of Dr. Jhā's translation of NBhā. and NV., Vol. II., p. 317.

[149] KP., Stavaka 5.

defined Him as the instrumental cause of the universe. Upon Him depends the acquisition of the fruits of one's past actions.[150] He is also defined as One whose worship is declared to be the means of heaven and liberation.[151] He is also known to us as One who possesses eternal consciousness, bliss and other similar qualities.[152]

III. *Characteristics of Paramātman*

He is endowed with such qualities as—absence of demerit, false knowledge and negligence; presence of merit, true knowledge and intuitiveness (*samādhisampad*). He also possesses the eight-fold powers consisting of *aṇimā*, *laghimā*, *mahimā*, *prāpti*, *prākāmya*, *vaçitva*, *īçitva* and *yatrakāmāvasāyitva*[153], as a result of His merit and knowledge. His merit follows the bent of His Will (*saṅkalpa*). He controls the activity of the residuum, of merit and demerit subsisting in each individual (*Jīvātman*), as also that of the earth and other material substances. He is Omnipotent in regard to His creation, not however, failing to be influenced by the results

[150] NS. and NBhā., IV. i. 19.

[151] KP., stavaka 1, Kārikā, 2.

[152] TD., p. 12.

[153] That power through which one can reduce himself to the form of *paramāṇu* is known as *aṇimā*; that which makes a man capable of making his body so light as to rise up even through the help of the rays of the sun is called *laghimā*; that which enables a man to make the subtlest possible thing as big as possible is known as *mahimā*; that which qualifies a man to touch even the moon through the tip of his little finger is called *prāpti*; that which makes him enjoy freedom of desire so as to even enter into the ground as if he is diving into water is known as *prākāmya*; that which makes him bring under his control everything without himself being under other's control is called *vaçitva*; that which qualifies him to produce, protect and destroy everything is called *īçitra*; and that which makes him achieve whatever he desires at whatever time is known as *yatrakāmāvasāyitva* or *satya-saṅkalpa*. YBhā., III. 44.

of acts, done by the beings He creates. He has obtained all the results of His deeds, and continues to act for the sake of His created beings; because, just as the father acts for his children, so does *Içvara* also act for living beings. He is the Seer, the Cogniser, and the Knower of all things.[154]

He is the instrumental cause of the universe. This is proved from the fact that the Primordial Matter, *paramāṇu*, and *karman*, being themselves unconscious, are found to act only when prior to beginning they have an intelligent agent to control them. Such an agent is the *Paramātman*[155]. He creates the universe by reason of His nature being so, just as the earth upholds things, because such is its nature. It is *Içvara* who makes the less-knowing *Jīva* go to heaven or to hell. The activities of the universe exist as long as He remains awake, and when He takes rest all the activities remain stopped in the state of Cosmic Rest. This proves that He is the instrumental cause of the universe.[156] His very nature consists of activity (*pravṛtti*).[157]

He is different from the *Jīvātman*, as He possesses distinct qualities, such as—eternity of intelligence, number, dimension, separateness, conjunction, disjunction, desire, and effort[158]. Uddyotakara lays emphasis on number, dimension, separateness, conjunction, disjunction and intelligence only as His qualities[159]. Further on, Uddyotakara asserts that He possesses desire which is not tainted with nescience and is not obstructed in regard to anything, like His intelligence[160].

[154] NBhā., IV. i. 21.
[155] NV., IV. 1. 21.
[156] NV., IV. 1. 21. p. 467.
[157] NV., IV. i. 21.
[158] BhāP., verse 34; NVṛ, p. 244; NV., IV., i. 21. p. 465.
[159] NV., p. 465.
[160] NV., p. 466.

He does not possess any organism[161]. Vācaspati also quotes *Çruti* in support of this[162]. He teaches us what is good and bad through the Vedas. He is the Father of the Universe[163]. He is only One[164].

The *Paramātman* is neither *baddha*, nor liberated. He is beyond these. As He does not possess nescience and pain, He is not under bondage. Again, there exists *dharma* in Him through *karman*, and through *dharma* again, there is the eight-fold *aiçvaryas* in Him, He cannot be called liberated as well. Uddyotakara says that as these are related terms, *Içvara*, who is never *baddha*, cannot be ever liberated[165]. It is, therefore, that He is called eternally liberated.

1. *A brief discussion about some of His characteristics*

(1) It has been told above that *Paramātman* eternally possesses knowledge. Now, a question is raised: whether *Içvara* is of the very nature of *Jñāna*, as some hold, or is only a substratum of *Jñāna*. Vātsyāyana, undoubtedly, holds the latter view and is of opinion that the *Çruti*—'*Paçyatyacakṣuḥ.........sa...vetti vedyam*'[166] also supports that *Içvara* is the substratum of knowledge. Even the *Çruti*—'*Yaḥ sarvajñaḥ sarvavit*'[167] speaks of the same. Again, it is said that the existence of the *Paramātman*, who is not qualified by intelligence, desire and effort, cannot be proved; so that, all these three qualities are the probans of the *Paramātman* also.[168]

[161] Tāt., p. 421; Laugākṣi Bhāskara says that there is the possibility of God's having an organism produced through our *adṛṣṭa* just as the *adṛṣṭa* of a man causes the production of the organism of his wife—TK., p. 5.

[162] Tāt., p. 426.

[163] NVr., p. 244.

[164] Kandalī., p. 57.

[165] NV., IV. i. 21. p. 466.

[166] ÇU., 3. 19.

[167] MU., II. ii. 7.

[168] NBhā., on NS., IV. i. 21. p. 686.

This also disapproves the view that *Içvara* is attributeless. Then again, it may be asked: What about the *çrutis* which directly speak of the *Paramātman* as attributeless? To this it is said that the *çrutis* speak of the *Paramātman* as such only to prevent the possibility of the devotees becoming attached to the various *Aiçvaryas* belonging to the *Paramātman* which would only drag them back to the world and be an obstacle in their way to the final liberation[169].

(2) About the number of qualities possessed by *Içvara* there is a difference of opinion between the Nyāya and the Vaiçeṣika systems. According to the Vaiçeṣikas, *Içvara* possesses the ordinary qualities of number, dimension, separateness, conjunction and disjunction, and the specific qualities of consciousness, desire and effort.[170] But Çrīdhara does not accept this view[171]. He further notes that others, however, hold that to God belongs unobstructed intelligence alone which constitutes His creative power through which alone the activities proceeding from desire and effort are also performed. Hence, according to these people, God does not possess these two qualities. In other words, He has only six qualities in all[172]. Although Çrīdhara attributes this view to others, yet he himself appears to have accepted it where he speaks of *Içvara* as the substratum of six qualities[173].

But then there is another difficulty. Praçastapāda clearly says that due to the desire of *Maheçvara* creation and dissolution take place[174]. While commenting upon this, Çrīdhara does not say anything and silently accepts the presence of desire in *Maheçvara*. Again, Ud-

[169] KP., Stavaka III. Kārikā. 17; KPP. on the same.
[170] BhāP., verse 34.
[171] Kandalī., p. 57.
[172] Kandalī., p. 57.
[173] Kandalī., p. 57.
[174] PPBhā., p. 48.

dyotakara also says that *Içvara* possesses six qualities only[175]. But just after this, again, he says that, of course, unchecked desire belongs to *Içvara*[176]. Similarly, Vācaspati also accepts that both desire and effort are eternally present in *Içvara*[177]. Jayanta also supports this view[178]

In order to remove this difficulty should we say that those who hold that both desire and effort do not exist in *Içvara* think that His unobstructed intelligence alone constitutes these two qualities, and therefore, these are not separately mentioned?

Jayanta makes his view clear in a different way. Even accepting the eternity of desire (*svarūpamātreṇa*) in *Içvara*, he says that sometimes during the interval of creation and dissolution, a desire, in the form 'may a particular man experience a particular kind of *bhoga* proceeding from a particular kind of action' is produced in *Içvara*[179]. This is also clear from the writings of Praçastapāda and others who in spite of the fact that they believe in the eternity of desire in *Içvara*, say that a desire is produced in *Maheçvara* to create the universe or to dissolve it. In other words, it appears that there is, no doubt, eternal desire in *Içvara*, but that is of no use for the worldly activities, just as in spite of the fact that the *Ātman* is ever in contact with the *Manas*, yet that contact does not produce any cognition, and for which another contact is required.

(3) Jayanta is of opinion that *Içvara* also possesses eternal bliss (*sukha*). This is supported by *Āgama*. If there be no eternal bliss in Him, then there cannot be the capacity to create and dissolve this universe[180]. But we know that almost all the Naiyāyikas are opposed to this

175 NV., IV. i. 22. pp. 464-65.
176 NV., IV. i. 21. p. 466.
177 Tāt., p. 425.
178 NM., p. 201.
179 NM., p. 201.
180 NM., p. 201.

view. They hold that even the word '*ānanda*' in the *çruti*—'*ānandam Brahma*' does not mean happiness or bliss. It means the absence of pain. The word '*sukha*' is very frequently used in the sense of the absence of pain[181]. Gangeça Upādhyāya, rejecting the view of Jayanta, even goes so far as to say that the use of the term '*ānanda*' in the neuter gender in the *çruti*—'*Nityam vijñānamānandam Brahma*' etc., shows that *Brahman* is not *ānandasvarūpa*. The reason is that the word '*ānanda*' in the sense of '*ānandasvarūpa*' is always masculine. Hence, according to Gangeça, by '*ānandam*' we should understand '*ānandaviçiṣṭa*.'[182] But in other place Gangeça himself uses the term '*ānanda*' in the sense of 'absence of pain.' It appears that as the Naiyāyikas do not believe in the existence of eternal bliss in the liberated *Ātman*, so they are not prepared to attribute it to the *Paramātman* also. But still there is a difference of opinion here also.

(4) It has been told above that *Īçvara* possesses *dharma* and the eight-fold powers. Now, Uddyotakara and Vācaspati say that He does not possess *dharma*. As regards the production of everything, the two eternal *Çaktis* of His, namely, *Jñāna* and *Kriyā* will help Him.[183]

(5) As regards His eight-fold *aiçvaryas* also there is a difference of opinion. Uddyotakara says that His *Aiçvarya* is eternal[184]. Vācaspati says that because His *Jñānaçakti* and *Kriyāçakti* are eternal, His *Aiçvarya* also is eternal. But as for the *aṇimā* etc., they are non-eternal, and this is clear from the Bhāṣya also when it says that this form of *aiçvarya* is the result of His *dharma*[185]. This makes it clear that according to Vātsyāyana there are two kinds of *aiçvaryas* in the *Paramātman*—eternal and

[181] NBhā., I. i. 22. p. 117.
[182] Īçvarānumāna, p. 181.
[183] NV., IV. i. 21. p. 464; Tāt., p. 420.
[184] NV., IV. i. 21. p. 464.
[185] Tāt., p. 420.

non-eternal. The latter is the result of His *dharma* produced by the particular *karman*. If it be not due to *karman*, then there will be the difficulty of reaping the fruit of those actions which have not been performed. And it is, therefore, that Vātsyāyana has said that He possesses *dharma*. Although, apparently, there is no *karman* in Him, yet it is the *karman* in the form of His Will (*saṅkalpa*) which is said to be the cause of this *dharma* which, in its turn, is the cause of the non-eternal *aiçvarya*. This makes it clear that the *dharma* of *Içvara* is not meant to lead to heaven but to produce the eight-fold *aiçvaryas* to move the *adrstas* of the *Jīvas* to form creation just after the Cosmic Rest is over.

IV. *Aim of Içvara in creating the Universe*

There is a view that *Içvara* cannot be the creator of the universe. The reason is—No wise man does anything without having any aim before him. God cannot have any selfish aim; for, He possesses all the *aiçvaryas* and is fully satisfied. There is nothing left unachieved for which God will desire and make efforts to create universe. To this it is said that it is not a fact that all our activities proceed from selfish motive alone. For instance, a father, even having nothing to do for his ownself, does make efforts to do things for the good of his children. Similarly, although God, does not do anything for His own good, yet He desires and makes efforts to create the universe for the good of the would-be created beings[186].

Now, an objection is raised here: If God creates the universe being compassionate towards the *Jīvas*, then He ought to have created only happy persons and not painful. To this an obvious answer may be given that God does not create the universe without taking into consideration the meritorious and the demeritorious

[186] NBhā., IV. 1. 21. p. 685.

deeds of the *Jīvas*. There may be an objection here to the compassionate nature of God, but otherwise, there will be the defect of reaping the fruits of the undone actions and not those of the actions which are performed[187]. Helping the *Jīvas* to reap the fruits of their past deeds in order to qualify themselves for liberation is itself a compassionate action of *Īçvara*[188].

Some, again, hold that *Īçvara* creates the universe for His sportive (*krīḍā*) motive. But it is untenable; for, only those, who do not otherwise experience bliss, take to *krīḍā* (*rati*). *Bhagavat* does not possess any pain, hence, He does not do anything for achieving bliss.

Others, again, think that God wants to make others know His own *aiçvaryas*, and therefore, creates the universe. But this is also rejected on the ground that as God is fully satisfied in every respect, why should He like to make a show of His *aiçvaryas* which does not add to Him anything; nor does He lose anything without making a show of His *aiçvaryas*[189].

After criticising these two views Uddyotakara gives his own. According to him God creates the universe, because it is His very nature to do so. It may be then asked: If that is His very nature, then as He cannot get rid of it, there will be a constant creation and never any dissolution. To this, again, Uddyotakara gives his reply that God possesses intelligence through which He creates only when the auxiliary causes of creation present themselves to Him. These auxiliaries do not appear simultaneously. Hence, there is bound to be succession in creation and also in dissolution[190].

Jayanta also holds a similar view. He says that it is the very nature of God that sometimes He creates

[187] NBhā., IV. i. 21.
[188] NM., p. 202; Kandalī., pp. 53-54.
[189] NV., IV. i. 21. pp. 462-63.
[190] NV., IV. i. 21. p. 463.

the universe and sometimes destroys it, like the rising and setting of the sun[191].

V. Difference between Jīvātman and Paramātman

Vātsyāyana distinguishing the *Paramātman* from the *Jīvātman* says that He is a different *Ātman* qualified by attributes. This leads some to doubt whether these two *Ātmans* are one or two different entities. But Vātsyāyana himself says that they do not belong to two different classes, for both of these two *Ātmans* are conscious, and as such, they cannot be classed under any of those categories which are non-conscious[192].

Although both are classed under the same category, that is, the *Ātman*, yet there is enough difference between them. The *Jīvātman* possesses demerit, nescience and carelessness[193]. It does not possess the eight-fold *aiçvaryas*. Bondage and liberation are attributed to this *Ātman*. There are infinite *Jīvātmans*. But *Paramātman* possesses none of these attributes.

It is needless to say that this difference is preached here only because we want to confine ourselves here within the limits of Nyāya and Vaiçeṣika, otherwise the fact is—

Ekamevādvitīyaṃ neha nānāsti kiñcana.

[191] NM., p. 202.
[192] NBhā., IV. i. 21. p. 685; NV., IV. i. 21. p. 464; NM., p. 201.
[193] NBhā., IV. i. 21. p. 684.

INDEX

A

B

D

N

Q

R

S

T

SOURCES AND AUTHORITIES

The following is the list of the sources and the authorities utilised in writing the present thesis:—

1. PUBLISHED

(1) *Nyāya*

1. Nyāya-Sūtra of Gautama, edited by Dr. Gangānātha Jhā, Benares, and MM. Kāmākhyānātha, Calcutta.
2. Nyāya-Bhāṣya of Vātsyāyana, the editions of Dr. Gangānātha Jhā and MM. Kāmākhyānātha, Calcutta.
3. Nyāya-Vārttika of Uddyotakara, edited by MM. Vindhyeçvarī Prasad, Benares.
4. Nyāyā-Vārttika-Tātparya-ṭīkā of Vācaspati Miçra I, edited by Paṇḍita Rājeçvara Çāstrī Drāviḍa, Chowkhamba, Benares.
5. Nyāya-Parīçuddhi-Prakāça of Varddhamāna, Bibliotheca Indica edition.
6. Nyāya-Bhāṣya-Vṛtti of Vīçvanātha, edited by Āshubodha Vidyābhūṣaṇa, Calcutta.
7. Nyāya-Mañjarī of Jayanta, Vizianagram Sanskrit Series edition.
8. Nyāya-Sīddhānta-Mañjarī of Jānakīnātha.
9. Bhāṣya-Candra of Raghūttama, edited by Dr. Gangānātha Jhā, Chowkhamba, Benares.
10. Khadyota of MM. Gangānātha Jhā, Chowkhamba, Benares, edition.
11. Tattvacintāmaṇi of Gangeça Upādhyāya, Bibliotheca Indica edition.
12. Tattvacintāmaṇi-Prakāça by Rucidatta Miçra, Published in the 'Paṇḍita', Benares.
13. Īçvarānumāna of Gangeça Upādhyāya, Bibliotheca Indica edition.
14. Ātmatattvaviveka by Udayana, edited by Jīvānanda Vidyāsāgara, Calcutta.
15. Kusumāñjaliprakaraṇa by Udayana, Bibliotheca Indica edition.

16. Prakāça, a commentary on No. 15, by Varddhmāna, Bibliotheca Indica edition.
17. Makaranda, a commentary on No. 16, by Rucidatta Miçra, Bibliotheca Indica edition.
18. Bodhanī, a commentary on No. 15, by Varadarāja Miçra, Sarasvatībhavana Text Series, Benares.
19. Haridāsī, a commentary on the Verses of Kusumāñjaliprakaraṇa, by Haridāsa Bhaṭṭācārya, edited by Mm. Kāmākhyānātha, Calcutta.
20. Nyāyakaustubha, by Mahādeva Puntamakar, edited by Dr. Umesha Mishra, The University, Allahabad.
21. Padārthatattvanirūpaṇa also known as Padārthatattvavivecana and Padārthakhaṇḍana, Reprint from the "Paṇḍita," Benares.
22. Padārthatattvavivecana-Prakāça, a commentary on No. 21, by Rāmabhadra Sārvabhauma, Reprint from the "Paṇḍita", Benares.
23. Padārthakhaṇḍana-Vyākhyā, a commentary on No. 21, by Raghudeva Nyāyālaṅkāra, Reprint from the "Paṇḍita", Benares.
24. Padārthamaṇḍana, by Veṇīdatta, Sarasvatībhavan Text Series, Benares.
25. Nyāyasāra, by Bhāsrvajña, edited by Dr. Satish Chandra Vidyābhuṣaṇa.
26. Nyāyasāra, by Mādhavadeva Paṇḍita, Reprint from the "Paṇḍita", Benares.
27. Padātharatnamālā, by Paṇḍita Raghunātha, Reprint from the "Paṇḍita".

(2) *Vaiçeṣika*

28. Vaiçeṣika-Sūtra, by Kaṇāda, Gujarati Press, Bombay edition.
29. Padārthadharmasaṅgraha, also known as Praçastapāda-Bhāṣya, by Praçastapādācārya, Vizianagram Sanskrit Series edition.
30. Vyomavatī, a commentary on No. 29, by Vyomaçivācārya, published from Chowkhamba, Benares.
31. Kiraṇāvali, a commentary on No. 29, by Udayanācārya, edited by Mm. Vindhyeçavarī Prasad, Benares.
32. Kandalī, a commentary on No. 29, by Çrīdharācārya, Vizianagram Sanskrit Series edition.
33. Lakṣanāvalī, by Udayana, Reprint from the "Paṇḍita", Benares.
34. Nyāya-Muktāvalī, a commentary on No. 33, by

Çeṣa-Çārṅgadharācārya, Reprint from the "Paṇḍita", Benares.

35. Upaskāra, by Çaṅkara Miçra, Gujarati Press, edition.
36. Vṛtti, a commentary on No. 28, attributed to Bharadvāja, quoted in the Upaskāra.
37. Vivṛti, a commentary on No. 28, by Jayanārāyaṇa Nyāyapañcānana, Gujarati Press edition.
38. Bhāṣya, a commentary on No. 28, by Candrakānta Tarkālaṅkāra, Gujarati Press edition.
39. Vaidika-Vṛtti, a commentary on No. 28, by Haridāsa, Nirnayasāgara, Bombay edition.
40. Setu, a commentary on No. 29, by Padmanābha Miçra, Chowkhamba, Benares edition.
41. Sūkti, a commentary on No. 29, by Jagadīça Bhaṭṭācārya, Chowkhamba, Benares edition.
42. Kiraṇāvalī-Bhāskara, a Commentary on No. 31, by Padmanābha Miçra, Sarasvatībhavan Text Series Benares edition.
43. Rasasāra, a commentary on No. 31, by Bhaṭṭa Vādīndra, Sarasvatībhavana Text Series, Benares edition.
44. Prakāça, a commentary on No. 31, by Varddhamāna, Bibliotheca Indica edition.
45. Nyāyalīlāvatī, by Vallabhācārya, Nirṇayasāgara, Bombay and Chowkhamba Sanskrit Series editions.
46. Kaṇṭhābharaṇa, a commentary on No. 45, by Çaṅkara Miçra, Chowkhamba, Benares edition.
47. Prakāça, a commentary on No. 45, by Varddhamāna, Chowkhamba, Benares edition.
48. Vivṛti, a commentary on No. 45, by Bhagīratha Ṭhakkura, Chowkhamba, Benares edition.
49. Kaṇādarahasya, by Çaṅkara Miçra, Chowkhamba Benares edition.
50. Saptapadārthī, by Çivāditya, Vizianagram Sanskrit Series edition.
51. Mitabhāṣiṇī, a commentary on No. 50, Vizianagram Sanskrit Series edition.
52. Tārkikarakṣā, by Varadarāja Miçra, Reprint from the "Paṇḍita," Benares.
53. Niṣkaṇṭaka, a commentary on No. 52, by Mallinātha, Reprint from the "Paṇḍita," Benares.
54. Padārthadīpikā, by Koṇḍa Bhaṭṭa, edited by Mm. Tātyā Çāstrī, Government Sanskrit College, Benares.

55. Tarkālaṅkārabhāṣyaparīkṣā, Chowkhamba Benares edition.
56. Çāstrārthasangraha, by Jayarāma, Gujarati Press edition.
57. Nyāyakoça, by Jhalkīkara, Bombay Sanskrit Series edition (Second and third editions).

(3) *Nyāya-Vaiçeṣika*

58. Bhāṣāpariccheda, by Viçvanātha.
59. Nyāya-Muktāvalī, a commentary on No. 58 by Viçvanātha, edited by Mm. Vindhyeçvarī Prasad, Benares.
60. Dinakarī or Prakāça, a commentary on No. 59, by Dinkara Bhaṭṭa, edited by Mm. Vindhyeçvarī Prasad, Benares.
61. Rāmarudrī, also known as Taraṅgiṇī, a commentary on No. 60, by Rāmarudra Bhaṭṭācārya, Mylapore, Madras edition.
62. Prabhā, a commentary on No. 59, by Rāya Narasiṃha Paṇḍita, Mylapore, Madras edition.
63. Mañjūṣā, a commentary on No. 59, by Paṭṭābhirāma Çāstrī, Mylapore, Madras edition.
64. Tarkabhāṣā, by Keçava Miçra, Reprint from the "Paṇḍita," Benares.
65. Nyāya-Prakāça, a commentary on No. 64, by Viçvakarman, Reprint from the "Paṇḍita", Benares.
66. Tarkasaṅgraha, by Annaṃ Bhaṭṭa, Bombay Sanskrit Series edition.
67. Dīpikā, or Tarkadīpikā, a commentary on No. 66, by Annaṃ Bhaṭṭa, Bombay Sanskrit Series edition.
68. Nīlakaṇṭhī, or Tarkadīpikāprakāça, a commentary on No. 67, by Nīlakaṇṭha, Nirṇayasāgara Press, Bombay edition.
69. Bhāskarodayā, a commentary on No. 68, by Lakṣmī-Nṛsimha, Nirṇayasāgara Press, Bombay edition.
70. Tarkakaumudī, by Laugākṣi-Bhāskara, Nirṇayasagara Press, Bombay edition.
71. Nyāyabodhinī, a commentary on No. 66 by Govardhana, Bombay Sanskrit Series edition.
72. Siddhānta-Candrodaya, a commentary on No. 66, by Çrīkṛṣṇa Dhūrjaṭī.

2. Manuscripts

73. Tarkaprakāça, a commentary on No. 8.
74. Tarkadīpikā, by Koṇḍa Bhaṭṭa.
75. An anonymous commentary on Padārthacandrikā a commentary on No. 50.
76. Nyāya-Pariçuddhi, a commentary on No. 4, by Udayanācārya, belonging to Dr. Gangānātha Jhā, Allahabad.
77. Dravyasārasaṅgraha by Raghudeva.
78. Padārthatattvavivecana by Raghunātha Çiromaṇi.
79. Siddhāntatattva, a commentary on Padārthaviveka by Gopinātha Maunin.
80. Dravya-Prakāçikā also known as Jalada, a commentary on the Dravya Section of No. 31, by Bhagīratha Ṭhakkura.
81. Pramāṇādipadārthaprakāçikā, by Laugākṣi-Bhāskara, quoted in Nyāyakoça.
82. Āloka, a commentary on No. 11, by Pakṣadhara Miçra.
83. Tātparyaṭīkā, the same as No. 4.
84. An anonymous commentary on Padārthatattvabodha.
85. Nyāyamālā, also known as Nyāyasiddhāntamālā, by Jayarāma.
86. Āmoda, a commentary on No. 15, by Çaṅkara Miçra, in possession of Paṇḍita Medhānātha Jhā, (Darbhanga).
87. Nyāyasiddhāntamañjarī, the same as No. 8.
88. Vivekavilāsa.

3. Published works of other schools of thought

89. Brahmasūtra, by Bādarāyaṇa.
90. Bhāṣya, a commentary on No. 89, by Çaṅkarācārya, Nirṇayasāgara Press, Bombay edition.
91. Bhāmatī, a commentary on No. 90, by Vācaspati Miçra I, Nirṇayasāgara Press, Bombay edition.
92. Ratnaprabhā, a commentary on No. 90, by Govindananda, Bombay edition.
93. Vedānta-Kalpataru, a commentary on No. 91, by Amalānanda Sarasvati, Nirṇayasāgara Press, Bombay edition.
94. Kalpataru-Parimala, a commentary on No. 93, by Appayya Dīkṣita, Nirṇayasāgara Press, Bombay edition.

95. Saṅkhṣepa-Çārīraka, by Sarvajñātma Muni, Kashi Sanskrit Series edition.
96. Pañcadaçī, by Vidyāraṇya Muni, Bombay edition.
97. Advaita-Brahmasiddhi, by Kashmīraka Sadānanda Yatī, Calcutta University Publication.
98. Prasthānabheda, the commentary on the 7th verse of the Mahimnaḥstotra, by Madhusūdana Saravatī, Vāṇīvilāsa Press edition.
99. Siddhantabindu, a commentary on Daçaçlokī of Çaṅkara, by Madhusūdana Sarasvatī, Kashi Sanskrit Series, Benares edition.
100. Nyāyaratnāvalī, a commentary on No. 99, by Gauḍa-Brahmānanda, Kashi Sanskrit Series, Benares, edition.
101. Nārāyaṇī also known as Laghuvyākhyā, a commentary on No. 100 by Nārāyaṇatīrtha, Kashi Sanskrit Series, Benares edition.
102. Siddhantaleçasaṅgraha, by Appayya Dikṣīta, Benares edition.
103. Vedānta-Siddhānta-Muktāvalī, by Prakāçānanda, Reprint from the "Paṇḍita", Benares.
104. Vedānta-Paribhāṣā, by Dharmarājādhvarīndra, Calcutta edition.
105. Vedāntasāra, by Sādānanda, Vāṇīvilāsa Press edition.
106. Tattvatraya, by Lokācārya, Chowkhamba Sanskrit Series, Benares edition.
107. Tattvatraya-Bhāṣya, a commentary on No. 106, Chowkhamba Sanskrit Series, Benares edition.
108. Siddhitraya, by Yāmunācārya, Chowkhamba Sanskrit Series, Benares edition.
109. Yatīndramatadīpikā, by Çrīnivāsācārya, Benares Sanskrit Series edition.
110. Nirṇayārṇava, by Bālakrisṇa Bhaṭṭa, Bombay edition.
111. Subodhinī, a commentary on Çrīmadbhāgavata, by Vallabhācārya, Bombay edition.
112. Prasthānaratnākara, by Puruṣottamajī, Bombay edition.
113. Çuddhādvaita-Mārtaṇḍa, by Giridharajī, Bombay edition.
114. Padārthasaṅgraha, by Padmanābha, Kumbhakonam edition.
115. Madhvasiddhāntasāra, Kumbhakonam edition.
116. Siddhāntadarçana, by an anonymous writer, Sacred Books of the Hindu Series, Allahabad.

117. Vedāntaratnamañjūṣa, by Puruṣottamācārya, Benares edition.
118. Daçaçlokī, by Nimbarkācārya, Benares edition.
119. Vedāntapārijātasaurabha, a commentary on Brahmasūtra, by Nimbārka, Benares edition.
120. Vedantatattvabodha, by Anantarāma, Benares edition.
121. Mīmāṃsāsūtra, by Jaimini, Benares edition.
122. Bhāṣya, on No. 121, by Çabara, Benares edition.
123. Çloka-Vārtika, by Kumārila, Benares edition.
124. Çāstradīpikā, by Çālikanātha Miçra, Nirṇayasāgara Press, Bombay edition.
125. Prakaraṇapañcikā, by Çālikanātha Miçra, Benares edition.
126. Gāgābhaṭṭī, by Viçesvara Bhaṭṭa *alias* Gāgā Bhaṭṭa, Benares edition.
127. Prabhākaravijaya, by Nandīçvara, Calcutta edition.
128. Sāṅkhyakārikā, also known as Sāṅkhyasaptati, by Īçvarakṛṣṇa.
129. Tattvakaumudī, a commentary on No. 128, by Vācaspati Miçra I, Dr. Gangānātha Jhā's edition.
130. Sāṅkhapravacana-Bhāṣya, by Vijñānabhikṣu.
131. Yogasūtra, by Patañjali, Bombay edition.
132. Yoga-Bhāṣya, on No. 131, by Vyāsa, Bālarāma Udāsīn's edition.
133. Tattvavaiçāradī, a commentary on No. 132, by Vācaspati Miçra I, Bombay edition.
134. Īçvarapratyabhijñā, Kashmir Sanskrit Series.
135. Īçvarapratyabhijñāvimarçinī, Kashmir Sanskrit Series.
136. Pratyabhijñāhṛdaya, by Kṣemarāja, Kashmir Sanskrit Series.
137. Tantrasāra, by Abhinavagupta, Kashmir Sanskrit Series.
138. Vivṛti, a commentary on Paramārthasāra of Abhinavagupta, by Yogarājācārya, Kashmir Sanskrit Series.
139. Parāpraveçikā, Kashmir Sanskrit Series.
140. Pāṇini-Sūtra.
141. Mahābhāṣya, on No. 140, by Patañjali.
142. Vākyapadīya, by Bhartṛhari, Benares edition.
143. A commentary on No. 142 by Helārājā and Puṇyarāja, Benares edition.
144. Mañjūṣā, by Nāgeça, Benares edition.
145. Kuñjikā, a commentary on No. 144, by Durbalācārya, Benares edition.

146. Sangītaratnākara. Anandaçrama Sanskrit Series edition.
147. A commentary on No. 146, by Caturakallinātha, Anandaçrama Sanskrit Series edition.
148. Ṣaḍdarçanasamuccaya, by Haribhadra, Bibliotheca Indica edition.
149. Guṇaratna's commentary on No. 148, Bibliotheca Indica edition.
150. Sarvamatasaṅgraha, by an anonymous writer, Gaṇapati Çāstrī's edition.
151. Sarvasiddhāntasaṅgraha, attributed to Çaṅkarācārya, Madras edition.
152. Sarvadarçanasangraha, by Mādhavācārya, Poona and Calcutta editions.
153. Mahimnaḥstotra, by Puṣpadanta, Bombay edition.
154. Tarkasangraha, by Anandajñāna, qouted by Çeṣa Çārngadhara in Nyāya-Muktāvalī.
155. Gurugītā of the Viçvasāra Tantra, quoted in Indian Logic by Dr. Vidyabhuṣaṇa.
156. Hayaçīrṣapañcarātra, quoted by Dr. Vidyabhūṣaṇa in his Indian Logic.
157. Arthaçāstra, by Kautilya, Madras edition.
158. Çabda-Kalpadruma.
159. Amarakoça.
160. Çrīmadbhāgavata Purāṇa.
161. Çridhara's commentary on No. 160.
162. Tattvaviveka, by Kamalākara Bhaṭṭa, Benares edition.
163. Çukla-Yajuḥprātiçākhya.
164. Ubbata-Bhāṣya on Yajurveda.
165. Taittirīyasaṁhitā.
166. Siddhāntaçiromani, by Bhāskarācārya, Benares edition.
167. Bṛhadāraṇyaka, along with the Çaṅkara-Bhāṣya.
168. Bhagavadgītā.
169. Kaṭhopaniṣad, along with the Çaṅkara-Bhāṣya.
170. Muṇḍaka Upaniṣad.
171. Taittirīya Upaniṣad.
172. Çvetāçvatara Upaniṣad.
173. Çvetāçvataropaniṣad-dīpikā, Ānandāçrama Sanskrit Series edition.
174. Mahābhārata.
175. Mahābodhijātaka.
176. Buddhacarita, by Açvaghoṣa.
177. Suçruta, Bombay edition.

178. Ḍalhaṇa's commentary on No. 177.
179. Manusmṛti.
180. Naiṣadhacarita.
181. Commentaries on Gītā, by Nīlakaṇṭha, Madhusūdana, Dhanapati and Çrīdhara.
182. Saṅkṣepaçaṅkarajaya, *vide* Catalogi Codicum Manuscriptorum, Bibliothecae Bodleianae, by Th. Aufrecht.
183. Abhidharmakoça, by Vasubandhu along with Rev. Rāhula's Sanskrit gloss, Benares edition.
184. Gommatasāra, by Nemicandra.
185. Dravyasangraha, Sacred Books of the Jain's Series.
186. Vṛtti, on No. 185, Sacred Books of the Jain's Series.
187. Nyāyāvatāra, Dr. S. C. Vidyabhūsaṇa's edition.
188. Vivṛti, on No. 187, Dr. Vidyabhūṣaṇa's edition.
189. Pañcāstikāyasāra, quoted from Dravyasaṅgraha.
190. Bhāskara-Bhāṣya on Brahmasūtra, Benares edition.
191. Siddhāntaratna, a commentary on Brahma-Sūtra, by Baladeva Vidyābhūṣaṇa, Śarasvatībhavana Text Series, Benares.
192. An anonymous commentary on the Pratāparudra Yaçobhūṣaṇa of Vidyādhara.
193. English Translation of Nyāya-Bhāṣya and Vārtika, by Dr. Gangānātha Jhā.
194. English Translation of Praçastapādabhāṣya by Dr. Gangānātha Jhā.
195. Positive Sciences of the Ancient Hindus by Dr. B. N. Seal.
196. Indian Philosophy by Dr. Sir. S. Radhakrishnan.
197. Introduction to the Pūrva-Mīmāṃsā, by Pashupatinatha Shastrī.
198. Prabhākara School of Purva Mīmāṃsā, by Dr. Gangānātha Jhā.
199. Karma Mīmāṃsā by Dr. A. B. Keith.
200. Indian Psychology-Perception, by Prof. Yadunatha Sinha, Meerut College.
201. Reality—"World as Power" Series.
202. History of Indian Logic by Dr. S. C. Vidyabhūṣaṇa, Calcutta.
203. Hindu Realism, by J. Chatterji.
204. Beyond Physics, by Sir Oliver Lodge.
205. Elements of Psychology, by M. Drumond and S. H. Mellone.
206. Introduction to Philosophy by Oswald Külpe.